GIANT BOOK
OF THE
DOG

GIANT BOOK

OF THE

DOG

CHARTWELL
BOOKS, INC.

A QUARTO BOOK

Published by Chartwell Books
A Division of Book Sales, Inc.
114, North Avenue
Edison, New Jersey 08837

This edition produced for sale in the U.S.A.,
its territories and dependencies only.

ISBN 0-7858-0947-3

This book was designed and produced by
Quarto Publishing plc
6 Blundell Street
London N7 9BH

Editor: Patricia Briggs

Designer: Louise Morley

Art Director: Moira Clinch

Manufactured in Singapore by Eray Scan Pte Ltd
Printed in China by Leefung-Asco Printers Ltd

The material in this book previously appeared in
the following titles: *Understanding your Dog* by Peter Messent;
The Illustrated Encyclopedia of Dog Breeds by Joan Palmer;
Dog Facts by Marcus Schneck and Jill Caravan; *The Dog
Care Manual* by David Alderton; *The Dog* by David Alderton

CONTENTS

INTRODUCTION

WHEN DID DOGS ORIGINATE?

The dog, in common with wolves, foxes and jackals, belongs to the family Canidae. This is one of seven families in the Carnivore, or meat-eating, order of mammals.

Above: The wolf (Canis lupus), which appeared 500,000 years ago and was much smaller than the wolf of today, could well be the ancestor of the dog.

THE EVOLUTION OF THE DOG, *Canis familiaris*, can be traced back to a small, tree-climbing, weasel-like carnivore, the Miacis, which dwelt in forests 50 million years ago. A descendant of the Miacis was the Tomarctus, a small, fox-like creature, which appeared some 35 million years later and is generally acknowledged as the forerunner of the dog, wolf, fox and jackal. But the Tomarctus had disappeared by the middle of the Pleistocene age, about one million years ago, and by then, wolves and jackals were well established.

Wolf in sheep's clothing

The saying that, "a dog is a wolf in sheep's clothing" is not far amiss. The most likely ancestor of the domestic dog is the gray wolf, with which it shares various characteristics. Another possibility is the jackel, but it is unlikely that the dog could have evolved from the fox.

Interestingly, matings between a wolf and dog do prove fertile – as do some between dog and jackal – and the dog that escapes into the wild will revert to the wolf-like behavior of its ancestors. Much of the behavior patterns of the domestic dog today, particularly when in the company of its own kind, can be traced back to those of the wolf pack.

The dog family is often divided into two distinct groups: the dogs and wolves, and the foxes and jackals. The two groups have much in common. They are meat-eaters with 42 teeth. They have four or five toes on their fore-feet, four on their hind-feet. They run on their toes, and their claws, unlike those of the cat, are non-retractable. The females have a 63-day gestation period. They give birth to fairly large litters, and the eyes of their young are closed at birth. It is also significant that members of these groups live in packs and respect a pack leader. This fact might explain why the domestic dog can readily accept the dictates of a human owner: the owner may have become a substitute pack leader!

Dogdom BC

The earliest identifiable remains of a pure-bred dog are those of a Saluki, a breed which took its name from the town of Saluk in the Yemen. Recent excavations of the Sumerian civilization in Mesopotamia (dated to 7000 BC) revealed rock carvings of dogs that bore a strong resemblance to the Saluki, the original ancestor of which is thought to have been a small-skulled desert wolf. The earliest domesticated dog in recorded history is the Pharaoh Hound: two hounds hunting gazelle are depicted on a circular disc dating back to around 4000 BC. The elegant and graceful Pharaoh Hound is known to have played an integral part in the daily lives of the kings of ancient Egypt.

Family likeness?

It is claimed that the Saluki and Pharaoh Hounds are the oldest pure-bred dogs on earth. However, it is interesting to note that a number of other dogs bear resemblance to their ancestral equivalents. They may have developed, through interbreeding, in response to climatic conditions or to the requirements of their new-found human friends.

Right: The Egyptian god, Anubis, ruler of the dead, symbolized both the dog and the jackal. This mythological son of Osiris, God of the underworld, resembles the Pharaoh Hound distinctly. It may be seen in the Louvre Museum, Paris. The Pharaoh Hound breed has changed little in 5,000 years.

DECENT OF THE MODERN DOG

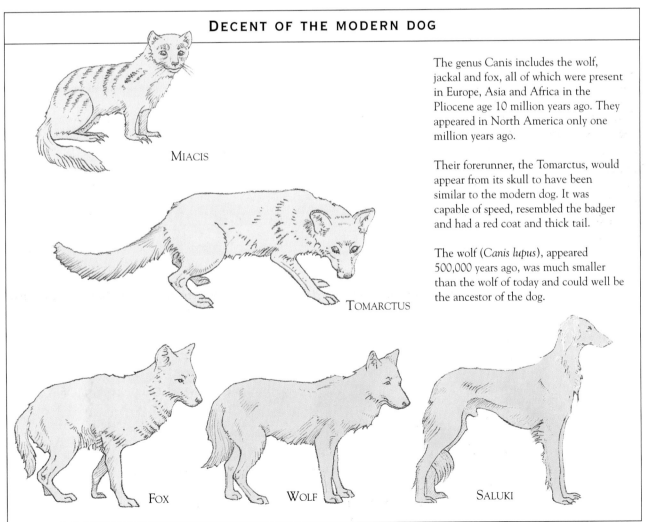

MIACIS

TOMARCTUS

FOX

WOLF

SALUKI

The genus Canis includes the wolf, jackal and fox, all of which were present in Europe, Asia and Africa in the Pliocene age 10 million years ago. They appeared in North America only one million years ago.

Their forerunner, the Tomarctus, would appear from its skull to have been similar to the modern dog. It was capable of speed, resembled the badger and had a red coat and thick tail.

The wolf (*Canis lupus*), appeared 500,000 years ago, was much smaller than the wolf of today and could well be the ancestor of the dog.

WHO DOMESTICATED THE DOG?

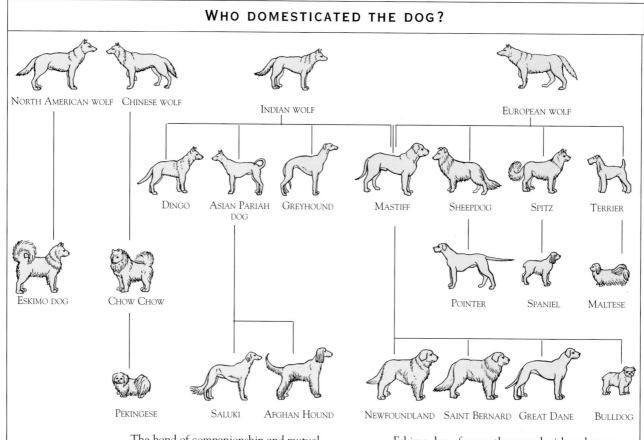

The bond of companionship and mutual affection between humans and dogs may have developed as prehistoric people realized that the dogs around their cave or camp fire sought nothing but food and warmth, and threw them scraps of meat to show they weren't predators.

In time, humans would have recognized the value of the dog as a guard, beast of burden, sled dog and hunter, and later would have made the first crude attempts at selective breeding to perpetuate their most-admired traits: conformation, temperament and ability.

Dogs, as we have seen, are descendants of the wolf and even today we can see the result of some of the early attempts at selective breeding.

Eskimo dogs, frequently crossed with wolves to maintain their size and stamina, are not dissimilar to the northern races of the wolf. The Samoyed is a descendant of the Siberian Wild Dog. Dogs owned by the North American Indians tend to be smaller animals – likely descendants of the coyote or prairie wolf. Of all European dogs, the German Shepherd, once known as the Alsatian Wolf Dog, is certainly the most wolf-like. Similarities such as these are readily found all over the world. Pariah dogs of India resemble the Indian wolf. Dogs in Africa, Asia and some parts of south-eastern Europe resemble the jackals of those regions, and the Australian dingo also resembles the jackal.

The Saluki, treasured by the Bedouin Tribes.

Early man's best friend

It is apparent that, in the early days of domestication, and despite the friendship that had developed between humans and dogs, little or no effort was made to produce other than "useful" breeds. The written history of domesticated dogs is – for 1000 years, starting with a work by Xenophon (c.430–c.350 BC) – essentially about hunting and hunting dogs. Indeed, it was not until 1685, in Nuremberg, that the first encyclopedia of dogs was published: the *Cynographia Curiosa oder Hundebeschreibung*, by Christian Franz Paullini.

An earlier glimpse of the changing role of the dog to meet social requirements, fashion and fancy, can be found in a letter penned in 1560 by the Cambridge scholar, John Caius, to the Swiss

OLDEST BREEDS

- The oldest pure-bred British dog is thought to be the Cardigan Welsh Corgi, traced back to dogs brought to Wales by the Celts from the Black Sea area around 1200 BC.

- The oldest pure-bred American breed is the American Foxhound. Robert Brooke, an Englishman, settled in Maryland in 1650 with his pack of foxhounds which he crossed with other strains imported from England, Ireland and France, to develop the American Foxhound.

naturalist, Gesner, in which he outlined the breeds of dog in England at that time:

"And we also have a small race of dogs that are specially bred to be the playthings of rich and noble ladies. The smaller they are, the more perfectly suited to their purpose, which is to be carried at the breast, in the bedchamber or in the lap, when their mistresses sally forth."

Hunting and watch dogs still predominated, but the lap dog had begun to make its mark.

Dog census

The domestic dog population of the world is roughly 150 million. The United States has the largest dog population; approximately 40 million. Britain has five-and-a-half million. But these figures are not all for pure-bred dogs, and account for two-and-a-half million mongrels.

A pact

The dog is a creature that humans have never had to subdue into subservience, or with which they have been forced to do battle, for there are no ancient rock carvings illustrating such situations. It appears that dogs formed an alliance with human of their own free will, and a partnership was formed on the basis of mutual friendship and trust.

Left: The Samoyed takes its name from the Siberian tribe of Samoyedes. A descendant of the Siberian Wild Dog it nonetheless "shows affection for all mankind." The explorer Nansen took a number of "Sammies" with him on his expedition to the North Pole. In its native land it guards and protects reindeer.

DOGGY BONES

- In 1979, Israeli archaeologists digging in the Middle East found the remains of a man and a puppy in close proximity. The hand of the man was resting on the puppy. This was among the remains of a 10,000-year-old Natufian settlement!

Far left: The Mastiff descends from the Molossus war dog of Rome. Left: the Pharaoh Hound is depicted in the tombs of the Pharaohs.

Above: While Moslems in the East scorned the dog – credited with devouring the body of the Prophet, Mohammed – fear of the animal was also prevalent in Europe, where the word dog, or 'cur', became an insult.

Were dogs always popular?

There have always been dog lovers and dog haters. Indeed, the rebellion in the United Kingdom in recent years against the registration of dogs is nothing new. In 1796 there was a motion to introduce the first duties on dogs in England: five shillings on "outdoor" dogs, three shillings on "indoor" dogs. It was proposed by one George T. Clark, who was

---

STARRY DOG

● In astrology, there are forty "dog days" – between July 3 and August 11 – when Sirius, the Dog Star, rises and sets with the sun. The superstition that Sirius greatly influences the canine race is found in Greek literature, as far back as Hesiod in the eighth century BC.

---

rewarded for his trouble with the receipt of dozens of dead dogs in hampers, packed as game. There was a massacre of dogs by owners who objected to paying the dues.

Generally, the dog has been more revered than reviled through the ages. The ancient Egyptians are known to have had faithful dogs buried alongside them, a practice also followed in ancient America by the Toltec people, and later by the Aztecs, whose dogs were sacrificed at funerals in the belief that they would guide their masters to a better world.

Holy dogs

The dog has played a large part in Eastern religions and that, although it is considered by Moslems to be an outcast of Allah, and unclean, the fleet-footed Saluki is still prized along with pure-bred Arab horses. Hindus believe that a person who ill-treats a dog will be punished by returning to earth in canine form. Often the fear of the unknown has made humans behave unreasonably towards animals. Here lies the source of Totemism (the identification of themselves by human families with an animal family) and of Metempsychosis (the belief in the transmigration of human souls, and their return in an animal's body).

The importance of shepherd dogs and guard dogs was stressed in the teachings of the

STATUS DOGS

- Wealth and snobbery have always played their part in dog ownership. In the time of King Richard I of England, any greyhound owner, unless he was worth ten pounds a year in land or inheritance, or 300 pounds a year in freehold, was liable to be summoned to the Forest Court, which met every year to determine whether his greyhound had been running in the forest.

- In the Middle Ages there were reckoned to be at least 69 Royal Forests, 800 Parks and 13 Chases in England and it was said that, to see a King of England, you need look no further than the hunting field.

- Common people were allowed to keep only watch dogs and dogs small enough to be incapable of bringing down game and therefore spoiling their betters' sport. Large dogs would be systematically and cruelly lamed.

- To this day there exists in the village of Lyndhurst in the County of Hampshire a measure, or stirrup, through which a dog had to pass so as to assess whether it was sufficiently small to be allowed to roam unhindered in the forest.

Persian prophet, Zoroaster (Zarathustra), almost three thousand years ago. Zoroaster's doctrine, which spread widely in the East, contained many references to dogs and their importance. He decreed: "Of these two dogs of mine, the shepherd dog and the guard dog, pass the house of any of my faithful people, let them never be kept away from it, for no house could exist, but for these two dogs of mine, the shepherd dog and guard dog."

Dog worship

Dogs were worshipped by the followers of Mithras, the ancient Persian light-god who was aided and accompanied by his dog. Mithraism later became very popular in the time of the Roman Empire and spread widely, from India to Spain and from Egypt to the south of Scotland.

There is a dog-worshipping sect to this day. It is called the Brotherhood of the Essenes. The Essenes maintain that there are animal planes in the celestial Kingdom from which one steps to the planes of knowledge. It is their view that animals have the power of speech in the Kingdom which they relinquish voluntarily as they journey through the gates of the zodiac into earth's sphere. According to the Essenes, dogs are beings without sin, sent to earth to test humans.

Above: A working sheepdog must be carefully trained. The intelligent Border Collie is one of the most popular breeds for herding dogs.

BEWARE OF THE DOG

- "Cave Canem": Beware the dog. Fierce dogs were highly prized throughout Ancient Rome. They were not, however, noted for their fidelity. They were various kinds of dogs, including watchdogs, messengers and combatants. Sometimes they would be starved before meeting their opponents so as to ensure they were at their most ferocious.

usual one is a bluish-gray, spotted with black. The tail is generally curled on the back."

At any rate, this sadly misused little animal was to survive until around 1870, by which time it had become so rare that owners of such treasures were able to hire them out by the day.

Lowly breeds

There were also, up until the 19th century, dogs such as the cur, a cross between sheepdog and terrier, and the drover's dog, a cross between a sheepdog and mastiff, the task of which was to guide a farmer's sheep to market. The cur was a watchdog with perhaps less than the social standing of the present day mongrel, and its title had become a derogatory term.

Have any breeds disappeared?

Many dogs have disappeared – some (like the unfortunate "Turnspit") into total extinction, others being sacrificed in the development of another or changed variety.

Canine historian, Carons Ritchie said the Turnspit was "the best-known representative of those worker-dogs which had once provided power for various purposes, such as raising water from a well by working a treadmill."

The Turnspit

Prior to the introduction of the Turnspit dog, meat in 18th century England was turned on the spit by a human, usually a small boy, protected from the fierce heat by a round, woven, straw shield, soaked in water. However, special treadmills were built near to the fires of large kitchens in great houses and dogs were trained to keep them turning. It would take at least three hours for a large side of beef to roast properly. The dog had to turn the wheel hundreds of times and was subject to beatings from the cook if it paused in its unenviable task. So exhausting was the work that sometimes two Turnspit dogs were kept, so that one might work on the other's day off.

What did Turnspits look like? They have been described as:

"extremely bandy legged, so as to appear almost incapable of running, with long bodies and rather large heads. They are very strong in the jaws, and are what are called "hard bitten." It is a peculiarity in these dogs that they generally have the iris of one eye black, and the other white. Their color varies, but the

THE QUEEN'S POM

- Queen Victoria, an avid lover of most breeds of dogs, became a champion of the Toy varieties, notably, and, before the arrival in England of the Pekingese, of the Pomeranian. Initially this was a much larger dog weighing as much as 13.5 kg (30 lb). The Pomeranian was however bred down and by 1896 show classes for the breed had been divided into those for exhibits under and over 3.5 kg (8 lb) in weight. By 1915 exhibits over that weight had all but disappeared.

RARE AND UNUSUAL DOGS

Left: The Portuguese Warren Hound (Pequeno) is usually fawn, but may be yellow, brown, gray-black or sooty, with or without white patches and spots. It is not currently recognized by the American or United Kingdom Kennel Clubs or by the International Canine Federation (FCI).

Nowadays, the world's rarest dog is reckoned to be the Tahltan bear dog which, as its name implies, was once used by the Tahltan Indians of western Canada for hunting bear, as well as lynx and porcupine. The Indians were thought to carry these dogs – the weight of which is around 13 kg (30 lb) – in hide sacks on their backs, so as to preserve their strength for when the quarry was sighted, at which time they would promptly be released. The job of the bear dog was to hold the proposed victim at bay, circling it until its masters moved in for the kill. There must be less than a handful of the breed now alive and it is sadly in danger of extinction. However, this was a fate which threatened the Chinese Shar Pei and the Chinese Crested dog not so long ago, and both

ON ICE

- The Broholmer is a breed recognized only in its native Denmark. It was believed to have become extinct in the 1960s but then, in December 1974, a dog of the breed appeared at the home of a pharmacist in Helsinki, Finland. The Royal Veterinary College in Copenhagen set up a frozen sperm bank for the dog – which was named Bjoern – in the hope that a bitch might eventually be found. But sadly, none was found, and Bjoern died in January 1975.

are now fairly commonplace, particularly in the British show ring.

The podengo

It would indeed be true to say that what is rare today may not be rare tomorrow, so one must hope that the future will be brighter for another breed threatened with extinction, the Portuguese Warren Hound, or Podengo, which is little known outside its country of origin where it is a hunter of rabbit, hare and deer. There are three sizes of this variety, the grande (large), which stands 56–68 cm (22–27 in) high, and whose numbers are diminishing, a small variety (pequeno), which resembles a large, smooth-coated Chihuahua, and a medium sized dog. The grande is not unlike the Ibizan Hound.

The Portuguese water dog

There is another Portuguese dog which is unusual albeit not so rare, and that is the

A ROCK DAY

- The Lundehund is a breed which for centuries has lived solely on two islands in the north of Norway. Unlike other dogs, which have four toes and possibly an atrophied fifth, the Lundehund has five toes and an atrophied sixth. Also, unlike other small dogs with five toe cushions, the Lundehund has seven or eight. Because of its small size and strange foot equipment the dog is enabled to scale rocks and cliffs so as to lift a Puffin gently from its nest and restore it unharmed to his master.

COURT FAVOURITES

● It is recorded by the famous diarist, Samuel Pepys, that King Charles II of England spent more time playing with his dogs in the Council Chamber than he did on affairs of state. However, credited as the most fanatical dog lover of all time was Henry III of France (1551–89). Indeed, he is said to have collected dogs as people collect stamps. When he saw one that took his fancy, and it wasn't for sale, he would think nothing of arranging for someone to steal it for him. It seems he had at least 2000 dogs spread around his palaces and, when he was in residence, there were never fewer than 100 dogs, mostly toy breeds, within patting distance. But then the love of British Royalty for dogs is well known, Edward VII's faithful dog (a Fox Terrier, like the one below), "Caesar", followed his late master's funeral procession, and "Slipper", a Cairn Terrier given by Edward VIII to the then Mrs. Wallis Simpson, featured largely in their much publicised courtship correspondence. The present Queen, Elizabeth II, is rarely photographed in home surroundings without a few Corgi dogs beside her.

Portuguese water dog, a fascinating animal, which was once readily to be seen at Portuguese and Spanish seaports working as a fisherman's dog, guarding his nets. It is remarkable in that it will catch an escaping fish in its jaws and swim back with it to its master. There are short, curly-coated and long-coated varieties, but it is the latter that calls for attention when it is presented in a smart lion clip similar to that of the elegant standard Poodle.

The Lowchen

The Lowchen, or "petit chien lion" (little lion dog), is a native French breed and member of the Bichon family. Though extremely rare 20 years ago, it is now a popular contender in the show ring – though rarely seen in a park. It is thought to be the dog shown with the Duchess of Albain in a portrait painted by Francisco Goya (1746–1828), and is undoubtedly the breed in the portrait, *A Lowchen Seated by a Quill* painted by Florent-Richard De Lamarre between 1630 and 1718, revealing then, as now, the distinctive lion clip.

Right: The Portuguese Water Dog is very muscular animal. It's toes are webbed, with soft membrane covered with hair. It may be black, white or various shades of brown; or a combination of brown with black or brown with white

WHAT IS A PURE BREED?

A pure-breed dog is one whose sire (father) and dam (mother) are of the same breed, the parents having themselves descended from dogs of the same breed. It has been explained how early people would have attempted planned matings of their canine companions so as to perpetuate those traits they admired and desired. They would have experimented with such things as height, weight and coat-type, with color patterns, with the shape of the dog's head and skull, and the setting of its tail until, in the course of a few generations, the desired canine type would breed true.

Registration introduced

Undoubtedly, dog fanciers would always have discussed the attributes of their animals much as people do today. It is, however, almost impossible to chart the progress of the different breeds of dogs through the ages, as we have little to refer to apart from many illustrations or paintings. It was not until 1873 that the UK's Kennel Club was established in London – the first of its kind in the world. The Kennel Club introduced a registration system that made it possible to determine the breeding of every pure-bred canine – in a kind of birth certificate. It also devised an approved

"Standard" for each variety of dog that was recognized.

The desire to introduce new breeds and improve existing breeds has, of course, continued, and there are remarkably few varieties now that do not owe their present existence to another breed. The Doberman, for example, owes much to the Rottweiler and Manchester Terrier, and the little Long Coat Chihuahua to the Papillon, or Butterfly dog (so named because of the shape of its ears).

Above: The Greyhound is a pure breed that has been used for coursing since Roman times. Nowadays it is bred along distinct lines for showing, coursing and track racing.

TALLEST AND SHORTEST

- The tallest dog breeds are the Great Dane, the Irish Wolfhound, the St. Bernard, the English Mastiff, the Borzoi and the Anatolian Karabash (Turkish Shepherd dog). All of these breeds can attain 90 cm (36 in) at the shoulder.

- The smallest dog breed is the Chihuahua, the recognized weight of which is between 0.9–2.75 kg (2–6 lb). Mexico City's Natural History Museum, however, has the skeleton of a fully grown Chihuahua measuring only 18 cm (7 in) in total length. There is no weight quoted for this dog, which was presented in 1910, but it is estimated that, if its bones are anything to go by, it could not have weighed more than one pound.

- The second smallest dog is reckoned to be the Yorkshire Terrier which "officially" should not weigh more than 3.20 kg (7 lb), although many pet "Yorkies" nowadays tend to be much heavier.

CROSSBREEDS AND PEDIGREES

Right: Mongrels come in all shapes and sizes. This example could well have a touch of Boxer in its makeup.

Above: Mongrels are wonderfully individual. You may be reasonably sure how a pure-bred pup will turn out, but with a mongrel you have to take pot luck!

What is a crossbreed?

A crossbreed is the progeny of a pure-bred bitch that has mated with a pure-bred dog of another pure breed – for example, the result of a Poodle–Spaniel mating.

There are those who favor a crossbreed believing that they will have the benefit of the known attributes of both breeds. In fact, a problem often arises where an owner who may have lost a crossbreed of a certain type wishes to replace it with another, for crossbreeds are rarely intentionally bred.

A mongrel is a dog or bitch whose sire and dam are likely to owe their make-up to any number of different breeds.

Old wives' tale

It is sometimes thought that mongrels are more robust than pure-bred dogs. In fact, a mongrel is unlikely to be any tougher, or any weaker, than its pure-bred contemporaries.

There is no doubt that mongrels make excellent pets, but there is always an element of uncertainty as to how they will turn out in either appearance or temperament.

MONGREL VARIETIES

- The result of the mating of two pure-bred dogs of different breeds can be either successful or somewhat startling, depending on the varieties involved.

PURE BREEDS OF SAME TYPE = PURE BREED

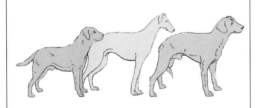

PURE BREEDS OF DIFFERENT TYPE = "X" BREED

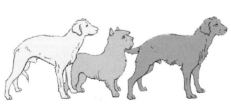

"X" BREED + "X" BREED = MONGREL

FEET FIRST

- To determine how large a mongrel puppy may grow, look at the size of its feet. A pup with really large feet is probably destined to be a mammoth-sized dog.

What is a certificate of pedigree?

It is a common mistake to use the term "pedigree dog". The correct term is a pure-bred dog. A Certificate of Pedigree is the document that should be handed to the buyer of a pure-bred puppy at the time of purchase. The buyer should also be given a Transfer form enabling him or her, for a fee, to register the pup in the buyer's name, in place of the vendor's name, with the respective national kennel club.

The Certificate of Pedigree which, like the Transfer form, should be signed by the breeder, must show the registered name and number of the puppy (obviously you can call your puppy whatever name you wish), its date of birth, and the registered names and registration numbers of its parents and ancestors for three, or preferably five, generations.

The Certificate of Pedigree

This Certificate of Pedigree is a valuable document which calls for careful scrutiny. Unless the puppy's parents are registered, and the signature of the breeder appears, the new owner will be unable to register a transfer of ownership and, perhaps more importantly, will be unable to enter the dog in pure-breed show classes, or to register and sell its subsequent progeny as pure-bred.

You will probably notice on a Certificate of Pedigree, that the dog's name bears a prefix; for instance, Merry Max of Penfold, or Penfold Merry Max. This is because breeders, again for a modest fee, are enabled to register a prefix with their respective kennel club, which enables stock from their kennels to be easily recognized. Where a dog has been bred by the prefix holder,

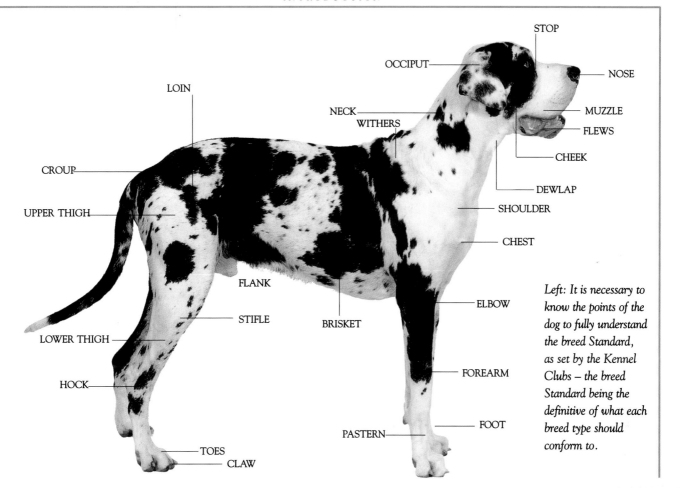

LOIN

CROUP

UPPER THIGH

FLANK

STIFLE

LOWER THIGH

HOCK

TOES

CLAW

NECK

WITHERS

OCCIPUT

STOP

NOSE

MUZZLE

FLEWS

CHEEK

DEWLAP

SHOULDER

CHEST

BRISKET

ELBOW

FOREARM

FOOT

PASTERN

Left: It is necessary to know the points of the dog to fully understand the breed Standard, as set by the Kennel Clubs – the breed Standard being the definitive of what each breed type should conform to.

the word will appear in front of the dog's name (called an affix). If the dog has been acquired, the prefix will follow the dog's name, for example "of" or "at," and this is called a suffix

How to detect prize-winning stock
If you attend dog shows and look at the catalogue entries for a specific breed, you may find it interesting to detect, from their affixes, those kennels that predominate and produce considerable prize-winning stock.

Pedigree certificates are usually completed by hand. Those that have entries written in red ink are highly prized, for only the names of champions can be honoured in this way.

The American and British championship systems are different. In the USA, a championship is attained through an accumulation of points. A dog that has accumulated 15 points is designated a

Champion. The dog may earn from one to five points at a show, and only one male and one female can win points a show. In Britain, champions are dogs that have been awarded three Challenge Certificates at three different Championship Dog Shows and by three different judges.

It is worth repeating that, when buying a puppy, the Certificate of Pedigree warrants careful scrutiny and that even if the puppy you intend to buy is an attractive and healthy example of its breed, and you have no intention of exhibiting or breeding from it, if the Certificate is incomplete, the puppy should not command as high a price as its fellows which are correctly documented.

Certificate of Pedigree

for ............TUDORA...HAPPY...PROSPECT.

PARENTS	GRAND-PARENTS	G.G.
SIRE	SIRE	SIRE GREML FAMOU
	CH.GREMLIN STORM	DAM GRE
CH.TYE FAMOUS		

REGISTERED NAME HALAMAR'S STORMY

BREED COLLIE

BREEDER/OWNER HAROLD & MARY SUN

LITTER IDENTIFICATION 4th

SOLD TO

THE KENNEL C

Registration Certificate for: TUDORA HAPPY PROSPECT NO1

Breed BOXER   Sex

Colour BRINDLE & WHITE   Bree

Sire TYEGARTH FAMOUS GROUSE CH   C11   1900BM

Dam TUDORA MYSTIC MAID   J10   1989BV

TRANSFERRED ON 04/06/88 FROM MRS R H NUGENT

TAYLOR

AMERICAN KENNEL C

HALAMAR'S STORMY DAWN

COLLIE

(610)   No. WD5

SABLE & WHITE   FEMA

LEAWOOD'S HOLIDAY BONUS   WC755107 (10-7   SEP 2

CH HALAMAR'S HERITAGE   WC074604 (2-74)

HAROLD SUNDSTROM

CHAMPION OF CHAMPIONS

- The greatest number of Challenge Certificates – or "CCs" as fanciers call them – to be won by a British dog, were the 78 awarded to Champion (Ch) U'Kwong King Solomon, a Chow Chow owned and bred by Mrs.

Joan Egerton of Bramhall, Cheshire in the north of England. Known as Solly, this magnificent Chow Chow died in 1978 aged 10 years. It is the life's ambition of some dog exhibitors to win even one Challenge Certificate.

ARE PEDIGREE DOGS SHOW DOGS?

The acquisition of a certificate of Pedigree proves that you own a pure-bred dog. It enables you to register ownership with the national kennel club, to legitimately enter the animal in pure-bred show classes and, if you wish to breed, to sell its progeny with a similar Certificate of Pedigree. But – contrary to a widely held belief – a pedigreed dog is by no means always a prospect for the show ring.

Falling short of perfection

Kennel clubs worldwide have what is known as a Standard laid down for each recognized breed. This Standard describes the perfect example of every variety and it is the dogs which meet this exacting requirement that compete against each other in the show ring. There are however countless breed members which fall short of their Standard of perfection, if only in some minor detail – they may be slightly too big, or too small, their teeth formation may be under or over-shot, or there could be a wrongful patch of colour on their coats – in which case, they would be sold (most pure-bred dogs are) as "pet" dogs rather than show dogs.

Pure-breed or show dog?

Most people who buy a dog simply want an attractive, faithful companion of their favorite

---

WHO DOMESTICATED THE DOG?

- A dog's mouth is overshot when the upper teeth project beyond the lower teeth. It is undershot if they don't project as far as the lower teeth. Correct alignment of the upper and lower teeth is known as a normal, or "scissor" bite.

OVERSHOT BITE

UNDERSHOT BITE

NORMAL OR SCISSOR BITE

TAILS OF A DOG

The correct shape and position of the tail varies according to the breed.

BOBTAIL: Dogs may be naturally tailless or the tail may be docked (Old English Sheepdog)

BRUSH: Tail like the brush of a fox (Alaskan Malamute)

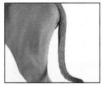

CRANK: Carried down and resembling a crank (Italian short-haired Segugio)

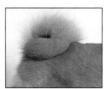

CURLED: Tail set high and curled over (Finnish Spitz)

FLAG: Long and carried high (Beagle)

KINK: Sharply bent (Lhasa Apso)

OTTER: Thick at the root, round and tapering. Used as rudder in swimming (Labrador)

RING: Carried up and around, almost in a circle (Basenji)

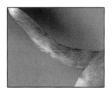

SABRE: Carried like a sabre (Basset Hound)

SICKLE: Carried out and up in a semi-circle (Affenpinscher)

SCREW: Naturally short, twisted in a spiral fashion (French Bulldog)

SPIKE: Short, thick, tapering along entire length (English Pointer)

STERN: Technical term for the tail of a sporting dog (English Pointer)

WHIP: Carried stiffly, straight and pointed (Bull Terrier)

SQUIRREL: Carried up and curving forward (Chow Chow)

EARS OF A DOG

The size, position and fall of the ears is also specified in the breed Standard. While ear-cropping is allowed in the US, it is banned in other countries, such as the UK.

PRICKED: STANDING ERECT AND GENERALLY POINTED AT THE TIPS (GERMAN SHEPHERD)

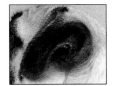

ROSE: SMALL DROP EAR THAT FALLS OVER AND BACK TO REVEAL THE BURR (PUG)

SEMI-DROP, OR *SEMI-PRICK EAR*: TIP OF THE EARS BREAKS AND FALLS FORWARD (SHETLAND SHEEPDOG)

BUTTON: FLAP FOLDS FORWARD, TIP LIES CLOSE TO SKULL, POINTING TOWARDS EYES (IRISH TERRIER)

DROP: END FOLDS OR DROPS FORWARDS, PENDENT OR PENDULOUS (ENGLISH COCKER SPANIEL)

FILBERT-SHAPED: HAZELNUT-SHAPED EARS (BEDLINGTON TERRIER)

HEART-SHAPED: SHAPED LIKE A HEART (PEKINGESE)

BAT: ERECT AND BROAD AT THE BASE. ROUNDED IN OUTLINE AT THE TIP.(FRENCH BULLDOG)

HOUND: ROUNDED, TRIANGULAR, FLAP FOLDING FORWARDS AND LYING CLOSE TO HEAD (BEAGLE)

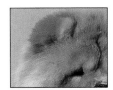

HOODED: SMALL, TRIANGULAR AND ERECT BUT TILTED FORWARDS SLIGHTLY (CHOW CHOW)

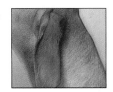

V-SHAPED: USUALLY CARRIED FORWARDS IN DROPPED POSITION (HUNGARIAN VIZLA)

Below: The Dalmatian's spots should be clearly defined. Those on the extremities should be smaller than those on the body.

breed. But some people assume their pure-breed pet is a show dog and may enter it in a show – with disastrous results. They may protest and claim they have been swindled, but they have been treated fairly: they have been sold a healthy example of the breed, but they never asked the breeder for a show dog.

Showing off

Obtaining a show prospect is not easy, particularly as it is rarely possible to determine a dog's true potential until it is six months old, or more. Often breeders will "run-on" a likely pup in their kennels, with a view to exhibiting and/or breeding from it themselves. A good dog is an advertisement for their kennels!

Potential exhibitors must first convince a breeder that they will prove to be a worthy owner and are keen to become involved in the breed, probably by joining the relevant Breed Club, attending many shows as a spectator and learning all they can about handling the variety. Having passed this test, and been rewarded with the acquisition of their first show dog, they will discover the world of show dogs is a completely new way of life.

THE SUPREME SHOW

● Crufts Dog Show is the largest dog show in the world, held annually in London since 1886 (except in 1918–20 and 1940–47, when it was cancelled). When the show was first held at the Royal Aquarium in Westminster, it was restricted to terrier breeds, but four years later, other breeds, including Toys, were added. The Golden Jubilee show held at the Royal Agricultural Hall, Islington, in 1936, attracted record numbers: 10,650 entries and 4,388 dogs. However this was before entry was restricted, as is now the case, to prizewinners in Championship Shows. Since 1948 the British Kennel Club has run Crufts, originally at London's Olympia Halls and then the Earls Court Exhibition Centre. In January 1991, celebrating its Centenary, the show moved to the National Exhibition Centre in Birmingham.

ARE DOGS INTELLIGENT?

Right: These curious Jack Russell pups enjoying tug of war are having a dress rehearsal for the more serious business of hunting rats and other small vermin.

This is a question which scientists have argued over for centuries. We know that dogs are incapable of logical thought as we know it. They cannot reason as we can, but in terms of a "domestic wolf" they are indeed intelligent, relying on association, scent, instinct and memory. They also display characteristics of guarding, loyalty and playfulness which are typical of the wolf pack and, I would add, a keen sense of humor.

It is known that pups, untouched by human hands during the first weeks of life, never become wholly domesticated. Similarly, the dog that is kenneled, fed, groomed and exercised, but otherwise given little attention, is unlikely to reach the same potential as its contemporary which is kept as a household pet, spoken to regularly, played with and introduced to any number of outside influences and experiences.

Teaching your dog

Dog training must be interpreted by the dog as an extension of play. Learning, however, is largely a matter of association. Some dogs, like some humans, are more intelligent than others, but, given time, there are few that, having recognized the key words, will not react to sentences such as: "Shall we go for a *walk*, Ben?", "Goodness, it's time for *bed*, Ben!", "Do you want your *dinner*?", "Here's *Mum* (or *Dad*)!" or "Let's go and meet *Jane*." The list is endless and the dog's reaction could reasonably

MOODY MONITORS

- One of the reasons why dogs bring great comfort to humans is their uncanny facility of picking up our moods. The dog, in common with its ancestor, the wolf, is sensitive to atmosphere. That is why it will come and sit quietly beside us when we are despondent or jump around enthusiastically when we are in high spirits.

- Dogs have an inbuilt sense of time. How else would they know to draw attention to themselves when a regular feeding time draws near?

- It has also been proved that dogs can recognize places, even if they have not visited them for months, or even years. Indeed, a dog that has been sleeping quietly in the back of a car may get up and show considerable excitement within a kilometer or so of a once familiar location.

be thought to mean that it understands the meaning of the word spoken. But it cannot; it simply associates the key word, whether or not used in conjunction with its name, with the action that takes place thereafter.

Actions rather than words

It is not just the spoken word that brings about this association in the canine mind. Actions can speak as loudly as words. The mere fact of a dog's owner walking into the hall, or kitchen, with a coat on may be enough for the dog to jump up from its basket in anticipation of a walk, while the sound of a car engine in the drive may be sufficient to send it running hurriedly to the door in anticipation of its master's arrival. Undoubtedly the more time one spends with one's dog the more it learns, and the more it learns, the more it endears itself to us.

Most pet owners have only one dog. They do not have the same opportunity, as those who keep several, of studying the behavior of the social pack.

Substitute pack leaders

It has been explained how humans became substitute pack leaders, whom our domesticated wolf knows he must respect. Where, however, there are a number of dogs, the biggest, strongest male will generally emerge as the canine pack leader. He will marshal his troops, standing aside, for instance, until all have been accounted for when going out of doors. He will guard the food bowls, sometimes literally forbidding another dog to eat until he allows it to do so – even, on some occasions, giving an unliked subordinate what amounts to the evil eye until the unfortunate animal creeps away into a corner. Much however depends on the breed and temperament of the dog.

Left: In a domestic situation the dog regards its human owner as a substitute pack leader. It feels secure in the subordinate role and wants only to win the leader's approval.

Below: Trained to find prey for the hunter, Pointers will stop still in this pose awaiting instruction.

Above: Sniffer dogs are used to help locate explosives or narcotics.

Often there is a second in command, even a third in pecking order, while some dogs do not aspire to leadership at all. Disagreements are rare except where three important factors raise their head: sex, food and jealousy.

Can dogs perform useful tasks?
Dogs undertake a vast range of useful tasks; here are a few.

Firstly, there are Search-and-Rescue Dogs, specially trained to detect missing persons or bodies in an area of scent. They are highly trained dogs, which frequently live the life of family pets when not on call. The dogs go out, with their masters, usually skillful hill climbers, in all weathers, and their value is being increasingly recognized in the case of avalanches, aircraft crashes and earthquakes.

Armed service dogs
There are dogs in the Armed Services, working for Customs and Excise and for the Police. They are variously used as Guards, Patrol Dogs, and as "Sniffer" Dogs trained in the detection of explosives and narcotics. Some dogs, particularly the Bloodhound, with its incredible scenting ability, are used to track criminals or find lost children.

Dogs that "see" and "hear"
Perhaps the best known worker dogs are Sheepdogs and Guide Dogs for the Blind. However, there are also Hearing Dogs for the Deaf. A "hearing" dog is taught to respond to sounds specified by the individual applicant (a

IT SEEMS LIKE PLAY

● Work must always be interpreted by a dog as play. When a Sniffer dog is being trained, his reward is to retrieve. When a young dog retrieves a package of cannabis he will be allowed to have a game with the package, but that will be the only game he is allowed when working.

A dog's instincts are channelled into retrieving a particular scent. The dog gets every individual scent, breaking it down until it finds the one that it knows its master desires, regardless of what else is with it. The dog builds up a "scent picture." Every picture given to the dog includes the drug or explosive that the dog has been trained to find as a common denominator.

knock at the door, a kettle's whistle, or the ring of a telephone or alarm clock), things that would go undetected by a deaf person but which a dog can draw to their attention.

Dogs for petting

Assistance Dogs for the Disabled are trained to answer special needs, and Pro-Dogs Active Therapy dogs visit hospitals, nursing homes and hospices with their owners, to brighten the lives of those who may no longer be able to keep a dog of their own.

The presence of dogs is being increasingly recognized as therapy, and canines are finding their way, as residents, into a growing number of psychiatric and geriatric hospitals and hospices. It has even been proved that the act of stroking a dog can help reduce a patient's blood pressure.

In the United Kingdom it is not permitted to allow a dog to pull a cart on a public highway. But in America it is not unusual for a large dog to bring home the groceries in this fashion, while in Switzerland the Bernese Mountain Dog may be seen drawing a milk churn. In its native Germany the Rottweiler was traditionally the butcher's dog.

DR DOG

- In January 1925, a case of diphtheria was discovered in Nome, Alaska. Insufficient supplies of antitoxin threatened an epidemic, so a relay of 22 native and mail teams forged across the rough interior of Alaska and the ice of the Bering Sea to bring the serum to the grateful citizens. Today, in Central Park, New York, a statue of Balto, one of the relay-team leaders, commemorates the Nome Serum Run. An inscription reads: "Dedicated to the indomitable spirit of the sled dogs that relayed antitoxin 600 miles over rough ice, treacherous waters, through arctic blizzards from Nemana to the relief of stricken Nome in the winter of 1925. Endurance, Fidelity, Intelligence."

Left: Dogs are always needed to join the Pro-Dogs Active Therapy team, but first they must pass a rigorous temperament test. Some top show dogs are on the register, as are cross breeds and mongrels.

Left: In 1916, a doctor in charge of a clinic for war-wounded in Germany was walking a blind man in the grounds when he was called away. He left his German Shepherd Dog in charge of the patient and, on his return, was so impressed with the way the dog had behaved that he vowed to begin training dogs as guides for the blind.

CAN DOGS LOVE?

Right: The bond between a child and a dog can become very strong, but in the first instance, the child must be taught not to tease or hurt the dog in any way. Mutual trust is important.

The story of Greyfriars Bobby

Perhaps the true story of Greyfriars Bobby best illustrates the lasting love of a dog for its master.

Bobby was a small, shaggy terrier – possibly a Skye terrier – and the much- loved companion of a Midlothian farmer named Gray.

Each Wednesday, Bobby accompanied his master to market in Edinburgh and, at about midday, the two would visit Traill's tea-rooms, where Gray had his midday meal and Bobby would be given a bun. In 1858 Gray died, and was laid to rest in Greyfriars Churchyard.

On the third day after the funeral, at the usual time of Gray's visit, Bobby, bedraggled and looking the picture of woe, presented himself at the tea-rooms where, out of pity, Traill gave the dog its customary bun.

The next day Bobby appeared again, and the day after that. Each time, Traill gave it a bun, and the dog trotted off with it.

Traill's curiosity was aroused, and he decided to follow Bobby. This he did, and was surprised to find the little dog heading for Greyfriars

Right: Play is a good way to build up friendship and loyalty between owner and dog, as well as reinforcing training lessons.

Although dogs do appear in films, television commercials and on the live stage, the most important role a dog can have is as companion to the lonely and elderly, who might have nobody to relate to were it not for their faithful friend, the dog.

The proverb says, "A dog never bites the hand that feeds it," and cynics may say that as dogs rely on us for their creature comforts, any show of affection is a self-motivated act to safeguard a meal ticket. There have, however, been far too many true stories illustrating the unselfish love dogs have for their masters for such arguments to carry much weight.

It is true that dogs thrive, and are happiest, when their routine is undisturbed. Like humans, they become attuned to sleeping on a familiar bed or basket, and eating their dinner and going out for walks at regular hours. A break in routine when, for example, a chief family dog-walker goes away, or the dog is sent to boarding kennels for a time, can account for loss of condition.

But there can be no doubt that dogs can literally pine to death if their owner predeceases them, especially when a dog has lived in close proximity with its owner, perhaps sharing the same sleeping quarters, and rarely leaving their side.

DOG POWER

● In canine weight-hauling contests, dogs' strength and endurance are tested as they pull heavy loads. The World Championship Weight Hauling Contest is held at Bothell, Washington, as part of the annual Northwest Newfoundland Club Working Dog Trials. There are five weight categories: under 45kg (100lb), 45–59kg (100–130lb), 59–75kg (130–165lb), 75–86kg (165–190lb) and over 86kg (190lb). But the greatest recorded load pulled was 2905kg (64001/2lb), by a 80kg (176lb) St. Bernard named Ryettes Brandy bear at Bothell on 21 July 1978, when the other dogs entered (three Newfoundlands, two Alaskan Malamutes and another St. Bernard) also pulled 25 times their own body-weight on their first haul.

Churchyard, where it lay down on its master's grave and ate its scanty lunch.

It soon became evident that Gray had been a loner and that no provision had been made for Bobby; also that the little dog was spending its days and nights lying on the grave, leaving its vigil only to go to the tea-rooms when forced to do so by pangs of hunger.

Normally, dogs were not allowed into Greyfriars Churchyard, but the rule was eventually waived in the case of Bobby who,

taking refuge only in wet weather in a nearby shelter, provided by compassionate friends, and refusing any attempt at re-homing, continued his vigil for the next fourteen years until his death in 1872, when he was buried, like his mater, in Greyfriars Churchyard.

Later, a statue in Bobby's likeness was erected by the people of Edinburgh to commemorate this little dog which, even following its master's death, could not be persuaded to leave his side.

TREKKER SETTER

● Some dogs love their home, almost as much as their master. In August 1976 an Irish Red Setter named Bede went missing while on holiday in Cornwall with his owner, Father Louis Heston. Almost six months later, Bede, footsore and weary, turned up at this master's home in Braintree, Essex, having traveled 480 km (300 miles).

The Kennel Club declared Bede the Bravest Dog of 1976 and he was presented with his award at Crufts Dog Show on 12 February 1977.

CARING FOR YOUR DOG

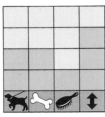

The care boxes located at the beginning of every entry in this book provide a ready reference for how to look after a dog. They show at a glance the basic requirements of each breed. The scales in the chart range from one shaded block (the least requirement) to four (the greatest requirement).

The first column indicates the amount of exercise a particular breed requires – in the case of the Bulldog, relatively little, whereas the Siberian Husky needs a great deal.

The second column shows the quantity of food that should be given – the Mastiff has a huge appetite, whereas the Sealyham Terrier has very modest requirements.

The third column gives an idea of the amount of grooming that is appropriate – the Bichon Frise should have daily, elaborate care, whereas the Bouvier de Flandres needs little grooming.

The fourth column is a guide to the suitability of the breed for a small house or apartment – with one block, the Dachshund is a good choice for limited living space; the Otterhound, with four blocks, needs a lot of room.

NON-SPORTING BREEDS

BOSTON TERRIER

The lively and intelligent Boston Terrier is a compactly built, well balanced dog with a rather short body. A joy to have around the house, it is nevertheless determined and self willed.

The Boston Terrier's head should be in proportion to its size; its teeth should be short and regular, with an even bite, and its neck of fair length, slightly arched, carrying the dog's head gracefully.

The Boston Terrier, formerly the American Bull Terrier, derives from a crossbred Bulldog/ Terrier that was imported into the United States from Britain in 1865. Barnard's Tom, the first example of the breed with the desired screw tail, was bred in Boston, Massachusetts, and registered with the American Kennel Club in 1893. The breed takes its name from the city where it was developed.

Character and care

It is a lively, intelligent dog and a loving family pet. It is easy to look after and requires little grooming. However, it is difficult to obtain a show specimen with the right markings – ideally, a white muzzle, even a white blaze over the head and down the collar, breast and forelegs below the elbows.

KEY CHARACTERISTICS
• **CLASS** Non-sporting. **Recognized** AKC, CKC, FCI, KC(GB).
• **SIZE** Weight not exceeding 11.4kg (25lb) divided by classes: *lightweight*, under 6.8kg (15lb); *middleweight*, under 9.1kg (20lb); *heavyweight*, under 11.4kg (25lb).
• **COAT** Short and smooth.
• **COLOUR** Brindle with white markings: brindle must show distinctly throughout body; black with white markings, but brindle with white markings preferred.
• **OTHER FEATURES** Square head, flat on top; round eyes set wide apart; broad, square jaw; ears erect at corners of head; broad chest; fine, low-set tail.

BULLDOG

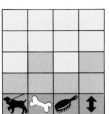

The Bulldog's proud ancestry can be traced back to the Molussus, the fighting dog named from an ancient Greek tribe, the Molossi. As its name suggests, it was bred to bait bulls. According to one story, this "sport" commenced in Britain in 1204 or thereabouts, when Lord Stamford of Lincolnshire in England was greatly amused by the sight of some butcher's dogs tormenting a bull. This gave his Lordship the idea of providing a field in which bull-baiting tournaments might take place on condition that the butcher would provide one bull a year for the "sport". Later, pits were set up in various parts of Britain where dogs would also fight other dogs.

When bull-baiting became illegal in 1835, the Bulldog was in danger of extinction. Fortunately, however, a Mr Bill George continued to breed Bulldogs and, in 1875, the first specialist club for the breed was formed, known as the Bulldog Club Incorporated. This was followed in 1891 by the London Bulldog Society, which still holds its annual meeting at Crufts Dog Show.

The Bulldog is not able to accompany its owner on long walks, but it does make a delightful companion.

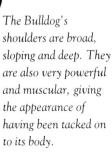

The Bulldog's shoulders are broad, sloping and deep. They are also very powerful and muscular, giving the appearance of having been tacked on to its body.

Character and care

Despite its fearsome appearance, the Bulldog is now a gentle, good natured dog. It adores children and makes a delightful pet. The only grooming it requires is a daily run through with a stiff brush and a rub-down. Care must be taken that it is not over exerted in hot weather.

KEY CHARACTERISTICS
• **CLASS** Non-sporting. **Recognized** AKC, ANKC, CKC, FCI, KC(GB), KUSA.
• **SIZE** Weight: dogs 22.7–25kg (50–55lb), bitches 18–22.7kg (40–50lb).
• **COAT** Short, smooth and close, and finely textured.
• **COLOUR** Uniform colour or with black mask or muzzle; reds, red brindle, piebald; black undesirable.
• **OTHER FEATURES** Large skull; eyes set low; ears small and set high on head; broad, sloping shoulders; tail set low and can be either straight or screwed.

DALMATIAN

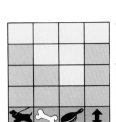

The nose of the black spotted Dalmatian is always black, but in the liver spotted variety it is brown.

The Dalmatian is named after Dalmatia on the Adriatic coast, but it is in Britain that the modern breed became well established. Heads would turn as a carriage of the British aristocracy went by with an elegant Dalmatian trotting alongside the horses. The breed still has an affinity with horses and will prove its worth as a ratter in the stables. Generally, however, the Dalmatian of today is kept solely as a pet and show dog.

Although already popular in Britain, the Dalmatian's registrations doubled following the filming in 1959 of Dodie Smith's book, *101 Dalmatians*. The breed received a further boost in 1978 when Mrs E. J. Woodyatt's Champion Fanhill Faune won the coveted Best in Show award at Crufts, in London. The breed's friendly character and elegant appearance have made it popular as a pet and show dog worldwide.

Character and care

This affectionate and energetic dog quickly becomes a family favourite. It requires plenty of exercise and a daily brushing but does tend to shed white hairs, which does not endear the breed to the houseproud. However, its intelligence and equable temperament should make up for this small failing.

KEY CHARACTERISTICS
● **CLASS** Non-sporting. **Recognized** AKC, ANKC, CKC, FCI, KC(GB), KUSA.
● **SIZE** Height at withers: 47.5–58.5cm (19–23in). Weight: 22.7–25kg (50–55lb).
● **COAT** Short, fine, dense and close; sleek and glossy in appearance.
● **COLOUR** Pure white ground colour with black or liver brown spots, not running together but round and well-defined, and as evenly distributed as possible; spots on extremities smaller than those on body.
● **OTHER FEATURES** Long head and flat skull; eyes set moderately far apart; medium-sized ears set high; deep chest; long tail that is carried with a slight upward curve.

A friendly, outgoing carriage dog capable of great speed, the Dalmatian should be free of any aggression or nervousness.

SCHIPPERKE

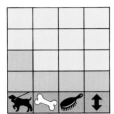

The Schipperke originated in Belgium but is often thought to be a Dutch dog, a confusion which may have arisen because the Netherlands and Belgium are relatively modern countries. The breed is thought by some to be 200 years old, although no records exist to prove this. It may have been established as long ago as the mid-1500s, because of a story that two black dogs without tails rescued Prince William of Orange (1533–84) from an assassin. Differences of opinion also exist on the breed's ancestry. Some think it arose from early northern spitz dogs, while others consider it a descendant of a now-extinct Belgian Sheepdog.

The Schipperke was once the most popular housepet and watchdog in Belgium. Traditionally its job there was to guard canal barges when they were tied up for the night, and it was this task that earned the breed its name. *Schipperke* is Flemish for "little captain", and has also been translated as "little skipper", "little boatman" and even "little corporal".

This breed was first exhibited in 1880. It was recognized by the Royal Schipperke Club of Brussels in 1886, and given an official standard in 1904. The Schipperke Club of England was formed in 1905 and the Schipperke Club of America in 1929. Miss F. Isabel Ormiston of Kelso Kennels is credited with being the greatest pioneer of the breed in the United States.

Character and care

The Schipperke is an affectionate dog which is good with children, usually very long lived, and an excellent watchdog. It is said to be able to walk up to 10km (6 miles) a day without tiring, but will make do with considerably less exercise. It should be housed indoors rather than in a kennel, and its coat needs very little attention.

Although other colours sometimes appear, the long lived and faithful Schipperke is generally pure black.

KEY CHARACTERISTICS
● **CLASS** Non-sporting. **Recognized** AKC, ANKC, CKC, FCI, KC(GB), KUSA.
● **SIZE** Height at withers: dogs 27.5–32.5cm (11–13in), bitches 25–30cm (10–12in). Weight: 5.4–8.1kg (12–18lb).
● **COAT** Abundant and dense, with longer hair on the neck, shoulders, chest and backs of rear legs.
● **COLOUR** Black, but the undercoat can be slightly lighter. Outside the USA other solid colours are permissible.
● **OTHER FEATURES** Broad head with flat skull; eyes oval, dark brown; ears moderately long; chest broad and deep; the tail is docked.

The Schipperke has a sharp, foxy expression; its back is short, straight and long; its feet are small and cat like.

FINNISH SPITZ

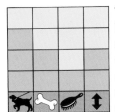

The Finnish Spitz is known in its native land as Suomenpystykorva, which means "cock-eared dog". It is the national dog of Finland, and is mentioned in a number of heroic Finnish national songs. It was once used by Lapp hunters to track elk and polar bears, but is now popular throughout Scandinavia for hunting grouse and other game birds. Related to the Russian Laika, the breed originated in the eastern area of Finland. It was introduced to and pioneered in Britain in the 1920s by the late Lady Kitty Ritson, who is responsible for the breed's nickname of Finkie.

Character and care

While still a favourite with hunters in Scandinavia, the Finnish Spitz is kept almost entirely as a companion and show dog elsewhere. It is appreciated as a faithful and home-loving pet, which is good with children and adept at guarding. It requires plenty of exercise and daily brushing.

KEY CHARACTERISTICS
• **CLASS** Non-sporting. **Recognized** AKC, CKC, FCI, KC(GB).
• **SIZE** Height at withers: dogs 43–50cm (17–20in), bitches 39–45cm (15–18in). Weight: 11.3–16kg (25–35lb).
• **COAT** Short and close on head and front of legs, longer on body and back of legs; semi-erect and stiff on neck and back.
• **COLOUR** Reddish-brown or red-gold on back, preferably bright; lighter shades permissible on the underside.
• **OTHER FEATURES** Medium-sized head and eyes; ears small and cocked, and sharply pointed; body almost square in outline; tail plumed, and curves vigorously from the root.

The Finnish Spitz is a breed that relishes being outdoors as much as it enjoys its home comforts.

FRENCH BULLDOG

The French Bulldog is gentle and peace-loving. It has distinctive "bat" ears and a natural screw tail, which people often wrongly imagine is docked.

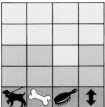

The French Bulldog, with its distinctive bat-like ears and screw tail, has had many famous owners, ranging from King Edward VII of England to the French novelist, Colette. It is obviously a descendant of small bulldogs, but it is not known whether these were English dogs taken to France by Nottingham laceworkers in the 19th century or dogs imported to France from Spain. Small English Bulldog ancestry is most generally accepted, despite the discovery of an ancient bronze plaque of a dog bearing an unmistakable likeness to the French Bulldog and inscribed: "Dogue de Burgos, España 1625".

A French Bulldog club was formed in Britain in 1902 and, in 1912, the breed was accepted by the British Kennel Club. By 1913, it had also achieved 100 entries at the Westminster Dog Show in New York.

Character and care

This breed is a popular and easy dog to show, and makes a delightful companion. It is good natured, affectionate and courageous, and usually gets on well with children and with other pets. Owners must become accustomed to its gentle snuffling, and be aware that it will invariably wander off and sulk on the rare occasions when it is in disgrace.

The "Frenchie" is easy to groom, requiring just a daily brush and a rub-down with a silk handkerchief, or piece of towelling, to make its coat shine. The facial creases should be lubricated to prevent soreness.

Warning This flat-nosed breed should not be exercised in hot weather.

KEY CHARACTERISTICS
● **CLASS** Non-sporting. **Recognized** AKC, ANKC, CKC, FCI, KC(GB), KUSA.
● **SIZE** Average height: 30cm (12in). Weight: dogs about 12.7kg (28lb), bitches 10.9kg (24lb).
● **COAT** Short, smooth, close and finely textured.
● **COLOUR** Brindle, pied or fawn.
● **OTHER FEATURES** Head square, large and broad; eyes dark and set wide apart; "bat ears", broad at base and rounded at tip, set high and carried upright; body short, muscular and cobby; tail very short.

SCHNAUZER

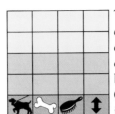

The Schnauzer or Standard Schnauzer is the oldest of three varieties of Schnauzer, the others being the Miniature and Giant. It has been depicted through the ages by artists including Albrecht Dürer (1471–1528), Rembrandt (1606–69) and Sir Joshua Reynolds (1723–92). The earliest likeness of the breed is probably that in Dürer's painting, *Madonna with the Many Animals 1492*.

Despite its many representations over the centuries, the Schnauzer's origin remains obscure. Some say that it was a cross between two now extinct breeds, the Beaver Dog of the Middle Ages and a rough-coated dog, perhaps a terrier, which was kept to dispel vermin. Others think that it evolved from the extinct Schafer Pudel and the Wire-haired German Pinscher. Still other researchers believe that the Schnauzer is descended entirely from drovers' dogs, including the Bouvier des Flandres to which it certainly bears a close resemblance. It was originally used as an all-purpose farm dog, and was a good ratter. It is also an excellent companion. The breed standard was first published in Germany in 1880. In 1918 the Bavarian Schnauzer Club united with the Pinscher Club of Cologne.

The Schnauzer's movement should be free, balanced and vigorous.

Character and care

The Schnauzer is an attractive, robust, intelligent and playful dog, which makes a good companion and is generally good with children. It enjoys plenty of exercise, and its hardy, harsh, wiry coat needs a certain amount of stripping and plucking. Pet dogs can be clipped but this will spoil the coat for showing, so owners wishing to exhibit are advised to discuss grooming with the breeder at the time of purchase.

KEY CHARACTERISTICS

- **CLASS** Non-sporting.
  Recognized AKC, ANKC, CKC, FCI, KC(GB), KUSA.

- **SIZE** *Standard* Height at shoulders: dogs 46–49cm (18½–19½in), bitches 44–46cm (17½–18½in). Weight: around 14.8kg (33lb). *Giant* Height at shoulders: dogs 65–70cm (25½–27¼in), bitches 60–65cm (23½–25½in). Weight: 32.8–34.6kg (73–77lb). *Miniature* Height: 30–35.5cm (12–14in). Weight 5.9–6.8kg (13–15lb).

- **COAT** Harsh and wiry, with a soft undercoat.

- **COLOUR** Pure black (white markings on head, chest and legs undesirable), or pepper and salt.

- **OTHER FEATURES** Strong head of a good length; dark, oval-shaped eyes; neat, pointed ears; chest moderately broad; tail set on and carried high, and is characteristically docked to three joints.

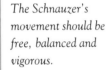

In this breed correct conformation is of more importance than colour or beauty points.

GIANT SCHNAUZER

The Giant Schnauzer or Riesenschnauzer was for many years known as the Münchener Dog, because it originated from an area near Munich. It is believed to have evolved from crosses between smooth-coated drovers' dogs and rough-coated shepherd dogs, as well as black Great Danes and the Bouvier des Flandres. It worked as a cattle dog until the need for such an animal declined.

The Giant Schnauzer made its first appearance in the show ring at Munich in 1909, when it was listed in the catalogue as a Russian Bear Schnauzer. The 30 breed representatives created such an impression that the Munich Schnauzer Club was formed the following month. Not as popular as the Standard and Miniature varieties, the Giant Schnauzer might have become extinct had it not proved itself an excellent guard dog in the First World War. However, it was not until after the Second World War that dedicated fanciers in Germany worked hard to secure deserved popularity for this fine dog.

Character and care
This intelligent dog makes a reliable, good natured companion, which requires a fair amount of exercise. It needs little grooming other than stripping and plucking. The coat may also be clipped but this will spoil it for showing, so it is best to discuss grooming with the breeder at time of purchase.

Regular stripping prevents the prized "hard coat" of the Giant Schnauzer from becoming soft and woolly.

MINIATURE SCHNAUZER

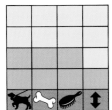

The Miniature Schnauzer, known in its native Germany as the Zwergschnauzer, was derived from crossing the Standard Schnauzer with smaller dogs – probably Affenpinschers. The breed was exhibited for the first time in 1899, and was established in Germany by the early 1920s. W. D. Goff is credited with taking the first breed member to the United States in 1923, while the first imports to the United Kingdom were made by a Mr W. H. Hancock in 1928.

In the United States and Canada, the Miniature Schnauzer is classed as a terrier and was at one time the most popular terrier there. In Britain, where it is regarded as a member of the utility group rather than a terrier, it is a popular family pet, and also does well in the obedience and show rings.

Character and care
The Miniature Schnauzer is a delightful small dog, which makes an excellent family pet and children's companion. Like its larger contem-

poraries, it needs a fair amount of exercise and its coat should be periodically stripped and plucked. The coat may also be clipped but this will spoil it for the show ring, so it is best to discuss grooming with the breeder at the time of purchase.

The Schnauzers are primarily companion dogs these days. They also make fine show dogs, but expert advice must be sought on how to trim them.

GERMAN SPITZ

The confident German Spitz should never show any sign of nervousness or aggression. Indeed, its buoyancy, independence and devotion to its human family are the breed characteristics.

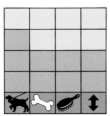

The only difference between the Small German Spitz (Kleinspitz) and Standard German Spitz (Mittelspitz) is size. Both are smaller versions of the Great German Spitz (Großspitz) or Wolfspitz. There are many varieties of spitz and, although it is difficult to pinpoint their origin, they were probably brought from Scandinavia by the Vikings. Spitz dogs were known as early as 1700 when white specimens were said to be kept in Pomerania and black ones in Württemberg. Some of the smaller varieties of the white

spitz bred in Pomerania became known and established in Britain under the name Pomeranian (see page 224). In 1899, the German Spitz Club was formed, and standards were issued for the separate varieties.

Character and care

This active, intelligent and alert dog is independent, yet devotion to its human family is a breed characteristic. The German Spitz can adapt to life in the town or country, and needs vigorous daily brushing and an average amount of exercise. If unchecked, the breed does have a tendency to yap.

KEY CHARACTERISTICS
• **CLASS** Non-sporting. **Recognized** ANKC, FCI, KC(GB), KUSA.
• **SIZE** *Small* Height: 23–28cm (9–11in). Average weight: 3.1kg (7lb). *Standard* Height: 29–35.5cm (11½–13in). Average weight: 11.3kg (25lb).
• **COAT** Soft, woolly undercoat and long, dense, straight outer coat.
• **COLOUR** All solid colour varieties.
• **OTHER FEATURES** A broad head; oval-shaped eyes; small, triangular ears; compact body; tail set on high and carried curled over the body.

KEESHOND

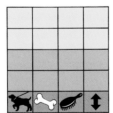

The Keeshond (plural Keeshunden, which is pronounced "kayshond") has been known as the Fik, Foxdog, Dutch Barge Dog and even as the Overweight Pomeranian in Victorian England. Its modern name is after a dog of this breed owned by the 18th century Dutchman, Kees de Gyselaer.

Like other spitz breeds, the Keeshond is believed to derive from an Arctic breed. It became popular in Holland as the companion of bargees and as a watchdog.

In 1905, Miss Hamilton-Fletcher, later Mrs Wingfield-Digby, arranged to import some puppies into England. In 1923, two of her dogs were shown at the Birmingham National

Dog Show as Dutch Barge Dogs. The Dutch Barge Dog Club (now the Keeshond Club) was formed in 1925 and, in 1928, challenge certificates were on offer for the breed. In 1920 Dutch fanciers again turned their attention to the breed. However, the FCI (Fédération Cynologique Internationale) has been reluctant to accept the standard that has been drawn up, believing that the Keeshond is identical to the German Wolfspitz.

Character and care

Good natured and long lived, the Keeshond tends to be a devoted one-person dog. It requires daily grooming using a stiff brush, and a fair amount of exercise. A choke chain will spoil the ruff.

JAPANESE SPITZ

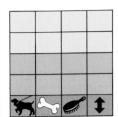

The Japanese Spitz shares a common ancestry with the Nordic Spitz. It is about half the size of the Samoyed, and is also closely related to the German Spitz and Pomeranian. Its ancestors are said to have been taken to Japan in the ships of traders many years ago, and there the breed was developed in isolation. The breed is a family favourite in Japan. It has only recently become known internationally, and is proving a popular show dog.

Character and care
Loyal to its owners but distrustful of strangers, this beautiful Spitz is alert, intelligent, lively and bold. It makes a fine small guard, and a number have been seen in Britain enjoying the role of companion and guard to long-distance lorry drivers. The breed requires daily brushing and, having an instinctive desire to herd other animals, enjoys a fair amount of exercise.

The Japanese Spitz has a snowy white coat, but its nose is black.

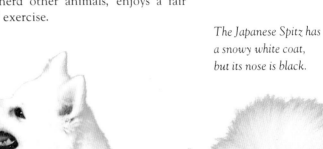

KEY CHARACTERISTICS

- **CLASS** Non-sporting.
  Recognized ANKC, CKC, FCI, KC(GB), KUSA.

- **SIZE** Height at shoulders: dogs 30–36cm (12–14in), bitches slightly smaller. Average weight: 5.9kg (13lb).

- **COAT** Straight, dense, stand-off outer coat; thick, short, dense undercoat.

- **COLOUR** Pure white.

- **OTHER FEATURES** Medium-sized head; dark eyes; small triangular ears standing erect; broad, deep chest; tail set on high and carried curled over back.

KEY CHARACTERISTICS

- **CLASS** Non-sporting.
  Recognized AKC, ANKC, CKC, KC(GB), KUSA.

- **SIZE** Height at shoulders: dogs, about 45.5cm (18in), bitches 43cm (17in). Weight: 25–29.7kg (55–66lb).

- **COAT** Long and straight with the hairs standing out; a dense ruff over the neck.

- **COLOUR** A mixture of grey, black and cream; undercoat pale.

- **OTHER FEATURES** Well-proportioned head that is wedge-shaped when seen from above; dark, medium-sized eyes; small, triangular ears; compact body; well-feathered, high-set tail that curls tightly over the back.

SHIBA INU

The Shiba Inu is an ancient breed associated with the prefectures of Gifu, Toyama and Nagano in central Japan ,and the name, in fact, means "little dog" in the Nagano dialect. Remains of a dog of this type were found in ruins dating back to the Joman era (500 BC). The Shiba Inu has, in recent years, become a firm favourite of exhibitors, following closely on the heels of the Japanese Akita (see page 64) onto the international scene. It is an excellent bird dog, guard and hunter of small game, with a considerable amount of native cunning.

Smallest of the spitz types, the fastidious, somewhat aloof Shiba is easily recognized by its deep set eyes and luxuriant coat.

Character and care
The Shiba is an affectionate, friendly and sensitive dog that makes a fine pet as well as a show dog and/or hunter. It needs a fair amount of exercise and a good daily brushing to keep it looking trim.

KEY CHARACTERISTICS
• **CLASS** Non-sporting. **Recognized** ANKC, FCI, KC(GB).
• **SIZE** Height at shoulders: dogs 37.5–40cm (15–16in), bitches 35–37.5cm (14–15in). Weight: 9–13.6kg (20–30lb).
• **COAT** Harsh, straight.
• **COLOUR** Red, salt and pepper, black, black and tan, or white.
• **OTHER FEATURES** Agile, sturdily built and well muscled; deep chest; long back; almond-shaped eyes; long sickle tail.

It is only in recent years that the Shiba Inu has been seen out of its native land. Now it has a growing band of devotees.

42

CHOW CHOW

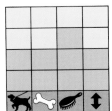

The Chow Chow is the only dog with a black tongue, a characteristic it shares with some small bears. This lion-like member of the spitz family has been known in its native China for more than 2000 years. It was bred variously for its flesh, its fur and as a hunter of game, its name possibly deriving from the Chinese Choo Hunting Dog. The Chow Chow is said to have been the original "Mastiff" of the Tibetan Lama, and is also referred to in early Chinese writings as the Tartar Dog and the Dog of the Barbarians.

The first Chow Chow imported into Britain in 1760 was exhibited in a zoo. In 1895, the Chow Chow Club was formed there, and in 1905 the first member of the breed was exported from Britain to America. This was Mrs Garnett Botfield's Chinese Chum which, in 1905, became the first American Chow Chow champion. In 1936, Mrs V. A. Mawnooch's Champion Choonam Hung Kwong won the Best in Show title at Crufts Dog Show. He was the recipient of 44 British Challenge certificates and was valued at the then immense sum of £5,250 (US$12,600).

Character and care

The Chow Chow has always had a reputation for ferocity but, although a formidable opponent, it is unlikely to attack unless provoked. It is a faithful, odour-free dog, which makes a good pet, but prefers to look to one person as its master and needs firm but gentle handling. A good daily walk will suffice, but the full coat requires considerable attention with a wire brush.

The Chow Chow is a good guard. Its tail, characteristic of the spitz breeds, is carried over its back.

A former hunter of wolves, today the Chow Chow is a successful show dog and companion.

KEY CHARACTERISTICS
● **CLASS** Non-sporting. **Recognized** AKC, ANKC, CKC, FCI, KC(GB), KUSA.
● **SIZE** Height at shoulders: dogs 48–56cm (19–22in), bitches 46–51cm (18–20in). Weight: 20.2–31.7kg (45–70lb).
● **COAT** Can be rough – abundant, dense and coarse textured, and varies in length, with pronounced ruff around head and neck and feathering on tail; or smooth – dense and hard, with no ruff or feathering.
● **COLOUR** Solid black, red, blue, fawn and cream.
● **OTHER FEATURES** Broad, flat head; dark, almond-shaped eyes; small ears slightly rounded at tips; long, nicely arched neck; broad, deep chest and compact body; tail set on high and carried curled over the back.

SHAR-PEI

The Shar-Pei's loose skin was an advantage in its fighting days. It is said that its opponents could not get a firm hold. No longer the rarest dog in the world, specimens still attract considerable attention.

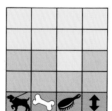

There are likenesses of the Shar-Pei or Chinese Fighting Dog dating back to the Han Dynasty (206BC to AD220), and it has been suggested that this loose-skinned breed may have originated in Tibet or China's Northern Province some 2000 years ago. Then it is likely to have been a larger dog, weighing some 39–75kg (85–165lb).

An unusual and attractive breed, the Shar-Pei was used to herd flocks and hunt wild boar in China. It was also matched against other dogs in trials of strength, although its nature is so affable that it may have had to be provoked to do so with the aid of drugs. It appears to have escaped the cooking pot, the fate of other Chinese breeds, because its flesh was not considered tasty.

It is not long since the Shar-Pei had the distinction of being the rarest dog in the world. Now it is drawing good entries in the show ring in the United Kingdom and elsewhere, and plans are afoot for breed members to be exported to Russia.

Character and care

A very affectionate dog with a frowning expression, the Shar-Pei is calm, independent and devoted. Its coat is never trimmed. It needs a reasonable amount of exercise.

KEY CHARACTERISTICS
• **CLASS** Non-sporting. **Recognized** AKC, ANKC, FCI, KC(GB), KUSA.
• **SIZE** Height at withers: 46–51cm (18–20in). Weight: 18–25kg (40–55lb).
• **COAT** Short, straight and bristly; no undercoat.
• **COLOUR** Solid colours only – black, red, light or dark fawn or cream.
• **OTHER FEATURES** Head rather large in proportion to body; dark, almond-shaped eyes; very small, triangular ears; broad, deep chest; rounded tail narrowing to a fine point, set on high and curling over to either side of the back.

LHASA APSO

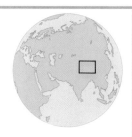

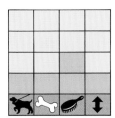

The Lhasa Apso originated in Tibet and is sometimes known as the Tibetan Apso. It is a small, indoor watchdog, possibly bred in the distant past from the Tibetan Mastiff. The word *apso* means goat-like, and the dog may have been so named because its coat resembled that of the goats kept by Tibetan herders. The breed was very highly regarded in its native land, and kept in temples and palaces. The Lhasa is often confused with the rather similar Shih Tzu from western China, but there are a number of physical differences between them, including the fact that the Lhasa Apso has a longer nose and its nose-tip is placed lower than that of the Shih Tzu. However, in the past there seems to have been some interbreeding between them outside their native lands, especially because it was the custom of the Dalai Lama of Tibet to give Lhasas from his court as gifts to visiting foreign dignitaries while, similarly, rulers in China gave the little Shih Tzu.

The Lhasa Apso first came to Britain in the 1930s, and the Tibetan Breeds Association was formed in 1934. The breed was recognized in America in 1935.

Character and care

The Lhasa Apso is happy, usually long lived, adaptable and good with children. It enjoys a good romp out of doors and has been seen in a stable yard, despite the need for careful daily grooming of its long coat.

KEY CHARACTERISTICS
• **CLASS** Non-sporting. **Recognized** AKC, ANKC, CKC, FCI, KC(GB), KUSA.
• **SIZE** Height at shoulders: dogs about 25.4cm (10in), bitches slightly smaller.
• **COAT** Top coat long, heavy, straight and hard; not woolly or silky. Moderate undercoat.
• **COLOUR** Solid golden, sandy, honey, dark grizzle, slate or smoke; black parti-colour, white or brown; all equally acceptable.
• **OTHER FEATURES** Long hair on head covering eyes and reaching towards floor; heavily feathered ears; dark eyes; compact, well-balanced body; tail set on high and carried over the back.

The Lhasa Apso is a firm family favourite, but its coat requires a great deal of grooming. Do not confuse it with the similar Shih Tsu, usually distinguished by its topknot.

SHIH TZU

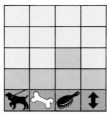

The upright head and round eyes are expressive of the Shih Tzu's alert, independent character. The nose should never be downpointed.

The Shih Tzu, whose Chinese name means "lion dog", is generally thought to have originated in western China. It resembles a Lhasa Apso except for its shortened face, and could be the result of crossing the Lhasa Apso and the Pekingese. Certainly it was the practice of the Dalai Lama of Tibet to give prize specimens of the Lhasa Apso to visiting dignitaries from foreign lands, including those from China.

An early standard for the breed written by the Peking Kennel Club, called the most flowery ever issued, reads: "should have lion head, bear torso, camel hoof, feather-duster tail, palm-leaf ears, rice teeth, pearly petal tongue and movement like a goldfish"!

The breed was first imported into England in 1930, but was not granted a breed register by the Kennel Club until 1946. The Shih Tzu was recognized by the American Kennel Club in 1969, and is now popular as a pet and as a show dog on both sides of the Atlantic.

Character and care
This happy, hardy little dog loves children and other animals and makes a good housepet suited to town or country living. It requires a good daily grooming using a bristle brush, and the topknot is usually tied with a bow.

KEY CHARACTERISTICS
• **CLASS** Non-sporting. **Recognized** AKC, ANKC, CKC, FCI, KC(GB), KUSA.
• **SIZE** Height at withers: 22.5–26.5cm (9–10½in). Weight: 4.1–8.1kg (9–18lb).
• **COAT** Long, dense, not curly, with a good undercoat.
• **COLOUR** All colours permissible; white blaze on forehead and white tip on tail highly desirable in parti-colours.
• **OTHER FEATURES** Broad, round head, wide between the eyes; large, dark, round eyes; large ears with long feathers, carried drooping; body longer between withers and root of tail than height at withers; tail heavily plumed and carried curved well over back.

Despite its elegant, slightly aloof bearing, the Shih Tzu is a courageous little dog that loves to play in the snow.

TIBETAN SPANIEL

Gentle and loving, the Tibetan Spaniel makes an ideal family pet, but tends to be fairly independent. It moves quickly on small, neat hare feet.

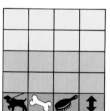

Despite its name, this breed is not related to the spaniels and is not known to have been used as a hunting companion or gundog. The Tibetan Spaniel is thought to have been in existence long before the history of Tibet started to be chronicled in the 7th century, and its origins are therefore obscure. The exchange of dogs between Tibet and China in ancient times means that Chinese dogs, such as early Shih Tzu or Pekingese-like dogs, could have contributed to it. It has also been said that the Tibetan Spaniel was crossed with the Pug to bring about the Pekingese. The Tibetan Spaniel was a favourite with monks, and was often kept in monasteries. It is said that it turned, and perhaps still turns, the prayer wheel of Tibetans. It is also said that, in common with the Hairless Dog in Mexico, it was used by humans for warmth.

The first Tibetan Spaniel recorded in the United Kingdom was brought by a Mr F. Wormald in 1905, but it seems to have been the late 1940s before the breed made any impact there.

Character and care

This charming, good natured dog is rarely seen outside the show ring. It is intelligent, good with children and makes a splendid housepet. It is energetic and enjoys a good romp, and its coat needs regular grooming.

KEY CHARACTERISTICS
• **CLASS** Non-sporting. **Recognized** AKC, ANKC, CKC, FCI, KC(GB), KUSA.
• **SIZE** Height: about 25.4cm (10in). Weight: about 4.1–6.8kg (9–15lb).
• **COAT** Moderately long and silky in texture; shorter on face and fronts of legs; feathering on ears, backs of legs and tail.
• **COLOUR** All solid colours and mixtures permissible.
• **OTHER FEATURES** Head small in proportion to body; dark brown, expressive eyes; medium-size pendant ears; tail set on high, richly plumed, and carried curled over the back.

This breed enjoys its daily walks. Watch that its collar does not mar the "shawl" of longer hair on its neck.

TIBETAN TERRIER

The Tibetan Terrier has a "resolute" expression and is intelligent and game. It looks like an Old English Sheepdog in miniature. Bred for farm work rather than going to earth, one wonders how it came to be called a terrier.

The Tibetan Terrier is not really a terrier at all, having no history of going to earth, but resembles a small Old English Sheepdog and, like those other little Tibetan dogs, the Tibetan Spaniel and Lhasa Apso, appears not to have been bred for any purpose other than that of companion dog.

Of ancient lineage, the Tibetan Terrier is said to have been bred in Tibetan monasteries, and specimens used to be presented to travellers as mascots and to bring luck. The breed was included in the Tibetan Breeds Association register in 1934 and now has its own standard. It has not yet become very popular in Britain and is even less well known in America, which may be to its advantage, as many breeds have been spoiled through over-popularization.

Character and care

The Tibetan Terrier might prove the ideal pet for those who admire the Old English Sheepdog but cannot house such a large animal. This appealing, shaggy little dog is also well worth choosing for its own sake. It is loyal, sturdy, a good walker, and devoted to its owners and to children, but a little apprehensive of strangers. Its long coat needs regular attention.

KEY CHARACTERISTICS
• **CLASS** Non-sporting. **Recognized** AKC, ANKC, CKC, FCI, KC(GB), KUSA.
• **SIZE** Height at shoulders: dogs 35.5–40.5cm (14–16in), bitches slightly smaller. Average weight: 9–10.8kg (20–24lb).
• **COAT** Soft, woolly undercoat; long, fine outer coat that can be straight or wavy.
• **COLOUR** Any colour or combination of colours permissible.
• **OTHER FEATURES** Large, round, dark eyes; pendant, feathered ears; compact and powerful body; medium-length tail set quite high and carried curled over the back.

BICHON FRISE

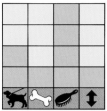

The word "bichon" is often used collectively to describe small, white dogs, such as the Coton de Tulear, Maltese, Frise, Bolognese and Havana. The Bichon Frise or Bichon à Poil Frise (curly haired bichon), or Tenerife Dog, is reputed to have been introduced to Tenerife in the Canary Islands by sailors in the 14th century. However, like the Poodle, it is thought to be a descendant of the French water dog, the Barbet, and its name comes from the diminutive, *barbichon*.

Similar in appearance to the Miniature Poodle, the Bichon Frise is recognized internationally as a Franco-Belgian breed. It was introduced into the United States in 1956 and registered by the American Kennel Club in 1972. A class for Bichon Frise was included at Crufts Dog Show in London in 1980.

Character and care

Happy, friendly and lively, this breed makes an attractive and cuddly small pet, which will enjoy as much exercise as most owners can provide. However, its long curly coat, resembling a powder puff, means that it is not the choice for anyone averse to grooming. The scissoring and trimming required to achieve this shape is intricate, and anyone intending to exhibit should discuss what is entailed with the breeder at the time of purchase.

KEY CHARACTERISTICS
● **CLASS** Non-sporting. **Recognized** AKC, ANKC, CKC, FCI, KC(GB), KUSA.
● **SIZE** Height at withers: 23–28cm (9–11in).
● **COAT** Long and loosely curling.
● **COLOUR** White, cream or apricot markings permissible up to 18 months. Dark skin desirable.
● **OTHER FEATURES** Long ears hanging close to head; dark, round eyes with black rims; relatively long, arched neck; tail carried gracefully curved over the body.

Friendly and outgoing, this little dog has grown steadily in popularity over the past 20 years.

The Bichon Frise has to have its coat regularly scissored. It is often to be seen in a canine beauty parlour.

STANDARD POODLE

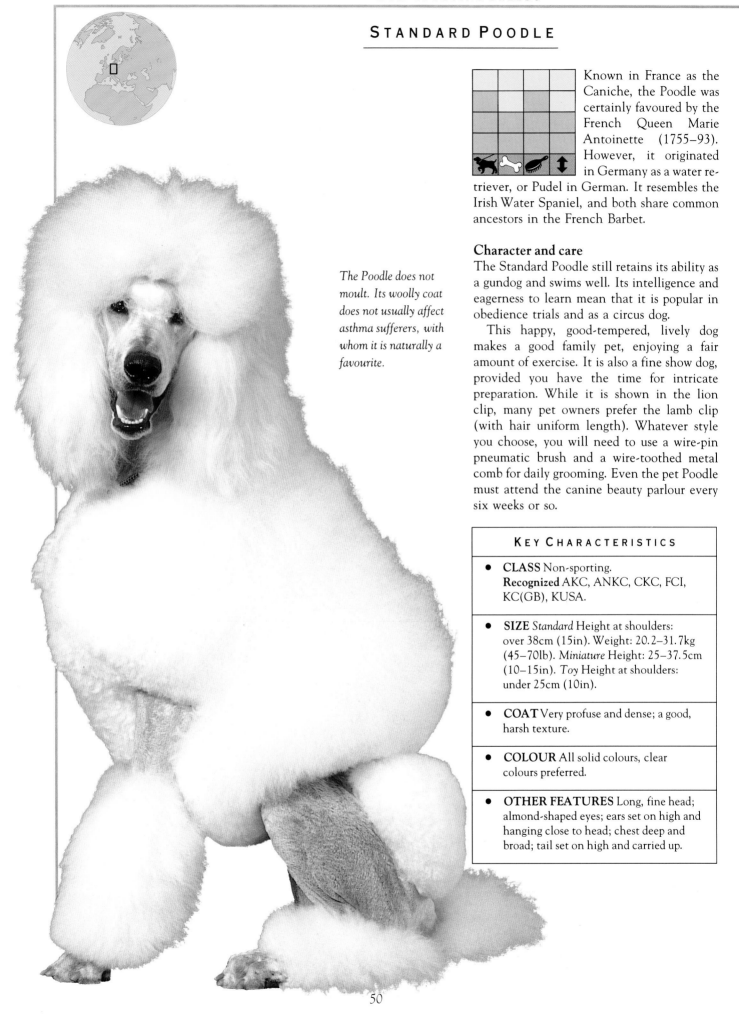

The Poodle does not moult. Its woolly coat does not usually affect asthma sufferers, with whom it is naturally a favourite.

Known in France as the Caniche, the Poodle was certainly favoured by the French Queen Marie Antoinette (1755–93). However, it originated in Germany as a water retriever, or Pudel in German. It resembles the Irish Water Spaniel, and both share common ancestors in the French Barbet.

Character and care

The Standard Poodle still retains its ability as a gundog and swims well. Its intelligence and eagerness to learn mean that it is popular in obedience trials and as a circus dog.

This happy, good-tempered, lively dog makes a good family pet, enjoying a fair amount of exercise. It is also a fine show dog, provided you have the time for intricate preparation. While it is shown in the lion clip, many pet owners prefer the lamb clip (with hair uniform length). Whatever style you choose, you will need to use a wire-pin pneumatic brush and a wire-toothed metal comb for daily grooming. Even the pet Poodle must attend the canine beauty parlour every six weeks or so.

KEY CHARACTERISTICS
• **CLASS** Non-sporting. **Recognized** AKC, ANKC, CKC, FCI, KC(GB), KUSA.
• **SIZE** *Standard* Height at shoulders: over 38cm (15in). Weight: 20.2–31.7kg (45–70lb). *Miniature* Height: 25–37.5cm (10–15in). *Toy* Height at shoulders: under 25cm (10in).
• **COAT** Very profuse and dense; a good, harsh texture.
• **COLOUR** All solid colours, clear colours preferred.
• **OTHER FEATURES** Long, fine head; almond-shaped eyes; ears set on high and hanging close to head; chest deep and broad; tail set on high and carried up.

MINIATURE POODLE

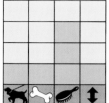

The Miniature Poodle was bred down from the Standard, presumably by using the smaller specimens, and in turn played its part in producing the even smaller Toy Poodle.

During the 1950s the Miniature Poodle became the most popular breed in many countries because it was believed, wrongly, that as more people migrated to the towns, interest in working breeds would lessen. This did not prove to be the case, and while there are those who say that it is not a proper dog at all – no doubt blissfully unaware of its origins as a gundog and water retriever – the Miniature Poodle remains a favourite.

Character and care

The Miniature Poodle has the same show standard as the larger and smaller breeds, except in the matter of size, and has similar characteristics. It requires frequent regular visits to the canine beauty parlour, even if it is not the intention to exhibit. Use a wire-pin pneumatic brush and a wire-toothed metal comb for daily grooming.

The intelligent and fun loving Miniature Poodle is often very long lived, and may survive for 17 years or more.

TOY POODLE

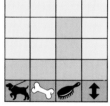

The origin of the Toy Poodle is exactly the same as that of its much larger relative, the Standard Poodle, for it is a descendant of the Miniature Poodle. The smaller specimens were so much in demand that, by the middle of the 1950s, the UK Kennel Club agreed to open a separate register for them. These are the least robust of the three varieties, however, so it is essential to select from sound stock.

Character and care

The Toy Poodle has the same characteristics and show standard as its larger contemporaries, except in the matter of size. It is happy and good tempered and makes a delightful pet that is ideal for the apartment dweller who nonetheless enjoys a canine companion. The Toy is exhibited in the same clips as the other two varieties. In any case it will require regular visits to the canine beauty parlour. Use a wire-pin pneumatic brush and a wire-toothed metal comb for daily grooming.

Even the Poodle kept solely as a pet companion must have its coat clipped about every six weeks.

WORKING BREEDS

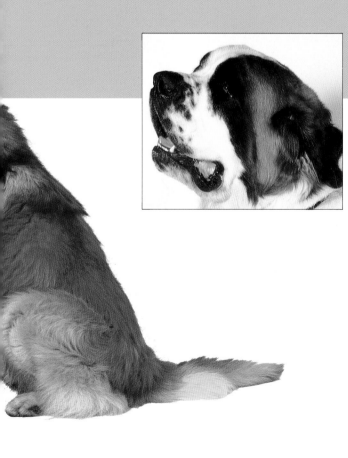

MASTIFF

Of great strength and dignity, the Mastiff is normally gentle, but can be a formidable guard.

The Mastiff is among the most ancient breeds of dog. Mastiff-like dogs were treasured by the Babylonians over 4000 years ago, and the Mastiff has been resident in Britain since the time of Julius Caesar. The breed has proved its worth as a formidable guard and as a hunter. The Mastiff was depicted on the 12th century Bayeux Tapestry and in a painting by Van Dyck (1599–1641) of the children of King Charles I. Shakespeare's play, *Henry V*, mentions ". . . mastiffs of unmatchable courage".

In the 19th century Saint Bernard blood was introduced. There were less than a dozen Mastiffs left in Britain after the Second World War because many kennels had been disbanded, and numbers declined in America as well. The situation is gradually improving.

Character and care
The Mastiff is large and dignified. It is usually devoted to its owner. It needs regular walking to build up its muscles. Many do not complete growth until their second year.

KEY CHARACTERISTICS
• **CLASS** Working. **Recognized** AKC, ANKC, CKC, FCI, KC(GB), KUSA.
• **SIZE** Minimum height: dogs 75cm (30in), bitches 68.5cm (27½in). Weight: 78.7–85.5kg (175–190lb).
• **COAT** Outer coat short and straight; undercoat dense and close-lying.
• **COLOUR** Apricot, fawn or brindle; in all, the muzzle, ears and nose should be black, with black around the eyes and extending up between them.
• **OTHER FEATURES** Broad skull; small eyes set wide apart; small ears; long, broad body; legs squarely set; tail set on high.

PYRENEAN MASTIFF

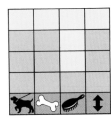

The Pyrenean Mastiff or Mastin de los Pirineos is a Spanish breed native to the southern slopes of the Pyrenees, where it was used for centuries to guard flocks during the annual migrations. The Mastiff is heavily built, with a short, broad muzzle and a deep stop. It carries its tail high when aroused.

Character and care
The Pyrenean Mastiff is intelligent, loyal and generally good natured but is a formidable guard. It is not a good choice for the inexperienced dog owner. It needs plenty of exercise; and grooming with a bristle brush.

KEY CHARACTERISTICS
• **CLASS** Working. **Recognized** CKC, FCI.
• **SIZE** Height at withers: dogs 70–80cm (27½–31½in), bitches slightly less. Weight: 55–70kg (121–155lb).
• **COAT** Medium length, thick, dense and rough to the touch.
• **COLOUR** White with golden or grey markings on head; some markings on body.
• **OTHER FEATURES** Large head; small, dark eyes; small ears; long, robust body; supple tail with good feathering.

TIBETAN MASTIFF

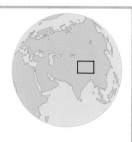

The tail of the Tibetan Mastiff curls over its back in the same manner as that of the Chow Chow. Its broad skull is generally well wrinkled.

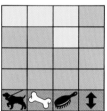

The Tibetan Mastiff is one of many breeds which is descended from the Molossus, a fighting dog of ancient Rome. It originated in central Asia, where it guarded flocks, and it can still be found in the central Asian steppes and around the Himalayan foothills performing the same task for nomadic shepherds. There is mention of the Tibetan Mastiff as early as the 13th century in the chronicles of the explorer Marco Polo, who referred to native mastiffs "as large as asses". This was possibly an exaggeration, but it is certainly imposing, as can be seen from the *New Book of the Dog* by Robert Leighton, in which he writes of the journey of "Bhotian", a Tibetan Mastiff exhibited at Crystal Palace, London in 1906: "Bhotian's journey through India was an expensive one as he had to have a carriage to himself. He effectively cleared the platform at all stations where he was given exercise."

The Tibetan Mastiff was imported into Britain by King George IV (reigned 1820–30) and reached America earlier this century, but is not numerous in either country. The breed was given an interim breed standard by the British Kennel Club in about 1986, and support for it appears to be growing.

Character and care

This breed makes a fine companion, watchdog and guard. It is aloof, protective and slow to mature, reaching its best at 2–3 years in females and at least 4 years in males. The Tibetan Mastiff has a reliable temperament unless provoked, and needs regular vigorous exercise on hard ground and daily brushing.

KEY CHARACTERISTICS
● **CLASS** Working. **Recognized** ANKC, FCI, KC(GB), KUSA.
● **SIZE** Minimum height: dogs 66cm (26in), bitches 61cm (24in). Minimum weight: 81.6kg (180lb).
● **COAT** Medium length, thicker on males than females, with a heavy undercoat.
● **COLOUR** Rich black, black and tan, brown, various shades of gold, various shades of grey, grey with gold markings.
● **OTHER FEATURES** Broad, heavy head; medium-sized, very expressive eyes; medium-sized ears; strong body with a straight back; tail medium length to long.

The lips of the Tibetan Mastiff are pendulous, and it often has tan markings over its eyes.

SPANISH MASTIFF

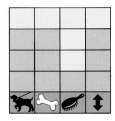

The Spanish Mastiff or Mastin de España (de Estremadura, de la Mancha) is an obvious descendant of the Molossus of ancient Rome. In common with many other mastiffs, this courageous and powerful animal was at one time used in organized dog fights, as a dog of war and as a hunter of wild boar. As a guard it protected stock during the traditional seasonal migrations across the mountains of southern Spain.

The Spanish Mastiff is not unlike the Neapolitan Mastiff in appearance, but has a longer coat and a more refined head. Traditionally, its ears were cropped and its tail docked to help reduce injuries in combat. These practices seem to be carried out less nowadays, greatly enhancing the appearance of this impressive animal.

Character and care

A superb guard of considerable strength and stamina, the Spanish Mastiff is loyal to its owner and responsive to training, but is not a suitable pet for the inexperienced dog owner. It needs wide open spaces and plenty of exercise. Groom with a bristle brush.

KEY CHARACTERISTICS
• **CLASS** Working. **Recognized** FCI.
• **SIZE** Height at shoulders: dogs 66–71cm (26–28in), bitches smaller. Weight: about 50–60kg (110–132lb).
• **COAT** Short, thick and coarse.
• **COLOUR** Wolf grey, fawn, brindle or white, with black, fawn or grey markings, grizzle.
• **OTHER FEATURES** Broad head with a rounded skull; small, dark eyes; pointed, pendant ears; powerful body; short thick tail carried low in repose and slightly curled in action.

NEAPOLITAN MASTIFF

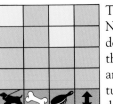

The massive, imposing Neapolitan Mastiff is doubtless a descendant of the fighting mastiffs of ancient Rome and, in turn, of the Molossus dogs prized by Alexander the Great in Greece. Bred as a fighting dog, it has also been employed as a guard. It is majestic in appearance, being one of the largest and heaviest of dogs. In its native land, it often wears a spiked collar and its ears are cropped to add an air of ferocity.

The Neapolitan was first exhibited at a dog show in Naples in 1946 and has since become known in other parts of the world, although it is not yet recognized in the USA.

Character and care

The Neapolitan Mastiff is generally a friendly animal, which is only likely to attack on command and makes an affectionate companion. However, it does need space and does best when given a job to do. It requires plenty of exercise, and its short coat needs grooming every few days.

KEY CHARACTERISTICS
• **CLASS** Working. **Recognized** ANKC, FCI, KC(GB), KUSA.
• **SIZE** Height: Dogs 65–72cm (25½–28½in), bitches 60–68.5cm (23½–27in). Weight: 50–68kg (110–150lb).
• **COAT** Short, dense and smooth.
• **COLOUR** Black, lead or mouse grey; sometimes there are small white spots on the chest or the tips of the toes.
• **OTHER FEATURES** Heavy head with a broad skull; eyes set forward and well apart; ears small in proportion to head; long, thick-set body; tail thick at root and tapering towards tip.

BULLMASTIFF

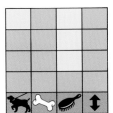

There have been bulldogs in Britain since the 13th century, but the Bullmastiff was developed some 200–300 years ago. It is the result of a cross between the Mastiff, an ancient breed which fought in the arenas of ancient Rome, and the British Bulldog. Like the Bulldog, it was used in bull-baiting until this "sport" was outlawed, and was a brave fighting dog, which could bear pain without flinching. It also had a considerable reputation for ferocity.

Later breeders worked towards a type which was 60 per cent Mastiff and 40 per cent Bulldog. The resultant Bullmastiff was registered by the Kennel Club in Britain in 1924.

Character and care

Despite its ferocious past, the Bullmastiff of today is a playful, loyal and gentle animal, an excellent guard and usually very dependable with children. However, it is too powerful for a child or slight adult to control, and should only be kept by experienced dog owners. It needs grooming every few days.

KEY CHARACTERISTICS
• **CLASS** Working. **Recognized** AKC, ANKC, CKC, FCI, KC(GB), KUSA.
• **SIZE** Height at shoulders: dogs 63.5–68.5cm (25–27in), bitches 61–66cm (24–26in). Weight: dogs 50–59kg (110–130lb), bitches 41–50kg (90–110lb).
• **COAT** Short, smooth and dense.
• **COLOUR** Any shade of brindle, fawn or red; a slight white marking on the chest is permissible, other white markings are undesirable; black muzzle.
• **OTHER FEATURES** Large, square, head; dark or hazel-coloured eyes; V-shaped ears set high and wide apart; strong, compact body; tail set on high.

This handsome breed was devised by crossing the Mastiff with the British Bulldog.

DOBERMAN

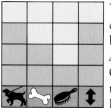

The Doberman was developed in the 1880s by Louis Dobermann of Apolda in Thuringia, Germany, who happened to be the keeper of the local dog pound. He wanted a ferocious, short-coated, medium- to large-sized dog with courage and stamina and developed his stock around the German Pinscher, which was both alert and aggressive. To this he introduced the Rottweiler with its stamina and tracking ability, the Manchester Terrier, then a much larger animal, from which the Doberman inherited its markings, and possibly also the Pointer.

The German National Doberman Pinscher Club was launched by Otto Göller in 1899, and the breed was given official recognition and a breed standard there in 1900. It was not until 1948 that the Doberman Pinscher Club was formed in Britain, and shortly afterwards the breed received recognition from the British Kennel Club.

BOXER

The Boxer traces back to the mastiff-type dogs taken into battle against the Romans by the Cimbrians, a Germanic tribe. The breed was first exhibited in Munich in 1895, and a Boxer was registered by the American Kennel Club as early as 1904. However, it was not until after the First World War that the Boxer was introduced into Britain. Within a few years, the breed had attained immense popularity worldwide.

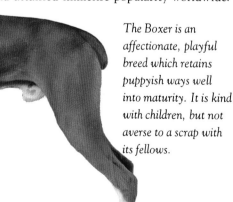

The Boxer is an affectionate, playful breed which retains puppyish ways well into maturity. It is kind with children, but not averse to a scrap with its fellows.

Character and care

The Boxer is affectionate and usually good with children. This obedient and loyal dog also makes a good guard. It is, however, a very strong dog and is not averse to a scrap with its fellows. It needs a reasonable amount of exercise, and its short coat is easy to care for.

KEY CHARACTERISTICS
• **CLASS** Working. **Recognized** AKC, ANKC, CKC, FCI, KC(GB), KUSA.
• **SIZE** Height: dogs 57–63cm (22½–25in); bitches 53–59cm (21–23in). Weight: 23.8–31.9kg (53–71lb).
• **COAT** Short, glossy and smooth.
• **COLOUR** Fawn or brindle with any white markings, not exceeding one third of ground colour.
• **OTHER FEATURES** Dark brown, forward-looking eyes; moderate-sized ears set wide apart; body square in profile; tail set on high and characteristically docked.

Character and care

The Doberman is a fine obedience and show dog and can make a good family pet, but it needs knowledgeable handling and training, being wary of strangers and constantly "on guard". It needs a lot of exercise, and should be groomed every couple of days.

KEY CHARACTERISTICS
● **CLASS** Working. **Recognized** AKC, ANKC, CKC, FCI, KC(GB), KUSA.
● **SIZE** Height at withers: dogs 65–70cm (26–28in), bitches 60–65cm (24–26in). Weight: 29.7–39.6kg (66–88lb).
● **COAT** Smooth, short, thick and close.
● **COLOUR** Solid black, brown, blue or fawn (Isabella), with rust markings on head, body and legs.
● **OTHER FEATURES** Almond-shaped eyes; small neat ears set high on head; well-arched neck; square body; tail characteristically docked at second joint.

The Doberman is constantly on the alert. It makes a first class companion and guard.

DOGUE DE BORDEAUX

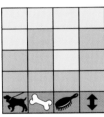

The Dogue de Bordeaux or French Mastiff is also known as the Dogue de Burgos in Spain and the Mastino Napolitano in Italy. It has recently come to international prominence because of the appearance of a breed member in a tear-jerking Hollywood movie. However, it has long been prized in France, where it is the national watchdog.

Of ancient lineage, the Dogue de Bordeaux is thought to be a descendant of the Tibetan Mastiff and the Molossus dog brought by the ancient Romans.

This impressive and appealing breed was once used to guard flocks against bear and wolf, and later in bull- and dogfights. In more recent times it has been kept mainly as a guard and companion.

Character and care

Of good and calm temperament, the Dogue de Bordeaux makes a first-class watchdog and guard, and an affectionate companion which is usually good with children. However, it is a powerful animal, and is not suitable for an inexperienced dog owner.

KEY CHARACTERISTICS
● **CLASS** Working. **Recognized** FCI.
● **SIZE** Height at withers: 69–75cm (27½–30in). Weight: 54.4–65.2kg (120–145lb).
● **COAT** Short and smooth.
● **COLOUR** Apricot, silver, fawn or brindle; muzzle, ears and nose can be black; nose can be lighter in dogs with a tan mask.
● **OTHER FEATURES** Massive head; large, wide-set eyes; pendant ears with slightly rounded tips; thick set body; tail carried low, but in line with back when on the alert.

MUDI

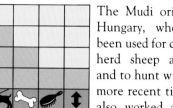

The Mudi originated in Hungary, where it has been used for centuries to herd sheep and cattle, and to hunt wild boar. In more recent times, it has also worked as a guard dog and as a dispeller of vermin. This versatile dog has something of the look of a Border Collie, but its tail, which hangs down, should be 5–7.5cm (2–3in) long – either by nature or by docking. The breed has only recently been recognized by the FCI and is rarely seen at dog shows.

Character and care

The Mudi is a brave, lively and intelligent animal, which is loyal and affectionate towards its human family and makes a good watchdog. It needs considerable exercise and daily brushing.

KEY CHARACTERISTICS
● **CLASS** Working. **Recognized** FCI.
● **SIZE** Height at shoulders: 35.5–48.5cm (14–19in). Weight: 8.1–13.1kg (18–29lb).
● **COAT** About 5cm (2in) long, shorter on head and front of legs; bristly and coarse, and tends to curl.
● **COLOUR** Black or white; sometimes a mixture of the two with scattered spots of more or less uniform size.
● **OTHER FEATURES** Dark brown oval eyes; erect, pointed ears; short, straight back; tail carried down.

GREAT DANE

One of the tallest dogs in the world, the Great Dane was a favourite of the German Chancellor Bismarck. A gentle giant which fits happily into its own special indoor space, the Great Dane sadly does not live much longer than 8 or 9 years.

BRAZILIAN GUARD DOG

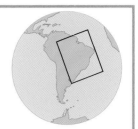

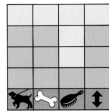

The Brazilian Guard Dog or Fila Brasileiro is descended from Spanish Mastiffs introduced into South America by the conquistadors in the 16th century. The Mastiffs were crossed with other dogs in Brazil to produce this mastiff-type breed, which has something of the expression of the Bloodhound about it. The Fila Brasileiro has been used as a drover, tracker and guard in its native land and is recognized by the FCI as a Brazilian breed.

Character and care

The Brazilian Guard Dog is obedient with its owner but distrustful of strangers, and makes a formidable guard. It needs firm training and handling to control its aggression. It should be groomed regularly with a hound glove.

KEY CHARACTERISTICS
• **CLASS** Working. **Recognized** CKC, FCI.
• **SIZE** Height: 60–74cm (24–29½in). Minimum weight: dogs 45kg (100lb), bitches 40.5kg (90lb).
• **COAT** Dense, soft and short; longer on throat.
• **COLOUR** Brindle or any solid colour except white; white allowed on tail tip and feet.
• **OTHER FEATURES** Large, heavy, square head; medium-sized, almond-shaped eyes; large ears; broad, deep chest; tail broad at the root and tapering to a point.

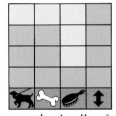

Among the tallest of the dog breeds, the Great Dane is known in its native Germany as the Deutsche Dogge. (German Mastiff). This statuesque dog, often referred to as the Apollo of the dog world, has existed in Britain for many centuries, and is said to be descended from the Molossus hounds of ancient Rome. In the Middle Ages, it was used as a wild boar hunter, companion and bodyguard, and the breed also played its part in bull-baiting.

In the 1800s the Chancellor of Germany, Bismarck, who had a particular interest in mastiffs, crossed the mastiff of southern Germany and the Great Dane of the north to produce dogs similar to the Dane we know today. They were first shown in Hamburg in 1863 under the separate varieties, Ulmer Dogge and Danisch Dogge. Then in 1876 it was decreed that the breed should be shown under the single heading Deutsche Dogge, and it was proclaimed the national dog of Germany. The Deutsche Doggen Klub was formed there in 1888. The Great Dane Club had already been formed in Britain, in 1882, and the breed has been in the British Kennel Club stud book since 1884.

Character and care

Despite its size, this breed should not be kennelled out of doors, but kept indoors as a member of the family. The Great Dane is good natured, playful and easy to train. However, it should not be teased lest an action be misinterpreted. It needs regular exercise on hard ground and daily grooming with a body brush. A sad fact for owners of this majestic breed is that it lives for only 8–9 years on average.

KEY CHARACTERISTICS
• **CLASS** Working. **Recognized** AKC, ANKC, CKC, FCI, KC(GB), KUSA.
• **SIZE** Minimum height over 18 months: dogs 76cm (30in), bitches 71cm (28in). Minimum weight over 18 months: dogs 54kg (120lb), bitches 46kg (100lb).
• **COAT** Short, dense and sleek.
• **COLOUR** Brindle, fawn, blue, black or harlequin (white, preferably with all black or all blue patches that have the appearance of being torn).
• **OTHER FEATURES** Large, wide and open nostrils; fairly deep-set eyes; triangular ears; very deep body; long tail, thick at the root and tapering towards the tip.

CANAAN DOG

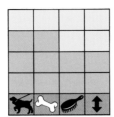

This breed has a long, bushy tail, pricked ears and an alert expression.

The Canaan Dog is an indigenous breed of Israel, which is said to have been developed through the selective breeding of the semi-wild Pariah dogs of the Middle East. A fine guard and protector of livestock, the Canaan has also proved its worth as a guard dog and as a messenger in the Israeli army. Other uses have been as a guide dog for the blind and as a search and rescue dog.

There are two varieties of Canaan Dog, one collie-like and the other Dingo-like, the latter being more heavily built.

Character and care

The Canaan is alert, home loving and loyal to its family. It has a distrust of strangers and will faithfully guard the humans and animals entrusted to its care, standing its ground if called upon to do so. It needs regular grooming with a brush and comb.

KEY CHARACTERISTICS
• **CLASS** Working. **Recognized** CKC, FCI, KC(GB), KUSA.
• **SIZE** Height at withers: 49.5–60cm (19½–23½in). Weight: 18–25kg (40–55lb).
• **COAT** Medium to long, straight and harsh; undercoat visible in winter.
• **COLOUR** Sandy to reddish brown, white or black; harlequin (black and/or blue-grey patches on a white background) also permissible.
• **OTHER FEATURES** Well-proportioned head; eyes slightly slanting, the darker the better; pricked ears; body generally strong but not massive; bushy tail set on high, carried curled over back when alert.

KOMONDOR

The Komondor was known as early as 1555, and has been used for centuries to guard flocks and property from predators and thieves on the Hungarian plains. It has worked with and without other dogs, first herding the semi-wild Hungarian sheep, and later protecting whatever required a large and commanding dog as guard. The breed was recognized in the United States in 1937, but is still comparatively rare in western Europe and has made its mark in the British show ring only over the last 10 years.

Very strong and agile for its size, the Komondor is hardy, healthy and tolerant of changing temperatures. It is a breed that can never be mistaken for any other because of its full white coat falling in tassels, or cords, which is thought by some to resemble an old-fashioned string mop. The cords of the coat form a kind of controlled matting which feels felty to the touch.

Character and care

The Komondor is a natural protector and will guard with its life sheep and cattle, or children and other pets if it is cast in the role of family companion. While it is utterly devoted to its human family, it is wary of strangers, does not take kindly to teasing and, if a warning growl goes unheeded, may attack without warning.

This breed needs plenty of exercise and meticulous grooming.

PINSCHER

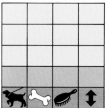

The Pinscher ("biter", in German) originated in Germany, where it has existed for several hundred years, as proved by likenesses in various works of art. The old Black and Tan Terrier may have contributed to its development at some stage.

Resembling the larger Doberman, to which it contributed, the Pinscher was officially recognized by the German Kennel Club as long ago as 1879. At the beginning of the 20th century, both smooth and coarse-haired puppies appeared in litters. However, the Pinscher Club ruled that a short-haired Pinscher would not be registered unless short-haired ancestors could be proved for three generations. However, it is only since 1988 that an interim breed standard has been set up for it by the British Kennel Club, and it will be interesting to see whether this good sporting and show breed makes an impact on the international show scene.

Character and care

The Pinscher's temperament has been described as high spirited and self possessed. It is a good natured, playful dog which is good with children and makes a fine guard, being alert, loyal, watchful and fearless. It needs exercise and grooming and can cope with life in an apartment.

KEY CHARACTERISTICS
• **CLASS** Working. **Recognized** FCI, KC(GB), KUSA.
• **SIZE** Height at withers: 43–48cm (17–19in).
• **COAT** Short and dense.
• **COLOUR** All colours from solid fawn (Isabella) to stag red; black or blue with reddish/tan markings.
• **OTHER FEATURES** Dark, medium-sized eyes; V-shaped ears set on high; wide chest; tail set on and carried high, and usually docked to three joints.

While sharing many characteristics with the Schnauzer, the Pinscher's smooth, glossy coat is similar to the Doberman's, to which this sturdily built dog contributed.

The Komondor's long, white, corded coat is a distinctive feature.

KEY CHARACTERISTICS
• **CLASS** Working. **Recognized** AKC, ANKC, CKC, FCI, KC(GB), KUSA.
• **SIZE** Minimum height at withers: dogs 63.5cm (25in), bitches 58.5cm (23½in). Weight: 36.3–68kg (80–150lb).
• **COAT** Long, coarse outer coat; may be curly or wavy; softer undercoat.
• **COLOUR** White.
• **OTHER FEATURES** Head is short in relation to its width; medium-sized eyes and ears; muscular, slightly arched neck; broad, deep body with a muscular chest; level back; tail continues line of rump, long and slightly curved at tip.

ROTTWEILER

Courageous and loyal, the Rottweiler can be a fearsome guard which will attack without warning, but many are gentle pets.

EURASIER

The Eurasier is a spitz breed, somewhere between the Chow Chow and Keeshond in appearance. It is a relative newcomer to the canine world, having emerged only in the 1950s as a separate breed. It was developed by a number of scientists, including the late Professor Konrad Lorenz, author of *Man Meets Dog*, who sought to revive what was once a Siberian dog. They did this by crossing the Chow Chow and the German Spitz, and then crossing again to another spitz, the Samoyed.

Character and care

This attractive, medium-sized dog has a good disposition, is easy to train and is relatively silent, barking only when provoked. It is also a vigilant and attentive guard, is loyal to its owner, hostile to intruders and needs time to accept newcomers. It has average exercise requirements and should be brushed regularly using a wire brush when necessary.

KEY CHARACTERISTICS

- **CLASS** Working. **Recognized** FCI.

- **SIZE** Height at shoulders: dogs about 60cm (23½in), bitches about 56cm (22in). Weight: dogs about 32kg (90lb), bitches about 26kg (57lb).

- **COAT** Abundant, short, dense undercoat and medium length top coat.

- **COLOUR** Red, wolf-grey, black, or black with fainter markings.

- **OTHER FEATURES** Fox-like head with flat skull and pronounced stop; almond-shaped eyes; erect ears; cat-like feet; tail reaching to hocks when resting, but carried curled over the back when on the move.

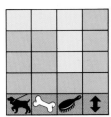

In its native Germany, this breed is still referred to as the Rottweiler Metzgerhund (Rottweil Butcher's Dog), because in the past it worked as a draught dog delivering the meat. It has also been used as a hunter of wild boar and a trusted cattle dog. Some fanciers believe that the Rottweiler is a descendant of the early German Shepherd Dog, while others consider that its ancestor was similar to the Tibetan Mastiff, brought as a guard by Roman soldiers. Certainly, this dog was prevalent from the Swiss canton of Argovie to the Nacker and Rottweil districts to the south of Württemberg, where the Romans had a military camp.

During the First World War, the Rottweiler proved itself to be an intelligent police dog and guard. It was recognized by the American Kennel Club in 1935, and the breed was introduced into Britain by the late Thelma Gray of the famous Rozavel Kennels in 1936. Surprisingly, another 30 years were to pass before the Rottweiler was given a separate register by the British Kennel Club. An inexperienced owner should never keep this breed. Nor should anyone who does not have considerable time to devote to its training.

Character and care

The Rottweiler is a large, courageous dog that makes an excellent companion-guard and responds to kindly but firm handling. It needs space and plenty of exercise. It also needs daily grooming with a bristle brush or hound glove and comb.

KEY CHARACTERISTICS
● **CLASS** Working. **Recognized** AKC, ANKC, CKC, FCI, KC(GB), KUSA.
● **SIZE** Height at shoulders: dogs 60–69cm (24–27in), bitches 55–63.5cm (22–25in). Weight: 40.5–48.6kg (90–110lb).
● **COAT** Medium length, coarse and lying flat, with undercoat on neck and thighs.
● **COLOUR** Black with clearly defined tan or deep brown markings.
● **OTHER FEATURES** Head broad between the ears; medium-sized, almond-shaped eyes; ears small in proportion to head; powerful, arched neck; broad, deep chest; tail docked at first joint and usually carried horizontally.

HUNGARIAN KUVASZ

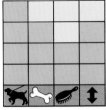

The Hungarian Kuvasz was established in Hungary many centuries ago, and has found its way to China, India, Tibet and Turkey. It bears a strong similarity to the Slovakian Kuvasz and, likewise, the Polish Sheepdog or Owczarek Podhalanski. These three, while regarded as separate breeds in their native lands, are in fact members of the same herding breed. The Polish and Slovakian types are sometimes called "Tatry" dogs after the mountain range that stretches between the two countries, and where each type has been long established.

Character and care

Brave, intelligent and lively, the Hungarian Kuvasz is an excellent guard – the name Kuvasz comes from the Turkish word *kavas* (guard). It has also been used to hunt big game. The Kuvasz may be kept as a pet, but it is wary of strangers. It needs plenty of exercise and a daily brushing to keep it looking trim.

KEY CHARACTERISTICS
● **CLASS** Working. **Recognized** AKC, CKC, FCI, KC(GB).
● **SIZE** Height at shoulders: dogs 70–73.75cm (28–29½in), bitches 65–68.75cm (26–27½in). Maximum weight: 50kg (110lb).
● **COAT** Harsh, wavy.
● **COLOUR** White or ivory.
● **OTHER FEATURES** Beautifully proportioned head; square in outline; almond-shaped eyes; tail set on fairly low, tip curving slightly upwards.

LEONBERGER

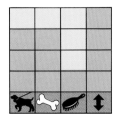

A German breed, the Leonberger is generally thought to have come about through the crossing of a Landseer and a Pyrenean Mountain Dog. However, some people believe that it is a descendant of the Tibetan Mastiff, while others consider it to be the product of selective breeding by Herr Essig of Leonberg. He is said to have used the Newfoundland, Saint Bernard and Pyrenean Mountain Dog to develop the breed. The breed was devastated by both World Wars and is considered a rare breed.

It was not until 1949 that a recognized standard for the breed clearly defined the differences between the Leonberger and the Saint Bernard. The Leonberger has worked in Germany, France, the Netherlands and Belgium as a watchdog, a protector of livestock, and as a draught dog, but has only become known outside these countries fairly recently.

Character and care

Good natured, intelligent and lively, the Leonberger is a fine-looking watchdog, produced from breeds of sound temperament. It is essentially a country dog, and needs daily brushing, regular exercise and plenty of space. It is very good with children, and has a great love of water.

KEY CHARACTERISTICS
● **CLASS** Working. **Recognized** ANKC, CKC, FCI, KC(GB), KUSA.
● **SIZE** Height at withers: dogs 72–80cm (28–32in), bitches 65–75cm (26–30in). Weight: 36.3–68kg (80–150lb).
● **COAT** Medium soft, fairly long and close to body.
● **COLOUR** Light yellow, golden to red-brown; preferably with black mask.
● **OTHER FEATURES** Top of head domed; eyes vary from light brown to brown; ears set high; long body; bushy tail carried at half-mast.

The Leonberger has a good natured expression. It is a strong, muscular dog, with webbed feet.

PORTUGUESE WATER DOG

Found mainly in the region of the Algarve, the Portuguese Water Dog is an invaluable member of the fisherman's crew. It is an exceptionally fine swimmer.

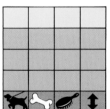

The Portuguese Water Dog (Cão d'Agua) was once a familiar sight throughout the fishing ports of the Iberian Peninsula, and is still commonly found in the Algarve region of Portugal. It is a fisherman's dog, a fine swimmer with great powers of endurance, and undertakes a wide variety of tasks. It will guard the catch, swim between boats, and dive and retrieve fish or objects lost overboard. It is also a good rabbiter.

There are two distinct varieties of the breed, one with a long, glossy, wavy coat and the other with a shorter, thicker, curlier coat, but conformation is identical. Although the Portuguese Water Dog was once a comparative rarity outside its native land, it is now a regular contender in the ring in Britain and elsewhere, and makes an attractive show dog.

Character and care

This intelligent and energetic dog is said to be self-willed but obedient to its owner, and somewhat apprehensive of strangers. It is a superlative swimmer and diver, needs ample exercise and regular brushing and combing. For exhibition purposes, the hindquarters are clipped from the last rib, and two-thirds of the tail are clipped.

KEY CHARACTERISTICS
● **CLASS** Working. **Recognized** AKC, ANKC, CKC, FCI, KC(GB), KUSA.
● **SIZE** Height at withers: dogs 50–57.5cm (19½–23in), bitches 43–52.5cm (17–21in). Weight: dogs 18.9–27kg (42–60lb), bitches 15.7–22.6kg (35–50lb).
● **COAT** Profuse and thick except under forelegs and thighs. There are two types, both without an undercoat: fairly long and loosely waved; and shortish with compact curls.
● **COLOUR** Solid black, white, or various shades of brown; black and white or brown and white; skin bluish under black, white, and black and white.
● **OTHER FEATURES** Large, well-proportioned head; round eyes set well apart; heart-shaped, dropped ears; wide, deep chest; tail thick at base and tapering towards point.

This dog's tail is set in line with its back and curls over. The tail is full and of natural length.

SWEDISH VALLHUND

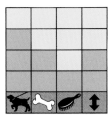

The Swedish Vallhund is known in its native land as Västgötaspets, which means "spitz of the West Goths". It closely resembles the Welsh Corgis, although the Vallhund is somewhat higher in the leg and shorter in the back. Undoubtedly there is a connection between the breeds, but whether Corgis taken by the Vikings to Sweden developed into the Vallhund or Swedish dogs brought to Britain developed into Corgis is not known. Like the Corgi, the Vallhund is a splendid cattle dog. Much credit for the development of the modern breed must go to the Swedish fancier, Bjorn van Rosen. Despite its antiquity, the Vallhund did not win recognition by any kennel club until 1950, but it is now gaining popularity in the international show ring.

Character and care

The Swedish Vallhund is a friendly, loyal, affectionate little dog, described in its standard as active and eager to please. It makes a good family pet and needs plenty of exercise.

Less than 50 years ago this charming breed was almost extinct, but is now a popular contender in the show ring. It is similar to the Pembroke Welsh Corgi, but is higher in the leg and has a shorter back.

The Vallhund has a foxy head and medium sized hazel eyes.

KEY CHARACTERISTICS

- **CLASS** Working.
  Recognized ANKC, FCI, KC(GB), KUSA.

- **SIZE** Height at withers: dogs 33–35cm (13–13¾in), bitches 31–33cm (12–13in). Weight: 11.4–16kg (25–35lb).

- **COAT** Medium length, harsh and close, with a soft, woolly undercoat.

- **COLOUR** Steel grey, greyish brown, greyish yellow, reddish yellow or reddish brown; darker guard hairs on back, neck and sides of body; lighter shade of same colour desirable on muzzle, throat, chest, belly, buttocks, feet and hocks; white markings acceptable in place of these lighter shades but never in excess of one-third of coat.

- **OTHER FEATURES** Head rather long; medium-sized eyes; medium-sized pointed ears; back level and well muscled; tail – if present – should not exceed 10cm (4in) in adults – puppies born with tails may be docked.

LAPLAND SPITZ

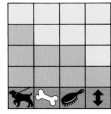

The Lapland Spitz or Lapphund is an ancient breed which was developed north of the Arctic Circle by the Lapp people to herd reindeer. It spread from there through the rest of Sweden, where it also herded sheep and other livestock. Today, it is kept as a household companion and guard, and is used for security by the Swedish army.

The Lapland Spitz is a medium-sized dog with strong jaws, prick ears, a long, thick double coat and a tail curled over its back in the manner typical of the spitz varieties. The breed was not recognized by the FCI until 1944, when a standard drawn up for it by the National Association of Swedish Dog Fanciers was approved.

Character and care

Affectionate and loyal to its owners and gentle with children, the Lapland Spitz tends to be aggressive towards and suspicious of strangers, making it a good watchdog. It is happiest kept in an outdoor kennel. It needs plenty of exercise and regular brushing.

KEY CHARACTERISTICS

- **CLASS** Working.
  Recognized FCI.

- **SIZE** Height at shoulders: dogs 44.5–49.5cm (17½–19½in), bitches 39.5–44.5cm (15½–17½in). Weight: 20kg (44lb).

- **COAT** Long, thick double coat, standing off from body. Dense undercoat, fringed belly and back legs, heavily plumed tail.

- **COLOUR** Dark brown, black, brown-white; solid colours preferred.

- **OTHER FEATURES** Characteristic pricked ears, thick coat and tail curled over back, but coat longer than some other spitz varieties.

JAPANESE AKITA

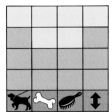

The Akita (or Akita Inu or Shishi Inu) is the largest and most well known internationally of the Japanese breeds. It originated in the Polar regions and has a history tracing back more than 300 years. The Akita was bred to hunt deer and wild boar, and has also, on occasion, hunted the Japanese black bear. It is an extremely swift-moving dog, which can work in deep snow. It also has webbed feet and is a strong swimmer, with the ability to retrieve wildfowl and to drive fish into fishermen's nets.

The Akita is revered in Japan, where it was officially appointed a national monument in 1931 in order to preserve the breed, and more recently was featured on a series of commemorative postage stamps. It is the recipient of a Japanese Dog Federation's "National Treasure" award, given under the auspices of the Japanese Government. Indeed, at one time this classic breed could only be owned by members of the Japanese nobility. The international popularity of the breed began when American servicemen took the Akita back to their homeland, after the Second World War.

AINU DOG

The Ainu Dog, also known as the Hokkaido, Kyushu or Ochi Dog, comes from the mountainous region of the Japanese island of Hokkaido and may have been taken there by the Ainu people when they emigrated thousands of years ago. The breed has changed little since its arrival, and with its smaller, heavy body it is said to resemble the Scandinavian spitz varieties more closely than other Japanese spitz breeds, such as the Akita. A medium-sized dog with a powerful physique, the Ainu is a guard and hunting dog, and is well behaved in the home.

Character and care

Despite its long history as a working breed, the Ainu Dog ideally combines the role of family pet and hunter. Intelligent and readily trained, it is fiercely loyal and affectionate towards an attentive master.

KEY CHARACTERISTICS
• **CLASS** Working. **Recognized** FCI.
• **SIZE** Height: dogs 49.5–53.5cm (19½–21in), bitches 42–48cm (16½–19in).
• **COAT** Double-coated: top coat medium short and dense, with dense undercoat.
• **COLOUR** Red, white, black, grizzle or black and tan.
• **OTHER FEATURES** Broad triangular head; ears upright and triangular; eyes dark and deep-set; muscular body; tail set on high, curling over back.

Character and care
The powerful but very trainable Akita is a versatile hunter and retriever, and a first class guard. It has a good temperament for a show dog and is now being kept widely as a pet. However, this alert and energetic dog should not be kept in confined conditions. It can be formidable if its hunting instincts become aroused and needs a good outlet, such as obedience classes, for its undoubted abilities. It also requires daily brushing and a reasonable amount of exercise.

The almond shaped eyes of the Akita are typical of the spitz type breeds.

The dignified and courageous Akita tends to show dominance over other dogs. This breed has been popular in the United States since the 1970s, and now has an equally large following in the United Kingdom and elsewhere.

KEY CHARACTERISTICS
• **CLASS** Working. **Recognized** AKC, ANKC, CKC, FCI, KC(GB).
• **SIZE** Height at withers: dogs 66–71cm (26–28in), bitches 61–66cm (24–26in). Weight: 33.7–48.6kg (75–101lb).
• **COAT** Outer coat coarse, straight and stand-off; soft, dense undercoat.
• **COLOUR** Any, including white, brindle and pinto (white with irregular black patches), with or without mask.
• **OTHER FEATURES** Large, flat skull; broad forehead; small eyes and ears; long body; large, full tail.

JAPANESE FIGHTING DOG

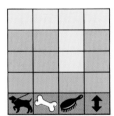

The Japanese Fighting Dog or Tosa was bred during the Meiji period (1867–1912), when dog fighting was a popular spectator sport in Japan. Local fighting dogs were crossed with the English Bulldog, English Bull Terrier, Saint Bernard and Great Dane, thus increasing height, strength and ferocity, and producing this massive, powerful yet agile dog. Named after Tosa on the Japanese island of Shikoku, the breed took on the roles of companion and guard when dog fighting was outlawed in Japan. It will fight to the death and is still reputed to take part in illegal fights in Japan.

Character and care
The Tosa can be fierce towards other dogs and needs experienced handling, but it is brave, patient and protective of its human family. Because of its aggressive past, people tend to regard this dog with caution and it is not permitted to be bred from in the United Kingdom. It should be groomed with a bristle brush and hound glove.

KEY CHARACTERISTICS
• **CLASS** Working. **Recognized** CKC, FCI.
• **SIZE** Minimum height at withers: 60cm (23½in). Weight: 45–90kg (100–200lb).
• **COAT** Short, smooth and hard.
• **COLOUR** Tan with or without markings in a different shade of tan; tan markings on white.
• **OTHER FEATURES** Large head; small amber-coloured eyes; small, high-set, dropped ears; powerful body; high-set tail reaching to the hocks.

ESTRELA MOUNTAIN DOG

A popular show dog in its native Portugal, the Estrela Mountain Dog is slowly but surely gaining international fame. It has great strength and is used for carting in its homeland.

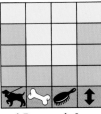

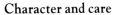

The Estrela Mountain Dog, also known as the Portuguese Mountain Dog or Cão da Serra da Estrêla, originated many centuries ago in the Estrêla mountains of central Portugal. It was bred as a herding dog and has in its make-up something of the Mastiff, and of the Saint Bernard, to which it bears some resemblance.

It has always been popular in its native Portugal, where it is still used as a guard dog. The breed standard was first published there in 1933. The breed was first introduced into the United Kingdom in 1974, and it is shown there at larger shows.

Character and care

The Estrela Mountain Dog is an excellent guard, with immense stamina. It is very loyal and affectionate to its owners but indifferent to other humans. This intelligent dog is said to need a great deal of love and firm, kindly handling. It requires plenty of exercise, regular brushing and a light diet, which should be discussed with the breeder at time of purchase.

The colour of the Estrela Mountain Dog is only seen when the young animal develops its outer coat. Its nose is always black.

KEY CHARACTERISTICS

- **CLASS** Working.
  Recognized FCI, KC(GB), KUSA.

- **SIZE** Height at shoulders: dogs 58–68cm (23–27in), bitches 51–61cm (20–24in). Weight: dogs 34–48kg (75–105lb), bitches 27–41kg (60–90lb).

- **COAT** Two types: long – thick, moderately harsh outer coat with feathering on backs of legs and thighs, and dense undercoat; short – short, thick and moderately harsh outer coat, with shorter, dense undercoat.

- **COLOUR** All colours, or combinations of colours, permissible.

- **OTHER FEATURES** Long, powerful head; eyes should be neither deep nor prominent; ears small in proportion to body; short back, higher at withers than loins; long, thick tail.

PYRENEAN MOUNTAIN DOG

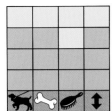

The Pyrenean Mountain Dog or Great Pyrenees probably originated in Asia before finding its way with immigrants to Europe. Its closest relatives are the Kuvasz and the Newfoundland to which it may have contributed. The breed has been used for centuries to guard flocks in the Pyrenean mountains bordering France and Spain, and throughout France. It was also a favourite at the French court prior to the French Revolution. A standard for this popular breed was approved in the mid-1960s.

Character and care

The Pyrenean can be kept in or out of doors, but must be well trained. It is a powerful dog, and I have witnessed one or two slight accidents when youngsters have thumped a strange Pyrenean on the head at dog shows. Generally, though, it is good natured, gets on with other pets and is a faithful protector. Provided you have sufficient space, food and time for regular exercise and brushing, the Pyrenean will make a good companion and/or show dog.

KEY CHARACTERISTICS
● **CLASS** Working. **Recognized** AKC, ANKC, CKC, FCI, KC(GB), KUSA.
● **SIZE** Height at withers: dogs 70–80cm (28–32in), bitches 65–72.5cm (26–29in). Minimum weight: dogs 50kg (110lb), bitches 40kg (90lb).
● **COAT** Long and coarse-textured, with a profuse undercoat of very fine hair.
● **COLOUR** White, with or without patches of badger, and wolf-grey or pale yellow equally acceptable.
● **OTHER FEATURES** Rounded crown; dark brown, almond-shaped eyes; small, triangular ears; broad chest; level back; tail thick at root and tapering towards tip.

The stately Pyrenean Mountain Dog was a favourite at the court of King Louis XIV of France.

The double dew claws in the Pyrenean's hindlegs are a distinguishing feature.

BERNESE MOUNTAIN DOG

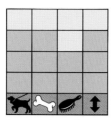

The Bernese Mountain Dog or Bernese Sennenhund is named after the canton of Berne in Switzerland, where it arrived with Caesar's army and was subsequently bred. Like other Swiss mountain dogs, such as the Great Swiss (see page 81), it has mastiff characteristics. The breed is believed to descend from the Molossus dog of ancient Greece and Rome, with some Rottweiler, Saint Bernard and Newfoundland blood discernible in its ancestry.

The Bernese has worked as herder and flock guardian in its native land, and is still used to pull milk carts up Swiss mountainsides. In Britain it frequently puts in an appearance, in harness, at fêtes and similar events in order to raise money for charity. This large, gentle dog has steadily gained popularity in the USA and Britain over the past few years, both as a pet and as a show dog, and is popular throughout Europe.

Character and care
The Bernese Mountain Dog makes a good pet for those with sufficient space, being amiable towards children and other pets. It needs regular brushing and plenty of exercise.

A capable worker, the Bernese Mountain Dog may also be kept as a loyal and affectionate pet.

KEY CHARACTERISTICS

- **CLASS** Working.
  Recognized AKC, ANKC, CKC, FCI, KC(GB), KUSA.

- **SIZE** Height at withers: dogs 64–70cm (25–27½in), bitches 58–66cm (23–26in). Weight: about 39.6kg (88lb).

- **COAT** Thick, moderately long, and straight or slightly wavy, with a bright, natural sheen.

- **COLOUR** Jet black, with rich, reddish brown markings on cheeks, over eyes, on legs and chest; some white markings on head, chest, tip of tail and feet are permissible.

- **OTHER FEATURES** Strong head with a flat skull; dark brown, almond-shaped eyes; medium-sized ears; compact body; bushy tail.

There should be a distinctive tan brand marking on each of its paws.

SAINT BERNARD

The Saint Bernard is intelligent, faithful and extremely gentle. It loves children, too, but does require plenty of space and large food rations.

The Saint Bernard is a gentle giant, despite being descended from the fierce Molossus dogs of ancient Rome. It is named after the medieval Hospice of St Bernard in the Swiss Alps, to which it was introduced between 1660 and 1670. It became famous for rescuing travellers and climbers on the Swiss Alps. One dog, Barry, saved 40 lives during the period 1800–10.

Prior to 1830, all Saint Bernards were short-coated, but in that year Newfoundland blood was introduced in an attempt to give the breed added size and vitality. As a result the modern Saint Bernard may be long- or short-haired. In 1810, a Saint Bernard called "Lion" was introduced into England and the breed was first exhibited in Britain in 1863. An international standard for the Saint Bernard was drawn up in Berne in 1887.

Character and care

True to its past, the Saint Bernard is intelligent, eminently trainable, loves children and is a kindly dog. Because of this, it is, unfortunately, sometimes kept in conditions which do not allow it nearly enough space. Like many heavyweights, the breed should not be given too much exercise in the first year of life, short regular walks being better than long ones. It needs daily brushing and requires generous quantities of food. It also slobbers. Sadly, like the Great Dane, this lovable, large dog has only a limited lifespan.

KEY CHARACTERISTICS
● **CLASS** Working. **Recognized** AKC, ANKC, CKC, FCI, KC(GB), KUSA.
● **SIZE** Minimum height at shoulder: dogs 69cm (27½in), bitches 64cm (23½in). Weight: 48.6–90kg (110–200lb).
● **COAT** Dense, short, smooth and lying close to body.
● **COLOUR** Orange, mahogany-brindle, red-brindle or white, with patches on body in any of these colours; white blaze on face, and white on muzzle, collar, chest, forelegs, feet and end of tail; black shadings on face and ears.
● **OTHER FEATURES** Massive, wide head; medium-sized eyes and ears; broad, muscular shoulders; broad, straight back; tail set on high.

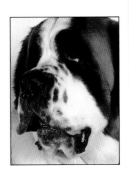

The white blaze that runs up the face of the Saint Bernard emphasizes its benevolent expression.

ESKIMO DOG

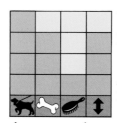

This hardy, strong spitz dog was developed to haul sleds in and around the Arctic Circle. The American polar explorer, Robert Peary (1856–1920), considered that there was only one breed of sled-dog with regional variations, but now a number of breeds are recognized. The beautiful Eskimo Dog probably originated in eastern Siberia, and shared common ancestry with the Alaskan Malamute, Siberian Husky and Samoyed. It bears a considerable resemblance to the Greenland Dog (which is not, at the time of writing, recognized in Britain), but the Eskimo Dog is shorter in the back and weightier.

Character and care

The Eskimo Dog is an excellent sled dog of remarkable endurance. It is a fine guard, which rarely lives indoors with its owners. It relishes vigorous outdoor exercise and a job of work, and benefits from regular brushing.

The Eskimo Dog, described by some as a miniature Husky.

KEY CHARACTERISTICS
• **CLASS** Working. **Recognized** FCI, KC(GB), KUSA.
• **SIZE** Height at shoulders: dogs 58–68cm (23–27in), bitches 51–61cm (20–24in). Weight: dogs 33.7–47.2kg (75–105lb), bitches 27.2–40.5kg (60–90lb).
• **COAT** About 15cm (6in) long, with a thick undercoat.
• **COLOUR** Any colour, or combination of colours.
• **OTHER FEATURES** Well-proportioned head; dark brown or tawny eyes; short, firm ears set well apart; broad, deep chest; large, bushy tail.

GREENLAND DOG

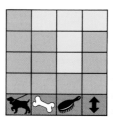

The Greenland Dog or Grönlandshund, like all the spitz breeds, originated in the Arctic Circle, probably in eastern Siberia. It shares common ancestry with other sled dogs, such as the Alaskan Malamute, Siberian Husky and Samoyed, but particularly resembles the Eskimo Dog which many consider to be the same breed. The Greenland is usually a little longer in the back than the Eskimo Dog and somewhat lighter.

Character and care

This sled dog has considerable powers of endurance, is faithful and obedient to its owner and makes a fine guard and a good show dog. However, it generally lives outdoors and is not suited to the house. It needs vigorous exercise, and regular brushing.

KEY CHARACTERISTICS
• **CLASS** Working. **Recognized** CKC, FCI.
• **SIZE** Minimum height at shoulders: dogs 61cm (24in), bitches 55cm (22in). Minimum weight: 29.7kg (66lb).
• **COAT** Straight, coarse and rather long, with a heavy undercoat.
• **COLOUR** Any colour or combination of colours except albino.
• **OTHER FEATURES** Cone-shaped muzzle; dark, slightly oblique eyes; small, triangular, erect ears; tail carried rolled over the back.

ALASKAN MALAMUTE

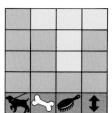

The Alaskan Malamute is a sociable member of the spitz family named after the Eskimo Mahlemut people who reside by the shores of Kotzebue Sound, a mountainous region in the Arctic Circle. According to stories, this and other similar arctic dogs derive partly from wolves. Whether this is true or not, the Malamute has developed great stamina and speed. It is highly prized as a sled dog, being capable of surviving in arctic temperatures, and of hauling heavy loads over rough terrain. The American explorer, Robert Peary (1856–1920), was of the opinion that there was only one breed of sled dog, which varied in name purely according to the region from which it came. However, there are distinguishing features between sled dogs, and a number of breeds have been identified. The Alaskan Malamute, which is one of the larger sled dogs, now has a standard of its own.

Character and care

Despite its rather wolfish appearance the Alaskan Malamute is a gentle, kind-natured dog, and makes a loyal and devoted companion, but is not very good with other canines. It needs a daily brushing and lots of exercise.

KEY CHARACTERISTICS
• **CLASS** Working. **Recognized** AKC, ANKC, CKC, FCI, KC(GB), KUSA.
• **SIZE** Height: dogs 64–71cm (25–28in), bitches 58–66cm (23–26in). Weight: 38.5–57kg (85–125lb).
• **COAT** Thick, coarse guard coat; dense, oily, woolly undercoat.
• **COLOUR** From light grey through intermediate shadings to black, or from gold through shades of red to liver; always with white on underbody, parts of legs, feet and part of mask markings; also other specific markings.
• **OTHER FEATURES** Broad, powerful head; almond-shaped brown eyes; ears small in proportion to head, triangular; strong, powerful body; tail moderately high-set.

Gentle and kind with humans, the Alaskan Malamute can be quarrelsome with its own kind.

SAMOYED

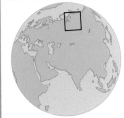

The Samoyed or Smiling Sammy takes its name from the Siberian tribe of Samoyedes. This beautiful and devoted spitz variety has great powers of endurance and was one of the breeds used by Fridtjof Nansen and Ernest Shackleton on their expeditions to the North Pole. It has also been used as a guard and to hunt reindeer. The Samoyed was introduced into Britain in 1889 by a Mr Kilburn Scott, who returned from the north coast of Russia with a pup. He subsequently mated a bitch "Whitey Pechora", said to have been obtained from a sailor in London, to a dog named "Musti" owned by Lady Sitwell, and many present-day Samoyeds descend from this pair. The standard originally drawn up by the Kilburn-Scotts has changed little over the years and British stock has been exported all over the world.

Character and care

Unlike many sled dogs, the Sammy lives in the homes of its owners in its native land. It is a devoted dog, which is good with children and makes an obedient, if slightly indepen-dent, housepet. Some breed members have excelled in obedience work. It revels in exercise, and its thick, water-resistant coat needs regular brushing and combing.

KEY CHARACTERISTICS
● **CLASS** Working. **Recognized** AKC, ANKC, CKC, FCI, KC(GB), KUSA.
● **SIZE** Height at withers: dogs 52.5–59cm (21–23½in), bitches 47.5–52.5cm (19–21in). Weight: 22.7–29.5kg (50–65lb).
● **COAT** Harsh, but not wiry, and straight, with thick, soft, short undercoat.
● **COLOUR** Pure white, white and biscuit, cream; outer coat silver-tipped.
● **OTHER FEATURES** Broad head; dark, almond-shaped eyes; thick ears, not too large, and slightly rounded at the tips; medium length back; long, profusely coated tail that is carried curled over the back.

The Samoyed's tail curls over its back in the characteristic manner of the spitz. Popular as a housepet, this dog has even made its mark in television and advertising.

SIBERIAN HUSKY

A dog of superb beauty, strength and stamina, the Siberian Husky has the Chukchi Sled Dog as an ancestor, and has a proud history of sled racing.

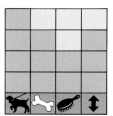

The Siberian Husky was developed in ancient times by the Chukchi people of north-east Asia who wanted a hardy sled dog with strength, speed and stamina. Wider recognition of its abilities came after the gold rush to Alaska at the turn of the century, when dog-hauled sleds were the only means of transportation available. There was considerable rivalry between the dog teams, and Huskies became famed sled racing dogs.

The breed became renowned, during the Second World War, for search and rescue work. In the following decade it gained considerable popularity in America, and by about 1960 had come into its own in the United Kingdom and elsewhere.

Character and care

The Siberian Husky is an intelligent and friendly animal with considerable stamina. It is not an aggressive dog and may be kept as a family pet, provided it is given some work and plenty of space and exercise.

KEY CHARACTERISTICS
• **CLASS** Working. **Recognized** AKC, ANKC, CKC, FCI, KC(GB), KUSA.
• **SIZE** Height at withers: dogs 53–60cm (21–23½in), bitches 51–56cm (20–22in). Weight: dogs 20–27kg (45–60lb), bitches 16–23kg (30–50lb).
• **COAT** Medium in length, giving a well-furred appearance; outer coat straight and lying smooth against body; undercoat soft and dense.
• **COLOUR** All colours and markings permissible; markings on head common, including striking ones not found on other breeds.
• **OTHER FEATURES** Medium-sized head in proportion to body; almond-shaped eyes; medium-sized ears; arched neck; strong body with a straight back; well-furred tail carried gracefully curled over back except when resting.

The Siberian Husky's head is rounded on top, and its ears – slightly rounded at the tips – are carried erect.

HERDING BREEDS

NEWFOUNDLAND

A gentle giant, the Newfoundland may seem ponderous on land but is in its element in water, swimming strongly and retrieving anything (or anyone) in its path.

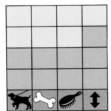

There are various theories on the origin of the Newfoundland, but that which seems most likely is that it is a descendant of the Tibetan Mastiff. In adapting to the rugged conditions in Newfoundland, eastern Canada, it developed webbed feet and an oily coat, which allows it to remain in the water for long periods of time. The breed aided fishermen and gained great fame as a life-saver. With the strong instinct to rescue anything, or anyone, in the water and retrieve it to safety, it became as valued by crews in Newfoundland waters as the Saint Bernard is by climbers in the Swiss Alps.

A particoloured variety of the Newfoundland, known as the Landseer, found fame in the paintings of Sir Edward Landseer (1802–73). The breed was also much admired by the English poet, Lord Byron.

Character and care

The large and beautiful Newfoundland is rarely bad tempered unless provoked. Indeed it is amazingly gentle with other breeds, one having been seen sitting quietly amid a bunch of squabbling Chihuahuas. It does, however, take up a fair amount of space, and needs regular exercise on hard ground and daily brushing using a hard brush.

KEY CHARACTERISTICS
• **CLASS** Herding. **Recognized** AKC, ANKC, CKC, FCI, KC(GB), KUSA.
• **SIZE** Average height at shoulders: dogs 71cm (28in), bitches 66cm (26in). Weight: dogs 64–69kg (130–150lb), bitches 50–54kg (110–120lb).
• **COAT** A double coat that is flat, dense and coarse textured; it is oily and water resistant. The outer coat is moderately long and can be straight or slightly wavy.
• **COLOUR** Black, brown, grey or Landseer (black head, black markings on a white ground).
• **OTHER FEATURES** Massive, broad head; small, dark brown eyes; small ears set well back; strong, broad, muscular body; thick tail.

The Newfoundland first began to appear in the show ring in the 1880s, its magnificent size and calm temperament soon attracting a loyal following.

LAPPONIAN HERDER

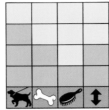

The Lapponian Herder, Lapponian Vallhund or Lapinporokoira is a Finnish breed which was developed by crossing the Lapphund with the German Shepherd Dog. Its task in life is to herd reindeer, which it is said to perform tirelessly, both guarding the herd against wolves and bears, and keeping the herd together. It is a medium-sized dog, strong-boned, muscular and longer than it is high. Its dense double coat, which is almost impervious to severe weather, may be medium length or short, but breeders are developing the short-haired type. The breed is recognized by the FCI but is not yet a contender in the European show ring.

Character and care

The Lapponian has strong herding instincts and is something of a barker, but is obedient and friendly and appears to make a good companion, provided that it receives vigorous exercise. It needs daily grooming with a bristle brush and slicker.

KEY CHARACTERISTICS
• **CLASS** Herding. **Recognized** FCI.
• **SIZE** Height at withers: dogs 48.5–56cm (19–22in), bitches 43–48.5cm (17–19in). Maximum weight: 29.7kg (66lb).
• **COAT** Long and glossy with a woolly undercoat.
• **COLOUR** Preferably black tinged with red, but also black and tan.
• **OTHER FEATURES** Pointed head; expressive eyes; erect ears; long in the back with a long tail.

BOUVIER DES FLANDRES

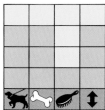

Traditionally the ears of the Bouvier des Flandres are clipped in its homeland, perhaps to give it a more alert attitude for guarding.

The Bouvier des Flandres or Belgian Cattle Dog originates, as might be expected, from the Flanders area, between the River Lys valley and the coast. This shaggy dog looks the picture of ferocity in its homeland, where its ears are traditionally cropped. It was bred as a farm dog from a multiplicity of working breeds with the purpose of producing a good all-rounder, and was used in the hunt over rough ground, and as a herder, drover, protector and guard.

A possible standard for the breed was discussed in 1912, but it was not until after the First World War that a standard was drawn up and finalized by the Club National Belge du Bouvier des Flandres.

Character and care

The Bouvier des Flandres can be rather fierce, but has a calm and sensible temperament, and is intelligent, hardy and trustworthy. It is extremely loyal to its family and is easily trained. The breed does, however, require a good deal of exercise and regular brushing. Its somewhat fearsome appearance belies its good nature. It is mainly kept as a pet or show dog.

KEY CHARACTERISTICS

- **CLASS** Herding.
  Recognized AKC, ANKC, CKC, FCI, KC(GB), KUSA.

- **SIZE** Height at withers: dogs 61–69cm (24½–27½in), bitches 59–66cm (23½–26½in). Average weight: 36kg (88lb).

- **COAT** Rough, thick and harsh with a soft dense undercoat.

- **COLOUR** From fawn to black, including brindle; white star on chest permissible; white predominating or chocolate brown highly undesirable; light, washed-out shades undesirable.

- **OTHER FEATURES** Eyes alert in expression; ears set on high; broad, deep chest and short, strong body; tail usually docked to 2–3 joints.

Descended from ancient rough-coated stock, the breed has a steel wool, all weather coat.

BOUVIER DES ARDENNES

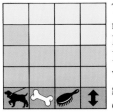

The Bouvier des Ardennes or Ardennes Cattle Dog is one of a number of Bouviers or cattle dogs which were developed to guard herds of cattle and drive them to market. For many years, these rough-coated drovers were unclassified, but then they started to be selectively bred and became known by their district of origin. The Bouvier des Ardennes, named after a high forested area in south-east Belgium, also herded pigs and is still often used for this task.

Character and care

This tireless, intelligent working dog is happiest in the wide, open spaces. It is a severe, rough-and-ready looking animal that tends to keep strangers at bay, but is obedient and deeply affectionate towards its owner. It needs regular brushing with a bristle or pin brush. It has a massive, rather short head and yellow eyes.

KEY CHARACTERISTICS
• **CLASS** Herding. **Recognized** FCI.
• **SIZE** Height: about 61cm (24in).
• **COAT** Long and bushy with a thick undercoat.
• **COLOUR** All colours permissible.
• **OTHER FEATURES** Large head with a short muzzle; dark eyes; upright ears; rounded ribcage; usually born without a tail, otherwise tail is docked.

HOVAWART

With roots in the farmyard, the Hovawart is an excellent watchdog and good with children and stock. The breed tends to require a firm hand in training.

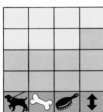

The Hovawart has been described as a relative newcomer. In fact, the breed has been recognized by the German Kennel Club since 1936, having appeared in Württemburg towards the end of the 19th century. The name Hovawart comes from the German "Hofewart", meaning estate or watch dog, but its role, for many years, seems to have been simply that of a companion dog that will rise to the occasion if required to do so. It has appeared on the European show circuit in recent years and is recognized by the Kennel Club in Britain.

Character and care

An excellent guard dog that is home loving, fond of children and easy to train, the Hovawart tends to be a one-man dog. It is slow to mature and will respond aggressively when provoked.

KEY CHARACTERISTICS

- **CLASS** Herding.
  Recognized FCI, KC(GB), KUSA.

- **SIZE** Height: dogs 63–70cm (24–27½in); bitches 58–65cm (23–25½in). Weight: dogs 30–40kg (66–88lb); bitches 25–35kg (55–77lb).

- **COAT** Medium soft, fairly long and close to the body.

- **COLOUR** Black and gold, blond and black.

- **OTHER FEATURES** Strong head, broad, convex forehead; ears triangular and set on high, in proportion with head; body longer than height at withers; tail well feathered and carried low.

GREAT SWISS MOUNTAIN DOG

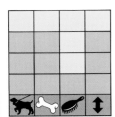

The Great Swiss Mountain Dog or Grosser Schweizer Sennenhund is the largest of four Swiss mountain dogs, of which the best known internationally is the Bernese (see page 68). All are thought to descend from Molossus dogs, brought north by ancient Roman armies, and local herding dogs, and they were used for guarding, herding and draught work. The Great Swiss, being an extremely robust dog with very strong hindquarters, is capable of moving quite heavy loads. At the beginning of this century it was threatened with extinction, but it revived and today, like the Bernese, is used for pulling carts loaded with dairy produce. Many members of the breed have also been used for search and rescue work, particularly detecting lost people, and objects, in the mountains.

Character and care

The Great Swiss Mountain Dog is a faithful, gentle animal that is generally devoted to children. It is alert and highly intelligent and makes a fine watchdog, willing to protect its human family with its life. It is essentially a country dog that thrives in wide open spaces, and needs plenty of exercise. It requires regular grooming with a bristle brush.

KEY CHARACTERISTICS
• **CLASS** Herding. **Recognized** CKC, FCI.
• **SIZE** Height: dogs 65–70cm (25½–27½in), bitches 59.5–65cm (23½–25½in).
• **COAT** Stiff and short.
• **COLOUR** Black with bright, symmetrical russet and white markings.
• **OTHER FEATURES** Flat, broad head; brown, medium-sized eyes; triangular, medium-sized ears; moderately long, strong, straight back; tail fairly heavy and reaching to the hocks.

An attractive and easily groomed pet, the Great Swiss Mountain Dog still enjoys a return to one of its traditional duties – pulling a cart or sled.

APPENZELL MOUNTAIN DOG

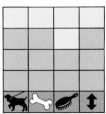

The Appenzell (Appenzeller Sennenhund) takes its name from a canton in northern Switzerland. It is one of four varieties of Swiss mountain dog, the others being the Entlebuch, the Great Swiss and, the best known internationally, the Bernese (see page 68). The Appenzell is similar in appearance to the Bernese but is generally smaller, more rectangular in shape and smooth coated.

Like all the Swiss mountain dogs, it is thought to descend from the Molossus dogs of ancient Rome, which were brought north with invading Roman soldiers, crossed with herding dogs. The Appenzell was used exten-

sively at one time as a herding dog and to haul carts of produce to market. It is still fairly common in its native land, where there is a thriving Appenzell club, but is rarely seen in other countries.

Character and care

A resilient, intelligent dog that is easily trained, the adaptable Appenzell makes an excellent farm and rescue dog, companion and guard. It needs plenty of food and exercise, and a daily brushing.

Easily recognized by the tail curling over its back, the Appenzell is smaller and more rectangular than its cousin, the Bernese.

KEY CHARACTERISTICS
• **CLASS** Herding. **Recognized** FCI, KUSA.
• **SIZE** Height: dogs 56–58.5cm (22–23in), bitches 46–50cm (18½–20in). Weight: 22–25kg (49–55lb).
• **COAT** Short, dense and hard.
• **COLOUR** Black and tan with white markings on head, chest and feet; tail tip is always white.
• **OTHER FEATURES** Head flat, broadest between ears; brown, rather small eyes; fairly small ears set on high; strong, straight back; medium-length, strong tail carried curled over the back.

ENTLEBUCH MOUNTAIN DOG

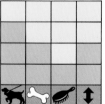

The Entlebuch (Entlebucher Sennenhund) is named after the Swiss town and river of Entlebuch. The breed is mostly found around Lucerne and in the Bernese Emmenthal. It is the smallest of the four Swiss mountain dogs thought to be crosses between Molossus dogs, brought by the Romans, and local herding dogs.

The Entlebuch was bred to tend and drive cattle and is still sometimes used for herding.

Character and care

This good natured dog is intelligent and makes a good companion and obedience worker, provided that it has plenty of space. It needs regular grooming with a bristle brush.

KEY CHARACTERISTICS
• **CLASS** Herding. **Recognized** FCI.
• **SIZE** Height: about 51cm (20in). Weight: 25–29.7kg (55–66lb).
• **COAT** Smooth-coated, short, thick, hard and glossy.
• **COLOUR** Black, white and tan.
• **OTHER FEATURES** Top of head flat, and head in proportion to size of body; small, lively, chestnut-coloured eyes; V-shaped, pendant ears; broad, deep chest; short tail.

NORWEGIAN BUHUND

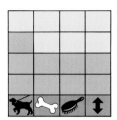

The Norwegian Buhund is a spitz type, and bears a strong resemblance to the Iceland Dog. The Icelandic Sagas (AD900–1300) record how dogs were brought to Iceland by Norwegian settlers in AD874.

In Norway, the Buhund is used as a guard and farm dog, for herding cattle, sheep and ponies, and is one of that country's national dogs. Despite its long history, it was little known outside its native land until 1920. Then it reached Britain, where it has never become really popular but does have a band of ardent devotees. It has been developing a following in other countries, but is not yet recognized in the USA.

Character and care

The Norwegian Buhund is a natural herder. It is also a gentle, friendly dog, and a natural guard and a reliable playmate for children. It needs a fair amount of exercise, and daily brushing and combing.

KEY CHARACTERISTICS
● **CLASS** Herding. **Recognized** ANKC, CKC, FCI, KC(GB), KUSA.
● **SIZE** Height: dogs about 42.5–45cm (17–18in), bitches smaller. Weight: 11.8–18.1kg (26–40lb).
● **COAT** Close, harsh and smooth, with a soft woolly undercoat.
● **COLOUR** Wheaten, black, red or wolf-sable; small symmetrical white markings permissible; black mask.
● **OTHER FEATURES** Light head, broad between the ears; ears set high; strong, short body; short, thick tail set high and carried tightly curled over back.

One of the earliest of the Nordic herding dogs, the Buhund is a good all-round working dog. It also makes an excellent pet.

The Australian Cattle Dog was purpose-bred from a number of breeds. A final cross was declared "pure" in 1893.

AUSTRALIAN KELPIE

The Australian Kelpie or Australian Sheepdog is descended from short-haired prick-eared collies imported from Scotland into Australia towards the end of the last century. The breed's ancestors are also thought to include the Old English Sheepdog. The mating of one pair of collies produced a bitch which became known as Gleeson's Kelpie. A dog called Caesar, also from imported stock, was bred to Gleeson's Kelpie and a pup from this litter was named King's Kelpie after the dam. The name Kelpie was thus adopted for the breed. In Scottish folklore, a "kelpie" is a water spirit in the form of a horse, and the Scottish writer, Robert Louis Stevenson,

refers to the "water kelpie" in his famous story *Kidnapped*, giving further credence to the breed's Scottish ancestry.

The Kelpie is a superb working sheepdog with the ability to sustain itself without water for considerable periods. It is also famed for running along the backs of the sheep to reach the head of the flock. Although it has always been well known in Australia it has come to the notice of fanciers during the 1980s, and the breed is now recognized in Britain and North America.

Character and care
The Kelpie is a fine sheepdog and makes a good, loyal companion. It requires considerable exercise and vigorous daily brushing.

AUSTRALIAN CATTLE DOG

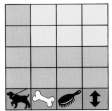

The Australian Cattle Dog is a superb worker which drives herds by nipping at the cattle's heels. The breed traces back to the now-extinct Black Bobtail, which has been described as large and rather clumsy. In 1840, new blood was introduced, including that of the extinct Smithfield, the native Dingo, the Kelpie, the Dalmatian and the blue merle Smooth Collie. The Dingo's contributions – its keen sense of smell and hearing, its stealth, speed and stamina, and its tolerance of a dry, hot climate – helped to create this unusual breed uniquely suited to the Australian outback. The addition of Kelpie made the AuCanDo an outstanding heeler as well. It has been said that ruthless culling took place during the early years of the breed, but the result has produced one of the most efficient herding dogs in the world.

At the beginning of this century, the first standard for the breed was drawn up by one Robert Kaleski and published in the *Agricultural Gazette* of New South Wales. This cattle dog was slow to become known internationally, but was recognized in the United States in 1980 and has made a welcome appearance in the British show ring over the past five years.

Character and care

The Australian Cattle Dog is intelligent and good tempered. This superlative working dog is capable of covering immense distances and so requires considerable exercise. It benefits from a vigorous daily brushing.

KEY CHARACTERISTICS

- **CLASS** Herding.
  Recognized AKC, ANKC, CKC, FCI, KC(GB), KUSA.

- **SIZE** Height at withers: dogs 46–51cm (18–20in), bitches 43–48cm (17–19in). Weight: 15.7–20.2kg (35–45lb).

- **COAT** Smooth, hard, straight, water-resistant top coat and short, dense undercoat.

- **COLOUR** Blue, blue mottled or blue speckled with or without black, blue or tan markings on head, evenly distributed for preference; there are other marking requirements; or red speckled with or without darker red markings on head.

- **OTHER FEATURES** Broad skull, slightly curved between the ears; alert, intelligent, oval-shaped eyes; moderate-sized to small ears; slightly long body; tail set low and follows slope of rump.

Born white, Australian Cattle puppies grow into medium height rangy creatures with blue or red speckled coats.

KEY CHARACTERISTICS

- **CLASS** Herding.
  Recognized AKC, ANKC, CKC, FCI, KC(GB), KUSA.

- **SIZE** Height at shoulders: about 51cm (20in). Weight: about 13.6kg (30lb).

- **COAT** A close outer coat and short, dense undercoat.

- **COLOUR** Black, black and tan, red, red and tan, fawn, chocolate and smoke blue, with or without tan.

- **OTHER FEATURES** Almond-shaped eyes; pricked ears; ribs well sprung; hindquarters show breadth and strength; at rest, tail hangs in very slight curve, when moving or excited it may be raised.

Unprepossessing to look at, the Australian Kelpie is an outstanding shepherd with strong natural herding and guarding instincts.

BEARDED COLLIE

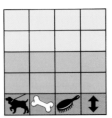

The Bearded Collie is believed to be one of the oldest herding dogs in Scotland. It is descended from three purebred Polish Lowland Sheepdogs (see page 102), a dog and two bitches, which were exchanged for a ram and a ewe brought by merchants on a trading voyage to Scotland in 1514.

A breed club was formed in Edinburgh, in 1912. Despite this, the Bearded Collie was in danger of extinction in the 1940s, but was saved by Mrs G. Willison of the former Bothkennar kennels in Ayrshire, Scotland. She obtained a Bearded bitch without pedigree in 1944 and started searching for a Bearded dog. Eventually she found one playing on the beach at Hove in East Sussex with his owners, who agreed to sell him to her. From this twosome, Jeannie and Baillie, all of today's Bearded Collies are descended.

Character and care

The Beardie is an alert, self-confident and active dog, and is good natured and reliable with children. It makes a good pet and a first-class obedience and show dog. It enjoys plenty of exercise, and requires daily brushing, very little combing and the occasional bath.

KEY CHARACTERISTICS
● **CLASS** Herding. **Recognized** AKC, ANKC, CKC, FCI, KC(GB), KUSA.
● **SIZE** Height at withers: dogs 53–56cm (21–22in), bitches 51–53cm (20–21in). Weight: 18.1–27.2kg (40–60lb).
● **COAT** Flat, harsh and shaggy; can be slightly wavy but not curly; soft, furry, close undercoat.
● **COLOUR** Slate grey, reddish fawn, black, blue, all shades of grey, brown or sandy, with or without white markings.
● **OTHER FEATURES** Broad, flat head; eyes toning with coat colour; medium-sized, drooping ears; long body; tail set low, without a kink or twist.

The Bearded Collie, a delightful family dog, needs careful grooming to prevent moulting of the coat.

BORDER COLLIE

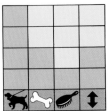

The present-day Border Collie is a descendant of working collies kept in the counties along the border of England and Scotland. It has participated in sheepdog trials since 1873, and has been exported as a working sheepdog all over the world. Bred for stamina and brains, the Border has the natural instinct to herd, and will crouch and circle from puppyhood and learn to work from more experienced dogs.

This collie has also made its mark as an unsurpassed contender in agility and obedience work. Prior to 1973, it was likely to be entered in the files of the International Sheepdog Society, and a standard for the breed was approved by the British Kennel Club in 1976. The popular Border now competes in both beauty and obedience classes in Britain.

Within the past 15 years, the Border Collie has been increasingly chosen as a domestic pet, despite being unsuited to an existence that does not offer sufficient outlet for its energy and intelligence.

Character and care

This loyal working dog requires considerable exercise but only a regular groom with a dandy brush and comb. It must be the ideal choice for anyone with their heart set on winning obedience competitions.

The Border Collie is still predominantly a working dog, much in demand to herd cattle and sheep. It also excels at obedience competitions.

KEY CHARACTERISTICS
• **CLASS** Herding. **Recognized** ANKC, CKC, FCI, KC(GB), KUSA.
• **SIZE** Height: dogs about 53cm (21in), bitches slightly less. Weight: 13.6–20.2kg (30–45lb).
• **COAT** Two varieties: moderately long, and smooth; both are thick and straight.
• **COLOUR** Variety of colours permissible; white should never predominate.
• **OTHER FEATURES** Oval-shaped eyes set wide apart; medium-sized ears set wide apart; body athletic in appearance; tail moderately long.

LANCASHIRE HEELER

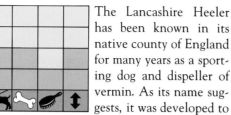

The Lancashire Heeler has been known in its native county of England for many years as a sporting dog and dispeller of vermin. As its name suggests, it was developed to herd cattle by nipping at their heels, but also has strong terrier instincts and is an excellent rabbiter and ratter. It is a small dog, and its coat is black with tan markings. The breed was little known outside the north of England prior to the 1980s. It was granted an interim standard by the British Kennel Club in 1986, and happily, breed members are now beginning to appear at dog training classes and in local exemption shows as well as at championship events.

Character and care
The Lancashire Heeler is a happy, affectionate little dog, which gets on well with humans and other pets. It requires an average amount of exercise and daily brushing.

The Lancashire Heeler is a small black and tan dog bred from Corgis and Manchester Terriers for its cattle-driving potential.

KEY CHARACTERISTICS
• **CLASS** Herding. **Recognized** FCI, KC(GB), KUSA.
• **SIZE** Height at shoulders: dogs 30cm (12in), bitches 25cm (10in). Average weight: 3.5–5.4kg (8–12lb).
• **COAT** Short and smooth.
• **COLOUR** Black and tan, with rich tan markings on muzzle, in spots on cheeks and often above eyes, from knees downwards, with desirable thumb-mark above feet, inside legs and under tail.
• **OTHER FEATURES** Richness of tan may fade with age. White to be discouraged, except for a very small white spot on forechest which is permitted but not desirable.

OLD ENGLISH SHEEPDOG

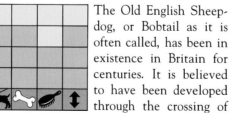

The Old English Sheepdog, or Bobtail as it is often called, has been in existence in Britain for centuries. It is believed to have been developed through the crossing of the Briard with the Russian Owtcharka, which in turn is related to the Hungarian sheepdogs. An early example is portrayed in a painting of 1771 by Gainsborough. The breed club for the Bobtail was set up in Britain as long ago as 1888, and its standard has altered little since then. In the past it was used as a drover's dog and for defending flocks of sheep. In the early 18th century in Britain drovers' dogs were exempt from taxes, and their tails were docked as a means of identification, hence the name Bobtail. In recent years the breed has enjoyed overwhelming popularity as a pet and show dog, owed in part to its frequent appearances in advertisements.

Character and care
The Old English Sheepdog is a kindly dog, which gets on well with people, children and other animals. The breed is of sound temperament and, provided that it has sufficient space and is adequately exercised, makes a splendid pet. However, parents of young children who wanted a dog "like the one on television" have sometimes found the breed too much to handle because it is fairly large, heavy and exuberant. Bobtails are also popular show dogs but do require many hours of grooming in preparation for exhibition.

SHETLAND SHEEPDOG

A small Collie-type dog with a handsome ruff, the Shetland Sheepdog, or "Sheltie", makes a most agreeable family pet.

Character and care

The Shetland Sheepdog is an excellent choice of family pet for those seeking an intelligent, faithful dog which enjoys exercise, gets on well with children and makes a fine show and obedience animal. It requires daily grooming using a stiff bristled brush and a comb. Despite having originated in cold climes, it should not be kennelled outside.

The Shetland Sheepdog or Sheltie originated in the Shetland islands off the north coast of Scotland where it has bred true for more than 135 years. It resembles a Rough Collie in miniature, with its thick double coat to protect it from the elements in its rigorous native habitat. It is believed to descend from working collies, the Iceland or Yakki Dogs which sometimes reached these islands on whalers and, possibly, the black and tan King Charles Spaniel.

The Sheltie was recognized by the British Kennel Club in 1909 and a breed club was formed in 1914.

KEY CHARACTERISTICS
● **CLASS** Herding. **Recognized** AKC, ANKC, CKC, FCI, KC(GB), KUSA.
● **SIZE** Height at withers: dogs about 37cm (14½in), bitches about 35.5cm (14in).
● **COAT** Outer coat of long, straight, harsh-textured hair; soft, short-haired, close undercoat.
● **COLOUR** Sable, tricolour, blue merle, black and white, and black and tan.
● **OTHER FEATURES** Refined head, with medium-sized, almond-shaped eyes, obliquely set; ears small and moderately wide at base; muscular, arched neck; back level; tail set low and tapering towards tip.

KEY CHARACTERISTICS
● **CLASS** Herding. **Recognized** AKC, ANKC, CKC, FCI, KC(GB), KUSA.
● **SIZE** Height at withers: dogs 55.8cm (22in), bitches 53.3cm (21in). Minimum weight: 29.7kg (66lb).
● **COAT** Profuse but not excessive, and a good harsh texture.
● **COLOUR** Any shade of grey, grizzle or blue is acceptable.
● **OTHER FEATURES** Head in proportion to body; eyes set well apart; small ears carried flat to the side of the head; short, compact body; tail docked close to body.

SMOOTH COLLIE

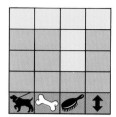

The Smooth Collie is identical to the Rough Collie except in coat, that of the Smooth being short and flat, with a harsh-textured top coat and a very dense undercoat. Both Collies' ancestors were brought over 400 years ago from Iceland to Scotland, where the breed worked as a sheepdog. Like the Roughs, the modern Smooth Collie can trace its ancestry to a tricolour dog called "Trefoil", which was born in 1873. The breed was exhibited alongside its more glamorous long-haired relative in the show ring until 1974, when the Smooth Collie was eventually given a separate standard.

Sadly, although the Smooth Collie has all the attributes of the Rough, it is seldom seen. However, the variety does have a dedicated small band of followers and there are many excellent examples with first-class temperament in the beauty and obedience rings.

Character and care

The Smooth Collie has the same character and temperament as the Rough, and its care requirements are also the same.

KEY CHARACTERISTICS
• **CLASS** Herding. **Recognized** AKC, ANKC, CKC, FCI, KC(GB), KUSA.
• **SIZE** Height at the shoulders: dogs 56–65cm (22–26in), bitches 51–60cm (20–24in). Weight: dogs 20.5–33.7kg (45–75lb), bitches 18–29.5kg (40–65lb).
• **COAT** Short, harsh and smooth with a dense undercoat.
• **COLOUR** Sable and white, tricolour, blue merle (not permissible in UK).
• **OTHER FEATURES** Head should appear light in proportion to body; medium-sized, almond-shaped eyes; ears small and not too close together; body slightly long in relation to height; long tail usually carried low.

Rough and Smooth Collies – both sometimes referred to as Scotch Collies – are really the same breed, and are identical except for their coats. The Smooth Collie is today much rarer than its long-haired stablemate.

ROUGH COLLIE

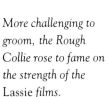

More challenging to groom, the Rough Collie rose to fame on the strength of the Lassie films.

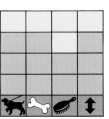

The Rough Collie, sometimes called the Scots or Scottish Collie, is still best known as the star of the "Lassie" films. This breed's ancestors were introduced into Britain from Iceland more than 400 years ago. The word "colley" is a Scottish term for a sheep with a black face and legs, and the breed worked as a sheepdog in the Highlands of Scotland for centuries.

In 1860, Queen Victoria admired the Rough Collie while on a visit to Balmoral, Scotland, and installed some breed members in the royal kennels at Windsor. In that same year, a Rough Collie was exhibited at a show in Birmingham, England, but its finer points were not agreed upon until some 25 years later. The beauty of the breed was enhanced, perhaps by the introduction of some Borzoi and Gordon Setter blood. The breed is no longer required to work, although it retains its intelligence, hardiness and keen eyesight.

Character and care

The Rough Collie makes an excellent guard, being suspicious of strangers. It is supremely loyal and affectionate to its owners, a joy to train and usually reliable with children. The breed needs a lot of exercise but, despite its thick coat, it is not difficult to groom.

KEY CHARACTERISTICS
● **CLASS** Herding. **Recognized** AKC, ANKC, CKC, FCI, KC(GB), KUSA.
● **SIZE** Height at shoulders: dogs 56–65cm (22–26in), bitches 51–60cm (20–24in). Weight: dogs 20.5–33.7kg (45–75lb), bitches 18–29.5kg (40–65lb).
● **COAT** Very dense, straight outer coat harsh to touch, with soft, furry, very close undercoat.
● **COLOUR** Sable and white, tricolour, blue merle (not permissible in UK).
● **OTHER FEATURES** Head should appear light in proportion to body; medium-sized, almond-shaped eyes; ears small, not too close together; body slightly long in relation to height; long tail.

WELSH CORGIS (PEMBROKE AND CARDIGAN)

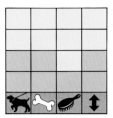

The Welsh Corgi Pembroke, a favourite of British royalty, has worked in South Wales at least since the time of the Domesday Book, instigated by William the Conqueror in the 11th century. Its job was to control the movement of cattle by nipping their ankles, which is an inherent characteristic as many protectors of the British royal family have discovered to their cost. The breed may have been introduced to Wales by Flemish weavers who settled in the area and crossed their own dogs with local stock, or it may descend from the Swedish Vallhund.

The rarer Welsh Corgi Cardigan, which has a similar history to the more popular Pembroke, is said to have a slightly more equable temperament. It is readily distinguishable from the tailless or docked Pembroke by its fox-like brush. The Welsh Corgis were first exhibited in Britain in 1925 and the Pembroke and Cardigan received separate classification in 1934. Both have among the keenest and most dedicated groups of exhibitors in the United Kingdom, and their classes are almost invariably of high standard.

Character and care
Corgis are extremely active and devoted little dogs, and are usually good with children. They make fine guards, and excellent show and obedience dogs. They have a tendency to put on weight if under-exercised, and their water-resistant coats need daily brushing.

Until the 1930s the two Welsh Corgis were inter-bred, and there is still today little difference between them. The better known Pembroke has straighter legs and a foxy face.

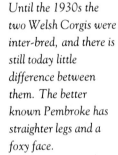

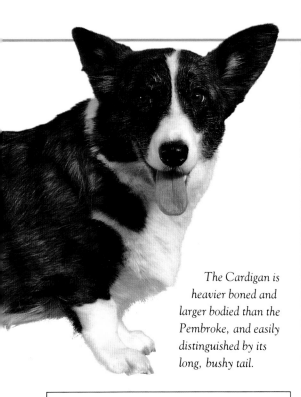

The Cardigan is heavier boned and larger bodied than the Pembroke, and easily distinguished by its long, bushy tail.

KEY CHARACTERISTICS

- **CLASS** Herding.
  Recognized AKC, ANKC, CKC, FCI, KC(GB), KUSA.

- **SIZE** *Pembroke* Height at shoulders: about 25.5–30.5cm (10–12in). Weight: dogs about 12kg (27lb), bitches about 11.3kg (25lb). *Cardigan* Height at withers: 26–31cm (10½–12½in). Weight: dogs 13.6–17.2kg (30–38lb), bitches 11.3–15.3kg (25–34lb).

- **COAT** *Pembroke* Medium length and straight, with a dense undercoat; never soft, wavy or wiry. *Cardigan* Short or medium length, with a hard texture, and weatherproof; short, thick undercoat.

- **COLOUR** *Pembroke* Red, sable, fawn or black and tan, with or without white markings on legs, brisket and neck; some white on head and foreface permissible. *Cardigan* Any, with or without white markings, but white should not predominate.

- **OTHER FEATURES** *Pembroke* Head foxy in shape and appearance; firm, upright ears with slightly rounded points; deep chest and moderately long body; short tail, docked if necessary. *Cardigan* Head foxy in shape and appearance; medium-sized eyes; upright ears; chest moderately broad with prominent breast bone; tail bushy and set in line with body.

PYRENEAN SHEPHERDS

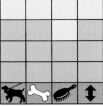

The Pyrenean Shepherds or Bergers des Pyrénées may be indigenous to the area, or are descendants of the Catalonian Shepherd. However, it is generally thought that they derive from Eastern shepherd dogs whose coats and abilities were adapted to the harsh conditions in the Pyrenean mountains on the border between France and Spain. The task of these sheepdogs was to herd flocks, while the much larger and heavier Pyrenean Mountain Dog or Great Pyrenees defended the flocks against predators. These lively herders are also protective of owners' property.

There are two varieties of Pyrenean Shepherd: one with long to medium-length hair all over, and the Smooth-faced Shepherd (Berger des Pyrénées à Face Rase), which has medium-length hair over most of its body but short hair on its face and the front of its legs. Both are still used for herding and are kept as companion dogs and watchdogs.

Character and care

These intelligent workers have a considerable amount of nervous energy and can be kept as pets, but are best given a job to do. The Smooth-faced Shepherd is easier to train, and likely to be more companionable and less aggressive to strangers. They require daily brushing and very little combing.

KEY CHARACTERISTICS

- **CLASS** Herding.
  Recognized FCI, KC(GB), KUSA.

- **SIZE** *Pyrenean Shepherd* Height: dogs 39.5–49.5cm (15½–19½in), bitches 38–49.5cm (15–19½in). *Smooth-faced Shepherd* Height: dogs 40.5–53.5cm (16–21in), bitches 40.5–52cm (16–20½in). Weight: 8.2–13.6kg (18–30lb).

- **COAT** Short or medium length.

- **COLOUR** Harlequin, black, salt and pepper, fawn in various shades.

- **OTHER FEATURES** Head strong; dark eyes; ears set on fairly high; body square; tail may be docked.

The Briard – official dog of the French army – developed as a large herding dog which could also protect livestock.

PICARDY SHEPHERD

Also known as the Berger de Picard, this breed has guarded flocks in its native France since time immemorial. It is said to be probably the oldest French herding dog and to be an unsurpassed worker with both sheep and cattle. It is a medium-sized, shaggy, somewhat rustic-looking dog and, when 12 Picards were entered in a dog show in Amiens in 1899, the eminent judge of sheepdogs refused to recognize them. Despite this the breed flourished until the First World War when its numbers were seriously depleted.

They built up again in the 1920s, only to have a further setback during the Second World War. In the 1950s, the breed finally revived and since then some fine examples have appeared in the show ring.

Character and care

The Picardy is an energetic, affectionate animal which superbly combines the role of working dog with that of family companion, and is almost always trustworthy with and devoted to children. It requires plenty of space and exercise, and regular brushing.

BRIARD

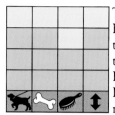

The Briard, or Berger de Brie, is the best known of the French sheepdogs, the others being the Beauce, Picardy and Pyrenean. The Briard is reputed to have come to Europe with Asian invaders before the end of the Middle Ages, along with other breeds of sheepdog such as the Hungarian Komondor and Kuvasz and the Russian Owtcharka, which have similar conformation.

"Les Amis du Briard" was formed around 1900 when a standard of sorts was drawn up. However, it was not approved until 1925 and then was amended in 1930. The Briard Club was formed in about 1928. By this time the breed had already become known in other parts of the world, partly through its work in the French Army during the First World War, when it carried ammunition and was employed by the Red Cross.

It is widely believed to have been introduced into the US during the 18th century, possibly by the Marquis de Lafayette or Thomas Jefferson. The first litter was registered with the AKC in 1922.

Character and care

The Briard has a gentle nature and makes a good family pet or farm dog, provided sufficient space is available. It is good with children, intelligent and fearless. It is a breed that takes pride in cleaning itself, but needs regular brushing. Like all sheepdogs, it requires plenty of exercise, and is not suited to a cramped environment.

KEY CHARACTERISTICS
● **CLASS** Herder. **Recognized** AKC, ANKC, CKC, FCI, KC(GB), KUSA.
● **SIZE** Height at withers: dogs 57.5–67.5cm (23–27in), bitches 55–64cm (22–25½in). Weight: about 33.7kg (75lb).
● **COAT** Long and slightly wavy, and dry to the touch, with a fine, dense undercoat.
● **COLOUR** Solid black, or with white hairs scattered through black coat; fawn in all its shades, darker shades preferred; fawns may have dark shading on ears, muzzle, back and tail.
● **OTHER FEATURES** Strong, slightly rounded skull; dark eyes, set wide apart and horizontally placed; ears set on high; back firm and level; broad chest; long well-feathered tail that has an upward hook at the tip.

With its rounded head and widely set eyes, the Briard looks out through a dense curtain of hair.

KEY CHARACTERISTICS
● **CLASS** Herding. **Recognized** FCI.
● **SIZE** Height at withers: dogs 61–66cm (24–26in), bitches 5cm (2in) less. Weight: 22.6–31.7kg (50–70lb).
● **COAT** Hard and moderate in length, with a heavy undercoat.
● **COLOUR** All shades of grey and fawn; white allowed only in spot on the chest and toes.
● **OTHER FEATURES** Large head with strong muzzle; dark eyes; ears carried erect; sturdy body; tail curved at the tip.

BELGIAN SHEPHERD DOGS

This breed includes four varieties: the Groenendael (long-coated black), the Tervueren (long-coated other than black), the Malinois (smooth-coated) and the Laekenois (wire-coated). All were developed from the many sheepdogs of varying colours and sizes that existed in Belgium towards the end of the 19th century. In about 1890, Monsieur Rose of the Café du Groenendael discovered a black, long-coated bitch in a litter. He bought a similar dog and, by selective breeding and considerable culling, produced the Groenendael, the most popular variety of Belgian Shepherd Dog. Further work began in 1891, when a collection of Belgian Sheepdogs was gathered at the Brussels Veterinary University. There it was agreed to recognize and develop three varieties and a fourth was subsequently added. They are recognized as separate breeds everywhere except in the UK.

Character and care

The medium-sized, well-proportioned, intelligent and attentive Belgian Shepherd Dog works well in obedience trials and makes an excellent guard. It is very protective, and can be kept in the home provided time is set aside for early training. It needs plenty of exercise and regular grooming.

First to establish type among the motley of Belgian Shepherd Dogs was the Malinois, which is named after its region of origin, Malines.

The Laekenois, today the rarest of the four breeds, comes from the district of Boom, near Antwerp, which is noted for its fine linens.

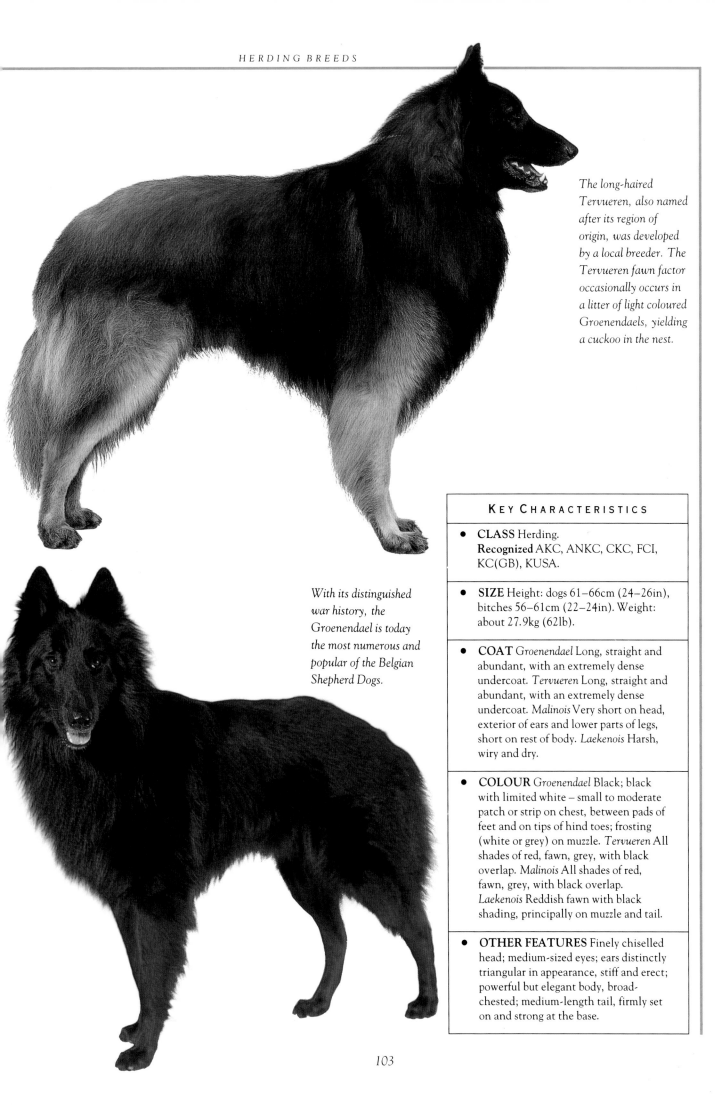

The long-haired Tervueren, also named after its region of origin, was developed by a local breeder. The Tervueren fawn factor occasionally occurs in a litter of light coloured Groenendaels, yielding a cuckoo in the nest.

With its distinguished war history, the Groenendael is today the most numerous and popular of the Belgian Shepherd Dogs.

KEY CHARACTERISTICS

- **CLASS** Herding.
  Recognized AKC, ANKC, CKC, FCI, KC(GB), KUSA.

- **SIZE** Height: dogs 61–66cm (24–26in), bitches 56–61cm (22–24in). Weight: about 27.9kg (62lb).

- **COAT** *Groenendael* Long, straight and abundant, with an extremely dense undercoat. *Tervueren* Long, straight and abundant, with an extremely dense undercoat. *Malinois* Very short on head, exterior of ears and lower parts of legs, short on rest of body. *Laekenois* Harsh, wiry and dry.

- **COLOUR** *Groenendael* Black; black with limited white – small to moderate patch or strip on chest, between pads of feet and on tips of hind toes; frosting (white or grey) on muzzle. *Tervueren* All shades of red, fawn, grey, with black overlap. *Malinois* All shades of red, fawn, grey, with black overlap. *Laekenois* Reddish fawn with black shading, principally on muzzle and tail.

- **OTHER FEATURES** Finely chiselled head; medium-sized eyes; ears distinctly triangular in appearance, stiff and erect; powerful but elegant body, broad-chested; medium-length tail, firmly set on and strong at the base.

BERGAMASCO

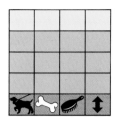

The Bergamasco or Bergamese Shepherd is a medium-sized, squarely built dog with soft, pendulous ears, almond-shaped slanted eyes and a long, rather harsh, wavy coat. Its ancestors almost certainly include the rather similar French Briard. Named after the city of Bergamo in northern Italy, the Bergamasco has worked for centuries in Italy, herding and guarding flocks. Unfortunately, relatively few Italian livestock keepers still use, or attempt to perpetuate, this fine sheepdog and its numbers are small. The breed is not well known outside its native country and it has yet really to make its mark upon the show rings of the world.

Character and care

The Bergamasco is a courageous, docile and loyal working dog. In common with all sheepdogs, it needs plenty of exercise. The cords of its coat need to be separated by hand and brushed and combed.

KEY CHARACTERISTICS
• **CLASS** Herding. **Recognized** FCI, KC(GB).
• **SIZE** Height: dogs about 61cm (24in), bitches about 56cm (22in). Weight: dogs 32–38kg (70–84lb), bitches 26–32kg (57–70lb).
• **COAT** Wiry at front, soft at back, very long with matted curls.
• **COLOUR** Solid shades of grey from light to almost black; solid white is not allowed, and white markings should not cover more than 20% of the coat.
• **OTHER FEATURES** Long head; large eyes; soft, thin ears; large chest; tail set on in last third of the rump, thick and robust at root.

BEAUCE SHEPHERD

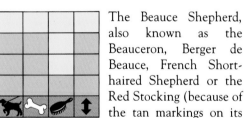

The Beauce Shepherd, also known as the Beauceron, Berger de Beauce, French Short-haired Shepherd or the Red Stocking (because of the tan markings on its lower legs and feet), could be mistaken for a Doberman and may have played a part in the development of that breed.

The Beauce is an ancient French breed, thought to have evolved from fiercer rough-coated stock, and bred to form the modern type. First used as a hunter of wild boar and later as a herder and guard of livestock, today it is often kept solely as a companion and guard. It has been exhibited since 1897 and is one of the most popular dogs in France.

Character and care

While retaining its herding instincts, the Beauce Shepherd is easily trained, good tempered but distrustful of strangers. It is not a house dog. It requires plenty of exercise and its short, smooth coat needs daily brushing. Its ears are cropped in its country of origin.

KEY CHARACTERISTICS
• **CLASS** Herding. **Recognized** FCI.
• **SIZE** Height: dogs 63.5–71cm (25–28in), bitches 61–68.5cm (24–27in). Weight: 29.7–38kg (66–85lb).
• **COAT** Reasonably short, close and dense.
• **COLOUR** Black with rich tan markings on face and legs and under tail; harlequin; or tricolour – grey with black patches and tan markings.
• **OTHER FEATURES** Long, flat head; blackish-brown eyes; ears set on high, pendant or, most usually, cropped; straight back; broad, well-arched loins; long tail curving slightly towards the end.

MAREMMA SHEEPDOG

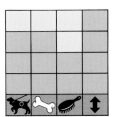

The Maremma Sheepdog has two names in its native Italy because for centuries the shepherd dogs spent from June until October in the Abruzzi, where there was good summer grazing, and from October until June in the Maremma. Called both Pastore Abruzzese and Pastore Maremmano, some people thought that they were two different breeds. Then, about 25 years ago at a meeting in Florence, the eminent judge, Professor Giuseppe Solaro, drew up a single breed standard under the name of Pastore Maremmano Abruzzese.

The Maremma has never worked sheep like the Border Collie, but defended the flock against wolves and bears. The first record of a Maremma Sheepdog appeared 2000 years ago when Columella (*c.* AD65) made reference to a white dog and Marcus Varro (116–27BC) produced a standard for a sheepdog almost identical to that for the Maremma of today. The breed has been known in the United Kingdom since 1872.

Character and care

The Maremma is a natural guard that will never forget a kindness or an injury. To quote an Italian expert, "If you want obedience and submission keep away from our breed, but if you appreciate friendship given and received, a trace of humour and much teaching of the lore of the wild, a typical Maremmano is the best you can have." The Maremma should be regularly groomed using a wire dog brush and, occasionally, a good cleansing powder.

KEY CHARACTERISTICS
• **CLASS** Herding. **Recognized** ANKC, CKC, FCI, KC(GB), KUSA.
• **SIZE** Height: dogs 65–73cm (25½–28½in), bitches 60–68cm (23½–26½in). Weight: dogs 35–45kg (77–99lb), bitches 30–40kg (66–88lb).
• **COAT** Long, plentiful and rather harsh; never curly.
• **COLOUR** All white.
• **OTHER FEATURES** Head conical in shape and appears large in proportion to body; bold eyes; ears small in proportion to head; strong, well-muscled body; tail set on low.

The Maremma is the serene master of all he surveys.

The Maremma is an ancient breed, descended from the original flock guarding dogs of the Middle East.

GERMAN SHEPHERD DOG

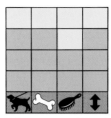

It has been suggested that the German Shepherd Dog (Alsatian or Deutscher Schäferhund) may be a descendant of the Bronze Age wolf. Certainly, around the 7th century AD, there existed in Germany a shepherd dog of similar type but with a lighter coat. By the 16th century, the coat is said to have darkened appreciably.

The German Shepherd was first exhibited at a dog show in Hanover in 1882. Credit for the formation of the modern breed is generally attributed to the German fancier, Rittmeister von Stephanitz, who worked tirelessly in the early 1900s to improve its temperament and conformation. The breed won dedicated fanciers in other countries, including Britain and America, among those who had seen the breed working in Germany in the First World War. It was at that time thought inappropriate to call the breed by a name that included the word "German", and it became known in the United Kingdom, and elsewhere, as the Alsatian because it had originated in the Alsace. In 1971, the British Kennel Club finally relented and the name German Shepherd Dog was restored.

Character and care

The popular German Shepherd is extremely intelligent and makes a first-class companion, show dog, obedience worker and guard. It is eminently trainable and so works as a police dog, in the armed services, as a guide dog for the blind, and in numerous other capacities. Its superior guarding ability can get it into trouble, because it may misread a sign and spring to its owner's defence. However, with knowledgeable handling and training it is a splendid canine companion. It needs vigorous daily grooming, plenty of exercise and, above all, a job to do, even if this only entails competing in obedience or agility tests. It is unfair and unwise for this intelligent animal to be subjected to a life of boredom.

Perhaps the most widely recognized of all breeds, the German Shepherd Dog is a versatile worker, renowned for its strength and agility.

106

KEY CHARACTERISTICS

- **CLASS** Herding.
  Recognized AKC, ANKC, CKC, FCI, KC(GB), KUSA.

- **SIZE** Height at top of shoulders: dogs 60–65cm (24–26in), bitches 55–60cm (22–24in). Weight: 33.7–42.7kg (75–95lb).

- **COAT** Medium length, straight, hard and close-lying, with a dense, thick undercoat.

- **COLOUR** Solid black or grey; black saddle with tan or gold to light grey markings; grey with lighter or brown markings (referred to as sables). Blues, livers, albinos and whites highly undesirable (a light-coated German Shepherd is included in the breed standards of some overseas countries).

- **OTHER FEATURES** Strong head; medium-sized eyes and ears; relatively long neck; long shoulder blades; straight back; strong hindquarters, broad and well muscled; long, bushy tail.

There is some colour variation among German Shepherd Dogs, with the familiar sable background with a black saddle being most prevalent. All white coloration is not acceptable in the show ring.

DUTCH SHEPHERDS

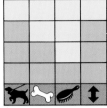

There are three varieties of Dutch Shepherd or Hollandse Herdershond, which differ only in coat and colour: the Short-haired, Long-haired and Wire-haired. Anatomically they are close to the Belgian Shepherd dogs, and, like them, probably descend from a variety of sheepdog breeds. They are recognized as separate breeds in their native Holland, but are rare elsewhere.

The Dutch Shepherds worked for many years as herding dogs. When the demand for this work lessened, they declined, but have now become quite popular again. They are kept as housepets, utilized as guard dogs, for police work, as guide dogs for the blind, and are known to be worthy retrievers.

Character and care
These obedient, hardy and trustworthy dogs make excellent guards, and are impervious to bad weather. They may be kept as pets, but preferably in rural surroundings, and are best kennelled out of doors. The Wire-haired's coat moults twice a year and must then be stripped, or plucked, using finger and thumb. All three types need daily brushing.

KEY CHARACTERISTICS

- **CLASS** Herding.
  Recognized FCI.

- **SIZE** Height at withers: dogs 58.5–63.5cm (23–25in), bitches 54.5–62cm (21½–24½in). Weight: about 29.7kg (66lb).

- **COAT** *Short-haired* Hard, woolly and not too short. *Long-haired* Long and rather stiff, lying close to the body. *Wire-haired* Hard and wiry all over body with little waviness, and close, woolly undercoat except on head.

- **COLOUR** *Short-haired* and *Long-haired* Gold or silver with streaks of black. *Wire-haired* Blue-black or grey-black.

- **OTHER FEATURES** Head in proportion to body and not coarse; dark, medium-sized, almond-shaped eyes; ears small in proportion to head, stiff and erect; solid body; tail carried low, with slight curve in it in repose, high in action.

HUNGARIAN PULI

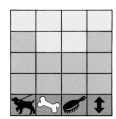

The Puli (plural Pulik), one of the best known of the Hungarian sheepdogs, is said to be a descendant of sheepdogs brought to Hungary by the Magyars over 1000 years ago. It has herded sheep on the edge of the Hungarian plain for many centuries and, more recently, has been used for police work. In 1935, the Puli was imported into the United States by the Department of Agriculture with the aim of improving local sheep- and cattle-herding breeds. However, the Puli was not recognized by the American Kennel Club until 1936. The breed has been in Britain for the past 20 years and now attracts a reasonable number of show entries.

Character and care

The Puli is a loyal, devoted, obedient and intelligent dog, which is good with other pets and slow to anger. It is, however, reserved with humans outside its own family. The breed requires a good amount of exercise and the cords of its coat, which give it a somewhat unkempt look, have to be separated by hand, brushed and combed.

KEY CHARACTERISTICS

- **CLASS** Herding.
  Recognized AKC, ANKC, CKC, FCI, KC(GB), KUSA.

- **SIZE** Height at withers: dogs 40–44cm (16–17½in), bitches 37–41cm (14½–16in). Weight: dogs 13–15kg (28½–33lb), bitches 10–13kg (22–28½lb).

- **COAT** Dense and weatherproof; outer coat wavy or curly, undercoat soft and woolly; correct proportion of each creates the desired cords.

- **COLOUR** Black, rusty black, white or various shades of grey and apricot, overall appearance of solid colour.

- **OTHER FEATURES** Small, fine head with slightly domed skull; medium-sized eyes; ears set slightly below top of skull; withers slightly higher than level of back; medium-length tail curling over loins.

POLISH LOWLAND SHEEPDOG

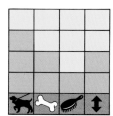

The Polish Lowland Sheepdog is also known as the Valee Shepherd Dog and the Owczarek Nizinny. It looks very much like the Old English Sheepdog and the Bearded Collie, which is descended from it. It probably resulted from crossing the Hungarian Puli with other herding breeds during the 16th century, with the aim of producing a natural herder and an animal with a tough, weather-resistant coat suitable for the harsh Polish climate. This sheepdog has been granted an interim breed standard by the British Kennel Club within the past five years and has begun to make its mark on the European show scene.

Character and care

This efficient herding dog is easily trained and generally good natured. A reasonable amount of exercise is essential, as is daily grooming with a brush and a steel comb.

KEY CHARACTERISTICS

- **CLASS** Herder.
  Recognized ANKC, FCI, KC(GB), KUSA.

- **SIZE** Height at withers: dogs 43–52cm (17–20in), bitches 40–46cm (16–18½in).

- **COAT** Long, dense, thick and shaggy with a harsh texture; soft undercoat.

- **COLOUR** All colours and markings are acceptable.

- **OTHER FEATURES** Medium-sized head and eyes; body rectangular in shape rather than square when viewed from side; often born without a tail, otherwise tail docked.

Still seen with flocks in present-day Hungary, the Puli is ideally clad for herding in Central Europe.

PUMI

A Hungarian breed, the Pumi was developed by crossing the Hungarian Puli with straight-eared French and German herding dogs in the 17th and 18th centuries. It also has some ancient terrier blood, which is apparent in its looks and temperament. It was originally bred to drive cattle, but is now used mainly as a herder and often as a guard. The Pumi looks unkempt but appealing, with semi-erect ears and a long, shaggy coat. Its eyes and muzzle are barely visible and the tail, which curls over the back, is naturally short or docked. It is rarely seen outside its country of origin.

Character and care

The Pumi is a lively, high-spirited, rather noisy dog, which is loyal to its owner and makes a good herder and watchdog. It can be very aggressive with strangers. It should be groomed with a slicker brush.

KEY CHARACTERISTICS
● **CLASS** Herding. **Recognized** FCI.
● **SIZE** Height at withers: 33–44.5cm (13–17½in). Weight: 8–13kg (17½–28½lb).
● **COAT** Medium-length and curling, tangled but not matted.
● **COLOUR** All shades of grey, also black or chestnut.
● **OTHER FEATURES** Muzzle small in proportion to head; ears like upside-down Vs; coffee-coloured eyes; square body; tail customarily docked.

ANATOLIAN SHEPHERD DOG

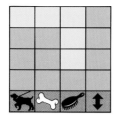

The Anatolian Shepherd Dog, previously known as the Anatolian Karabash, has existed for centuries, from the Anatolian plateau of Turkey right across Afghanistan. Such large, powerful and heavy headed dogs have lived in the area since Babylonian times (2800–1800BC) and were once used as war dogs and to hunt big game such as lions and even horses. However, their more usual job was to guard sheep, and shepherds would crop their ears and fit them with spiked collars to help them defend flocks from predators. They still perform this task today, watching flocks from high ground and then, at the slightest suspicion of trouble, splitting up and converging silently upon the scene at great speed.

Character and care
This powerful, loyal and loving dog is good with children, makes a fine watchdog and is eminently trainable. However, it cannot be kept in a confined space, is not suited to town life and does not take kindly to strangers. It requires considerable exercise and, although the breed has a natural ability to keep itself clean, it should be brushed regularly.

A black mask and black-fringed ears are identifying features in a breed which varies considerably in colour.

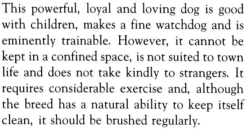

KEY CHARACTERISTICS
• **CLASS** Herding. **Recognized** ANKC, FCI, KC(GB), KUSA.
• **SIZE** Height at shoulders: dogs 74–81cm (29–32in), bitches 71–79cm (28–31in). Weight: dogs 50–64kg (110–141lb), bitches 41–59kg (90½–130lb).
• **COAT** Short and dense, with a thick undercoat.
• **COLOUR** All colours acceptable, but most desirable is solid cream to fawn with black mask and ears.
• **OTHER FEATURES** Large, broad head, flat between the ears; small eyes; medium-sized, triangular ears rounded at the tips; deep chest; long tail.

A big, powerful breed, the Anatolian Shepherd Dog will guard flocks tirelessly in extremes of heat or cold.

RUSSIAN SHEEPDOG

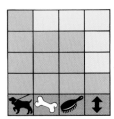

There are four breeds of Russian Sheepdog or Owtcharka: the Mid-Asian, the South Russian, the Steppe and the Transcaucasian. All are descendants of spitz breeds crossed with local dogs to produce types suited to the requirements and climatic conditions of the area in which they were bred. They are all excellent herding and guarding dogs, and are also often employed to protect military camps and installations. The Owtcharka are rarely seen outside their country of origin, and particularly little is known about the rare Steppe Owtcharka.

The South Russian Owtcharka, which originated in the Crimean area, resembles an Old English Sheepdog. The Mid-Asian Owtcharka is a more powerful animal, designed to defend the herd against wolves and robbers, and likely to have Mastiff blood in its ancestry. The Transcaucasian comes from around the Caucasus Mountains, and, like the Mid-Asian, it has Mastiff ancestors. Its long tail is rarely docked. The Steppe (North Caucasian) is found in the desert regions of North Caucasia and the low country round the Caspian Sea. It is a squarely built dog, lighter in the body and longer in the leg than the Transcaucasian.

Character and care

Although said to be easy to train and intelligent, these dogs are strong-willed, fearless guards and are unlikely to be suitable as pets. The South Russian is reputed to be the most biddable of the four. All need abundant exercise and regular brushing.

KEY CHARACTERISTICS
• **CLASS** Herding. **Recognized** FCI.
• **SIZE** Height at withers: *South Russian* about 51cm (20in); *Mid-Asian* 61–66cm (24–26in); *Transcaucasian* about 66cm (26in); *Steppe* no height recorded.
• **COAT** *South Russian* Long and dense. *Mid-Asian* Hard and straight. *Transcaucasian* Long, dense and rough. *Steppe* Short.
• **COLOUR** *South Russian* White or pale grey, with or without small white or fawn spots. *Mid-Asian* black white, grey, fawn or brindle. *Transcaucasian* White, fawn, grey, tan or brindle, solid or combination of colours. *Steppe* Various.
• **OTHER FEATURES** *Mid-Asian* often has ears cropped and tail docked.

RUMANIAN SHEPHERD DOG

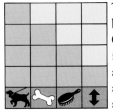

This breed is reputed to be descended from the Greek Simocyon which, in turn, is related to the ancient Molossus. Large and powerful with a massive head, the Rumanian Shepherd looks rather like a Saint Bernard. It has been used to hunt wolf and bear, and is still kept extensively in its native land as a flock guard. It was recognized by the Rumanian Kennel Club in 1937, but is little known outside its country of origin.

Character and care

The Rumanian Shepherd is kept for its working abilities rather than as a domestic pet. It makes a fine guard, being loyal to its owner and distrustful of strangers. It needs regular exercise, and its heavy coat requires regular brushing.

KEY CHARACTERISTICS
• **CLASS** Herding. **Recognized** AKC, ANKC, CKC, FCI, KC(GB), KUSA
• **SIZE** Height at shoulders: 63.5–66cm (25–26in). Weight: 50kg (110lb).
• **COAT** Medium-length, soft and smooth; onger on flanks and hindquarters.
• **COLOUR** White, or tricolour, sable with darker head points, black and tan, and various brindles.
• **OTHER FEATURES** Distinct stoop and slightly domed skull; dark amber eyes; small ears set wide apart, rather low and folded back; tail usually medium length, but may be docked very short.

GUNDOGS

CHESAPEAKE BAY RETRIEVER

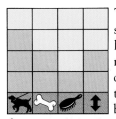

The ancestry of the Chesapeake Bay Retriever is less obscure than that of many breeds. Indeed, its origins can be pinpointed to 1807, when an English brig was shipwrecked off the coast of Maryland. An American ship, the *Canton*, rescued the English crew and two Newfoundland puppies. One puppy was a male called Sinbad, which has been described as dingy red in colour, while the other was a black bitch, which became known as Canton after the rescue ship. The pups were presented to the families that had given shelter to the English sailors and were trained as duck retrievers. In time, they mated with various working breeds in the Chesapeake Bay area. It is likely that the cross bloods added were those of the Otterhound and the Curly-coated and Flat-coated Retrievers. The matings produced a variety with the swimming ability of the Newfoundland and the duck retrieving abilities of local dogs.

Until fairly recently, the Chesapeake Bay Retriever was kept strictly as a sporting dog. However, it is now finding its way into the family home and becoming a contender in the show ring.

Character and care
The Chesapeake is good natured and does well in field trials. It has an oily coat which needs regular brushing and gives off a slight, but not unpleasant, odour. It has yellow-orange eyes. Like all gundogs it needs plenty of exercise and does best in an environment where it has space to roam freely.

The reddish-brown coat of this Chesapeake Bay Retriever clearly shows the typical waviness on the neck, back and loins.

Yellow-amber eyes are a characteristic of this retriever.

NOVA SCOTIA DUCK TOLLING RETRIEVER

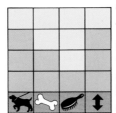

The Nova Scotia Duck Tolling Retriever originated in the Maritime Provinces of Canada and has only recently become known outside its native area. It is believed to be of Chesapeake Bay and Golden Retriever stock. With the head of the Golden it is well boned down to its strong webbed feet. Although the breed has been set for over 100 years, it only received a breed standard in the 1940s. It was given full international recognition by the FCI in 1982. This dog's job in life is to thrash about at the water's edge in order to attract the attention of wildfowl, a performance known as tolling. Eventually the wildfowl become curious or angry enough to swim within range of the hunter on the bank. The dog will retrieve the fowl shot down.

Character and care
The Nova Scotia Duck Tolling Retriever is quiet and easy to train. Like many gundogs it makes a good family pet provided that it receives plenty of exercise. It needs regular grooming with a bristle brush and comb.

KEY CHARACTERISTICS

- **CLASS** Gundog.
  Recognized AKC, ANKC, CKC, FCI, KC(GB), KUSA.

- **SIZE** Height: dogs 58.4–66cm (23–26in), bitches 53.3–60.9cm (21–24in). Weight: dogs 29.5–36.3kg (65–80lb), bitches 25–31.75kg (55–70lb).

- **COAT** A distinctive feature: thick and reasonably short (not over 3.8cm (1½in) long), with harsh, oily outercoat and dense, fine, woolly undercoat.

- **COLOUR** Dead grass (straw to bracken), sedge (red-gold), or any shade of brown; white spots (the smaller the better) on chest, toes and belly permissible.

- **OTHER FEATURES** Broad, round head; medium-sized eyes; small ears; strong, deep, broad chest; tail should extend to hock.

KEY CHARACTERISTICS

- **CLASS** Gundog.
  Recognized ANKC, CKC, FCI, KC(GB).

- **SIZE** Height at shoulders: 41–52cm (17–21in). Weight: 16.6–23kg (37–51lb).

- **COAT** Moderately long and close lying, with a thick, wavy undercoat.

- **COLOUR** Red fox, with white marking on chest, feet and tip of tail, and sometimes on face.

- **OTHER FEATURES** Broad head with well-defined stop; webbed feet.

The sleek, slightly wavy coat of this dog is a feature of the breed. White markings on the face, feet and/or the tip of the tail are common.

CURLY-COATED RETRIEVER

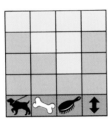

Everything about the Curly-coated Retriever points to the Irish Water Spaniel or the Standard Poodle contributing to its ancestry. The Labrador Retriever obviously also played some part in producing this fine breed, of which far too little is seen.

The Curly-coated was first exhibited at dog shows in the United Kingdom as long ago as 1860, and one of the first breeds to be used seriously for retrieving purposes in England. However, despite its attractive appearance, stamina and working ability, it is now rarely seen outside the show ring. It has been said that its popularity as a sporting dog declined because of its reputation of being hard-mouthed, a fault that certainly does not exist in the breed today.

Character and care

The Curly-coated Retriever has an excellent nose and a good memory. It is a better guard than other retrievers, and while a little anti-social with its canine colleagues in the shooting field, it generally combines its working life admirably with that of a reliable family dog. It requires vigorous exercise, and fares best in a country environment with plenty of opportunities to run free. Its curly coat does not need to be brushed or combed, just dampened down and massaged with circular movements. Advice should be sought on the necessary trimming if it is the intention to exhibit.

KEY CHARACTERISTICS
• **CLASS** Gundog. **Recognized** AKC, ANKC, CKC, FCI, KC(GB), KUSA.
• **SIZE** Height at withers: dogs about 67cm (27in), bitches about 62cm (25in). Weight: 31.7–36.3kg (70–80lb).
• **COAT** A mass of crisp, small curls all over, except on face.
• **COLOUR** Black or liver.
• **OTHER FEATURES** Long, well-proportioned head; black or dark brown eyes; small ears, set on low; muscular shoulders and deep chest; moderately short tail.

FLAT-COATED RETRIEVER

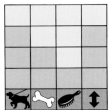

When a Flat-coated Retriever won the Best in Show award at Crufts Dog Show in London in 1980, reporters clamoured around its owner anxious to know what the breed did. "Picking up," they were told. In fact, the Flat-coat is superlative at picking up game, and it is an excellent wildfowler and water dog. It is loyal and affectionate, and although it can be kept as a pet, most Flat-coats are maintained for the job for which the breed was originally bred and they are happiest when doing this.

Once known as the Wavy-coated Retriever, the breed is thought to have evolved from the Labrador Retriever and spaniels. It is likely that Collie blood was introduced to produce the flat coat. This was achieved around the 1800s, when a Mr Shirley of Ettington Park, Warwickshire (now the West Midlands), in England, made tremendous efforts on the breed's behalf. The Flat-coat went on to become the most popular retriever in Britain, a position it held until after the Second World War when it was eclipsed by the Golden and Labrador Retrievers.

Character and care

An intelligent and sound dog with a kindly temperament, it is a hardy breed and many owners choose to keep their Flat-coats in outside kennels, although this is a matter of preference. Like most gundogs, Flat-coats need plenty of exercise and a daily brushing.

KEY CHARACTERISTICS
● **CLASS** Gundog. **Recognized** AKC, ANKC, CKC, FCI, KC(GB), KUSA.
● **SIZE** Height: dogs 58–61cm (23–24in), bitches 56–59cm (22–23in). Weight: dogs 25–35kg (60–80lb), bitches 25–34kg (55–70lb).
● **COAT** Dense, fine to medium texture, medium length and lying flat.
● **COLOUR** Solid black or solid liver.
● **OTHER FEATURES** Long, clean head; medium-sized eyes; small ears well set on, lying close to side of head; deep chest and strong body; tail short, straight and well set on.

A gaily-held tail is a hallmark of the alert Flat-coat, keen to get to work in the field.

LABRADOR RETRIEVER

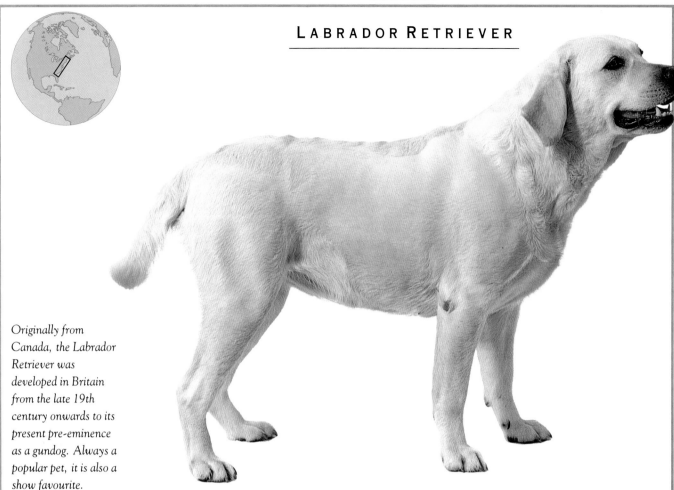

Originally from Canada, the Labrador Retriever was developed in Britain from the late 19th century onwards to its present pre-eminence as a gundog. Always a popular pet, it is also a show favourite.

Despite its association with Britain, the Labrador Retriever arrived in the 1830s with Newfoundland fishermen who used the dogs to help them land their nets. The Earl of Malmesbury, who appears to have named the breed, bought his first Labrador in 1870 from a fisherman plying between Newfoundland and Poole, Dorset. A great authority on the Labrador was the late Countess Howe, whose dog, Champion Bramshaw Bob, became a UK field trials champion and then went on to win Best in Show at Crufts on two occasions.

At one time, Labrador Retrievers were invariably black. Yellow Labradors are now much more popular, though a good black is a joy to behold in the field. Unfortunately, there are so many crossbred blacks that the beauty of the purebred black Labrador is now little seen outside show and sporting circles.

This breed remains among the most popular of dogs. A first-class gundog and fine swimmer, it ideally combines the role of family pet and sporting companion. It is also a worthy contender in obedience competitions, draws large entries in the show ring and works as a guide dog for the blind.

Character and care

Exuberant in youth, but easy to train, the Labrador is good with children and rarely seems to get itself into any kind of trouble. It needs plenty of exercise and regular brushing. It can be kept indoors as a family pet or in an outdoor kennel.

KEY CHARACTERISTICS
• **CLASS** Gundog. **Recognized** AKC, ANKC, CKC, FCI, KC(GB), KUSA.
• **SIZE** Height at shoulders: dogs 56–61cm (22½–24½in), bitches 54–59cm (21½–23½in). Weight: dogs 27.2–33.7kg (60–75lb), bitches 25–33.7kg (55–70lb).
• **COAT** Short and dense, without wave or feathering; weather-resistant undercoat.
• **COLOUR** Wholly black, yellow or liver/chocolate; yellows range from light cream to red fox; small white spot on chest permissible.
• **OTHER FEATURES** Head broad with defined stop; medium-sized eyes; ears not large or heavy; chest of good width and depth; distinctive "otter" tail.

GOLDEN RETRIEVER

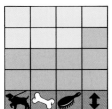

Some controversy surrounds the Golden's origin. One tale tells that, in 1858, Sir Dudley Marjoribanks (later Lord Tweedmouth) saw a troupe of eight Russian sheepdogs performing in a circus in the seaside resort of Brighton in England. So impressed with them was Sir Dudley that, following the show, he approached the owner and offered to buy two of them. The offer was declined on the grounds that the circus act would be spoilt if the troupe was split up, whereupon Sir Dudley agreed to buy all eight dogs. According to this tale, the troupe provided the foundation stock for the Golden Retriever breed to which Bloodhound blood was introduced. Although this story still persists, it is more generally believed that the Golden Retriever was the progeny of retriever/spaniel stock born on His Lordship's Scottish estate.

Character and care

The Golden Retriever ideally combines the role of sportsman's companion and family pet, being an excellent gundog, of sound temperament and gentle with children. This beautiful animal also makes a popular show dog and works well in obedience competitions. Requiring regular brushing and ample exercise, the Golden Retriever is best suited to a country environment. It will, however, adapt to suburban conditions provided that good walks and a garden are available.

KEY CHARACTERISTICS
● **CLASS** Gundog. **Recognized** AKC, ANKC, CKC, FCI, KC(GB), KUSA.
● **SIZE** Height at withers: dogs 56–61cm (22–24in), bitches 51–56cm (20–22in). Weight: dogs 29.5–33.7kg (65–75lb), bitches 25–29.5kg (55–65lb).
● **COAT** Flat or wavy with good feathering; dense, water-resistant undercoat.
● **COLOUR** Any shade of gold or cream, but neither red nor mahogany; a few white hairs on chest only are permissible.
● **OTHER FEATURES** Head balanced and well chiselled; dark brown eyes; moderate-sized ears; deep chest and well balanced body; tail set on and carried level with back.

Varying in colour from cream to warm gold, the Golden Retriever is an excellent family dog with a kind, brown eye.

119

AMERICAN COCKER SPANIEL

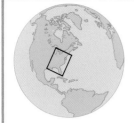

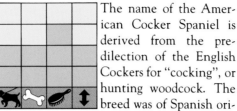

The name of the American Cocker Spaniel is derived from the predilection of the English Cockers for "cocking", or hunting woodcock. The breed was of Spanish origin, but the American Cocker can be traced back to an English-bred bitch, Obo Obo, brought over from Britain in the 1880s.

The English Cocker Spaniel Club of America, formed in 1935, helped establish the breed. It is distinguished by its small stature – suited to the lighter New World game birds – shorter head and extremely dense coat. This smallest of American gundogs, and the most popular breed in the country, was recognized by the AKC in 1946 as the American Cocker Spaniel.

For many years the American Cocker was shown exclusively in the ring. Recently, however, field trials have been reintroduced.

Character and care

The American Cocker has a much thicker coat than the English Cocker and elegant trousers. It is a useful, all-purpose gundog, able both to flush out and retrieve. It is a popular show dog, makes a fine housepet and is usually good with children. The American Cocker needs plenty of exercise, daily brushing and combing, and, if it is the desire to exhibit, fairly intricate trimming using scissors and electric clippers.

No longer bearing much resemblance to its English cousins, the American Cocker Spaniel ranks among top dog breeds in the United States.

Careful attention is needed to the American Cocker Spaniel's long, silky coat, which is much thicker than that of the English Cocker.

KEY CHARACTERISTICS

- **CLASS** Gundog.
  Recognized AKC, ANKC, CKC, FCI, KC(GB), KUSA.

- **SIZE** Height: dogs 36.25–38.75cm (14½–15½in), bitches 33.75–36.25cm (13½–14½in). Weight: 10.8–12.5kg (24–28lb).

- **COAT** Short and fine on head, medium length on body, with enough undercoat to give protection.

- **COLOUR** Black, jet black, shadings of brown or liver in sheen of coat undesirable; black and tan and brown and tan, with definite tan markings on jet black or brown body; particolours and tricolours (those wishing to exhibit are advised to check breed standard for lengthy colour requirements).

- **OTHER FEATURES** Head rounded and well developed; eyes full and looking directly forwards; back slopes slightly downwards from shoulders to tail; tail characteristically docked.

AMERICAN WATER SPANIEL

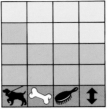

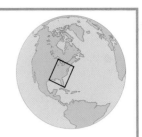

The American Water Spaniel is a comparatively modern breed. It was officially recognized by the American Kennel Club in 1940, and, while its development can be traced to the American Midwest, it probably descends from the Irish Water Spaniel, which owes its ancestry to crosses with the Poodle and the Curly-coated Retriever and in its present form dates from the late 1800s. The American Water Spaniel, which is a fine swimmer and bird dog, is smaller than its Irish counterpart. However, like the latter, it has a good nose and will work and quarter much like a Springer Spaniel.

Character and care

The American Water Spaniel is an affectionate, hardy and intelligent dog, much esteemed by huntsmen. It makes a good pet, but can be too boisterous with other animals. It needs regular combing, using a steel comb, and occasional stripping and trimming.

KEY CHARACTERISTICS

- **CLASS** Gundog.
  Recognized AKC, CKC, FCI, KC(GB).

- **SIZE** Height at shoulders: 37.5–45cm (15–18in). Weight: dogs 12.7–20.4kg (28–45lb), bitches 11.3lb–18.2kg (25–40lb).

- **COAT** Tightly curled.

- **COLOUR** Solid liver or dark chocolate (a small amount of white on chest or toes is permissible).

- **OTHER FEATURES** Body sturdy, not too compact; head of moderate length; skull quite broad; ears lobular; eye colour should tone with coat; tail moderately long.

121

CLUMBER SPANIEL

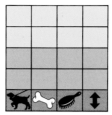

The Clumber's silky coat is free of markings, except for some freckling on the ears and face.

The Clumber is the heaviest of the spaniels, with the Basset and the now extinct Alpine Spaniel in its ancestry. It is a reliable, slow but sure dog mainly confined to country areas where it excels in flushing game over rough ground and as a retriever.

A favourite of British royalty, the Clumber has a romantic history. In the years just prior to the French Revolution it was promoted by the Duc de Noailles and became renowned as a beater and retriever. At the beginning of hostilities, the French Duke brought his dogs to England and entrusted them to the Duke of Newcastle at Clumber Park, near Nottingham, from which the breed gets its name. The French Duke met his death in the Revolution but the breed lived on, a fitting memorial to its aristocratic master.

Character and care

The Clumber is of good temperament and may be kept as a pet but its ideal role is as a working gundog in the countryside. It needs a fair amount of brushing, and care must be taken that mud does not become lodged in between its toes.

KEY CHARACTERISTICS
● **CLASS** Gundog. **Recognized** AKC, ANKC, CKC, FCI, KC(GB), KUSA.
● **SIZE** Height at withers: dogs 48–50cm (19–20in), bitches 42.5–48cm (17–19in). Weight: dogs 31.7–38kg (70–85lb), bitches 25–31.7kg (55–70lb).
● **COAT** Abundant, close and silky.
● **COLOUR** Plain white body with lemon markings preferred; orange permissible; slight head markings and freckled muzzle.
● **OTHER FEATURES** Massive, square, medium-length head; clean dark amber eyes, slightly sunk; large, vine-leaf shaped ears; long, heavy body close to ground; chest deep; tail set low and well feathered.

A favourite of royalty, the Clumber is slower than lighter-boned dogs in the field, but is nevertheless a good, steady gundog.

ENGLISH COCKER SPANIEL

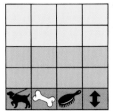

The Cocker Spaniel is also called the Merry Cocker because of its wagging tail. It originated in Spain (the word "spaniel" comes from *Espagnol*, meaning Spanish). Spaniels have been known since the 14th century and were used in falconry.

In the 19th century, the breed came into its own in the task of flushing out woodcock and small game, and became known as the cocking or Cocker Spaniel.

Recognized by the British Kennel Club in 1892, the English Cocker Spaniel is still the smallest spaniel in the gundog group. It is a favourite contender in obedience and working trials as well as in the show ring. The breed soared in popularity in the years leading up to the Second World War when Mr H. S. Lloyd's famous "Of Ware" Kennels won the coveted Best in Show Award at Crufts in London on no less than six occasions. These kennels continue under his daughter today.

Character and care

It is a gentle and popular pet, as well as being a first-class gundog, which is able both to flush out and retrieve. It needs careful brushing and combing every day, and immense care must be taken to dislodge any mud that may have become caked in its paws or its ears. Some owners gently peg back their spaniel's ears when it is eating.

KEY CHARACTERISTICS
● **CLASS** Gundog. **Recognized** AKC, ANKC, CKC, FCI, KC(GB), KUSA.
● **SIZE** Height: dogs approx. 39–42.5cm (15½–17in), bitches approx. 38–41cm (15–16in). Weight: approx. 12.7–14.5kg (28–32lb).
● **COAT** Flat and silky in texture.
● **COLOUR** Various; self (pure) colours, no white allowed on chest.
● **OTHER FEATURES** Square muzzle; eyes full but not prominent; strong, compact body; tail set on slightly lower than line of back.

Long, silky ears frame the English Cocker Spaniel's square muzzle.

The English Cocker is the smallest spaniel in the gundog group, but is excellent in the field, tending to work close to the guns.

ENGLISH SPRINGER SPANIEL

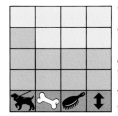

The English Springer is one of the oldest of the British spaniels, with the exception of the Clumber. The land spaniel written about in 1570 by the historian Dr Caius was obviously a forerunner of the Springer. It was originally used for flushing or springing game from cover before shotguns were in use. For a time it was known as the Norfolk Spaniel, named after either a Norfolk family that kept a strain of "springing" spaniels prior to 1900 or the breed's place of origin in the county of Norfolk in England.

Sir Thomas Boughey, who helped establish the modern breed, had Springers with a pedigree traceable to a bitch that whelped in 1812. One of her descendants was Field Trials Champion Velox Powder, bred in 1903, which won 20 field trial stakes. Sir Thomas's family retained an interest in the breed until the 1930s and many of today's field trials champions are descendants of his strain. The English Springer Spaniel Club was formed in the UK in 1921, but the breed had found fame as a "bird dog" in America long before.

Character and care

The English Springer Spaniel is an intelligent, loyal and popular gundog, which also makes a reliable housepet and is good with children. The breed needs plenty of exercise, a daily brushing and regular checks to ensure that mud does not become lodged in its paws or its ears. The Springer may not be a good choice for the houseproud because it tends to have a good shake when it comes indoors out of the rain!

Spaniels bred to flush game were often known as "springers" because in effect they sprang from cover. The English Springer Spaniel was for a time called the Norfolk Spaniel, reflecting its county of origin.

Outstanding in the field, the English Springer is also an attractive family pet.

KEY CHARACTERISTICS

- **CLASS** Gundog.
  Recognized AKC, ANKC, CKC, FCI, KC(GB), KUSA.

- **SIZE** Height at shoulders: dogs 51cm (20in), bitches 48.5cm (19in). Weight: 22–25kg (49–55lb).

- **COAT** Close, straight and weather-resistant; never coarse.

- **COLOUR** Liver and white, black and white, either of these with tan markings.

- **OTHER FEATURES** Medium-length skull; medium-sized eyes; long, wide ears; strong body; tail set low, and never carried above the level of the back.

WELSH SPRINGER SPANIEL

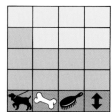

The Welsh Springer Spaniel, or its forerunner, is mentioned in the earliest records of the Laws of Wales, dating back to about AD1300. It is also possible that these red and white spaniels are a cross between the English Springer and the Clumber. Certainly, the breed has the Brittany in its ancestry, being similar both in its marked ability as a gundog and in conformation, although the Welsh Springer is higher in the leg and lighter boned. In the UK it was exhibited as a Welsh Cocker prior to 1902, when it was recognized by the Kennel Club. Over the last 20 years it has been exported to North America and other parts of the world.

Character and care

This loyal and hard-working gundog is somewhere between the Merry Cocker and the English Springer Spaniel in size. It is a good swimmer, has an excellent nose, and combines the role of family dog and sportsman's companion provided the need for exercise is met. It needs brushing daily, and regular checks to make sure that mud does not become lodged in its paws or ears.

KEY CHARACTERISTICS
• **CLASS** Gundog. **Recognized** AKC, ANKC, CKC, FCI, KC(GB), KUSA.
• **SIZE** Height at withers: dogs 45–48cm (18–19in), bitches 42.5–45cm (17–18in). Weight: 15.8–20.2kg (35–45lb).
• **COAT** Straight and flat, silky in texture; some feathering on chest, underside of body and legs.
• **COLOUR** Rich red and white only.
• **OTHER FEATURES** Slightly domed head; medium-sized, hazel or dark eyes; ears set moderately low; strong, muscular body; tail well set on and low.

With a more tapered head and higher-set ears, the Welsh Springer Spaniel is smaller than the English Springer.

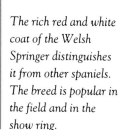

The rich red and white coat of the Welsh Springer distinguishes it from other spaniels. The breed is popular in the field and in the show ring.

FIELD SPANIEL

Little known outside Britain, the Field Spaniel shares its origins with the Cocker Spaniel, although the two types became separate breeds in 1892.

This resulted in a better proportioned standard type evolving, which is breeding true and producing some very nice specimens. Despite this, the Field Spaniel is still rarely seen in its country of origin outside the show ring. It is recognized in the United States, but very few specimens are registered there.

Character and care

The Field Spaniel has an equable temperament and makes a good household pet and gundog. Like other spaniels, it thrives on plenty of exercise, and needs to be brushed and combed every day, taking care that its coat does not become matted.

The Field Spaniel has the same origin as the Cocker Spaniel, being, in effect, a larger version of it, and early litters sometimes contained both. Then, in 1892, the varieties went their separate ways. While the Cocker was improved greatly, the Field Spaniel was bred to produce an exaggeratedly long body and short legs, and its popularity and numbers declined sharply.

In 1948 the Field Spaniel Society was reformed in Britain and considerable work was undertaken by dedicated enthusiasts.

KEY CHARACTERISTICS
• **CLASS** Gundog. **Recognized** AKC, ANKC, CKC, FCI, KC(GB), KUSA.
• **SIZE** Height at withers: dogs about 45–47cm (18in), bitches about 42.5cm (17in). Weight: 15.7–25kg (35–55lb).
• **COAT** Long, flat and glossy, without curls; silky in texture.
• **COLOUR** Black, liver or roan with tan markings; clear black, white or liver and white unacceptable.
• **OTHER FEATURES** Head conveys impression of high breeding, character and nobility; eyes wide open; moderately long and wide ears; deep chest; tail set low and characteristically docked.

At one time bred for extreme characteristics, the Field Spaniel has been rehabilitated by enthusiasts over the past half century.

IRISH WATER SPANIEL

The tallest of the spaniels, the Irish Water Spaniel comes into its element in the wetlands, often diving beneath the surface to retrieve injured waterfowl.

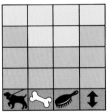

Documentary evidence for water dogs and water spaniels traces back to AD17, and some form of water spaniels has been known in Ireland for more than a millennium.

Writing about 80 years ago, the canine historian Hugh Dalziel suggested that the Irish Water Spaniel was the forerunner of all modern spaniels. However, the contemporary view is that this breed developed through crosses with Poodles and Curly-coated Retrievers which, from its appearance, would seem very likely. Prior to 1859, there were two separate strains of the breed in Ireland, one in the north and one in the south. It would seem that the southern strain, which resembled the Standard Poodle, formed the basis of the modern breed.

Character and care

The tallest of the spaniels, the Irish Water Spaniel is a brave, loving and intelligent animal. It excels in retrieving wildfowl, has a fine nose, and will work and quarter as a spaniel. Maintaining this breed's coat of curls and thick undercoat is not such a chore as might be expected. However, it does need to be groomed at least once a week using a steel comb. Some stripping of unwanted hair is necessary, as is trimming around the feet.

KEY CHARACTERISTICS
● **CLASS** Gundog. **Recognized** AKC, ANKC, CKC, FCI, KC(GB), KUSA.
● **SIZE** Height: dogs 53–60cm (21–24in), bitches 51–58cm (20–23in). Weight: dogs 25–29.5kg (55–65lb), bitches 20.2–26kg (45–58lb).
● **COAT** Dense, tight ringlets on neck, body and top part of tail; longer, curling hair on legs and topknot; face, rear of tail and back of legs below hocks smooth.
● **COLOUR** Rich, dark liver.
● **OTHER FEATURES** Good-sized, high-domed head; small, almond-shaped eyes; long, oval-shaped ears; long, arching neck; deep chest; short tail.

Tight curls and a knowing look are part of the appeal of the Irish Water Spaniel.

SUSSEX SPANIEL

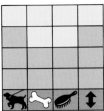

Once popular with farmers, Sussex Spaniels have been known in the county of Sussex in southern England for around two centuries. The breed was originated by a Mr Fuller of Rosehill, Sussex, in 1795. It was first exhibited at Crystal Palace, London, in 1862. Later a bigger strain, known as the Harvieston, was developed. This owed something to the Clumber Spaniel and the Bloodhound, and to this day some Sussex Spaniels have a hound look about them.

The breed has always been relatively rare and credit must go to the British breeder Mrs Freer for keeping it going during the two World Wars. In the early to mid 1950s, more Clumber blood was added, which resulted in improved bone and temperament.

The Sussex is used mainly for partridge and pheasant, being too small to take a hare. It works in thick cover, giving tongue as it works so that its handler knows where it is.

Character and care

The Sussex is a working spaniel with an excellent nose, which makes an ideal country dog. It tends to attach itself to one person, and is loyal and easy to train. It requires a daily brush and comb and, as with all spaniels, care must be taken that mud does not become caked in its ears and feet.

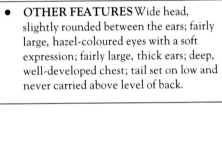

KEY CHARACTERISTICS
● **CLASS** Gundog. **Recognized** AKC, ANKC, CKC, FCI, KC(GB), KUSA.
● **SIZE** Height at withers: 32.5–40cm (13–16in). Weight: 15.7–23kg (35–50lb).
● **COAT** Abundant and flat, without a tendency to curl; ample weather-resistant undercoat.
● **COLOUR** Rich golden liver shading to golden at tips of hairs, gold predominating; dark liver or puce is undesirable.
● **OTHER FEATURES** Wide head, slightly rounded between the ears; fairly large, hazel-coloured eyes with a soft expression; fairly large, thick ears; deep, well-developed chest; tail set on low and never carried above level of back.

There is more than a hint of hound about the Sussex, now one of the rarest of spaniel breeds.

POINTER

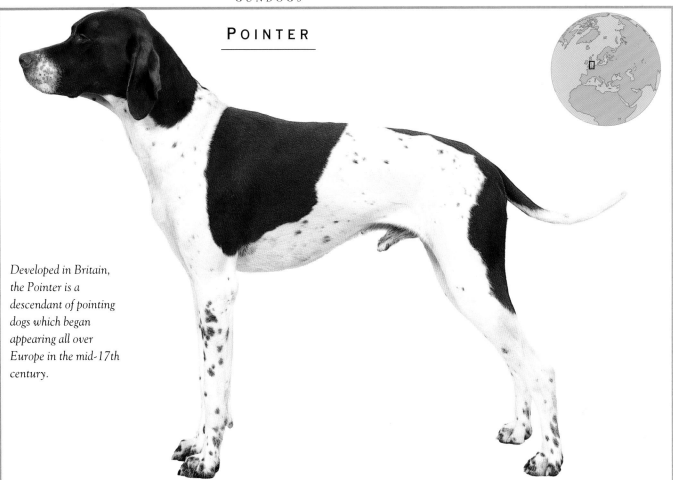

Developed in Britain, the Pointer is a descendant of pointing dogs which began appearing all over Europe in the mid-17th century.

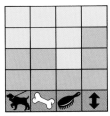

Like the setters, the Pointer is famed for its classic stance, pointing with nose and tail in the direction of game. It is thought by many to have originated in Spain. There is, however, a school of thought that it may be of English origin, developed through crossings of Foxhound, Bloodhound and Greyhound. Also, in the opinion of William Arkwright, who spent a lifetime researching the history of the breed, the Pointer originated in the East and found its way to Italy before arriving in Spain.

William Arkwright, from Sutton Scarsdale near Chesterfield in England, compiled *Arkwright on Pointers* during the period 1890–1919. This work is still regarded as the bible on the breed. In the United Kingdom, the Pointer was accepted by the then Setter and Pointer Club in 1937, and reassessed and confirmed by the Pointer Club as recently as 1970. It is popular internationally and recognized throughout the world.

Character and care

The Pointer is a popular show dog, and admirably combines the roles of sportsman's companion and family pet. It is an affectionate, obedient dog, which is easy to train, good with children and needs only regular brushing to keep its coat in good condition. It does, however, need plenty of exercise and so is not ideally suited to town life.

KEY CHARACTERISTICS
● **CLASS** Gundog. **Recognized** AKC, ANKC, CKC, FCI, KC(GB), KUSA.
● **SIZE** Height at withers: dogs 62.5–70cm (25–28in), bitches 57.5–65cm (23–26in). Weight: dogs 25–33.7cm (55–75lb), bitches 20.2–29.5kg (45–65lb).
● **COAT** Short, dense and smooth.
● **COLOUR** Lemon and white, orange and white, liver and white, black and white; self (pure) colours and tricolours also correct.
● **OTHER FEATURES** Medium-width head with pronounced stop; dark, round, intense eyes; ears set on level with eyes; thin, sloping shoulders; deep chest; tail thicker at root, tapering to a point.

ENGLISH SETTER

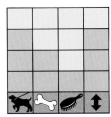

A distinctive feature of the English Setter is the curving feathered tail.

The English is the oldest and most distinctive of the four breeds of setter – which sit or "set" when they find prey – the others being the Irish, (commonly called the Red Setter), the Gordon and the Irish Red and White.

The English Setter has been known since the 14th century, but the name most closely associated with the breed is that of Edward Laverack (1815–77) whose setter pedigrees trace back to about 1860. The breed was registered by the British Kennel Club in 1873. Laverack wrote that "this breed is but a Spaniel improved", and undoubtedly it does derive from spaniels. It was Laverack, too, who, through interbreeding, developed the strain upon which the present-day English Setter breed standard was founded.

Another breeder, Mr R. L. Purcell Llewellin, helped establish the English Setter in America. Mr Llewellin bought several of Mr Laverack's best dogs and crossed them with new blood in the north of England. He introduced a Mr Slatter and Sir Vincent Corbet's strain, which thereafter became known as the Duke–Kate–Rhoebes strain. His Setters found fame in the United States and Canada, where they proved unsurpassed in field trials and firmly established the breed line in North America.

Character and care
Strikingly beautiful, loyal and affectionate, the English Setter is a breed that admirably combines the role of family pet and sportsman's dog. It is good with children, can live as one of the family or be kennelled out of doors, and needs only daily brushing with a stiff brush and the use of a steel comb. Straggly hairs must be removed before exhibition. Like most gundogs, the English Setter requires a good amount of exercise and is not ideally suited to town life, though many do seem to survive in an urban setting.

GORDON SETTER

The heaviest of the setters, the Gordon is Scotland's only native gundog.

KEY CHARACTERISTICS

- **CLASS** Gundog.
  Recognized AKC, ANKC, CKC, FCI, KC(GB), KUSA.

- **SIZE** Height: dogs 62–68cm (25–27in), bitches 60–62cm (24–25in). Weight: 18.1–31.7kg (40–70lb).

- **COAT** Short, straight and dense.

- **COLOUR** Black and white (blue belton), orange and white (orange belton), lemon and white (lemon belton), liver and white (liver belton), or tricolour (blue belton and tan or liver belton and tan); those without heavy patches of colour but flecked (belton) all over are preferred.

- **OTHER FEATURES** Head lean and noble; eyes neither deep nor prominent; ears moderately low set; back short, level and well muscled; high withers; tail set on almost in line with back, scimitar shaped but not turning upwards, soft feathering.

Arguably the most elegant of the group, the English Setter was developed mainly to hunt in open country.

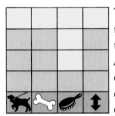

The Gordon, formerly the Gordon Castle Setter, owes its existence to Alexander, Fourth Duke of Richmond and Gordon, who bred Scotland's only gundog in the late 1770s. He aimed to produce a larger, heavier setter by introducing Bloodhound and, it is widely thought, collie blood. Gordons are not so fast or stylish as other setters.

Gordons were exhibited at the world's first dog show, held at Newcastle Town Hall, England, on the 28 June, 1859. The setter prize was won by "Dandy", a Gordon which was owned by the pointer judge! Around this time, the breed was introduced into the United States, where there are now more members registered than in Britain.

Character and care

The Gordon is a tireless worker, able to withstand the heat of grouse shooting in August better than other setters and able to work without water for longer. It will combine the role of gundog admirably with that of a family pet and it is a better watchdog than other setters. The Gordon needs plenty of space and lots of exercise, and is not best suited to town life.

KEY CHARACTERISTICS

- **CLASS** Gundog.
  Recognized AKC, ANKC, CKC, FCI, KC(GB), KUSA.

- **SIZE** Height at shoulders: dogs 60–70cm (24–27in), bitches 57–65cm (23–26in). Weight: dogs 25–36.3kg (55–80lb), bitches 20.2–31.7kg (45–70lb).

- **COAT** Short and fine on head, fronts of legs and tips of ears; moderately long over rest of body, flat and free from curl.

- **COLOUR** Deep, shining coal black, without rustiness, and with lustrous tan (chestnut red) markings; black pencilling on toes and black streak under jaw permissible.

- **OTHER FEATURES** Head deep rather than broad; dark brown eyes; medium-sized ears; body of moderate length; tail straight or slightly curved, not too long.

IRISH SETTER

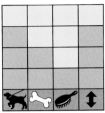

The Irish Red Setter (or Big Red) was developed through the crossing of Irish Water Spaniels, the Spanish Pointer and both the English and Gordon Setters. This resulted in a beautiful, exuberant, pointer-like dog, which is notable for its classic pointing stance.

The person most closely associated with the modern breed is Edward Laverack (1815–77), who spent a lifetime perfecting the Irish (and the English) Setter. Although it originated in Ireland, the breed came into its own in Victorian England, where its speed and energy, developed for the conditions found in Ireland, made it ideally suited to work as a gundog in large open expanses of countryside.

Character and care

While undoubtedly having hunting ability, this breed is widely sought after as a popular and loving family pet. It is good with children and other pets, and has a particular affinity with horses. The Irish Setter has boundless energy and, therefore, needs plenty of exercise, as well as a daily brushing. It will adapt to a suburban home, but is far better suited to country life where it has plenty of freedom. It is, incidentally, far too good natured to be used as a guard dog.

The Irish Setter, the most popular and perhaps most light-hearted of the setter group, took on its solid red appearance in the 19th century.

KEY CHARACTERISTICS
● **CLASS** Gundog. **Recognized** AKC, ANKC, CKC, FCI, KC(GB), KUSA.
● **SIZE** Height: 63.5–68.5cm (25–27in). Weight: 27.2–31.7kg (60–70lb).
● **COAT** Short and fine on head, fronts of legs and tips of ears; moderately long, free and as straight as possible on rest of body; good feathering.
● **COLOUR** Rich chestnut with no trace of black; white markings on chest, throat, chin or toes, or small star on forehead or narrow streak or blaze on nose or face permissible.
● **OTHER FEATURES** Long, lean head; dark hazel to dark brown eyes; moderate-sized ears; chest as deep as possible, rather narrow in front; tail moderate in length in relation to size of body.

IRISH RED AND WHITE SETTER

At one time almost eclipsed by the stylish solid Red Setter, the Irish Red and White Setter has enjoyed a revival over the last half century.

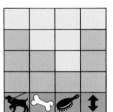

The Irish Red and White Setter evolved from spaniels, probably red and white spaniels, that were brought to Ireland from France and crossed with pointers, and by the 18th century, Red and White Setters were being bred to type. Then setter fanciers began to prefer the Red Setter and by the end of the 19th century the Red and White all but disappeared. Since the 1940s the breed has undergone a revival in Ireland. Red and Whites are recognized by the Kennel Club in Britain, have their own breed standard, and have been recognized by the FCI.

Fortunately the breed has recently begun to make its mark on the show scene.

Character and care

The Irish Red and White Setter is a happy, good natured and affectionate dog, which admirably combines the role of sportsman's dog and family pet. It needs space and plenty of exercise, and requires daily brushing.

KEY CHARACTERISTICS

- **CLASS** Gundog.
  Recognized ANKC, FCI, KC(GB), KUSA.

- **SIZE** Height: 59–67cm (23½–27in).
  Weight: 18.1–31.7kg (40–70lb).

- **COAT** Flat, straight and finely textured with good feathering.

- **COLOUR** Clearly particoloured with pearl white base and solid red patches; mottling and flecking, but not roaning, permitted around face and feet, and up foreleg to elbow and up hind leg as far as hock.

- **OTHER FEATURES** Head broad in proportion to body; hazel or dark brown eyes; ears set level with eyes; body strong and muscular; tail strong at root and tapering to fine point.

Particoloured with red patches on a solid white base, the breed is allowed some mottling on the face and paws.

BOURBONNAIS SETTER

The Bourbonnais Setter, little known outside its native France, is distinguished by its abundant freckles and rudimentary tail.

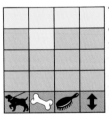

The Bourbonnais Setter or Braque du Bourbonnais is associated with the area of central France after which it is named. However, it seems to derive from the Pyrenees, where a number of other French gundogs also originated. The ancestors of these dogs gradually spread out to other regions, and crossings with local dogs produced varieties which took the name of their new home.

The Bourbonnais is often described as the short-tailed setter because it is almost always born without a tail. It has a striking Dalmatian-like coat pattern on a distinctly thickset body.

Character and care

The Bourbonnais is a good-natured sporting and family dog, which is easy to train. Like most gundogs, it requires a fair amount of exercise, and needs a brush and rub down every few days.

KEY CHARACTERISTICS

- **CLASS** Gundog.
  Recognized FCI.

- **SIZE** Average height: 53cm (21in). Weight: 18.2–25.9kg (40–57lb).

- **COAT** Short.

- **COLOUR** White and light brown, giving a colour that has been described as "like dregs of wine"; fawn without large markings, but having small spots fused into the white, distributed uniformly over the body.

- **OTHER FEATURES** Very long head with arched skull and slight stop; large, dark amber eyes, not sunken; long ears reaching to throat; broad, slightly convex back; tail very short and set low.

SAINT-GERMAIN SETTER

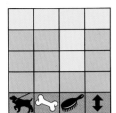

The Saint-Germain Setter is also known as the Saint-Germain Pointer, the Compiègne Setter or, more commonly, the Braque Saint-Germain. This attractive gundog bears a strong resemblance to the English Pointer and has a similar tail carriage, although it is not so heavily boned. It is said to have derived from the crossing of an English Pointer "Miss", owned by King Charles X of France (reigned 1824–30), and a French Setter or Braque at the beginning of the 19th century. According to De La Rue in *Les Chiens d'Arrêt Francais et Anglais*, "Miss produced seven puppies and four of these were given to the Compiègne forest wardens; the latter transferred to Saint-Germain, and took their dogs with them. Their elegance was pleasing to the hunters of Paris."

Character and care

This strong hunting dog, with less refinement and sense of smell than the English Pointer, may be used against large game, and also hunts pheasant and rabbit. It has a good gallop. It is an affectionate dog and is gentle and intelligent, but can be stubborn. It needs a brush and rub down every few days, and requires plenty of exercise.

KEY CHARACTERISTICS
• **CLASS** Gundog. **Recognized** FCI.
• **SIZE** Height: dogs 51–63.5cm (20–25in), bitches 53–58cm (21–23in). Weight: 18.1–25.6kg (40–57lb).
• **COAT** Short and soft.
• **COLOUR** White with orange markings.
• **OTHER FEATURES** Fairly broad head; large, well-set, golden-brown eyes; ears set on level with eyes; short, straight back; loins strong, short and slightly arched; tail undocked.

A refined and stylish dog, the Saint Germain Setter is said to have derived from a 19th century mating between an English Pointer and a French Setter.

PUDELPOINTER

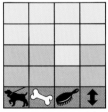

The Pudelpointer is the result of a cross between various pointer breeds and the old Barbet (now extinct) or the Poodle. It is a good all-purpose gundog with a hard, rough, thick coat, enabling it to cope with difficult terrain and cold water. In build it resembles a heavy pointer rather than a Poodle, and has a short, straight back, large round eyes and what has been described as a "bird of prey" expression. Unfortunately, it is becoming rare in Europe as a distinct breed, but some Pudelpointers are now owned by hunters in the USA and Canada.

Character and care

The Pudelpointer is an intelligent, good natured dog, which is eager to learn and possesses great stamina.

KEY CHARACTERISTICS
• **CLASS** Gundog. **Recognized** CKC, FCI.
• **SIZE** Height at withers: over 61cm (24in). Weight: 25–31.7kg (55–70lb).
• **COAT** Short, hard and coarse.
• **COLOUR** Light to chestnut brown.
• **OTHER FEATURES** Medium-length head; long eyebrows and slight beard; round, lively eyes; ears flat and hanging tight to side of head; chest deep but in proportion to rest of body; tail starts high, thick at root and grows thinner towards tip.

BRITTANY

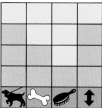

The Brittany, formerly known as the Brittany Spaniel, is the only spaniel in the world that points to game. It is a fine woodcock dog and will also retrieve wildfowl. Believed to have originated in Spain or the Argoat forests of Brittany, it has also been suggested that the Brittany may be the progeny of an English Red and White Setter dog and a Breton bitch. English sportsmen liked to shoot woodcock in Brittany and took their dogs with them, presumably before the quarantine laws which now exist.

The breed was first exhibited in Paris in 1900 and was officially recognized in France in 1905. The standard was prepared in 1907 and altered in 1908.

Character and care

The Brittany has an excellent nose and needs gentle handling. It is a relative newcomer to Britain, but has done well in field trials in the United States. It requires daily brushing and plenty of exercise.

KEY CHARACTERISTICS
• **CLASS** Gundog. **Recognized** AKC, ANKC, CKC, FCI, KC(GB), KUSA.
• **SIZE** Height at shoulders: 44–51cm (17½–20½in). Weight: 13.6–18.1kg (30–40lb).
• **COAT** Body coat flat and dense, never curly; a little feathering on legs.
• **COLOUR** Orange and white or liver and white in clear or roan patterns, or tricolour (also black and white in UK).
• **OTHER FEATURES** Rounded, medium-length head; expressive eyes; drop ears; deep chest reaching to the level of the elbows; tail naturally short or usually docked to 10cm (4in), with a small twist of hair on the end, carried level with back.

Really a small setter, the Brittany is a keen hunting dog, single minded in the field.

The Brittany's well defined stop and tapering muzzle resemble the features of the setter.

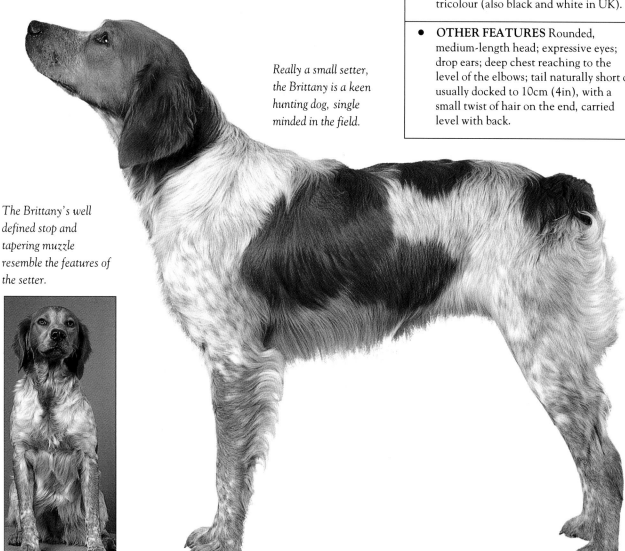

DUPUY SETTER

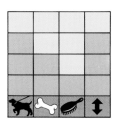

Some sources say that the Dupuy Setter or Pointer or Braque Dupuy owes its existence to a Monsieur Pierre Dupuy, a hunter from Poitou, who mated his white and chestnut setter bitch, Leda, with a dog of unknown breed named Mylord. Others claim that it came about through a setter and greyhound cross. The writer gives most credence to the belief that the Dupuy is an ancient French setter, a few examples of which survived the French Revolution (1789–99) due to the dedication of a game warden at the Anneu d'Argensois who was named Dupuy.

Character and care

A good-sized gundog, the Dupuy is of noble bearing. The expression in its eyes is said to be both gentle and dreamy. It is suitable for any kind of hunting, but is not too keen on water. The Dupuy is fast, keen and obedient. It needs plenty of exercise, and should be groomed every day or two with a bristle or pin brush and given a rub down to make its coat shine. The tail is not docked.

KEY CHARACTERISTICS
• **CLASS** Gundog. **Recognized** FCI.
• **SIZE** Height: dogs 67.5–68.5cm (26½–27in), bitches 65–66cm (25½–26in); males generally leaner than females.
• **COAT** Short and smooth.
• **COLOUR** White and dark brown; the white should be a good white with more or less broad markings or a brown saddle, with or without flecking or streaking.
• **OTHER FEATURES** Fine, long head, narrow and lean; golden or brown eyes, well open and having very little stop; very small neck; small, narrow ears; deep chest, well let down; tail set on neither too high nor too low.

FRENCH SPANIEL

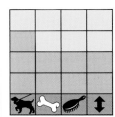

The French Spaniel or Épagneul Français has been written of as "the mainspring of all other breeds of long-haired pointers, commonly called spaniels". The descendant of dogs imported into France from England in the 14th century, it bears a resemblance to the English Springer and Cavalier King Charles Spaniel. Its ancestors, like those of all French and English spaniels, are widely believed to have originated in Spain. Little known today outside France, the French Spaniel is well muscled with a strong head and a long, soft, slightly wavy coat.

Character and care

The French Spaniel is a willing gundog, with considerable stamina. It has an intelligent expression and is good natured. It makes a good family pet provided that it is given plenty of exercise. It is best suited to a country home. It needs grooming daily with a bristle brush or slicker brush and comb.

KEY CHARACTERISTICS
• **CLASS** Gundog. **Recognized** CKC, FCI.
• **SIZE** Average height at shoulders: dogs 56–61cm (22–24in), bitches 53.5–58.5cm (21–23in). Weight: 19.9–25kg (44–55lb).
• **COAT** Long and supple, with some feathering.
• **COLOUR** White with chestnut markings only, tan not permissible.
• **OTHER FEATURES** Strong, fairly long head, not clumsy; medium-sized, dark amber eyes; long ears framing the head; deep, fairly broad chest; tail set on rather low, in many dogs slightly long, carried horizontally and obliquely with slight S-curve, undocked.

GERMAN POINTER

Slower to catch on with the show fraternity, the Wire-haired Pointer differs from its Short-haired relative mainly in its bristly coat.

The German Short-haired Pointer (Deutscher Kurzhaariger Vorstehhund or Kurzhaar) is of Spanish origin, probably derived through crossing the Spanish Pointer with a scenthound, thereby producing a versatile gundog that would both point and trail. English Foxhound blood is also believed to have been added.

Developed some 100 years ago, it was entered in the stud book of the American Kennel Club in 1930. A similar club was set up in Britain in 1951, and since then field trials for the breed have been held there.

The German Wire-haired Pointer (Deutscher Drahthaariger Vorstehhund or Drahthaar) is very similar to the German Short-haired Pointer, except in coat, and obviously had a hand in its make-up, as did the Wire-haired Pointing Griffon and the Stichelhaar, as well as the Airedale Terrier.

Although popular in its homeland, the German Wire-haired took longer than the Short-haired to become established overseas. It was recognized by the American Kennel Club in 1959 and it is still more widespread in the USA than in Britain.

Although pointers had been known in Germany for centuries, the Short-haired did not begin to emerge as a distinct breed until about a century ago.

Character and care

Both varieties are powerful, strong and versatile hunting dogs. They are equally at home on land or in the water, and excellent at working wildfowl and most game. The forest, in water, and for hunting bigger game, especially if the quarry is dangerous. The German Short-haired also makes a good household pet, provided that it receives enough exercise. It is easy to train, usually enough exercise. It is easy to train, usually good with children and does not require a lot of grooming. The Wire-haired, although it can adapt to the role of household pet, has had certain aggressive qualities bred into it, and is best kept purely as a hunting dog.

KEY CHARACTERISTICS
● **CLASS** Gundog. **Recognized** AKC, ANKC, CKC, FCI, KC(GB), KUSA.
● **SIZE** *Short-haired* Height at withers: dogs 58–64cm (23–25in), bitches 53–59cm (21–23in). Weight: dogs 25–31.7kg (55–70lb), bitches 20.2–27.2kg (45–60lb). *Wire-haired* Height at shoulders: dogs 60–67cm (24–25in), bitches 56–62cm (22–24in). Weight: dogs 25–34kg (55–75lb), bitches 20.5–29kg (45–64lb).
● **COAT** *Short-haired* Short and flat, coarse to the touch. *Wire-haired* Thick and harsh, no longer than 3.8cm (1½in) long, with dense undercoat.
● **COLOUR** *Short-haired* Solid liver, liver and white spotted, liver and white spotted and ticked; liver and white ticked; the same variations with black instead of liver; not tricoloured. *Wire-haired* Liver and white, solid liver, also black and white in UK; solid black and tricolour highly undesirable.
● **OTHER FEATURES** *Short-haired* Broad, clean-cut head, with slightly moulded crown; medium-sized eyes; broad ears set on high; chest should appear deep rather than wide, but in proportion to body; tail starts high and thick, growing gradually thinner towards tip. *Wire-haired* Broad head balanced in proportion to body; slightly rounded crown; medium-sized, oval eyes; ears medium-sized in relation to head; chest should appear deep rather than wide but not out of proportion to rest of body; tail starts high and thick, growing gradually thinner towards tip.

FRENCH SETTER

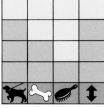

This breed is known in its native France as the Braque Français. The word "Braque" comes from the French *braquer* (to aim) and is used for dogs that point or "set" themselves in the direction of game. The breed is, therefore, called in English either the French Setter or the French Pointer.

The French Setter appears to have originated in the Pyrenees area of Spain and thereafter to have spread throughout Europe. The catalogue of a championship dog show held in Paris described this breed as "the oldest breed of pointer in the world, it has been the origin of nearly all the continental fled, hardy hunting dog, with a powerful nose even in hot and dry weather."

There is a smaller variety of this gundog called the French Pointer.

There is a smaller variety of this gundog called the French Pointer.

Character and care

The French Setter of today is a noble, powerful animal, with a docked tail, a good nose and fine working abilities. It makes a gentle pet as well as gundog, being good natured and getting on well with children and other animals. However, in common with other gundogs, it thrives on a considerable amount of exercise. It needs grooming to make the coat shine.

KEY CHARACTERISTICS
● **CLASS** Gundog. **Recognized** FCI.
● **SIZE** Height at withers: about 61cm (24in). Weight: about 27kg (60lb).
● **COAT** Smooth and rather thick.
● **COLOUR** White and tan with tan or cinnamon flecking; roans and red speckled examples also popular.
● **OTHER FEATURES** Head not too heavy; eyes well open and well set in sockets, affectionate, pensive expression; average-length ears; chest broad when viewed from the front, deep when viewed in profile; tail characteristically docked.

GERMAN SPANIEL

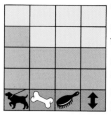

The German Spaniel, Quail Dog or Deutscher Wachtelhund was created in the 1890s in Germany. Its breeders used a variety of long-haired European hunting dogs, including waterdogs, and the resultant dog bears a marked resemblance to the English Springer Spaniel and the German Long-haired Pointer, although it is not so long in the leg. The old German hunting dog, the Stöber, may also have given the breed its keen scenting ability.

The Wachtelhund's long coat protects it in thick forests, where it flushes and retrieves quail and other feathered game and is also used to hunt fox and hare. This enthusiastic worker and fine swimmer is valued by German foresters and hunters, but is little known outside its country of origin.

Character and care

This good all-round gundog has a hardy constitution and reliable temperament. It makes an excellent hunting companion but Germans say that it should "only be in sportsmen's hands". It requires a lot of exercise, daily brushing and regular checks to make sure that mud has not become embedded in its ears or paws.

KEY CHARACTERISTICS
• **CLASS** Gundog. **Recognized** FCI.
• **SIZE** Height: dogs 39.5–49.5cm (15½–19½in), bitches 39.5–44.5cm (15½–17½in). Weight: 19.8–29.7kg (44–66lb).
• **COAT** Strong, glossy and slightly wavy.
• **COLOUR** Roan or brown.
• **OTHER FEATURES** Head clean with slightly rounded crown; expressive eyes, any shade of brown; ears set on high with broad bases; body longer than high; tail set on high, well feathered, and not raised much.

LARGE AND SMALL MÜNSTERLÄNDERS

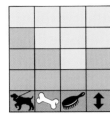

Münsterländers combine the best qualities of the setter and the spaniel. According to Edward Laverack, the setter "is but a spaniel improved": Münsterländers have the setter's build and the spaniel's head.

While officially recorded as one of the newest pointing and retrieving gundog breeds, the Large Münsterländer has been well established in its native Germany as an all-purpose gundog since the beginning of the 18th century. Then it was regarded as a German Long-haired Pointer, but in the early days of the German Kennel Club it was decided that only brown and white German Long-haired Pointers would be eligible for registration and pups of other colours were given away. The "odd-coloured" puppies fell into the hands of farmers whose aim was to perpetuate the best working qualities, irrespective of colour. Thus, the farmers were able to build up and save an interesting and attractive variety of gundog, known today as the Large Münsterländer.

The Small Münsterländer is a more recent breed, derived by crossing the Brittany with the German Long-haired Pointer in the early 20th century.

Character and care

The Münsterländers are loyal, affectionate and trustworthy dogs, which admirably fulfil the roles of sportsmen's companions and family pets. They are energetic and so need plenty of exercise, and a daily brushing.

The Large Münsterländer is an all-purpose pointing/retrieving dog, but also makes an excellent family pet.

KEY CHARACTERISTICS
• **CLASS** Gundog. **Recognized** *Large* ANKC, FCI, KC(GB), KUSA. *Small* FCI, KC(GB).
• **SIZE** *Large* Height: dogs about 61cm (24in), bitches about 58–59cm (23in). Weight: dogs 25–29kg (55–65lb), bitches about 25kg (55lb). *Small* Height: 47.5–55cm (19–22in). Average weight: 15kg (33lb).
• **COAT** Moderately long and dense, with feathering.
• **COLOUR** *Large* Head solid black, white blaze, strip or star allowed; body white or blue roan with black patches, flecks, ticks, or a combination of these. *Small* Liver and white with ticking.
• **OTHER FEATURES** Head well proportioned in relation to body and slightly elongated; medium-sized, intelligent eyes; broad, high-set ears; strong back; tail well set on in line with back.

WEIMARANER

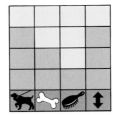

The Weimaraner or "Silver Ghost" bears a striking resemblance to a painting by Van Dyck (*circa* 1631). However, it is said to have been purpose-bred as a gundog in the 1800s by the Grand Duke Karl August of Weimar (the capital of the former state of Thuringia in central Germany), after which the breed is named. Breeds which are likely to have played a part in its make-up include the Saint Hubert or other French hounds, Short-haired Pointers, Spanish Pointers, Bloodhounds and the German Schweisshunds. The result is a fine gundog, which was originally used against big game and, in more recent times, has worked as a police dog.

The Weimaraner made an impact in the United States and Canada after the Second World War. It did not reach the United Kingdom until the 1950s, but it has since become very popular there.

Character and care
The Weimaraner is good natured and distinctive looking, with a metallic silver-grey coat and amber or blue-grey eyes. It excels in obedience and agility, and makes a fine pet provided that it has an outlet for its keen intelligence. It is best housed indoors rather than in a kennel and requires little grooming.

KEY CHARACTERISTICS
• **CLASS** Gundog. **Recognized** AKC, ANKC, CKC, FCI, KC(GB), KUSA.
• **SIZE** Height at withers: dogs 61–69cm (24–27in), bitches 56–64cm (22–25in). Weight: 31.7–38kg (70–85lb).
• **COAT** Short, smooth and sleek.
• **COLOUR** Preferably silver grey; shades of mouse or roe grey permissible.
• **OTHER FEATURES** Head moderately long and aristocratic; medium-sized eyes; long ears; deep chest and moderately long body; tail characteristically docked.

PORTUGUESE SETTER

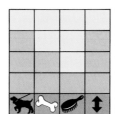

The Portuguese Setter or Pointer (Perdiguerio Português) probably traces back to the Segugio hounds and the Assyrian Mastiff. The Portuguese Setter has been known since the 14th century and, with the Spanish Pointer, may have been the ancestor of other pointer-type breeds. Originally used as a bird dog (*perdiguerio* means partridge), this is a good all-round gundog with an excellent nose. It is popular with hunters in Portugal but little known outside that country.

Character and care
This prodigious hunter is speedy, attentive, skilful and intelligent. Its aim in life is to please its master and it will retrieve game with the utmost joy. It is also very affectionate, and often fills the role of house dog as well as hunting companion in its native land. It should be given a brush and rub-down every few days.

KEY CHARACTERISTICS
• **CLASS** Gundog. **Recognized** FCI.
• **SIZE** Height: dogs 52–61cm (20½–24in), bitches 48–56cm (19–22in).
• **COAT** Short, strong and dense.
• **COLOUR** Yellow or brown, with or without plain markings.
• **OTHER FEATURES** Head in good proportion to body; eyes full, symmetrical and large; ears medium length and width; body deep and broad, indicative of ample heart and lung room; tail characteristically docked at third joint, if not, should not reach further than hocks, preferably shorter.

The Weimaraner, a favourite at the 19th century Court of Weimar, developed into a versatile utility dog, working for the police as well as in the field.

STABYHOUN

The Stabyhoun originated in the Friesland area of the Netherlands, where it was bred as an all-purpose gundog. It is known to have existed at least since 1800 but was not recognized by the Dutch Kennel Club until 1942. This first-class retriever and pointer is an extremely popular dog in its native land, but is little known outside the Netherlands. In appearance it is somewhere between a setter and a spaniel, and is said to produce a formidable rat-catcher when crossed with the Wetterhoun.

Character and care

Although it is a good versatile sporting dog, the Stabyhoun is now kept mainly as a family pet and has adapted well to this role. It is good with children, easy to train, affectionate, and requires only regular brushing to keep its coat in good condition. It requires a lot of exercise.

KEY CHARACTERISTICS
● **CLASS** Gundog. **Recognized** FCI.
● **SIZE** Maximum height: dogs 49.5cm (19in), bitches somewhat smaller. Weight: 14.8–19.9kg (33–44lb).
● **COAT** Long and sleek, but short on head; bushy feathering on tail.
● **COLOUR** White with black, blue, liver or orange markings.
● **OTHER FEATURES** Lean head narrowing to a black nose; brown eyes; folded, "trowel-shaped" ears; long tail, set on low and hanging straight.

WIRE-HAIRED POINTING GRIFFON

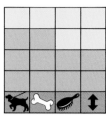

The Wire-haired Pointing Griffon or Griffon à Poil Dur is commonly known as the Korthals Griffon after its originator, Edward Karel Korthals, a Dutchman and dedicated dog-fancier. It was Korthals' desire to produce a gundog that could be used against all game over a variety of terrain. He used various types of griffon, setter and water spaniel, including the French Setter (Braque) and Barbet. Korthals succeeded in producing a versatile gundog of extreme endurance and with a good sense of smell. Unfortunately it is now comparatively rare.

Although listed as a French breed, the Wire-haired Pointing Griffon was developed by a Dutchman from French and German stock.

Character and care

The Wire-haired Pointing Griffon boasts all the fine qualities of its ancestors – strength, good nature, docility, intelligence and fine working ability. It is favoured by the one-dog huntsman, and it can be kennelled out of doors or live in the house as a member of the family. It requires plenty of exercise. Its coat should not be groomed too vigorously, and it needs some trimming.

KEY CHARACTERISTICS
● **CLASS** Gundog. **Recognized** AKC, CKC, FCI.
● **SIZE** Height: dogs 56–60cm (22–24in), bitches 51–56cm (20–22in). Weight: 22.7–27.2kg (50–60lb).
● **COAT** Coarse and hard.
● **COLOUR** Steel grey with chestnut markings; white and chestnut; white.
● **OTHER FEATURES** Large, long head; large eyes, with mild but lively expression; pendant ears; slightly arched neck; muscular tail, customarily docked and carried horizontally.

HUNGARIAN COARSE-HAIRED VIZSLA

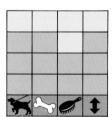

The Hungarian Coarse-haired Vizsla or Setter is the result of crossing the Hungarian Vizsla (a smooth-haired setter) with the German Wire-haired Pointer or Drahthaar in the 1930s. The Hungarian Vizsla probably descended from the Weimaraner (see page 136) and Transylvanian pointing dogs. The product of the cross is a keen-looking, medium-sized hound of regal bearing, with a tough coat, strong bone and considerable powers of endurance.

Character and care

The Hungarian Coarse-haired Vizsla has good scenting ability, and is a hardy all-round gundog. It is good natured and easy to train. It needs plenty of exercise, and should be given a brush and rub down every few days.

KEY CHARACTERISTICS
● **CLASS** Gundog. **Recognized** FCI, KC(GB).
● **SIZE** Height at withers: dogs 57.5–64cm (22½–25½in), bitches 53.5–59.5cm (21–23½).
● **COAT** Short and hard, bearded; hair slightly longer on ears, but fine.
● **COLOUR** Dark yellow.
● **OTHER FEATURES** Lean, noble head; eyes neither protruding nor deep set; ears set on at medium length; back straight, short and very muscular; medium-thick tail set on rather low, should be docked to two thirds of its natural length.

HUNGARIAN VIZSLA

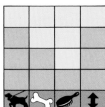

The Hungarian Vizsla or Magyar Vizsla is the national hunting dog of Hungary. This smooth-haired setter was bred on the central Hungarian plain (Puszta), the habitat of a wide variety of game. The Vizsla was developed as an extremely versatile dog, able to hunt, track, point and retrieve hare, ducks, geese and other prey. It is likely that the German Weimaraner, to which it bears a strong resemblance, and Transylvanian pointing dogs played a part in its early development. However, Magyar noblemen took immense care not to introduce new blood that might prove in any way detrimental to the ability of this breed.

It was not until after the Second World War, when many sportsmen had to leave Hungary and took their dogs with them, that the Vizsla became widely known. The breed was recognized by the American Kennel Club in 1960 and now there are also some splendid Vizsla kennels in the United Kingdom.

Character and care

The Vizsla is a versatile, easily trained gundog which also makes a first-class pet and is good with children. It needs plenty of exercise and its coat should be brushed regularly.

KEY CHARACTERISTICS
● **CLASS** Gundog. **Recognized** AKC, ANKC, CKC, FCI, KC(GB), KUSA.
● **SIZE** Height at withers: dogs 57–64cm (22½–25in), bitches 53–60cm (21–23½in). Weight: 20–30kg (48½–66lb).
● **COAT** Short, dense and straight.
● **COLOUR** Russet gold; small white marks on chest and feet acceptable.
● **OTHER FEATURES** Lean head; ears moderately low set; short, level, well-muscled back; tail moderately thick.

Bred for the temperature extremes of the central Hungarian plain, the Vizsla is an all weather sportsman.

KOOIKERHONDJE

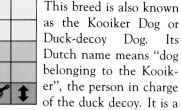

The Kooikerhondje is an old breed, familiar from paintings of 17th century Dutch masters such as Vermeer.

This breed is also known as the Kooiker Dog or Duck-decoy Dog. Its Dutch name means "dog belonging to the Kooiker", the person in charge of the duck decoy. It is a fairly old breed, native to the Netherlands, whose job was to draw ducks out of their cover by walking in and out of low reed fences by the banks of a dyke that was covered with netting. When the ducks investigated, the dyke was closed. Since the Second World War, efforts have been made to improve its breeding, and it has recently been introduced into the United Kingdom.

Character and care

The Kooikerhondje is an intelligent, affectionate dog, which is lively but not over-excitable. A good companion dog, it is a handy size for a household pet. It needs plenty of exercise and daily brushing.

ITALIAN SPINONE

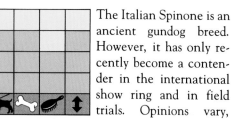

The Italian Spinone is an ancient gundog breed. However, it has only recently become a contender in the international show ring and in field trials. Opinions vary, even in Italy, about the dog's origin, as to whether it is of setter descent – climatic conditions alone accounting for its thick coat – or a relative of the coarse-haired Italian Segugio or, indeed, a Griffon cross.

Other authorities believe that this powerful, versatile hunter originated in the French region of Bresse, later finding its way to Piedmont in Italy, and that its evolution is attributable not only to the French Griffon, but also to German Pointers, the Porcelaine, the now extinct Barbet and the Korthals Griffon. Or the Spinone may be the result of a mating between a Coarse-haired Setter and a white mastiff.

Character and care

Affectionate, agreeable and of loyal temperament, the Italian Spinone has a soft mouth and will both point and retrieve. It needs plenty of vigorous exercise, is a fine swimmer and is best suited to country life.

KEY CHARACTERISTICS
• **CLASS** Gundog. **Recognized** AKC, ANKC, CKC, FCI, KC(GB), KUSA.
• **SIZE** Height at shoulders: dogs 58.75–68.75cm (23½–27½in), bitches 57.5–63.75cm (23–25½in). Weight: dogs 31.75–37kg (70–82lb), bitches 28.2–32.02kg (62–71lb).
• **COAT** Rough, thick, fairly wiry.
• **COLOUR** White, white with orange markings, solid white peppered orange, white with brown markings, white speckled with brown (brown roan), with or without brown markings.
• **OTHER FEATURES** Expressive eyes; ears triangular; body length equal to height at withers; tail thick at base, carried horizontally.

A newcomer to the international show ring, the Spinone is still hunted throughout the Piedmont.

KEY CHARACTERISTICS

- **CLASS** Gundog.
  Recognized FCI.

- **SIZE** Height at shoulders: about 38cm (15in). Weight: 9–10.8kg (20–24lb).

- **COAT** Moderately long and slightly wavy; feathering on chest, legs and tail.

- **COLOUR** Clear white with red patches.

- **OTHER FEATURES** Head broad, with long hair on ears, pointed nose; tail long and curled to one side, bushy.

ITALIAN SETTER

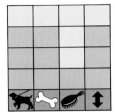

The Italian Setter (or Pointer) or Bracco Italiano has a most attractive hound-like appearance with pendulous ears and a kindly expression. It is thought to be one of the oldest of the setters having certainly been well established in the 18th century. The breed was probably derived through crossings with the Italian Segugio and the now-extinct Assyrian Mastiff. In its country of origin, the Italian Setter is divided into two varieties according to colour – the white and orange, and the chestnut roan. The white and orange is believed to have originated in Piedmont and is usually thought of as the original. The roan, which is attributed to Lombardy, is considered by some fanciers to trace back to crosses between imported setters and the old Saint Hubert Hound. However, there is no recognized difference in conformation between the two varieties.

Character and care

The Italian Setter is a good natured, intelligent gundog, and is docile yet powerful. It combines the role of gundog and family companion. It needs plenty of exercise, and a brush and rub down every day or two.

KEY CHARACTERISTICS

- **CLASS** Gundog.
  Recognized FCI, KC(GB).

- **SIZE** Height: 54.5–62cm (21½–26½in) but varies considerably. Weight: 25–40kg (55–88lb).

- **COAT** Short and fine.

- **COLOUR** Generally orange and white, or chestnut roan.

- **OTHER FEATURES** Long, angular head with pronounced, arched eyebrows; yellow or ochre eyes; well-developed, pendant ears; prominent withers; back almost straight as far as 11th vertebra; tail characteristically docked to 15–25cm (6–10in).

HOUNDS

THE PHARAOH HOUND

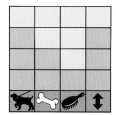

In typical pose, the Pharaoh Hound recalls the Egyptian dog-god Anubis, whose task it was to guide the souls of the newly departed into the after-life.

The Pharaoh Hound is a medium-sized sight breed which will also hunt by scent. It has been described as the oldest domesticated dog in recorded history because it so closely resembles the likenesses of dogs carved on the tomb walls of the pharaohs and on ancient Egyptian artefacts dating back to at least 2000BC. In 1935, archaeologists working in the great cemetery west of the Pyramid of Cheops, at Giza, found an inscription recording that such a dog, named Abuwtiyuw, had been buried with all the ritual ceremony of a great man of Egypt by order of the kings of Upper and Lower Egypt.

It is thought that these hounds were taken to Malta and Gozo by the Phoenicians. First imported into the UK in the 1920s, the breed was re-established in Britain in 1968 when eight examples were imported from Gozo and Malta, and it was soon recognized. It was introduced into North America in the late 1960s and was subsequently recognized.

Character and care
The affectionate and intelligent Pharaoh Hound has a happy, confident personality, likes children and makes a good family pet. Its coat needs little attention but the breed does require plenty of exercise and is not suited to cramped conditions.

KEY CHARACTERISTICS
• **CLASS** Hound. **Recognized** AKC, ANKC, CKC, FCI, KC(GB).
• **SIZE** Height at withers: dogs 55–62.5cm (22–25in), bitches 52.5–60.5cm (21–24in).
• **COAT** Short and glossy.
• **COLOUR** Tan or rich tan with white markings; white tip on tail strongly desirable; white star on chest, white on toes and slim white blaze on centre line of face permissible; flecking or white other than above undesirable.
• **OTHER FEATURES** Long, lean, well-chiselled head; eyes amber, blending with coat; medium-sized ears set high; lithe body with almost straight top line; tail medium set, fairly thick at base and tapering towards tip, reaching just below point of hock in repose.

Large, erect ears designed to radiate heat betray the Pharaoh Hound's desert origins.

SICILIAN HOUND

Bred in Sicily for 3000 years, the Sicilian Hound is a close relative of the Pharaoh Hound.

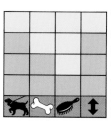

The Sicilian Hound is also known as the Cirneco dell'Etna after the volcano, Mount Etna, on the Italian island of Sicily. It is thought to have been brought from Egypt to Sicily over 3000 years ago by the Phoenicians. They are reputed to have carried on a most profitable trade in greyhounds and other sighthounds, which they acquired in Africa and Asia and unloaded in Aegean and Mediterranean mainland ports and islands, including Sicily. This ancient breed of sighthound is smaller than the obviously related Pharaoh and Ibizan Hounds. The length of its muzzle is approximately that of its skull, its eyes are oval and deep set, and its coat is short and fine. It is a mysterious, wise-looking hound which is said by some to have supernatural powers as well as serving the more practical purpose of hunting wild rabbit, hare and other game on the slopes of Mount Etna.

Character and care
The Sicilian is a quiet hunter with an excellent nose, even though it is primarily a sighthound. It will adapt to the role of a companion. Its coat needs little attention. Its ethereal looks belie a strong constitution.

KEY CHARACTERISTICS
● **CLASS** Hound. **Recognized** FCI.
● **SIZE** Height at shoulders: dogs 45.5–51cm (18–20in), bitches 43–45.5cm (17–18in). Weight: dogs about 12–13.5kg (26–30lb), bitches 10–12kg (22–26lb).
● **COAT** Harsh to the touch.
● **COLOUR** Any shade of fawn, small white markings acceptable; solid white, or white with orange markings.
● **OTHER FEATURES** Long head with oval-shaped skull; triangular ears with stiff, straight points, carried erect; body as long as it is high; fairly long tail set on low, without brush or long hair.

IBIZAN HOUND

The Ibizan Hound, seen above in wire-haired form, is descended from the same stock of Middle Eastern prick-eared dogs as the Pharaoh and Sicilian Hounds.

The Ibizan Hound (Podenco Ibicenco, Ca Eivessenc) is native to Ibiza, one of the Spanish Balearic Isles. Like the Pharaoh Hound, which it strongly resembles, it is descended from hunting dogs kept by the ancient Egyptians. In the 9th century BC, Egypt was invaded by the Romans, and the neighbouring Carthaginians and Phoenicians were driven out to the island of Ibiza, where they lived for about a century. However, the hounds they took with them remained on Ibiza for the next 3000 years, still retaining the colours depicted on Egyptian drawings of their ancestors. The breed was also used for hunting in southern Spain and France. The Ibizan Hound comes in three varieties: smooth-, coarse- and long-haired.

Character and care

This noble-looking animal has a kindly nature, is good with children, rarely fights and makes a fine gundog or housepet. It is extremely sensitive and has acute hearing, so must never be shouted at, but responds well to kind treatment. Like all hounds it needs a lot of exercise. Its coat is easy to maintain, needing only a daily brushing.

SPANISH GREYHOUND

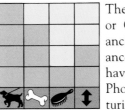

The Spanish Greyhound or Galgo Español is an ancient breed, whose ancestors are believed to have been brought by the Phoenicians many centuries BC. Favoured by the Spanish nobility, it is used mainly for coursing. It is smaller and slightly sturdier than the English Greyhound. There is also an Anglo-Spanish variety produced by crosses to the English Greyhound for use on the race-track. The Anglo-Spanish is closer in appearance to the English Greyhound but has darker eyes and a longer tail.

Character and care

Like all greyhounds, the Spanish is a gentle dog and, once de-trained, makes a very good pet, provided that care is taken around livestock. Greyhounds kept for coursing are accustomed to being kennelled in fairly confined spaces and a pet greyhound quickly adapts to the confines of an average-sized home. Regular exercise is more important than speed or distance travelled, and regular brushing is also required.

KEY CHARACTERISTICS
● **CLASS** Hound. **Recognized** FCI.
● **SIZE** Height: dogs 65–70cm (25½–27½in), bitches slightly smaller. Weight: 27.2–29.7kg (60–66lb).
● **COAT** Close, shiny and short.
● **COLOUR** Tawny with black mask, or black usually streaked with light undercoat; white muzzle, belly and feet.
● **OTHER FEATURES** Long, narrow head; dark, bright, vivacious eyes; rose-type ears falling down back; very long, slightly sabred tail carried low.

KEY CHARACTERISTICS
• **CLASS** Hound.   **Recognized** AKC, ANKC, CKC, FCI, KC(GB), KUSA.
• **SIZE** Height at withers: dogs 59–69cm (23½–27½in), bitches 56–65cm (22½–26in). Weight: dogs about 22.7kg (50lb), bitches about 20.2kg (45lb).
• **COAT** Smooth or rough; always hard, close and dense.
• **COLOUR** Solid white, chestnut or lion, or any combination of these.
• **OTHER FEATURES** Long, fine head; flat skull with prominent occipital bone; clear amber, expressive eyes; large, thin, stiff, highly mobile ears; level back; long thin tail set on low.

A fast, silent hunter, the Ibizan is extremely agile, and can jump up to 2.5m (8ft) in height from a standstill.

PORTUGUESE PODENGO

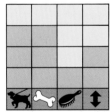

The Podengo or Portuguese Hound is known, but rarely seen, outside its native Portugal, but it is popular there, particularly in the north. It is kept as a companion, and as a hunter of rabbit, hare and deer.

The breed is descended from a number of ancient sighthounds, and over the years three size varieties have been developed to suit different terrains and prey. The Large (Grande) chases larger, fleet quarry over flat ground, the Medium (Medio) is used over rougher terrain, while the Small (Pequeño) can go down burrows to flush out rabbits. The Small Podengo looks rather like a big Chihuahua, indeed, the Chihuahua was originally a larger dog with the same large prick ears. The Medium closely resembles the Ibizan Hound.

Character and care

The Podengo is an attractive, good-natured hunter, which also makes a fine guard and a lively companion. All three varieties need plenty of exercise and daily brushing.

KEY CHARACTERISTICS
• **CLASS** Hound.   **Recognized** FCI.
• **SIZE** Height: *Small* 20.5–30.5cm (8–12in); *Medium* 50–56cm (20–22in); *Large* 56–58.5cm (22–27in).
• **COAT** Long and harsh; short and silky.
• **COLOUR** Predominantly fawn or yellow, with or without white markings.
• **OTHER FEATURES** Sharp nose; large ears set high and carried erect, open at front; tail carried like a sickle; moderately long, muscular body.

153

BASENJI

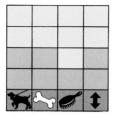

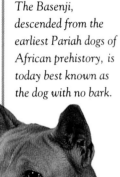

The Basenji, descended from the earliest Pariah dogs of African prehistory, is today best known as the dog with no bark.

The Basenji (meaning "bush thing") comes from central Africa and is also called the Zande Dog, Belgian Congo Dog, Congo Bush Dog, Bongo Terrier, Congo Terrier and Nyam Nyam Terrier. Its likeness is depicted on the tombs of the pharaohs and its very expression seems to hint at inner wisdom and antiquity. Used as a hunting dog in its native land, the Basenji is famed for the fact that it does not bark, instead giving a kind of yodel.

European explorers came upon the breed in the mid-19th century in the Congo and southern Sudan and the first Basenjis reached Britain in 1895. They were exhibited at Crufts as Congo Terriers and evoked considerable interest. Unfortunately, they succumbed to distemper before any breeding programme could be attempted, and further imports in the 1920s and 1930s also perished. Then, in 1941, two African-bred pups imported into Massachusetts survived, and the Basenji Club of America was established in 1942. Later, Miss Veronica Tudor Williams pioneered the breed in the United Kingdom.

Character and care

The Basenji is playful, extremely loving, dislikes wet weather and needs a reasonable amount of exercise. It washes itself like a cat and has no doggie smell, so a daily rub-down with a hound glove will suffice. In common with certain other breeds, the bitch comes into season only once a year. Pups may be destructive if unchecked. Some good friends who took in a misplaced Basenji frequently complained about the damage their young dog had done. That period soon passed, however, and 15 years later the family were inconsolable at Benji the Basenji's passing.

KEY CHARACTERISTICS
• **CLASS** Hound. **Recognized** AKC, ANKC, CKC, FCI, KC(GB), KUSA.
• **SIZE** Height at withers: dogs about 43cm (17in), bitches 40cm (16in). Weight: dogs about 10.8kg (24lb), bitches 9.9kg (22lb).
• **COAT** Short, sleek, close and very fine.
• **COLOUR** Black, red, or black and tan; all should have white on chest, on feet and tail tips; white blaze, collar and legs optional; black and tan with tan melon pips and black, tan and white mask.
• **OTHER FEATURES** Dark, almond-shaped eyes: small, pointed ears, erect and slightly rounded; well balanced body with short, level back; tail set on high, curling tightly over spine and lying close to thigh, with a single or double curve.

Though Basenjis may vary in colour, the white "shirt front" is a standard feature.

BLACK AND TAN COONHOUND

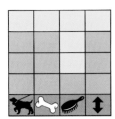

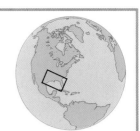

The (American) Black and Tan Coonhound is one of a number of varieties of coonhound recognized by America's United Kennel Club, the others including the Redbone (see below) and Treeing Walker (see page 249). All were purpose bred to hunt raccoon and opossum, and will chase their quarry up a tree and hold it there for the hunters. The energetic Black and Tan also has the endurance needed to trail larger game such as stags and bears.

The Black and Tan is a descendant of the extinct Talbot Hound and various Bloodhound crosses to which the blood of the American Virginia Foxhound has been added. It bears a close resemblance to the Bloodhound and has similar, long pendulous ears, but lacks the skin folds. Although a frequent contender in field trials, it is rarely seen in the show ring except at special coonhound shows.

Character and care
This friendly, intelligent dog is able to cope with both extremes of climate and difficult terrain. It is a hard worker and obedient to its master. A secure, high fence is needed to keep it in, and it is usually kennelled out of doors. Its ears need regular checking as they need to be kept clean.

KEY CHARACTERISTICS
• **CLASS** Hound. **Recognized** AKC, CKC, FCI.
• **SIZE** Height at shoulders: dogs 63.5–68.5cm (25–27in), bitches 58.5–63.5cm (23–25in). Weight: dogs 27–36.5kg (60–80lb), bitches 25–34kg (55–75lb).
• **COAT** Short and dense.
• **COLOUR** Black and tan only.
• **OTHER FEATURES** Finely modelled head; round, chestnut-coloured eyes; long, pendant ears; well-proportioned body; strong tail carried freely.

REDBONE COONHOUND

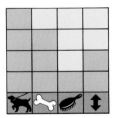

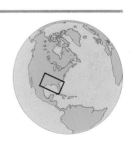

This is one of six varieties of Coonhound recognized by the United Kennel Club of America (UKC), the others being the Black and Tan, English, Bluetick, Treeing Walker and Plott. All are mainly descended from foxhounds. However, other hounds played a part in their development and, in common with the Black and Tan, the Redbone resembles more closely the English Bloodhound than a foxhound.

As their name suggests, the coonhounds were bred to hunt the raccoon, a quarry that is prevalent throughout the United States except for Alaska and Hawaii, and is also found in Canadian forests. Since the raccoon is nocturnal, it is hunted at night. The Redbone has excellent scenting and hunting abilities. It also adapts well to working in a variety of terrains. As well as being popular in the US, the Redbone is also now found in Central and South America and Japan.

Character and care
The Redbone Coonhound is an efficient and handsome working dog, which is faithful to its owner and generally good natured. It requires plenty of exercise and grooming with a hound glove.

KEY CHARACTERISTICS
• **CLASS** Hound. **Recognized**
• **SIZE** Height: 63.5–68.5cm (25–27in), bitches 58.5–63.5cm (23–25in).
• **COAT** Dense, short and harsh.
• **COLOUR** Red, sometimes with small white marks on chest and feet.
• **OTHER FEATURES** Eyes hazel to dark brown; ears set low and well back; strong tail with base slightly below level of back line.

BLOODHOUND

The world's finest tracker, the Bloodhound can follow a cold trail after hours or even days have passed.

Long, drooping ears, wrinkles and dewlaps give the Bloodhound an expression of inconsolable sadness.

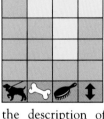

The Bloodhound or Chien de Saint Hubert is one of the oldest hound breeds. It is believed to have been brought to Britain by William the Conqueror in 1066, and the description of it written by the dog historian, Doctor Caius, in 1553 differs little from that of the dog we know today.

It is generally believed that the earliest ancestors of the Bloodhound were dogs bred in Assyria, in Mesopotamia, around 2000–1000BC. Some of these were probably taken to the Mediterranean region by Phoenician traders, and from there spread north through Europe. A concentration of hounds developed in Brittany in the 7th and 8th centuries, from which emerged the Saint Hubert, thought to be the direct ancestor of the Bloodhound.

The Bloodhound has the keenest sense of smell of any domestic animal. Able to follow a days-old scent, it has been used to track down lost people as well as game and, having found its quarry, this gentle animal does not kill it. To help develop its skills, owners join a Bloodhound Club and participate in what is known as "Hunting the Clean Boot". Pups learn early on how to "follow a line", beginning by playing simple games of hide and seek with their owners. There are Bloodhound clubs in many countries.

Character and care

Good with children and exceedingly affectionate, the Bloodhound makes an ideal companion for those who have the room to accommodate it, the energy to exercise it, and neighbours who do not object to its baying. It can be kept in an average-sized home provided that it has adequate exercise, but is best suited to a rural environment. It should be groomed daily with a hound glove.

KEY CHARACTERISTICS
• **CLASS** Hound. **Recognized** AKC, ANKC, CKC, FCI, KC(GB), KUSA.
• **SIZE** Height: dogs 63–67.5cm (25–27in), bitches 58–63cm (23–25in). Weight: dogs 40.5–48.6kg (90–110lb), bitches 36.3–45kg (80–100lb).
• **COAT** Smooth, short and weatherproof.
• **COLOUR** Black and tan, liver (red) and tan, or red.
• **OTHER FEATURES** Head narrow in proportion to length, and long in proportion to body; medium-sized eyes; thin, soft ears set very low; well-sprung ribs; tail (stern) long, thick and tapering to a point.

OTTERHOUND

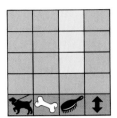

The big, strongly built British Otterhound is believed to trace back to the Griffon Vendéen and the now extinct rough-coated Griffon de Bresse. According to the Otterhound Club, these hounds were imported into Britain in significant numbers before 1870. Shortly afterwards, the Comte le Couteuix de Canteleu sent his entire pack of Griffons to a Mr Richard Carnaby Forster who gave them to his stepdaughter, Lady Mary Hamilton. In 1906, the Hamilton Otterhounds were sold individually to masters of Otterhounds.

The Otterhound has keen scenting abilities almost on a par with the Bloodhound. The dogs, which are fine swimmers, would swim upriver, following the otter's "wash" (trail of bubbles). When otter hunting was outlawed in the United Kingdom in the late 1970s, the Master of the Kendal and District Otterhounds in the Lake District set up the Otterhound Club to ensure its survival. In 1981, a breed standard was approved by the British Kennel Club and since then, the attractive Otterhound has become a popular contender in the show ring on both sides of the Atlantic.

Character and care

The Otterhound makes an amiable though stubborn pet, which can be somewhat destructive within the household, if undisciplined. Like other thick-coated breeds it can be kennelled outdoors, if the owner wishes, though many Otterhounds do live indoors. It needs a considerable amount of exercise and its rough coat should be groomed once a week, and bathed as necessary.

KEY CHARACTERISTICS
• **CLASS** Hound. **Recognized** AKC, ANKC, CKC, FCI, KC(GB), KUSA.
• **SIZE** Height: dogs 60–67.5cm (24–27in), bitches 57.5–65cm (23–26in). Weight: dogs 33.7–51.7kg (75–115lb), bitches 29.5–45kg (65–100lb).
• **COAT** Long (4.8cm/1½–3in), dense, rough and harsh, but not wiry.
• **COLOUR** All hound colours permissible.
• **OTHER FEATURES** Clean, very imposing head; intelligent eyes; long, pendulous ears – a unique feature of the breed – set on level with corner of eyes; deep chest with fairly deep, well-sprung rib-cage; tail (stern) set on high, carried up when alert or moving.

The Otterhound is a shaggy breed with a majestic head framed by long, pendulous ears.

Said to possess scenting abilities almost on a par with those of the Bloodhound, the Otterhound is increasingly rare now that otter are a protected species.

ITALIAN SEGUGIO

The Italian Segugio or Segugio Italiano comes in two coat types, Short-haired (a Pelo Raso) and Coarse-haired (a Pelo Forte). The origins of this ancient Italian hunting dog trace back to the coursing dogs of ancient Egypt and it still has something of the Greyhound in its appearance. As well as having keen eyesight, it is blessed with an exceptional sense of smell, and was used against a wide variety of game. Today it is used mainly to hunt hare. The Segugio will remain bravely within firing distance once it has found its quarry.

Character and care

It can cope with most types of terrain, and is a natural hunter, but it should be trained in its working role during its early months. It is generally good natured, if a little strong willed, and can be kept as a companion dog. It needs plenty of exercise, but its coat needs little attention apart from regular brushing.

Fixed in type at least since the Renaissance, the Italian Segugio stands midway between the sight- and scent hounds.

RHODESIAN RIDGEBACK

Ancestors of the modern Ridgeback came originally from South Africa – the product of European dogs crossed with Hottentot hounds.

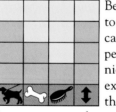

Before Europeans began to settle in southern Africa, the local Khoikhoi people were accompanied on their hunting expeditions by a dog with the distinctive ridge of hair growing in the reverse direction along its back. During the 16th and 17th centuries, Dutch, German and Huguenot immigrants to southern Africa brought as guards and hunters their own working dogs including Pointers, Mastiffs, Greyhounds and Bulldogs. These crossed with the Ridgeback, gradually producing an animal with the best qualities of the imported and local dogs.

The Rhodesian Ridgeback was named after the country of Rhodesia (now Zimbabwe), where it was highly valued by the settlers. It was also known once as the Lion Dog because it was used in packs to hunt lions and other big game, as well as to guard property. The standard was drawn up by the South African Kennel Club in 1922 and has altered little since. It attracts good entries in shows in North America and Britain and behaves well in the ring.

Character and care

This attractive animal is obedient, good with children and will guard its owners with its life. It has a gentle temperament but can move with great speed when it spies a rabbit or some other prey. It needs plenty of exercise and daily grooming with a hound glove.

KEY CHARACTERISTICS
• **CLASS** Hound. **Recognized** AKC, ANKC, CKC, FCI, KC(GB), KUSA.
• **SIZE** Height at withers: dogs 63–67cm (25–26½in), bitches 61–66cm (24–26in). Weight: 29.5–33.7kg (65–75lb).
• **COAT** Short, dense, sleek and glossy.
• **COLOUR** Light wheaten to red wheaten.
• **OTHER FEATURES** Flat skull, broad between ears; round eyes, set moderately well apart; ears set rather high; chest very deep but not too wide; tail strong at root and tapering towards tip.

The Segugio's long muzzle is slightly convex, with very little stop and no excess skin. The ears are long and narrow.

KEY CHARACTERISTICS
• **CLASS** Hound. **Recognized** FCI, KC(GB).
• **SIZE** Height: dogs 53–58.5cm (21–23in), bitches 48–56cm (19–22in). Weight: 17.7–28kg (39–62lb).
• **COAT** Dense, glossy and smooth; or coarse on head, ears, body, legs and tail.
• **COLOUR** Various shades of red, fawn or black and tan.
• **OTHER FEATURES** Large, luminous eyes; ears flat, should hang and be flat for almost their entire length; length of body from the shoulder to the buttock should equal the height at the withers; tail set on high in line with croup.

Bred as a guard dog by European settlers, the Rhodesian Ridgeback also developed the speed, stamina and courage to hunt lion.

TAHLTAN BEAR DOG

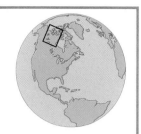

This Canadian breed, native to mountainous areas of north-west Canada, is named after the Tahltan Indians, who used it for hunting bear, lynx and porcupine. The Indians would carry the dogs on their backs in sacks to preserve their strength until the quarry was sighted. Then the dogs would be released and would hold the quarry at bay, circling it, nipping its ankles and barking like a fox, until the hunters went in for the kill.

The Tahltan Bear Dog's courage and ferocity are belied by its appealing looks. It is an attractive, fox-like little dog with enormous ears, an alert expression and, most unusually, a tail which is some 12.5–20.5cm (5–8in) long, and carried erect and thick from tip to stern. The breed was recognized by the Canadian Kennel Club in 1941 but, sadly, has not adapted to living outside its native environment and is now almost extinct. Its decline has been aggravated by breeding difficulties. The Tahltan Bear Dog only mates once a year, has a maximum of four pups and the dam will kill her offspring if she is in any way disturbed.

Character and care

A lively, fearless hunter, powerful for its size, the Tahltan Bear Dog is said to have shared a tent with its human family and to have been gentle and affectionate with them. Its coat requires regular brushing.

KEY CHARACTERISTICS
• **CLASS** Hound. **Recognized** CKC.
• **SIZE** Height: 30.5–40.5cm (12–16in). Weight: about 6.8kg (15lb).
• **COAT** Thick and long, with a soft undercoat.
• **COLOUR** Black, black and white, greyish blue or white.
• **OTHER FEATURES** Fox-like head; dark, medium-sized eyes; erect, bat-like ears; flexible body; wiry tail, very thick from root to tip, carried vertically.

ANGLO-FRENCH HOUNDS

The Middle-sized Anglo-French White and Orange Hound, more delicate than the larger variety, was produced by crossings with the Harrier, Poitevin and Porcelaine.

Great Anglo-French Hounds like this pack of Tricolours are hunting dogs and are almost never seen in the show ring. They have heavier bodies and smaller ears than the Medium-sized and Small varieties.

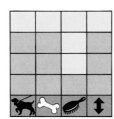

As its name suggests, the Anglo-French or Anglo-Français de Moyen Venerie came about through crossings between French medium-sized hounds and an English hound, the Harrier. At one time, the dogs were named after the breeds that had produced them, such as Harrier-Poitevin and Harrier-Porcelaine. In addition, as the experts George Johnston and Maria Ericson have recorded, the word Bâtard (meaning crossbred hounds) was often used as a prefix, as in, for example, the Bâtard-Anglo-Gascon-Saintongeois. In 1957, the Anglo-French was given its current title and categorized by colour as Anglo-French White and Black, Anglo-French White and Orange, and Anglo-French Tricolour. The latter is one of the most popular hounds in France and all are used to hunt deer, wild boar and other quarry.

Like the Anglo-French, the Great Anglo-French or Grande Anglo-Français was pro-

duced by crossing French and English hounds. In the case of this larger breed the English blood introduced was that of the English Foxhound. At one time the dogs tended to be identified by the crossing, for instance, the Anglo-French-Poitevin and Anglo-Gascon-Saintongeois. Then, in 1957, the breed was given its current name and categorized by colour as the Great Anglo-French Tricolour, Great Anglo-French White and Black, and Great Anglo-French White and Orange.

It is usually kept in packs, and used to hunt large and small game. The Small Anglo-French or Anglo-Français de Petite Venerie is the result of crossings between the Beagle or Beagle Harrier and short-haired, medium-sized French hounds. Except for size, it is similar in appearance to its larger relatives, the Anglo-French and the Great Anglo-French. The Small has fine attributes and is used for hunting rabbit, pheasant and other small game. However, it has never become popular. It is recognized by the FCI, but there is still too much variation for it to achieve a breed standard.

Character and care

The Anglo-French are, in the main, robust and good natured hounds. They are usually kept as one of a pack, looked after by professional hunt staff.

KEY CHARACTERISTICS
• **CLASS** Hound. **Recognized** FCI.
• **SIZE** *Anglo-French* Height: about 50cm (20in). Weight: 22–25kg (49–55lb). *Great Anglo-French* Height at withers: 61–68.5cm (24–27in). Weight: 29.7–31.9kg (66–71lb). *Small Anglo-French* Height: 48–56cm (19–22in).
• **COAT** Short and smooth.
• **COLOUR** *Anglo-French* Tricolour – black, white and orange; white and black; white and orange. *Great Anglo-French* As for Anglo-French. *Small Anglo-French* Usually tricolour – black, white and orange; may have black saddle covering upper torso and back.
• **OTHER FEATURES** *Anglo-French* Head moderate in size in relation to body; dark eyes; pendulous ears; tail carried low. *Great Anglo-French* Kindly eyes; large, hound-like ears; large, big-boned body; tail carried low. *Small Anglo-French* As for Anglo-French.

BILLY

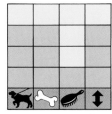

The Billy was devised by Monsieur Hublot du Rivault on his estate in Poitou, south-west France, for the express purpose of hunting wild boar and deer. His pack of dogs, formed in 1877, were known as the Chiens de Haut Poitou. He commenced selective breeding in 1888, using the wolf-hunter, the Poitevin, the Céris, a hunter of both wolf and hare, and the Montembœuf a large, noble hound that would follow only those animals selected as quarry. He called the new breed Billy after a town of that name.

Character and care

The Billy is a tall, intelligent dog, with exceptional hunting and scenting abilities and a melodious voice. It is known to be somewhat argumentative with its fellows. It is usually kept in a pack.

KEY CHARACTERISTICS
• **CLASS** Hound. **Recognized** FCI.
• **SIZE** Height at shoulder: dogs 61–66cm (24–26in), bitches 58.5–63.5cm (23–25in). Weight: 25–29.7kg (55–66lb).
• **COAT** Short and hard to the touch.
• **COLOUR** White or "café au lait"; white with orange or lemon blanket or mottling.
• **OTHER FEATURES** Large, dark, expressive eyes; rather flat ears, set high for a French hound; very deep narrow chest; long, straight tail, sometimes lightly feathered.

With its long legs and streamlined body, the Billy is swift in pursuit of prey across open ground and through thick woodland.

FRENCH HOUNDS

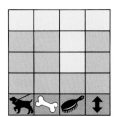

There are three varieties of French Hounds (Chiens Français): the French Tricolour (Chien Français Tricolore), the French White and Black (Chien Français Blanc et Noir) and the French White and Orange (Chien Français Blanc et Orange). Like the Anglo-French (see pages 154–5) they are the result of matings between French and English hounds, particularly the English Foxhound and the Harrier. Until 1957 they were known by a wide variety of names. Then an inventory was made of all hound packs in France and those of French type were given the title French Hounds.

Of the three varieties the White and Black is the most popular and widely represented, being a strong and fast hunter of roe and other deer. The French White and Orange, which was produced by an English Foxhound and Poitevin or Billy cross, is very similar to the Tricolour except in colour.

The Tricolour is a fairly muscular, sophisticated-looking hound of medium build. Its cheeks are more substantial than those of the Poitevin and its stop is more accentuated.

Character and care
These hounds are quiet, affectionate and obedient. However, they are bred only for hunting. They are kept in packs, kennelled out of doors, and looked after by professional hunt staff.

Packs of large hunting dogs have been kept on the great estates of France for centuries. Many varieties have become extinct, but the Tricolour, Orange and White and Red and White have survived.

KEY CHARACTERISTICS
• **CLASS** Hounds. **Recognized** FCI.
• **SIZE** *Tricolour* and *White and Orange* Height: dogs 62–72.5cm (24½–28½in); bitches 62–68.5cm(24½–27in). Weight: 27.2kg (60lb). *White and Black* Height: dogs 65–71cm (25½–28in); bitches 62–68.5cm (24½–27in). Weight: 27.9kg (62lb).
• **COAT** *Tricolour* Smooth and rather fine. *White and Orange* Short and smooth. *White and Black* Smooth, strong and close.
• **COLOUR** *Tricolour* White, black and tan with extensive saddle. *White and Orange.* White and orange *White and black* White and black; extended black saddle or markings; some blue mottling permissible; tan mottling permissible only on legs.
• **OTHER FEATURES** *Tricolour* and *White and Orange* Head not too large; large brown eyes; wide ears; deep chest descending to level of elbows; rather long tail, carried elegantly, hound-fashion. *White and Black* Large, rather long head; dark, intelligent, confident eyes; ears set on above the line of the eyes; chest deep rather than wide; rather long tail, strong at the base and carried elegantly.

POITEVIN

An outbreak of rabies in 1842 nearly wiped out the Poitevin, but, happily, this stylish scenthound has been revived.

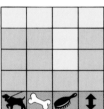

The Poitevin was developed in the late 1600s in the Poitou, south-west France, where wolves existed in large numbers. In 1692, the Marquis François de Larrye of Poitou obtained a dozen Foxhounds from the kennels of the Dauphin of France and crossed these with his own Céris dogs. This produced hounds that were unsurpassed as wolf hunters, possessing great speed, courage and scenting ability. Sadly, most were destroyed during the French Revolution (1789–99) but a few were saved by loyal supporters. Despite crossings thereafter, the Poitevin's original qualities survived and were enhanced by an infusion of English Foxhound blood. The Poitevin now closely resembles the English Foxhound, although it differs in colour and its ears are longer and more slender.

Character and care

The Poitevin is a large, distinguished hound, which is swift and intelligent, but timid and reserved. It is usually happiest when kept as a member of a pack, and looked after by professional hunt staff.

KEY CHARACTERISTICS
● **CLASS** Hound. **Recognized** FCI.
● **SIZE** Height at shoulders: 61–71cm (24–28in). Weight: around 30kg (66lb).
● **COAT** Short and glossy.
● **COLOUR** Tricolour with black saddle; tricolour with large black patches; sometimes orange and white or badger-pied.
● **OTHER FEATURES** Head long but not exaggerated; large, brown, expressive eyes; medium-width ears; very deep chest; back well muscled and very well coupled; medium-length, fine, smooth tail.

GRIFFONS VENDÉEN, GRAND AND BASSET

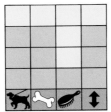

The Griffons Vendéen are French sporting dogs which occur in a number of varieties, including the Grand, the Briquet, the Basset and the Petit Basset. The Grand Griffon Vendéen is the largest and is reputed to be the oldest, of the varieties. It is thought to be a descendant of a white Saint Hubert Hound crossed with a tawny and white Italian bitch, and the resultant dogs were known as the King's White Dogs. The introduction of Nivernais Griffon and setter blood is said to have added stamina and endurance. The Basset Griffon Vendéen, descended from the Grand, is now comparatively rare. It is short legged but otherwise rather similar to the Grand. It has been bred by the Desamy family in the Vendée for more than a century. The Grand was initially used to hunt wolves and, when this role became obsolete, proved itself an agile wild boar hunter. The Grand, Basset and other varieties are also used against hare and rabbit.

Character and care

The Griffons Vendéen are extremely attractive, intelligent dogs which make good family pets as well as hunters. They are independent and love to wander, so all escape routes should be sealed. They require a considerable amount of exercise, and the Grand needs regular grooming with brush and comb to prevent its coat from matting.

KEY CHARACTERISTICS
● **CLASS** Hound. **Recognized** *Grand, Basset* and *Petit Basset* AKC, ANKC, CKC, FCI, KC(GB), KUSA. *Briquet* FCI.
● **SIZE** *Grand* Height at shoulders: 61–66cm (24–26in). Weight: 30–35kg (66–77lb). *Basset* Height at shoulders: 38–43cm (15–17in). Weight: 18–20kg (40–44lb). *Petit Basset* Height at shoulders: 34–38cm (13½–15in). Weight: 11.3–15.7kg (25–35lb). *Briquet* Height at shoulders: 51–56cm (20–22in). Weight: 15.7–23.8kg (35–53lb).
● **COAT** Rough, long and harsh to the touch – never silky or woolly – with a thick undercoat.
● **COLOUR** Solid fawn or hare; white with red, fawn, grey or black markings; bicolour or tricolour.
● **OTHER FEATURES** *Grand, Basset* and *Briquet* Domed head; large, dark eyes, without white, and with a kindly expression; narrow, supple ears; long, wide back; tail set on high, and strong at the base. *Petit Basset* Head medium length and not too wide; large, dark eyes; narrow, fine, supple ears; deep chest with a prominent sternum; medium-length tail, set on high and strong at base.

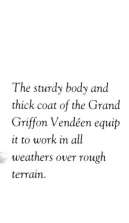

The bewhiskered face and floppy ears give the Grand Griffon Vendéen a disarming expression.

The sturdy body and thick coat of the Grand Griffon Vendéen equip it to work in all weathers over rough terrain.

PETIT BASSET GRIFFON VENDÉEN

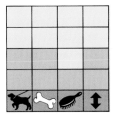

The Petit Basset Griffon Vendéen is a short-legged, rough-coated hound, developed in the Vendée district of southwest France. It was bred down from the Grand Griffon Vendéen, a larger variety originally used in France for wolf hunting and now used against wild boar.

The Petit Basset Griffon Vendéen has been described by Monsieur P. Doubigne, an expert on this breed, as a miniature Basset reduced proportionately in size while retaining all its qualities – a passion for hunting, fearlessness in the densest coverts, activity and vigour. It is now used for hunting hare and rabbit, but can also manage larger game.

It is very popular in France, particularly in its native Vendée region. It is becoming popular in the UK show ring, and is also recognized in the USA.

Character and care

This most attractive animal makes a good family pet provided that it receives plenty of exercise. It needs little grooming and considers humans its friends.

Unlike its larger relatives, the Petit Basset Griffon Vendéen works well in thick undergrowth. It is also strong enough to pursue sizeable prey.

BRIQUET GRIFFON VENDÉEN

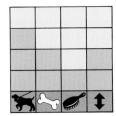

The Briquet Griffon Vendéen is a medium-sized hound from the Vendée region of France. The modern breed was established around 1910. It is popular in Europe both as a tracker and gundog, and is used for hare coursing, like the Grand and Basset Griffon Vendéen, being a smaller version of the former. Strong, fast and agile, this hound is kept in many small packs, or used on its own as a single hunter, in its native France. It is popular in France, but is little known elsewhere.

Character and care

It is courageous and good natured, but difficult to handle. It is usually kept as a member of a pack and looked after by professional hunt staff. It needs a considerable amount of exercise, and regular grooming with brush and comb to prevent its coat from matting.

BEAGLE HARRIER

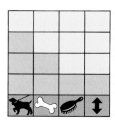

The Beagle Harrier is a French breed which was produced by crossing the Beagle and the larger Harrier. It was developed by the Frenchman, Baron Gérard, whose intention was to produce a hound with the stature of the Harrier and the scenting and hunting ability of the Beagle. Solidly built but graceful, the breed was designed to hunt deer, fox and hare, and has the stamina to run for hours without tiring. It is still used in France today but is not seen outside that country. Like its forebears, it is a typical English hound.

Character and care

The Beagle Harrier is courageous, lively, intelligent and good natured. Like the Beagle, it is affectionate but is much better suited to the role of hunter than as a pet and prefers to live as a member of a pack. It should be groomed with a hound glove.

The vivacious Beagle Harrier is a graceful, compact hunting dog bred expressly to work in small packs.

KEY CHARACTERISTICS
• **CLASS** Hound. **Recognized** FCI.
• **SIZE** Average height at shoulders: 43–48cm (17–19in). Average weight: 20kg.
• **COAT** Short, thick and rather flat.
• **COLOUR** Most colours are acceptable, but it usually occurs in grey or tricolour.
• **OTHER FEATURES** A typical hound with a somewhat regal appearance and flat, high-set ears; deep chest with slightly curved ribs; legs long and muscular; tail carried "sabre" fashion.

HANOVER HOUND

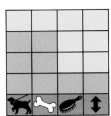

The Hanover Hound or Hannoverischer Schweisshund is a descendant of heavy German tracking dogs, which were closely related to the Saint Hubert Hound and performed similar tasks to the Bloodhound in England and the Saint Hubert Hound in France. From the 5th century, this ancestor was made leader of the pack and sent ahead to rouse game because of its keen scenting ability. It would also follow a cold trail and track down wounded animals.

In about 1800, near Hanover, hunters crossed the ancient German hound with the lighter Harz Hound (Harzerbracke) to produce a faster tracking dog. The Hanover inherited its Bloodhound ancestors' keen nose, its sad expression and characteristic skinfolds.

Character and care

Highly valued by gamekeepers and wardens in Germany, the Hanover Hound is a calm, trustworthy dog, devoted to its owners. It requires a lot of exercise and a rub down with a hound glove from time to time.

KEY CHARACTERISTICS
• **CLASS** Hound. **Recognized** FCI.
• **SIZE** Height: dogs 51–60cm (20–24in), bitches somewhat less. Weight: 37.8–44.5kg (84–99lb).
• **COAT** Dense, abundant, smooth and glossy.
• **COLOUR** Grey-brown with a dark brown mask on the cheeks, lips and around the eyes and ears; brown-red, yellow-red, yellow-ochre, dark yellow or speckled brown.
• **OTHER FEATURES** Long, strong head; forehead slightly wrinkled; clear, expressive eyes; very broad ears, rather more than medium length, set on high, and with rounded tips; long back; loins broad and slightly arched; slanting croup; belly only slightly drawn up; tail long, and straight at the root.

NIVERNAIS GRIFFON

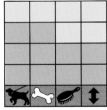

The Nivernais Griffon or Griffon Nivernais is descended from the Saint Louis Grey Dog. Packs of these shaggy hounds were used for hunting wolves and wild boar in central France; but as larger prey diminished in number, various crosses, including one to a Foxhound named Archer, produced a hound used mainly for smaller prey. It was called the Griffon-Vendéen-Nivernais, but towards the end of the last century the word Vendéen was omitted. At that time the Nivernais was in danger of extinction, but survived due to the efforts of a small band of enthusiasts, and was officially recognized in 1925.

Character and care

This large, thickset and rather mournful-looking shaggy dog is built for endurance rather than speed. It is brave, affectionate and companionable. Its long coat needs regular grooming with brush and comb, and it requires a lot of exercise.

KEY CHARACTERISTICS
• **CLASS** Hound. **Recognized** FCI.
• **SIZE** Height at shoulders: dogs 53.5–58.5cm (21–23in), bitches proportionately less. Weight: 22.7–25kg (50–55lb).
• **COAT** Long, unkempt and shaggy.
• **COLOUR** Preferably wolf grey or slate grey; can also be black, with or without tan markings, or fawn.
• **OTHER FEATURES** Head fleshless and light without being small; skull almost flat; eyes preferably dark; supple ears set on slightly above the line of the eye; deep chest; tail well set on and carried "sabre" fashion.

PORCELAINE

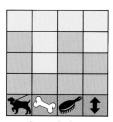

The Porcelaine is also known as the Chien de Franche-Comté after a former French region bordering Switzerland. Following the French Revolution (1789–99) examples of the Porcelaine were found at the Franco-Swiss border, leading to confusion over whether it is of French or Swiss origin. However, the breed is recognized as French, and is thought to descend from the English Harrier and ancient French hounds. The breed has been recorded in France since 1845, and in Switzerland since 1880, when the first hunting packs were established.

Bred to hunt hare and roe deer, the Porcelaine has a glossy white coat like fine porcelain. As befits one of the most popular hounds of France, it looks every inch purebred and has dark eyes, a medium-length tail and thin, well-curled ears.

The modern Porcelaine is smaller than the original breed of that name which flourished in the 18th century.

Character and care
The Porcelaine is an energetic and fierce hunter, but gentle at home and easy to handle. It needs a lot of exercise, but its coat requires only an occasional sponge over, for example before a show.

KEY CHARACTERISTICS
• **CLASS** Hound. **Recognized** FCI.
• **SIZE** Height at withers: dogs 56–58.5cm (22–23in), bitches 53.5–56cm (21–22in). Weight: 25–27.9kg (55–62lb).
• **COAT** Sparse and fine, particularly in summer, giving appearance of porcelain.
• **COLOUR** White with round, orange spots, particularly on ears.
• **OTHER FEATURES** Head rather long and finely sculpted; dark, slightly hooded eyes with sweet expression; fine, well-folded ears; deep, medium-width chest; well-attached tail.

ARTOIS HOUND

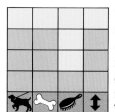

The Artois Hound or Chien d'Artois is more commonly known in its native France as the Briquet, which appears to mean "small braque". The original Briquet hounds were large and ponderous, and were replaced in the hunting field by the shorter-legged Basset Artésien Normand. The Artois of today results from the crossing of a hound with a braque and it differs from the Basset Artésien Normand only in the matter of its flatter ears and narrower head.

Character and care
With its sweet and melancholy expression, the intelligent and courageous Artois Hound is now mainly used for hunting hare. It is usually kept only in packs, kennelled out of doors and looked after by the hunt staff.

KEY CHARACTERISTICS
• **CLASS** Hound. **Recognized** FCI.
• **SIZE** Height at shoulders: 53–59cm (20¾–23¼in). Weight: 18.1–23.8kg (40–53lb).
• **COAT** Short and smooth.
• **COLOUR** Tricolour – white, black and deep fawn – mantle pattern or light patches; head generally fawn or charcoal grey.
• **OTHER FEATURES** Small, short head; medium-length ears that turn inwards; wide chest; sturdy body.

HAMILTONSTÖVARE

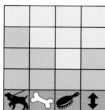

The Hamiltonstövare or Hamilton Hound is named after Count Adolf Patrick Hamilton, founder of the Swedish Kennel Club, who standardized the breed about a century ago. This medium-sized hound, used to flush game in the forests of Sweden, resulted from cross-breedings between the English Foxhound, the Holstein Hound, the Hanoverian Haidbracke, Hanover and Kurland Beagles (now extinct). The Hamiltonstövare is currently the most popular hunting hound in its native land and has achieved international publicity over the past 20 years, becoming a popular contender in the show ring.

Character and care

This smart, affectionate and intelligent dog makes a good companion which may be kept in the home, provided that it receives plenty of exercise. It is easily trained and needs daily grooming using a hound glove.

KEY CHARACTERISTICS
• **CLASS** Hound. **Recognized** ANKC, FCI, KC(GB), KUSA.
• **SIZE** Height: dogs 50–60cm (19½–23½in), bitches 46–57cm (18–22½in). Weight: 22.7–27.2kg (50–60lb).
• **COAT** Strongly weather-resistant upper coat lying close to body; short, close, soft undercoat.
• **COLOUR** Black, brown and white – upper side of neck, back, sides of trunk and upper side of tail, black; head, legs, side of neck, trunk and tail, brown; blaze on upper muzzle, underside of neck, breast, tip of tail and feet, white; mixing of black and brown undesirable, as is predominance of any one of the three colours.
• **OTHER FEATURES** Fine long head, flat; expressive, clear amber eyes; large, thin, stiff ears; level back; long, thin, low-set tail.

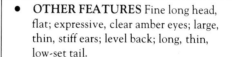

The Hamilton was developed by the founder of the Swedish Kennel Club, a hound connoisseur, using English and German stock.

SWISS, BERNESE AND LUCERNESE HOUNDS

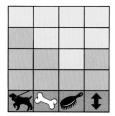

The scenthounds or *laufhunde* of Switzerland include the Swiss Hound (Schweizer Laufhund), the Bernese Hound (Berner Laufhund) and the Lucernese Hound (Luzerner Laufhund). The similar and closely related Jura Hounds (Bruno de Jura and Saint Hubert Jura) are described on page 165. There are also short-legged versions of all these hounds, produced by crossing the Dachshund with some of the full-size versions, to produce specialized hunters for certain types of terrain. They are used to hunt deer and fox.

The ancestors of the *laufhunde* trace back to pre-Christian times when hunting dogs of similar type were brought to southern Europe by the Greeks and Phoenicians, and spread to Switzerland when it was under Roman rule. By the Middle Ages, they had developed into dogs very similar to the *laufhund* of today as shown by 12th-century illustrations that adorn the cathedral in Zurich. The modern Swiss, Bernese and Lucernese Hounds are very similar in abilities, character and in appearance, except for colour of coat. They have keen noses, great powers of endurance and will work over any terrain. They make excellent tracking dogs and are used to hunt a variety of game, including hare, fox and deer.

Character and care

The *laufhunde* are calm companions but have strong hunting instincts and are powerfully built, and so are not suitable as household pets. They need a lot of exercise, and should be groomed with a hound glove, and a slicker for the rough-coated varieties.

KEY CHARACTERISTICS
• **CLASS** Hound. **Recognized** FCI.
• **SIZE** Minimum height: 44.5cm (17½in), generally 45.4–56cm (18–22in). *Short-legged varieties* 30–37.5cm (12–15in).
• **COAT** *Swiss* Rough and wiry, with a thick undercoat. *Bernese* As for the Swiss. *Lucernese* Short and very dense.
• **COLOUR** *Swiss* White with orange markings. *Bernese* Tricolour – white, black, strong tan markings. *Lucernese* White with grey or blue speckling and broad dark or black markings.
• **OTHER FEATURES** Clean, refined head; long muzzle; mouth with scissor bite; eyes as dark as possible; very long ears; long, sloping shoulders; good-length back, tail not too long, carried horizontally. *Short-legged varieties* Medium-sized head; mouth with scissor-bite; fairly large eyes with tight lids; ears long enough to reach tip of nose; body of good hound type, proportionately built; medium-length tail, set neither too low nor too high.

Living near the French border, the Swiss Hounds are closely related to Orange and White French Hounds.

JURA HOUNDS

The Jura Hounds, named after the mountain range, are closer to the older pure Celtic hounds; they have no white in their coat.

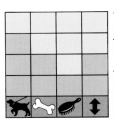

There are two varieties of Jura Hound, the Bruno (Bruno de Jura, Bruno Jura Laufhund) and the Saint Hubert (Saint Hubert Jura Laufhund). Both are native to the Jura mountains area in western Switzerland and have a similar origin to the other Swiss hounds (see page 164), which they resemble. However, they are closer in appearance than the other Swiss hounds to the Saint Hubert Bloodhound, particularly the Saint Hubert Jura which has a heavier head, larger ears and more pronounced folds of skin on the chin and neck than the Bruno. There are also short-legged versions of the Jura Hounds.

Strong, enthusiastic hunters, the Jura Hounds are used mainly against hare. They have a good nose, a strong, clear voice, and can cope with any type of terrain.

Character and care

Like the other Swiss Hounds, the Bruno and Saint Hubert varieties of Jura Hounds are gentle, affectionate dogs which make excellent hunting companions, but have strong hunting instincts and are not really suited to life as a household pet. They need plenty of exercise and grooming with a hound glove.

KEY CHARACTERISTICS
• **CLASS** Hound. **Recognized** FCI.
• **SIZE** Minimum height: 44.5cm (17½in), generally 45.5–56cm (18–22in).
• **COAT** Short.
• **COLOUR** Yellowish or reddish brown, with or without large black saddle; black with tan markings over eyes, on cheeks and on underparts of body; may have white mark on chest.
• **OTHER FEATURES** Heavy, domed head; eyelids not close fitting; large, very long ears, set on low and well back; moderate-length tail.

BASSET HOUND

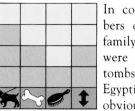

In common with members of the Greyhound family, Basset-type dogs were depicted on the tombs of the ancient Egyptians and so have obviously existed for a long time. However, the Basset Hound is fairly recent, having been developed in Britain from the late 1800s. It was bred from the French Basset Artésien Normand crossed with the Bloodhound to produce a slow but sure dog, which was used in tracking rabbits and hare. The Basset Artésien Normand first reached Britain in 1866 when the Comte de Tournow sent a pair, later named Basset and Belle, to Lord Galway. In 1872 a litter produced by them was acquired by Lord Onslow, who increased his pack with further imports from France. It is from this stock that the best British Basset Hounds are descended.

Character and care

The Basset Hound is now mainly kept as a companion, pet and show dog. It is a lovable animal, which gets on well with children, but needs lots of exercise. Sweet-voiced and a superb tracker, it also has a propensity to wander, and fencing is essential if you own a Basset. The breed requires daily grooming with a hound glove and, in the writer's opinion, is unsuited to a hot climate. One of the saddest sights I have ever seen was a Basset Hound in such an environment.

With its Bloodhound expression and short legs, the Basset is among the few hound breeds to have become popular household pets.

KEY CHARACTERISTICS
• **CLASS** Hound. **Recognized** AKC, ANKC, CKC, FCI, KC(GB), KUSA.
• **SIZE** Height at withers: 33–35cm (13–14in). Weight: 18.1–27.2kg (40–60lb).
• **COAT** Hard, smooth, short and dense.
• **COLOUR** Generally black, white and tan (tricolour) or lemon and white (bicolour), but any recognized hound colour acceptable.
• **OTHER FEATURES** Head domed, with some stop and occipital bone prominent; lozenge-shaped eyes; ears set low; body long, and deep throughout length; tail (stern) well set on.

The Basset was bred to work close to the ground, hunting in thick cover.

BEAGLE

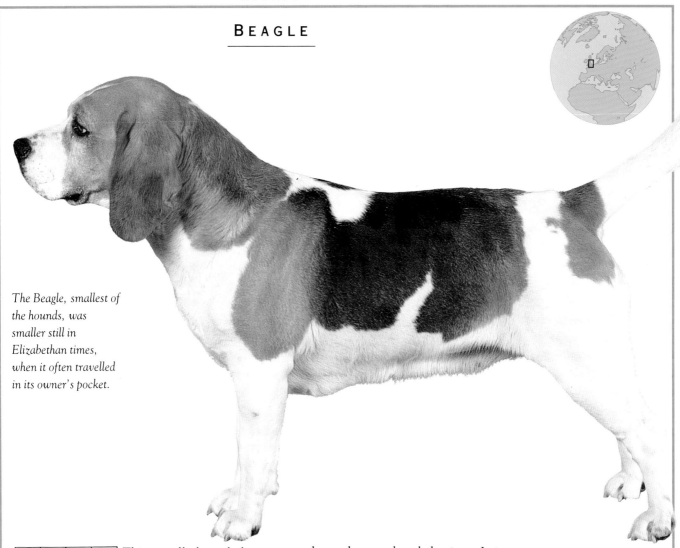

The Beagle, smallest of the hounds, was smaller still in Elizabethan times, when it often travelled in its owner's pocket.

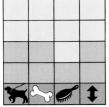

This small hound has existed in Britain at least since the reign of King Henry VIII (1509–47). His daughter Elizabeth I of England (1533–1603) kept numerous Beagles, some of which were so small they could be put in one's pocket and so became known as Pocket Beagles (now extinct).

The breed is often known as the "singing Beagle" but is not noisy indoors, reserving its voice for the chase. In Britain it is adept at hunting hare and wild rabbit, and it has been used against wild pig and deer in Scandinavia, and the cottontail rabbit in the United States. In the latter country and in Canada it works as a gundog both seeking out and retrieving. It is also a favourite companion and was the most popular dog in the United States in 1954.

Character and care

This affectionate, determined and healthy dog is usually long-lived and good with children. It makes a fine show dog, and is a good choice of family pet for those who do not demand exemplary behaviour. It is not renowned for obedience and, in common with other hounds, will take advantage of an open gate, possibly ending up some distance away. Its short, weatherproof coat requires little or no attention, and the Beagle needs only average exercise when kept as a pet.

KEY CHARACTERISTICS
● **CLASS** Hound. **Recognized** AKC, ANKC, CKC, FCI, KC(GB), KUSA.
● **SIZE** Height: USA two varieties: under 33cm (13in), and 33–37.5cm (13–15in); UK at withers: 33–40cm (13–16in).
● **COAT** Short, dense and weatherproof.
● **COLOUR** Any recognized hound colour other than liver; tip of stern, white.
● **OTHER FEATURES** Head fairly long and powerful without being coarse; dark brown or hazel eyes; long ears with pointed tips; top-line straight and level; moderately long, sturdy tail.

With its lively intelligence and easy going nature, the Beagle is as happy in the family home as in the hunt.

ARIÉGEOIS

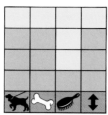

The Ariégeois originated in the Ariège, a French province on the Spanish border. It is the result of a crossing between the native medium-sized hounds, the Gascon Saintongeois and the Gascony Blue. While not a very fast hound, it does have considerable stamina and a keen nose, and this intelligent, eager worker has hunted hare throughout this century. A breed standard was drawn up by the Gaston Phoebus Club, which was formed in 1908 with the aim of encouraging the selective breeding of both the Ariégeois and the French Setter (Braque).

A superb scenthound, the Ariégeois combines the fine head and long ears of the Gascon-Saintongeois and the endurance of the Blue Gascony.

Character and care

The Ariégeois is a finely built hound with a calm disposition and friendly expression, and is altogether a most pleasant animal. Like all hounds, it requires a lot of exercise. Its short coat requires little attention.

KEY CHARACTERISTICS
• **CLASS** Hound. **Recognized** FCI.
• **SIZE** Height at shoulders: dogs 56–61cm (22–24in), bitches 53.5–58.5cm (21–23in). Weight: about 29.7kg (66lb).
• **COAT** Fine and close.
• **COLOUR** Usually white with black markings and small tan spots over eyes; black puppies occasionally occur; rich tan should not be encouraged.
• **OTHER FEATURES** Long, light, narrow head with no wrinkle or dew lap; dark eyes well open and with a sweet expression; fine supple ears; back generally level and well supported; tail well attached and carried "sabre" fashion.

HARRIER

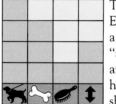

The name of this ancient English breed comes from a Norman word meaning "all-round hunting dog" and its ancestors may have arrived on British shores with the invading Norman armies of William the Conqueror in 1066. The first Harrier pack, established in England in 1260, was descended from the old Talbot and Saint Hubert Hounds, possibly crossed with a basset-type hound.

The Harrier is a very fast hound with considerable powers of endurance, a short, smooth coat, drop ears and a lengthy tail. Packs were mainly used to hunt hare and the Master of the Pack would selectively breed those dogs best suited to the local terrain. The Harrier is usually kept in packs. It is now rare, even in the UK, and is not recognized by the British Kennel Club.

Character and care

The Harrier is usually gentle and good natured. It should be groomed occasionally.

KEY CHARACTERISTICS
• **CLASS** Hound. **Recognized** AKC, ANKC, CKC, FCI.
• **SIZE** Height: 47.5–52.5cm (19–21in). Weight: 21.6–27.2kg (48–60lb).
• **COAT** Short and hard.
• **COLOUR** Usually black, tan and white, but all hound colours acceptable.
• **OTHER FEATURES** Head fairly long and shallow in the muzzle and stop; small, oval eyes; V-shaped, pendant ears; deep body; medium length tail carried somewhat high.

GREAT GASCONY BLUE

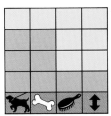

The Great Gascony Blue (Grand Bleu de Gascogne) is famed for its ability to pick up a "cold" scent. It descends from the scenting dogs of pre-Roman times and the ancient Saint Hubert Hound. Developed by the Count of Foix, Gaston Phoebus, in the 14th century, it became a favourite of the French King Henry IV (1553–1610) who kept a pack. Even though this aristocratic animal is taller and lighter than many other it is very strong and is possessed of great stamina and a strong melodious voice. It excelled at hunting wolves, which it pursued to extinction.

French explorers probably brought the Great Gascony Blue to North America in the 17th century, and, in 1785, General Lafayette gave a small pack to George Washington, who also bred them. They were crossed with other American hounds to produce a breed with improved tracking ability and stamina.

Character and care

The Great Gascony Blue has a calm and friendly temperament. However, it requires a great deal of exercise and is not a suitable housepet. It should be groomed regularly and the long ears checked frequently.

KEY CHARACTERISTICS
• **CLASS** Hound. **Recognized** AKC, FCI, KC(GB).
• **SIZE** Height: dogs 63.5–70cm (25–28in), bitches 60–65cm (23½–25½in). Weight: 34.2–36kg (71–77lb).
• **COAT** Short, smooth, weather resistant and somewhat coarse.
• **COLOUR** White with black patches and extensive black ticking to give appearance of blue dog; tan markings on head.
• **OTHER FEATURES** Large, elongated head; ears set low, elongated and folded; chest deep and slightly rounded; legs long and muscular; tail well set on, slight upward curl.

The large head and melancholy expression of the Great Gascony Blue give it a distinguished appearance.

The Great Gascony Blue is a classic French scenting dog, long legged and with a square body, capable of hunting over great distances.

TAWNY BRITTANY BASSET

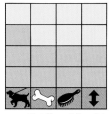

The Tawny Brittany Basset or, as it is more commonly known, the Basset Fauve de Bretagne, originated in Brittany, north-west France. It was developed from the Basset Griffon Vendéen and other short-legged bassets to track over moorland and other rough terrain, where it is fast and active. A pack of these first-rate fox hunters was maintained by Francis I of France (1515–47), but by the mid 1800s the type had become all

The Basset's wheaten colour and rough coat come directly from its taller ancestor, the Tawny Brittany Griffon.

Swift for its size, the Brittany Basset was developed to track over rough country, after small game.

but extinct, possibly due to their somewhat headstrong temperament despite undoubted courage. Resembling a large, rough-haired dachshund in appearance, this hound has large, pendulous ears, a rough close coat and is described as being "dumpy overall".

It has been granted an interim breed standard by the British Kennel Club in the past seven years and is gradually gaining impetus in the British show ring.

Character and care

This short-legged, wire-coated hound has courage and a good nose. It requires a generous amount of exercise but its rough coat needs little attention.

KEY CHARACTERISTICS
• **CLASS** Hound. **Recognized** AKC, FCI, KC(GB), KUSA.
• **SIZE** Height: 33–43cm (13–17in).
• **COAT** Harsh and close.
• **COLOUR** Golden, wheaten or fawn; white spot on neck or chest permissible.
• **OTHER FEATURES** Moderate-length skull; dark, alert eyes; thin ears set on at eye level; chest quite wide and well let down; tail thick at root and tapering towards the tip.

DACHSBRACKES

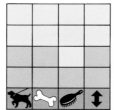

There are three varieties with this name – the Dachsbracke, Westphalian Dachsbracke and the Erz Mountains Dachsbracke. The Dachsbracke is native to the Austrian Alps, the Westphalian to western Germany, and the Erz Mountains variety originated in the Erz mountains of Bohemia. All are short-legged versions of longer-legged local hounds or brackes that were crossed to Dachshunds. Heavier and longer in the leg than the Dachshunds, the Dachsbrackes are used to hunt hare, fox and other game in the mountains, tracking and locating their quarry by scent. The Dachsbracke and Erz Mountain variety are similar in size but differ in colour, while the Westphalian Dachsbracke is smaller.

Character and care

The Dachsbrackes are all splendid small hounds of considerable endurance and hunting ability. They are good natured and make fine family pets despite their propensity to dig the garden and their somewhat loud bark. They need plenty of exercise and should be groomed with a hound glove.

KEY CHARACTERISTICS
• **CLASS** Hound. **Recognized** ANKC, CKC, FCI, KC(GB), KUSA.
• **SIZE** Height at shoulders: *Dachsbracke* and *Erz Mountains Dachsbracke* 33–43cm (13–17in). *Westphalian Dachsbracke* 30.5–35.5cm (12–14in).
• **COAT** Short and dense with little undercoat.
• **COLOUR** *Dachsbracke* Black with tan markings; shades of tan or white with tan markings. *Westphalian Dachsbracke* Reddish fawn with white markings or tricolour. *Erz Mountains Dachsbracke* Red or black and tan.
• **OTHER FEATURES** Long narrow head; dark, medium-sized, almond-shaped eyes; broad, medium-length ears with rounded tips; back fairly long; tail set on relatively high and carried horizontally.

DACHSHUND

The oldest of the Dachshund varieties, the Smooth-haired is a favourite in Britain and the United States.

There are six varieties of the Dachshund (Teckel or Badger Hound): Smooth-haired, Long-haired and Wire-haired, each occurring as both Standard and Miniature.

The Dachshund derives from the oldest breeds of German hunting dogs, such as the Bibarhund, and is known to have existed as long ago as the 16th century. It was bred to go to ground, as most owners who garden know to their cost! It has been said that the English inability to translate the Dachshund's name caused the dog to be placed in the hound group rather than with the terriers, and it has remained there ever since.

The British Queen Victoria was the first person to own a Dachshund in England, in 1839. The following year, when she married the German Prince Albert, he brought over more Dachshunds to Britain and the breed gained in popularity there. Dachshunds were exhibited in Britain in 1866 and given breed status in 1873. The English Dachshund Club was formed in 1881, the first club of its kind in the world. The Dachshund Club of America was formed in 1895.

Originally there was only one variety, the Smooth-haired Dachshund, whose wrinkled paws are a characteristic now rarely seen. The Wire-haired was produced through the introduction of Dandie Dinmont and other terrier blood, while the Long-haired was formed by introducing the German Stöber, a gun-dog, to a Smooth-haired Dachshund and Spaniel cross.

KEY CHARACTERISTICS

- **CLASS** Hound.
  Recognized AKC, ANKC, CKC, FCI, KC(GB), KUSA.

- **SIZE** Weight: *Standard* USA 7.2–14.4kg (16–32lb); UK 9–12kg (20–26lb). *Miniature* USA under 5kg (11lb); UK about 4.5kg (10lb).

- **COAT** *Smooth-haired* Dense, short and smooth. *Long-haired* Soft and straight, and only slightly wavy. *Wire-haired* Short, straight and harsh, with a long undercoat.

- **COLOUR** All colours but white permissible; small patch on chest permitted but not desirable; dappled dogs may include white but should be evenly marked all over.

- **OTHER FEATURES** Long head, conical in appearance when seen from above; medium-sized eyes; ears set high; body long and full muscled; tail continues along line of spine but is slightly curved.

The Wire-haired Dachshund results from cross-mating with various terrier breeds.

Cross-breeding between the Smooth-haired and gundog types yielded the Long-haired Dachshund.

Character and care

Sporty and devoted, the Dachshund makes an excellent family pet and a good watchdog, with a surprisingly loud bark for its size. It can walk fairly long distances provided that these are worked up to from an early age. The Short-haired is easy to groom, requiring only daily attention with a hound glove and soft cloth. The Wire-haired and Long-haired should be brushed with a stiff bristled brush and also combed.

Warning The Dachshund is prone to disc trouble so care must be taken to prevent it jumping on, or from, heights.

179

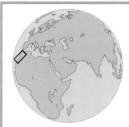

SLOUGHI

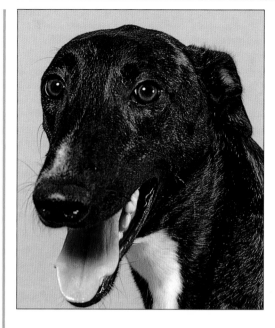

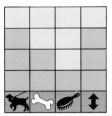

The Sloughi, Slughi or Eastern Greyhound, is one of the rarest sight-hounds in the West. It is known by the Arabs in its native lands as El Hor and is the only dog they recognize apart from the Saluki. Like the Saluki, which it resembles, the Sloughi has keen eyesight, is capable of immense speed and is a hunter of gazelle. Its success at this task is said to be helped by its sandy colour which makes it difficult for gazelle to detect the dog against the desert sands until danger is upon them.

Character and care

The Sloughi is a gentle, healthy, intelligent dog, which makes a first-class pet provided that it has plenty of space in which to exercise and is not allowed to roam near livestock. It requires only a daily grooming with a soft brush and a hound glove.

The Greyhound has been prized for thousands of years as a dog of war, a keen sight- and scent-hound, a racing dog and companion.

KEY CHARACTERISTICS
• **CLASS** Hound. **Recognized** ANKC, FCI, KC(GB), KUSA.
• **SIZE** Height: 60–70cm (23½–27½in). Weight: 20.2–27.2kg (45–60lb).
• **COAT** Tough and fine.
• **COLOUR** Sable or fawn in all shades with or without black mask; white, brindle or black with tan points; brindle pattern or fawn pattern on head, feet and sometimes breast. Dark with a white patch on chest, undesirable; parti-colours not permissible; solid black or white undesirable.
• **OTHER FEATURES** Head fairly strong without being heavy; large, dark eyes, set well into orbit; triangular ears, not too large, with rounded tips; chest not too broad; tail fine and well set on.

GREYHOUND

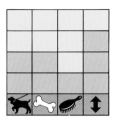

The Greyhound is arguably the purest breed on Earth, appearing to have changed little from dogs depicted on the tombs of Egyptian pharaohs. It also has the distinction of a mention in the Holy Bible in the Book of Solomon. It is likely that the Greyhound found its way to Afghanistan, where its coat thickened to contend with the colder climate, and was then brought by Celts to Britain. The breed became a favourite with the nobility there, and in 11th- and 14th-century England, only persons of royal or noble blood were permitted to own one.

Possessing keen eyesight and capable of great speed, this sighthound was highly valued as a courser and, more recently, as a competitor on the racing track. Greyhounds are still widely used as racing dogs, and now appear with regularity in the show ring.

Character and care

The Greyhound does have a propensity to chase anything that moves, but is also a gentle, faithful animal, which is good with children. Even the ex-racer, once retrained, makes a fine and often long-lived companion. It needs a daily brush and average but regular exercise on hard ground, and takes up relatively little space, having a liking for its own special corner.

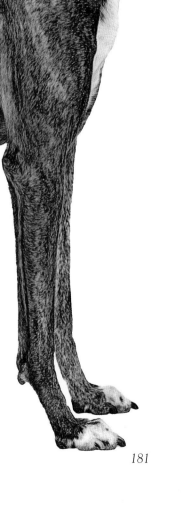

Reputedly the fastest dog on earth, the Greyhound has fanciers dating back to the Egyptian Fourth Dynasty.

KEY CHARACTERISTICS
• **CLASS** Hound. **Recognized** AKC, ANKC, CKC, FCI, KC(GB), KUSA.
• **SIZE** Height: dogs 71–76cm (28–30in), bitches 68–71cm (27–28in). Weight: dogs 29.5–31.7kg (65–70lb), bitches 27.2–29.5kg (60–65lb).
• **COAT** Fine and close.
• **COLOUR** Black, white, red, blue, fawn, fallow brindle, or any of these colours broken with white.
• **OTHER FEATURES** Long, moderately broad head; bright, intelligent eyes; small, close-shaped ears; long, elegant neck; deep, capacious chest; long tail set on rather low.

ENGLISH FOXHOUND

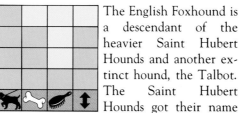

The English Foxhound is a descendant of the heavier Saint Hubert Hounds and another extinct hound, the Talbot. The Saint Hubert Hounds got their name from the Bishop of Liège, later Saint Hubert, the patron saint of hunters, and were brought to England by the invading Normans in the 11th century.

The Foxhound's prime function is to hunt foxes alongside mounted huntsmen. It can work for several hours without a break in various types of terrain.

Character and care

In Britain, the strong, lively and noisy English Foxhounds are never kept as pets but are the property of individual hunting packs. They cannot be bought in Britain by individuals and, unlike the American Foxhound, are not exhibited other than at special hound shows. It is, however, sometimes possible for hunt supporters to walk a Foxhound pup, and accustom it to various road hazards, before returning it to its pack.

KEY CHARACTERISTICS
• **CLASS** Hound. **Recognized** AKC, ANKC, CKC, FCI, KC(GB).
• **SIZE** Height: dogs 55–62.5cm (22–25in), bitches 50.5–60cm (21–24in). Weight: 29.5–31.7kg (65–70lb).
• **COAT** Short and hard.
• **COLOUR** Tricolour – black, white and tan – or bicolour with a white background.
• **OTHER FEATURES** Head not heavy, and with pronounced brow; ears set on low and hanging close to head; muscular, level back; straight legs; tail (stern) well set on and carried gaily.

The English Foxhound has a deep girth and long back which allow it to run well over varied terrains.

AMERICAN FOXHOUND

Since its arrival in the New World, the American Foxhound has produced many strains to work in diverse conditions. The AKC Foxhound resembles its English progenitor, but with a lighter body and longer legs.

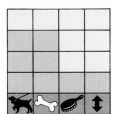

The American Foxhound is a descendant of English Foxhounds taken to Maryland, United States, by Robert Brooke in 1650. These were later crossed with other British and French hounds to obtain dogs well suited to hunting the red fox. George Washington is also known to have imported Foxhounds from England in around 1770 and to have received a gift of some French hounds in 1785. A pack from Ireland was introduced in 1830. The Gloucester Fox-hunting Club (founded in 1808) and the Baltimore Club obtained the best type of English Foxhounds and used them as foundation stock. While the English Foxhound is never kept within a family or exhibited except in special hound shows, the rangier American Foxhound is a popular show dog as well as a highly valued hunting dog.

Character and care
The American Foxhound is good natured, but can become less attentive and more wilful as it grows older. It needs a large amount of exercise. It is not groomed in the manner of a pet dog, and needs only an occasional sponge over before a hound show.

KEY CHARACTERISTICS
• **CLASS** Hound. **Recognized** AKC, CKC, FCI, KC(GB).
• **SIZE** Height: dogs 55–62.5cm (22–25in), bitches 52.5–60cm (21–24in).
• **COAT** Hard and close.
• **COLOUR** All colours acceptable.
• **OTHER FEATURES** Large skull; large, broad, pendant, wide-set ears, flat to head; streamlined body; sabre-shaped tail.

The square-cut muzzle and soft eyes are characteristic of the American Foxhound.

WHIPPET

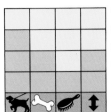

The Whippet looks like a Greyhound in miniature, and the Greyhound undoubtedly played a part in its make-up. It is uncertain whether the Pharaoh Hound, as seems likely, or some other imported hound or terrier, was the other half of the cross. The Whippet was bred expressly as a racing dog, and is the fastest breed in the world. It has been timed at 8.4 seconds over a standard 137m (150yd) straight course (58.76km/h, 36.52mph). Known as the "poor man's racehorse", it became the sporting pet of miners in the north of England, where Whippet racing is still very popular. It has spread to other countries as well. Originally, the dogs raced after live rabbits but now artificial lures are used instead.

The Whippet was recognized by the Kennel Club in Britain in 1902, having been exhibited in 1897 at Crufts Dog Show in London. It is also popular in the United States, where a slightly larger dog is preferred.

Character and care

The Whippet is a gentle dog, which is good with children and makes a fine pet and show dog, and a splendid watchdog. While it can adapt to domestic life, this powerful runner needs plenty of exercise. Its short coat requires little other than a brush and rub-down, but it does mean that the dog is better housed indoors year round rather than kennelled outside.

KEY CHARACTERISTICS
• **CLASS** Hound. **Recognized** AKC, ANKC, CKC, FCI, KC(GB), KUSA.
• **SIZE** Height: dogs 47–51cm (18½–20in), bitches 44–47cm (17½–18½in). Weight: about 12.5kg (28lb).
• **COAT** Short, fine and close.
• **COLOUR** Any colour or mixture of colours.
• **OTHER FEATURES** Long, lean head; bright, oval-shaped eyes with a very alert expression; rose-shaped ears; very deep chest with plenty of heart-room; long, tapering tail with no feathering.

Developed in Britain as the poor man's racehorse, the Whippet was taken to America by emigrant Lancashire textile workers.

HUNGARIAN GREYHOUND

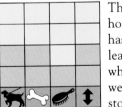

The Hungarian Greyhound or Magyar Agăr has a history traceable at least to the 9th century, when likenesses of it were depicted on tombstones in its native Hungary. Its ancestors were Asiatic sighthounds that arrived in Hungary with the Magyars, probably crossed with local hounds.

A dog of great speed and beauty, the Agăr is used to course hare and to catch and kill both fox and hare in its native land. In the 19th century crosses were made to the English Greyhound to produce faster dogs, and by the Second World War it is estimated that this blood was present in all but a handful of Agărs. Since then, breeders in Hungary have been working to revive the original type.

Character and care

Like most Greyhounds, the Hungarian is gentle and affectionate by nature and makes a calm, devoted housepet, once it has been re-trained and provided that it is kept away from livestock. It requires little grooming and needs regular rather than extensive exercise.

Note: This dog has a fine coat, feels the cold and must be provided with a coat when it is taken out of doors in winter.

KEY CHARACTERISTICS

- **CLASS** Hound.
  Recognized FCI.

- **SIZE** Weight: dogs 27–32kg (60–70lb), bitches 22.5–27kg (50–60lb).

- **COAT** Short, smooth and fine.

- **COLOUR** Black, Isabella, grey, brindle, ash, piebald, often white.

- **OTHER FEATURES** Head broad between the ears; brown, medium-sized eyes with a lively expression; ears broad and set well back, the upper third folded forward; broad back; long, thin tail with a hook-like curve at the tip, carried low.

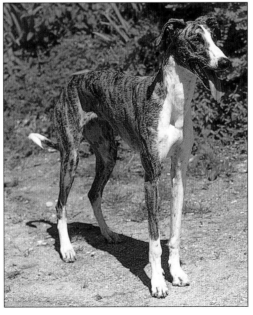

Smaller than its English cousin, the Hungarian Greyhound was used for hunting and coursing on the Central European steppe.

DEERHOUND

At one time, when deer were still hunted by hound packs, it was illegal for anyone below the rank of Earl to own a Deerhound.

Immortalized in the paintings of Landseer, the Deerhound is almost as evocative of the Highlands as the red deer it used to hunt.

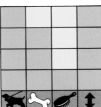

The Scottish Deerhound is the emblem of the Kennel Club in Scotland. It also features largely in the writings of the novelist, Sir Walter Scott (1771–1832), who referred to his bitch, Maida, as "the most perfect creature of heaven", and was a favourite subject of the British painter, Edwin Landseer (1802–73).

One of the most ancient of British breeds, the Deerhound may have arrived in Scotland with Phoenician traders about 3000 years ago, and thereafter developed its thick weather-resistant coat to combat the colder climate. Very similar hounds were certainly in existence there in the early centuries AD. The breed became a favourite of chieftains in the Scottish Highlands, hunting with them by day and gracing their baronial halls by night. Then, with the advent of breech-loading rifles, the dog's use as a hunter came to an end. The Deerhound does, however, still have a staunch band of devotees.

Character and care
Today, the Deerhound is used for coursing, draws good entries at dog shows, and makes a faithful and devoted pet for the energetic. Although gentle in the home, the breed needs careful training around livestock, for it can kill when its hunting instincts are roused. With its shaggy coat it is no hardship for this breed to be kennelled out of doors – in fact, it does not like intense heat. It needs lots of exercise but the minimum of grooming – just the removal of stray hairs for showing.

KEY CHARACTERISTICS
• **CLASS** Hound. **Recognized** AKC, ANKC, CKC, FCI, KC(GB), KUSA.
• **SIZE** Height: dogs 76–80cm (30–32in), bitches at least 71cm (28in). Weight: dogs 38–48.6kg (85–110lb), bitches 33.7–42.7kg (75–95lb).
• **COAT** Shaggy but not overcoated.
• **COLOUR** Dark blue grey and lighter greys; brindles and yellows; sandy red or red fawn with black points.
• **OTHER FEATURES** Head broadest at ears, tapering slightly towards eyes; dark eyes; ears set on high, folded back in repose; body and general formation that of a Greyhound, with larger size and bone; long tail, thick at root.

IRISH WOLFHOUND

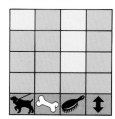

The Irish Wolfhound is the tallest dog in the world, and the national dog of Ireland. Bred to kill wolves, it is thought to be descended from dogs brought by the Celts as they spread across Europe from Greece, which they invaded in about 279BC, to Ireland. The Irish Wolfhound became highly prized and many were exported to Europe, including a brace presented to the king of Spain in the 16th century. In 1652 Oliver Cromwell (1599–1658) forbade their future export on the grounds that they were far too valuable in keeping down wolves.

By 1800, the last wolf in Britain and Ireland had been killed, and the Wolfhound was redundant and in danger of extinction. Then, in 1885, Captain George Graham, a Scot serving in the British army, commenced a 23-year breeding programme which restored the breed to its former glory.

Character and care

The Irish Wolfhound is a breed that many people would choose to own if only their lifestyle and house size enabled them to. However, the Wolfhound does not require more exercise than average-sized breeds and, although it can be kennelled out of doors, it has a calm temperament, and many of these giants have a place by the fireside. The breed is popular in the show ring and, since it is exhibited in what is deemed a "natural state", brushing and the removal of straggly hairs are all the preparation that is required.

KEY CHARACTERISTICS
• **CLASS** Hound. **Recognized** AKC, ANKC, CKC, FCI, KC(GB), KUSA.
• **SIZE** Minimum height: dogs 80cm (32in), bitches 75cm (30in); 80–85cm (32–34in) to be aimed for. Minimum weight: dogs 54.5kg (120lb), bitches 48kg (105lb).
• **COAT** Rough and harsh.
• **COLOUR** Grey, steel grey, brindle, red, black, pure white, fawn or wheaten.
• **OTHER FEATURES** Long head carried high; dark eyes; small, rose-shaped ears; very deep chest; long, slightly curved tail.

More than two centuries after the last wolf disappeared from Britain and Ireland, the Irish Wolfhound remains a coveted breed. It is the tallest dog in the world.

SALUKI

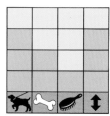

The Saluki, graceful hound of the desert.

The Saluki, like the Sloughi, is an ancient breed whose likeness appears on the tombs of Egyptian pharaohs. It takes its name from the ancient city of Saluk in the Yemen, or possibly from the town of Seleukia in the ancient Hellenic empire in Syria. It is also known as the Gazelle Hound, the Arab Gazelle Hound, the Eastern Greyhound and the Persian Greyhound.

The Saluki is esteemed by the Arabs, including the nomadic Bedouin, who prize it for its ability to keep pace with fleet-footed Arab horses and, paired with a falcon, to hunt gazelle. Elsewhere in the world it is kept as a companion and show dog.

In 1895, an Englishwoman, Lady Florence Amherst, was given two Saluki puppies, and was so impressed by the breed that she imported others and did her best to popularize it. Despite this the Saluki was not recognized by the Kennel Club in Britain until 1923. The breed was recognized in the US in 1927.

Character and care

This elegant, if somewhat aloof, breed is loyal, affectionate and trustworthy, and is now sought after both as a pet and show dog. It requires plenty of exercise, and care should be taken in the countryside that its hunting instincts are kept under control. The Saluki's coat should be groomed daily, using a soft brush and a hound glove.

KEY CHARACTERISTICS
• **CLASS** Hound.   **Recognized** AKC, ANKC, CKC, FCI, KC(GB), KUSA.
• **SIZE** Height: dogs 58.4–71cm (23–28in), bitches smaller.
• **COAT** Smooth, silky in texture.
• **COLOUR** White, cream, fawn, golden red, grizzle, silver grizzle, deer grizzle, tricolour (white, black and tan) and variations of these colours.
• **OTHER FEATURES** Long, narrow head; eyes dark to hazel; long, mobile ears, not set too low; fairly broad back; strong hip bones set wide apart; tail set on low from long, gently sloping pelvis.

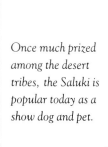

Once much prized among the desert tribes, the Saluki is popular today as a show dog and pet.

BORZOI

Another of the world's great hounds is the Borzoi, bred to run down wolves for Russian noblemen.

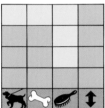

The noble Borzoi or Russian Wolfhound was used in Russia from the 17th century for wolf hunting and coursing, a sport of the tsars and noblemen of imperial Russia. The Borzoi tracked the wolf, when it was beaten from cover, but did not kill it. The dog's task was to grab the wolf by the neck and throw it, whereupon it would be finished off with a blow from a dagger.

Originally there were various strains of Borzoi, including the Sudanese Borzoi, the Turkoman Borzoi and the Borzoi Tartar. However, it was a strain developed in Russia which formed the basis of the present breed standard, the others having become extinct. The Borzoi reached Britain in the mid-1800s and went from there to America in 1889. Then in 1903, Mr Joseph B Thomas started importing the Borzoi into the United States direct from Russia, his source being the Grand Duke Nicholas Romanoff. The Revolution in 1917 brought breeding to a halt.

Until fairly recently, information about the Borzoi in its native land was sketchy. Now, breeders in Russia appear anxious to cooperate in exporting their stock, there is a Borzoi database in Moscow, and information can be obtained from the Russian Cyndromic Association "Dromos" (Borzoi section).

Character and care

The Borzoi has made its mark in Europe and America as an elegant, intelligent and faithful, albeit somewhat aloof, pet and a reasonably popular show dog. It is not ideally suited to being a child's pet as it does not take kindly to teasing. It requires a considerable amount of space and exercise, and care must be taken that it does not, true to its hunting instincts, worry livestock. Its coat needs surprisingly little attention.

KEY CHARACTERISTICS
● **CLASS** Hound. **Recognized** AKC, ANKC, CKC, FCI, KC(GB), KUSA.
● **SIZE** Minimum height at withers: dogs 74cm (29in), bitches 68cm (27in). Weight: dogs 33.7–65kg (75–105lb), bitches about 6.8–9kg (15–20lb) less.
● **COAT** Silky, flat, and wavy or rather curly; never woolly.
● **COLOUR** Any colour acceptable.
● **OTHER FEATURES** Long, lean head, in proportion to overall size; dark eyes with intelligent, alert expression; small ears, pointed and delicate; chest deep and narrow; long tail, rather low set.

The Borzoi has a long, tapering head, slightly convex and with almost no stop.

ELKHOUND

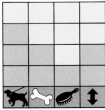

The Grey Norwegian Elkhound has probably existed in its native Scandinavia for millennia. Archaeologists have discovered bones of similar dogs dating back to 5000–4000BC. Its task was to seek an elk and hold it at bay until its master moved in for the kill.

The breed was first exhibited in 1877, when the Norwegian Hunters' Association began holding shows. In 1923, the British Elkhound Club was formed and the breed was officially recognized by the British Kennel Club. The Norwegian Elkhound Association of America was recognized by the American Kennel Club in about 1930. There is also a Miniature Elkhound, although no breed standard is yet available for it. There is also a Black Elkhound, but it is little known outside its native Norway.

The Elkhound – one time hunter, herder and sled dog.

AFGHAN HOUND

The Afghan – a fearless hunter turned elegant status symbol.

As its aloof oriental expression suggests, the Afghan Hound is an ancient breed, said by legend to have been one of the animals taken aboard Noah's Ark at the time of the flood! This member of the Greyhound family, possibly related to the Saluki, has certainly existed for centuries. Its ancestors somehow found their way from their original home Persia (Iran) to Afghanistan, where the breed undoubtedly developed its long, shaggy coat to withstand the harsh climatic conditions. Its speed and stamina meant that, in its native land, it was used to hunt leopards, wolves and jackals. It is only in the West that it has become a status symbol.

The first Afghan Hound breed club was formed in Britain in 1926 and, in that same year, the breed was officially recognized by the American Kennel Club. It has since become one of the most popular show dogs and, in recent years, has also been utilized in the growing sport of Afghan racing.

Character and care

Although somewhat wilful in youth, the Elkhound is generally a good natured household pet, which has no doggie odour and is reliable with children. It requires daily brushing and combing and plenty of exercise.

KEY CHARACTERISTICS
• **CLASS** Hound. **Recognized** AKC, ANKC, CKC, FCI, KC(GB), KUSA.
• **SIZE** Height at shoulders: dogs about 52cm (20½in), bitches about 49cm (19½in). Weight: dogs about 23kg (50lb), bitches about 20kg (43lb).
• **COAT** Close, abundant and weather-resistant; outer coat coarse and straight, undercoat soft and woolly.
• **COLOUR** Various shades of grey with black tips to hairs on outer coat; lighter on chest, stomach, legs, underside of tail, buttocks and in a harness mark.
• **OTHER FEATURES** Wedge-shaped head; slightly oval eyes; ears set high; powerful body; strong tail, set on high.

Character and care

The Afghan is an elegant, beautiful and affectionate dog, which is generally good natured but does not tolerate teasing. It is intelligent, somewhat aloof and requires plenty of exercise. The coat should be groomed with an air-cushioned brush and will soon become matted if it is not given sufficient and regular attention.

KEY CHARACTERISTICS
• **CLASS** Hound. **Recognized** AKC, ANKC, CKC, FCI, KC(GB), KUSA.
• **SIZE** Height: dogs about 68cm (27in), bitches about 63cm (25in). Weight: dogs about 27.2kg (60lb), bitches about 22.7kg (50lb).
• **COAT** Long and fine.
• **COLOUR** All colours acceptable.
• **OTHER FEATURES** Head long and not too narrow; eyes preferably dark, but golden, not debarred; ears set low and well back; moderate-length, level back; tail not too short.

JÄMTHUND

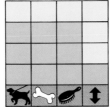

The Jämthund or Swedish Elkhound, named after the area of Jämtland in Sweden, is popular in its native land but is seldom seen elsewhere. It is closely related to the Norwegian Elkhound, which is considerably better known internationally. The Jämthund has existed in northern Scandinavia for many years, having been developed by keen Swedish huntsmen who wanted an improved local variety of Elkhound. It was recognized as a breed distinct from the Norwegian Elkhound in 1946.

This powerful spitz is similar in appearance to the Norwegian Elkhound, but is about 10cm (4in) taller and has light facial markings. Like its Norwegian relative, the Jämthund was bred to hunt large game, including elk, bear and wolf, and is now used against a variety of quarry. Opinions differ on whether it is actually a better elk hunter than the Norwegian.

Character and care

The Jämthund is assertive and intelligent, but is friendly and good with children. It requires plenty of exercise and daily grooming with a bristle brush and comb.

KEY CHARACTERISTICS
• **CLASS** Hound. **Recognized** FCI.
• **SIZE** Height: dogs 58.5–63.5cm (23–25in), bitches 53.5–58.5cm (21–23in).
• **COAT** Harsh and dense, with a short, soft undercoat.
• **COLOUR** Grey with lighter grey or cream markings on muzzle, cheeks, throat and underside of body.
• **OTHER FEATURES** Long, narrow head; small, dark, lively eyes; erect, pointed ears; deep chest; tail tightly rolled on the back.

TERRIERS

BULL TERRIER

Some people consider this breed the picture of ugliness, while others, like myself, have only admiration for the Bull Terrier, which is described somewhat poetically in its standard as "the gladiator of the canine race".

Like the Staffordshire Bull Terrier, the Bull Terrier began life as a fighting dog and was the result of crossing an Old English Bulldog with a terrier. The first Bull Terriers were said to have closely resembled the Staffordshire but then Dalmatian and possibly other blood was introduced. Much work on the breed's refinement was done by James Hinks of Birmingham, England, in the 19th century. He selected for white colour and Bull Terriers were invariably white, until after the Second World War, when coloureds appeared.

Character and care

If you admire the Bull breeds, you will adore the Bull Terrier. Despite its fierce appearance and strength, it makes a faithful and devoted pet. The bitch, in particular, is utterly reliable with children. However, this breed is too strong for other than the able bodied to handle, and needs careful training. Its short, flat coat is easy to look after.

Unique among dog breeds, the Bull Terrier's head shape is set off by naturally erect ears. The eyes are small and triangular.

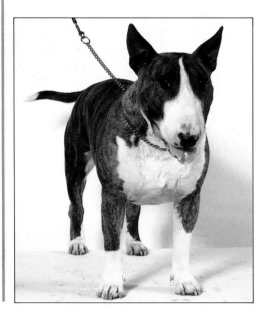

KEY CHARACTERISTICS

- **CLASS** Terrier.
  Recognized AKC, ANKC, CKC, FCI, KC(GB), KUSA.

- **SIZE** Height: 52.5–55cm (21–22in). Weight: 23.5–27.9kg (52–62lb).

- **COAT** Short and flat.

- **COLOUR** For white, pure white coat; for coloureds, brindle preferred; black, red, fawn and tricolour acceptable.

- **OTHER FEATURES** Long, straight head, and deep right to end of muzzle; eyes appear narrow; small, thin ears set close together; short tail, set on low and carried horizontally.

Bred originally to be white, the Bull Terrier is now seen also in colours, with brindle preferred.

MINIATURE BULL TERRIER

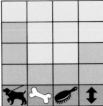

This dog is a smaller replica of the Bull Terrier (see page 188) and shares the same breed standard apart from height. Bull Terriers weighing as little as 4.5kg (10lb) were recorded early in the breed's history, but it was not until 1939 that the Miniature was given a separate breed register by the Kennel Club in Britain. It has never been very popular and few specimens are seen in the show ring.

Character and care

This loving and companionable little dog has the same characteristics as its larger relative, making an excellent pet and being generally good with children. It requires daily brushing and plenty of exercise.

KEY CHARACTERISTICS

- **CLASS** Terrier.
  Recognized AKC, ANKC, CKC, FCI, KC(GB), KUSA.

- **SIZE** Height at shoulders: 25–35.5cm (10–14in). Weight: 4.5–18.1kg (10–40lb).

- **COAT** Short, flat, with a fine gloss.

- **COLOUR** Pure white, black, brindle, red, fawn and tricolour acceptable.

- **OTHER FEATURES** Eyes appear narrow, obliquely placed and triangular in shape; thin ears set close together; very muscular, long, arched neck, tapering from shoulders to head, free from loose skin; short tail, set on low and carried horizontally.

The Miniature Bull Terrier was bred to help out its larger relative when ratting.

STAFFORDSHIRE BULL TERRIER

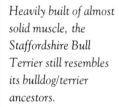

The Staffordshire Bull Terrier should not be confused with the American Staffordshire Terrier, or Pit Bull, which has been developed along quite different lines. The lovable Staffordshire or Staffy has a bloody history. It derived from the crossing of an Old English Bulldog and a terrier, most likely the extinct Black and Tan, at a time when bull-baiting and dog fighting were two of the most popular "sports" in Britain. The resultant dogs had the ideal attributes for combat: the strength and tenacity of a bulldog coupled with the agility and quick wits of a terrier. When bull-baiting and, thereafter, dog fighting were outlawed in Britain, the Staffy was developed along gentler lines as a companion dog. It was recognized by the British Kennel Club as a pure variety in 1935, and by the American Kennel Club in 1974.

Heavily built of almost solid muscle, the Staffordshire Bull Terrier still resembles its bulldog/terrier ancestors.

Character and care

The Staffy is one of the most popular pets and show dogs. It makes a fine household dog as well as guard, being an affectionate and game companion which adores children. However, it is not averse to having a scrap with its fellows, usually emerging the victor, and so it is sensible to keep it on the leash while out walking. This totally reliable, smooth-coated dog is easy to look after, requiring little other than regular brushing.

KEY CHARACTERISTICS
● **CLASS** Terrier. **Recognized** AKC, ANKC, CKC, FCI, KC(GB), KUSA.
● **SIZE** Height at shoulders: 35.5–40.5cm (14–16in). Weight: dogs 12.7–17.2kg (28–38lb), bitches 10.9–15.4kg (24–34lb).
● **COAT** Smooth, short and dense.
● **COLOUR** Red, fawn, white, black or blue, or any one of these colours with white; any shade of brindle, or any shade of brindle with white.
● **OTHER FEATURES** Short, deep through, broad skull; eyes preferably dark, but may bear some relation to the coat colour; rose or half-pricked ears; close-coupled body; medium-length tail.

Since bull-baiting and dog fighting became illegal, the "Staffy" has gained widespread popularity as a family pet.

AIREDALE TERRIER

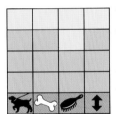

The Airedale is the king of the terriers, being the largest member of the terrier group. Originally known as the Waterside Terrier and sometimes also as the Bingley Terrier, the Airedale was named after the Valley of Aire in Yorkshire, England. It was the progeny of a working terrier probably crossed with the Otterhound. The breed was first classified separately for show purposes in 1879, but did not really come into its own as a show dog until the 1930s. Airedales were introduced into the United States by 1910.

An expert ratter and duck-catcher, the Airedale can also be trained to the gun and is a splendid guard. It has therefore undertaken a multitude of tasks ranging from service in both the British and Russian armies to acting as messenger and collector of money for the Red Cross and as a railway police patrol dog. It seems to have lost its niche as a guard since the emergence of the German Shepherd Dog.

Character and care

The multi-purpose Airedale is a good choice for the terrier devotee who wants a bigger dog. As a family pet, it is good with children, extremely loyal and, despite its size, seems to adapt well to fairly cramped conditions – provided that it has plenty of exercise. It will, however, need to be hand stripped twice a year, if it is the intention to exhibit.

KEY CHARACTERISTICS
• **CLASS** Terrier. **Recognized** AKC, ANKC, CKC, FCI, KC(GB), KUSA.
• **SIZE** Height: dogs about 58–61cm (23–24in), bitches 56–59cm (22–23in). Weight: about 19.9kg (44lb).
• **COAT** Hard, dense and wiry.
• **COLOUR** Body-saddle, top of neck and top surface of tail, black or grizzle; all other parts tan; ears often a darker tan, and shading may occur round neck and side of skull; a few white hairs between forelegs is acceptable.
• **OTHER FEATURES** Long, flat skull; small, dark eyes; V-shaped ears; deep chest; short, strong, straight, level back; tails set on high and carried gaily, customarily docked.

The Airedale, the largest of the terrier group, has a distinguished record in the police, military and rescue services.

Half-drop ears, small dark eyes and a beard combine to give the Airedale its benign look.

BEDLINGTON TERRIER

The Bedlington may look like a lamb, but its past record ranges from poaching to pit fighting.

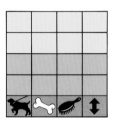

The Bedlington Terrier looks like a shorn lamb with its distinctive thick and linty coat standing well out from the skin. This breed was once a favourite with poachers and is still known by some as the Gypsy Dog. It is believed that the Greyhound or Whippet played a part in its ancestry and possibly also the Dandie Dinmont Terrier. The Bedlington probably originated in Northumberland, England, and the first of its kind is thought to have been a dog known as Old Flint, owned by Squire Trevelyan.

The dog, which whelped in 1782, is said to have had descendants traceable until 1873. Then the British Kennel Club was formed, making record-keeping more reliable.

A strain of similar terriers, known as Rothbury Terriers, existed in the Rothbury Forest of Northumberland in the 18th century. In 1820, Mr J. Howe came to the village of Bedlington in that county with a bitch Phoebe, which was given to Joseph Ainsley. Ainsley mated Phoebe to a dog called Old Piper producing Young Piper, the first dog to bear the new name of Bedlington Terrier. The breed was first exhibited in the United Kingdom during the 1860s and the British Bedlington Terrier Club was formed in 1875. It is moderately popular in the US and UK.

Character and care

The Bedlington is a true terrier: lovable, full of fun, and a terror when its temper is provoked. It is, however, easy to train and usually adores children. It does not need a great deal of space, enjoys average exercise and, while its coat needs regular trimming, a good grooming every day using a stiff brush will normally keep it tidy.

KEY CHARACTERISTICS
• **CLASS** Terrier. **Recognized** AKC, ANKC, CKC, FCI, KC(GB). KUSA.
• **SIZE** Height at withers: dogs 40.5–44cm (16–17½in), bitches 37.5–41cm (15–16½in). Weight: 8.2–10.5kg (18–22lb).
• **COAT** Thick and linty.
• **COLOUR** Blue, liver or sandy, with or without tan; darker pigment to be encouraged; blues, and blue and tans must have black noses; livers and sandies must have brown noses.
• **OTHER FEATURES** Narrow skull; small, bright, deep-set eyes; moderate-sized, filbert-shaped ears; muscular body; moderate-length tail, thick at root and tapering to a point.

FOX TERRIER (SMOOTH AND WIRE)

The Smooth Fox Terrier started life as a stable dog, its job being to hunt vermin. It probably descends from terriers in the English counties of Cheshire and Shropshire with some Beagle blood added. The Wire, which is a great rabbiter, originated in the coal-mining areas of Durham and Derbyshire in England, and in Wales. As their names imply, they will also go in pursuit of the fox.

For many years, the Smooth and Wire Fox Terriers were bred together, regardless of coat. All the great Wires resulted from the mating of a Smooth Fox Terrier called Jock with a bitch of unknown antecedents, but definitely wire-haired, called Trap. The Smooth was given its own register in 1876, three years after the British Kennel Club was founded, but the conformation of the two breeds still remains the same.

Both varieties of Fox Terrier were much sought after in Britain in the 1930s. Sadly, they are now seen less frequently. The Wire is more popular than its smooth-coated relative, which is rarely seen outside the show ring.

Character and care

The Fox Terriers are affectionate, and trainable, and make the ideal small child's companion for rabbiting. The Smooth needs daily grooming with a stiff brush, and trimming and chalking before a show. The Wire needs to be hand-stripped three times a year, and to be groomed regularly.

The Wire-haired was probably developed some years before the Smooth, although it was slower to make its début in the show ring.

Today fairly rare, the Smooth differs from its wiry relative only in the texture of its coat.

KEY CHARACTERISTICS
● **CLASS** Terrier. **Recognized** AKC, ANKC, CKC, FCI, KC(GB), KUSA.
● **SIZE** Maximum height at withers: dogs 39cm (15½in), bitches slightly less. Weight: 7.2–8.2kg (16–18lb).
● **COAT** *Smooth* Straight, flat and smooth. *Wire* Dense and very wiry.
● **COLOUR** *Smooth* All white; white with tan or black markings, white should predominate; brindle, red or liver markings highly undesirable. *Wire* White should predominate with black or tan markings; brindle, red, liver or slate-blue markings undesirable.
● **OTHER FEATURES** *Smooth* Flat, moderately narrow skull; dark, small eyes, rather deep set; small, V-shaped ears dropping forward close to cheek; chest deep, not broad; tail customarily docked. *Wire* Topline of skull almost flat; dark eyes, full of fire and intelligence; small, V-shaped ears, of moderate thickness; short, strong, level back; tail customarily docked.

GLEN OF IMAAL TERRIER

A game little dog, the Glen of Imaal Terrier is little known outside its home territory.

Character and care

The Glen of Imaal is nowadays to be found mainly as a family pet and/or working terrier on Irish farms and small holdings. It is affectionate, brave, good with children and very playful. Maintaining its charming, "shaggy dog" appearance requires only a good daily brushing.

KEY CHARACTERISTICS
• **CLASS** Terrier. **Recognized** ANKC, FCI, KC(GB), KUSA.
• **SIZE** Height: about 35.5cm (14in). Weight: about 15.7kg (35lb).
• **COAT** Medium length and harsh textured, with a soft undercoat.
• **COLOUR** Blue, brindle or wheaten, all shades.
• **OTHER FEATURES** Head of good width and fair length with a strong foreface; medium-sized, brown eyes; small ears, rose-shaped or pricked when alert, thrown back in repose; powerful jaws; deep, medium-length body; tail strong at root, well set on and carried gaily, docking optional.

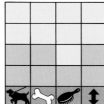

This short-legged terrier derives from the Glen of Imaal in County Wicklow, Ireland, where it has existed for a very long time. It was used to dispel vermin, including fox and badger, and in dog fights. Badger hunting and dog fighting are now illegal, but its other skills continue to be employed.

The Glen of Imaal Terrier received official breed recognition in its own country in 1933. It is now also recognized by the British Kennel Club but remains little known outside its native Ireland.

The Glen still serves as a working terrier on Irish farms.

IRISH TERRIER

Similar in appearance to the Airedale, but smaller, the Irish Terrier is a keen ratter and can also be trained to the gun.

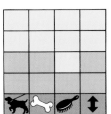

The Irish or Irish Red Terrier is reminiscent of a small Airedale Terrier, except for its fiery coat colour. The Irish claim that this, their national terrier, is a smaller version of the Irish Wolfhound and has been in existence in Ireland for centuries. However, the first official record of it did not occur until 1875, and the breed did not rate a mention in Idstone's *Book of Dogs*, published in 1872. It seems more likely that the Irish Terrier is a descendant of wire-haired Black and Tan Terriers, whose job was to repel vermin and hunt some 200 years ago. One study of the very similar Welsh and Lakeland Terriers adds substance to this suggestion. In the case of the Irish, the blood of a large Wheaten Terrier said to have existed around County Cork may also have been introduced.

Whatever its ancestry, the Irish Terrier varied greatly in size, conformation and colour until 1879. In that year, a specialist breed club was formed in Ireland, standardization began, and the Irish Terrier went on to become a firm favourite internationally.

Character and care

The attractive Irish is an expert ratter and has been trained to the gun with success. It also makes an affectionate pet. Its coat should be stripped two or three times a year, and it should be groomed regularly.

KEY CHARACTERISTICS
● **CLASS** Terrier. **Recognized** AKC, ANKC, CKC, FCI, KC(GB), KUSA.
● **SIZE** Height at shoulders: about 46cm (18in). Weight: 11.3–12.1kg (25–27lb).
● **COAT** Harsh and wiry.
● **COLOUR** Whole-coloured, preferably red, red wheaten, or yellow-red; small amount of white on chest acceptable; white on feet or any black shading highly undesirable.
● **OTHER FEATURES** Long head, flat and narrow between ears; small, dark, unprominent eyes; small, V-shaped ears; deep, muscular tail, customarily docked.

Though the Irish Terrier had been around for centuries, it varied greatly in type until a breed club was formed.

KERRY BLUE TERRIER

Once a mascot for Irish patriots, the Kerry Blue is very game, even tackling otters in deep water.

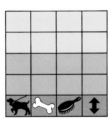

The Kerry Blue Terrier originated in County Kerry, south-western Ireland. An excellent sporting dog and fine swimmer, it was used there to hunt badgers, foxes and otters. Its ancestors are thought to have included the Irish, Bedlington and Bull Terriers. As with the Irish Terrier, there is a school of thought that the Irish Wolfhound also contributed to its make-up. According to a legend, however, the Kerry Blue traces its lineage back to a blue terrier survivor from a shipwreck in Tralee Bay, County Kerry. This dog was so ferocious that it killed every opponent with which it did battle, establishing the right to found its own strain. Whatever its true origin the Kerry Blue is certainly not the breed one would wish to encounter off the lead when exercising one's Peke or Chihuahua.

The breed was first exhibited at Crufts Dog Show in England, and in the United States, in 1922. It was recognized by the British Kennel Club in the same year, and in the United States two years later.

Character and care

Although it began life as a sporting dog, the Kerry Blue is now mainly kept as a pet. It is good with children, while retaining excellent guarding qualities. However, it may display a fierce temper against dogs or other pets when roused and so, if you own a fiery Kerry, you would be wise to insure yourself against other people's veterinary bills. The Kerry is not the easiest dog to prepare for the show ring, requiring knowledgeable trimming. It needs daily grooming with a stiff brush and metal-toothed comb.

KEY CHARACTERISTICS
● **CLASS** Terrier. **Recognized** AKC, ANKC, CKC, FCI, KC(GB), KUSA.
● **SIZE** Height: dogs 45–49cm (18–19½in), bitches 44–47.5cm (17½–19in). Weight: 14.8–18.1kg (33–40lb).
● **COAT** Soft, spiky, plentiful and wavy.
● **COLOUR** Any shade of blue, with or without black points; a small white patch on chest should not be penalized.
● **OTHER FEATURES** Eyes as dark as possible; small to medium-sized, V-shaped ears; short-coupled body with good depth of brisket and well-sprung ribs; tail set on high and carried erect, customarily docked.

LAKELAND TERRIER

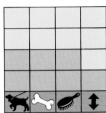

The Lakeland Terrier, originally known as the Patterdale Terrier, comes from the Lake District in the old English county of Cumberland. It was developed with the aim of protecting lambs from foxes. To meet this aim, there were various terrier crossings, and it is thought that the Border, the Bedlington and the Dandie Dinmont Terriers, and probably later the Fox Terrier, all contributed. The result is a practical and courageous working animal, resembling an Airedale Terrier in miniature, which is small enough to follow prey underground.

Although the Lakeland worked with local hunts for years, it did not appear in the show ring until 1912. After the First World War a breed club was formed, and the Lakeland was recognized by the Kennel Club in Britain in 1921. In 1964, a Lakeland Terrier, Champion Stingray of Derryabah, won Best in Show at Crufts Dog Show in London and, a year later, repeated this triumph at the Westminster Dog Show in New York.

Character and care

The Lakeland Terrier has retained its sporting instincts yet makes an excellent handy-sized housepet, being a smart little guard and good with children. However, it is a lively dog, needing a fair amount of exercise. Its coat requires daily brushing and, if it is the intention to exhibit, will have to be stripped three times a year.

KEY CHARACTERISTICS
• **CLASS** Terrier. **Recognized** AKC, ANKC, CKC, FCI, KC(GB), KUSA.
• **SIZE** Maximum height at shoulders: 37cm (14½in). Weight: dogs about 7.7kg (17lb), bitches about 6.8kg (15lb).
• **COAT** Dense and harsh, with weather-resistant undercoat.
• **COLOUR** Black and tan, blue and tan, red, wheaten, red grizzle, liver, blue or black; mahogany or deep tan not typical; small tips of white on feet and chest undesirable but permissible.
• **OTHER FEATURES** Flat skull; refined, dark or hazel eyes; moderately small ears; reasonably narrow chest; tail customarily docked.

Another breed resembling a small-scale Airedale, the Lakeland Terrier hunted foxes across rugged terrain.

MANCHESTER TERRIER

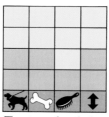

The Manchester Terrier is a professional ratter turned household pet.

The Manchester Terrier and English Toy Terrier (known in the United States as the Toy Manchester Terrier) were once exhibited under the name of Black and Tan Terrier, divided only by weight. Nowadays the two breeds are classified separately.

Although not well documented, the history of the Manchester Terrier suggests that the breed has been long established. Its ancestors were sporting terriers that would demolish rats in a pit for the amusement of spectators in the mid 19th century. This sport was popular among poorer people in areas such as the city of Manchester in northern England. The Manchester Terrier appears to descend from the now extinct White English Terrier, with the addition of Dachshund, Whippet and King Charles Spaniel blood. The Doberman and Italian Greyhound also contributed, both accounting for the Manchester's smooth shiny coat and colouring, and the latter for its slightly arched back.

PARSON JACK RUSSELL TERRIER

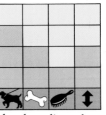

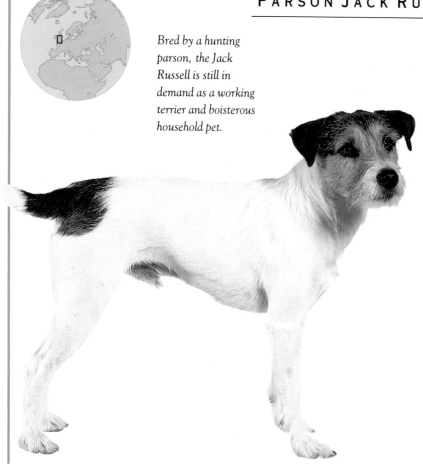

Bred by a hunting parson, the Jack Russell is still in demand as a working terrier and boisterous household pet.

The Parson Jack Russell Terrier was only recognized by the British Kennel Club in January 1990. Until then it was believed that there was far too much variation in the breed's colour, conformation, size and coat texture for it to be granted pure-bred status. The Kennel Club recognized one type of Jack Russell only, the Parson Jack. Although people have got into the habit of calling similar terriers Jack Russells, they are not recognized as such. They are often also referred to as hunt terriers, and are very popular in North America and the UK.

This breed takes its name from a sporting parson, Jack Russell, who lived in the county of Devon, England, in the 1800s. He was a horseman, a terrier judge and one of the early members of the British Kennel Club. Parson Russell developed this strain of terriers from various early types of wire-haired fox terriers to obtain dogs that would run with hounds and bolt the fox from its lair. Their coat may be either rough and broken or smooth.

Character and care

The long-lived Manchester Terrier tends to be a one-person animal and, regardless of its sporting past, is often a pampered pet of old ladies. It also makes an extremely good family pet, and is suited to a town or country existence. The only grooming required is a daily brush and rubdown.

KEY CHARACTERISTICS
• **CLASS** Terrier. **Recognized** AKC, ANKC, CKC, FCI, KC(GB). KUSA.
• **SIZE** Height at shoulders: dogs about 40.5cm (16in), bitches 38cm (15in). Weight: 5.4–9.9kg (12–22lb).
• **COAT** Close, smooth, short and glossy.
• **COLOUR** Jet black and rich tan.
• **OTHER FEATURES** Long, flat, narrow skull; small, dark, sparkling eyes; small, V-shaped ears; chest narrow and deep; short tail, set on where arch of back ends.

Character and care

The Parson Jack Russell is still an extremely good working terrier, and has become enormously popular as a household pet with many people, including the elderly. However, it can be somewhat excitable and is really better suited to being the companion of an active child. It requires little grooming.

KEY CHARACTERISTICS
• **CLASS** Terrier **Recognized** ANKC, FCI, KC(GB), KUSA
• **SIZE** Height at withers: dogs 33–35cm (13–14in), bitches 30–33cm (12–13in).
• **COAT** Smooth, or rough and broken.
• **COLOUR** Entirely white or with tan, lemon or black markings, preferably confined to head and root of tail.
• **OTHER FEATURES** Strong-boned head; almond-shaped eyes; V-shaped ears; strong hindquarters; tail is customarily docked.

GERMAN HUNT TERRIER

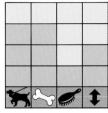

The German Hunt Terrier or Deutscher Jagdterrier was developed in Germany, probably by crossing the English Fox Terrier with the Lakeland Terrier. Careful selection achieved a terrier that would go to earth and retrieve small game from land or water. The German Hunt Terrier is a courageous hunter, which will take on fox and boar as well as small rodents.

Character and care

This hunter and gundog possesses an aggressive temperament and is not a suitable pet. It should be kennelled outdoors, and can be groomed with a hound glove.

KEY CHARACTERISTICS
• **CLASS** Terrier. **Recognized** FCI.
• **SIZE** Maximum height at withers: 40.5cm (16in). Weight: dogs 8.7–9.9kg (19½–22lb), bitches 7.2–8.1kg (16–18lb).
• **COAT** *Smooth* Smooth, harsh, dense and lying flat; *Rough* Harsh and wiry.
• **COLOUR** Predominantly black, greyish black or dark brown with small, even tan markings.
• **OTHER FEATURES** Rather heavy head; small, dark eyes set obliquely; V-shaped ears, folded so that tips fall forward; long back; tail set on high and carried erect, characteristically docked.

Although ideal for its purpose, the German Hunt Terrier is not suitable as a pet.

SOFT-COATED WHEATEN TERRIER

One of the oldest Irish Terriers, the Wheaten did not emerge from the farmyard until fairly recently.

HARLEQUIN PINSCHER

The Harlequin Pinscher or Harlekinpinscher is the newest pinscher breed, having been recognized by the FCI in 1958. It was bred down from the Pinscher, possibly with the addition of other blood. The main difference between the Harlequin and its larger relative is coat colour. It was bred for beauty and companionability rather than for work. It is rarely seen outside Germany.

Character and care

The Harlequin Pinscher is alert and, like all terrier-type dogs, will warn its owner of intruders, but its main purpose is as a companion and pet. It has an excellent temperament. It is lively and needs some exercise, and requires grooming with a brush or hound glove once or twice a week.

KEY CHARACTERISTICS
● **CLASS** Terrier. **Recognized** FCI.
● **SIZE** Height at withers: 30.5–35.5cm (12–14in).
● **COAT** Short, smooth, dense and glossy.
● **COLOUR** Pied on a white or pale-coloured ground; grey dappled with black or dark patches; brindle with or without tan points.
● **OTHER FEATURES** Skull and muzzle proportionate, forming smooth line; eyes not too large, too round or too small; small ears erect, with pointed or forward-hanging tips (cropped); muscular body; tail, characteristically docked.

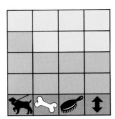

One of the oldest native dog breeds of Ireland, the Soft-coated Wheaten Terrier is believed to be a progenitor of the Irish and Kerry Blue Terriers. It is said that a blue dog swam ashore from a ship wrecked in Tralee Bay, Ireland, around 180 years ago. This dog mated with the native Wheaten and the result of the union was the Kerry Blue Terrier.

The Soft-coated Wheaten was developed as a farm dog to hunt rabbits, rats and other prey. It will work any kind of covert and no respectable Irish farmer would be without one. Recognized by the Irish Kennel Club in 1937 and by the British Kennel Club in 1971, the breed first appeared in the United States at the beginning of the 1970s and was recognized by the American Kennel Club in 1973. It is now making progress in the show ring on both sides of the Atlantic.

Character and care

Despite being bred as a farmyard dog the Soft-coated Wheaten does best when housed indoors as a family pet. It is gentle and devoted, and generally loves children. It revels in plenty of exercise, and the coat should be groomed regularly using a medium-toothed metal comb and a wire brush.

KEY CHARACTERISTICS
● **CLASS** Terrier. **Recognized** AKC, ANKC, CKC, FCI, KC(GB), KUSA.
● **SIZE** Height at withers: dogs 45.5–49.5cm (18–19½in), bitches slightly less. Weight: 15.7–20.2kg (35–45lb).
● **COAT** Soft and silky.
● **COLOUR** A good, clear wheaten, the shade of ripening wheat; white and red equally objectionable; dark shading on ears not untypical.
● **OTHER FEATURES** Head and skull flat and moderately long; clear, bright, dark hazel eyes; V-shaped ears; compact body; tail customarily docked.

With a stocky body and profuse, silky coat, the Wheaten has small ears and a docked tail.

JAPANESE TERRIER

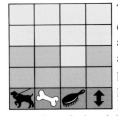

This Japanese breed was developed in the 1700s around the ports of Kobe and Yokohama, using imported British terriers, particularly the Smooth Fox Terrier. These were crossed with local breeds to produce a dog that is lighter throughout and lacks the heavy bone, short, strong body and clean-cut reach of Smooth Fox Terriers. Kept principally as a pet in Japan, it is thought to have gone through so many changes that it is now described as a terrier with some reservation. It is rarely seen outside the country of origin.

Character and care

The Japanese Terrier is a lively pet and so probably retains something of the terrier temperament. Its smooth coat needs little grooming, but it requires regular exercise.

KEY CHARACTERISTICS
● **CLASS** Terrier. **Recognized** FCI.
● **SIZE** Height: 30.5–38cm (12–15in).
● **COAT** Smooth and sparse.
● **COLOUR** Predominantly white with black and tan markings.
● **OTHER FEATURES** Small head; small eyes; small V-shaped ears; muscular body; small tail, customarily docked.

WELSH TERRIER

Of Celtic origin, the Welsh Terrier was used to hunt badger, fox and otter.

Like the Airedale, the Welsh Terrier has half-drop ears and small, deep-set eyes.

The Welsh Terrier resembles very closely both the Lakeland Terrier and the larger Airedale Terrier. Like another similar terrier, the Irish, the Welsh Terrier is of Celtic origin. Two strains of it were evolved by the Welsh, a Celtic strain using a coarse-haired Black and Tan Terrier and an English strain using an Airedale and a Fox Terrier cross, and appeared as a distinct breed in the late 18th century. The English strain is said to have died out, though, to the writer's way of thinking, both the Airedale and Fox Terrier influences are visibly apparent. In any event, the Celtic strain was presented in 1885 and a Welsh Terrier Club was formed a year later. In 1887, the Kennel Club in Britain awarded the breed championship show status. The first Welsh Terriers reached America in about 1901, and there a smaller dog is preferred. These terriers were originally popular for hunting badger, fox and otter.

Character and care

A fun dog, the Welsh Terrier is energetic, affectionate and good with children. It enjoys plenty of exercise and will need to have its coat stripped at least twice a year, if it is the intention to exhibit. Many owners of pet Welsh Terriers have their dog's coat clipped.

KEY CHARACTERISTICS
● **CLASS** Terrier. **Recognized** AKC, ANKC, CKC, FCI, KC(GB), KUSA.
● **SIZE** Maximum height at shoulders: 39cm (15½in). Weight: 9–9.5kg (20–21lb).
● **COAT** Abundant, wiry, hard and close.
● **COLOUR** Black and tan for preference; also black, grizzle and tan; free from black pencilling on toes; black below hocks most undesirable.
● **OTHER FEATURES** Head flat and moderately wide between ears; small, dark eyes well set in; small, V-shaped ears carried forward; short, well ribbed-up body; long, muscular legs; tail well set on but not carried too gaily, customarily docked.

BORDER TERRIER

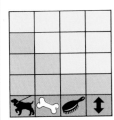

This attractive, tough little dog derives from the Border country, the area around the boundary between England and Scotland, and is probably still seen in its largest numbers there. The Border Terrier was bred in the middle of the 19th century to run with hounds and yet be small enough to bolt the fox from its lair.

Recognized by the British Kennel Club in 1920 the breed has been less spoilt by the dictates of fashion than many others. It has always been a working terrier. When James Davidson wrote in 1800 that he had purchased "twa red devils o' terriers, that has hard wiry coats and would worry any demned thing that crepit", he could have been describing the Border Terrier of today.

Character and care

The smallest of the working terriers, the Border makes a first-class pet. It usually loves all children, is long lived, will literally walk its owners off their feet, and is a good watchdog. It requires little routine grooming, and only a slight tidying up before exhibiting.

KEY CHARACTERISTICS
● **CLASS** Terrier. **Recognized** AKC, ANKC, CKC, FCI, KC(GB), KUSA.
● **SIZE** Height: about 25cm (10in). Weight: dogs 6–7kg (13–15½lb), bitches 5.1–6.4kg (11½–14lb).
● **COAT** Harsh and dense with close undercoat.
● **COLOUR** Red, wheaten, grizzle and tan, blue and tan.
● **OTHER FEATURES** Dark eyes with keen expression; small, V-shaped ears; deep, narrow, fairly long body; moderately short tail.

The Border, smallest of the working terriers, was sent in to bolt the fox from its lair.

CAIRN TERRIER

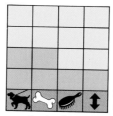

This popular Scottish terrier, or one very similar, has been known and used for putting down vermin for 150 years or more. It was named after the cairns (a Scottish word which means a heap or pile of stones), which often harboured vermin. The Cairn Terrier originated in the Western Highlands, where the Skye Terrier is well known. There appears to have been some confusion between the breeds at one time, and the Cairn, predominantly a working breed, used to be known as the Short-haired Skye Terrier.

The oldest known strain of Cairn Terriers is that founded by the late Captain MacLeod of Drynoch in the Isle of Skye. Mr John MacDonald, gamekeeper to the Macleod of Macleod at Dunvegan Castle for more than 40 years, kept this strain alive.

The Cairn Terrier made its first appearance in the show ring in 1909, and is now known and admired the world over. However, like the Border Terrier, it still tends to be seen most in the North of England and in its native Scotland.

Character and care

This intelligent, lively little working terrier is still well able to prove its worth as a dispeller of vermin and is also a popular and affectionate pet. It is hardy and enjoys plenty of exercise though it can adapt to most living situations. The Cairn is an easy dog to show, requiring little grooming other than brushing, combing and removing of excess feathering.

Bright eyes, erect ears and a short muzzle help give the Cairn its attitude of keenness.

KEY CHARACTERISTICS
• **CLASS** Terrier. **Recognized** AKC, ANKC, CKC, FCI, KC(GB), KUSA.
• **SIZE** Height: 24–30cm (9½–12in). Weight: 5.9–7.5kg (13–16lb).
• **COAT** Profuse, harsh but not coarse, with short, soft, close undercoat; weather resistant.
• **COLOUR** Cream, wheaten, red, grey or nearly black; brindling acceptable in all these colours; not solid black, solid white, nor black and tan; dark points, such as ears and muzzle, very typical.
• **OTHER FEATURES** Small head; eyes set wide apart; small, pointed ears; level back; short, balanced tail, well furnished with hair but not feathery.

DANDIE DINMONT TERRIER

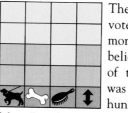

The appealing and devoted little Dandie Dinmont Terrier is generally believed to be a relative of the Skye Terrier. It was originally bred to hunt badgers and foxes. Most Dandies trace back to a pack owned by "Piper" Allan of Northumberland (now Northumbria), England, in the 1700s. His dogs are also credited with helping in the development of the Bedlington Terrier.

James Davidson, a farmer in the Borders (the area around the boundary between England and Scotland), kept a pack of these short-legged, rough-haired terriers, and Sir Walter Scott (1771–1832), the novelist, acquired some of them. Though Scott subsequently denied that there was any connection, his famous novel *Guy Mannering*, published in 1814, includes a character called

One of several terriers originally bred in the Western Highlands, the Cairn was used to clean vermin out of wayside cairns.

An engaging little character, the Dandie Dinmont takes its name from a novel by Sir Walter Scott.

Dandie Dinmont, who is a Borders farmer with a pack of little terriers. Thereafter, the dogs became known as Dandie Dinmont's Terriers, and, in time, as Dandie Dinmonts. They were also known as Pepper and Mustard Terriers after the colours for which David-son's dogs were renowned.

When the Dandie Dinmont Terrier was first shown at the Birmingham Dog Show in 1867, the judge, Mr W. Smith, refused to award the exhibits a prize, being of the opinion that they were "just a bunch of mongrels". The breed has been vastly improved since then.

Character and care

Now kept mainly as a pet, the Dandie Dinmont makes a most affectionate, playful and intelligent companion, and is in its element as the family's sole pet. It will be happy with as much exercise as its owner is able to provide. This breed is also fairly simple to groom, use of a stiff brush and comb, and the removal of surplus hair, being all that is necessary.

KEY CHARACTERISTICS
● **CLASS** Terrier. **Recognized** AKC, ANKC, CKC, FCI, KC(GB), KUSA.
● **SIZE** Height at shoulders: 20–27.5cm (8–11in). Weight: 8.1–10.8kg (18–24lb).
● **COAT** Soft, linty undercoat and harder topcoat, not wiry and feeling crisp to the hand.
● **COLOUR** Pepper (from bluish black to pale silvery grey) or mustard (from reddish brown to pale fawn).
● **OTHER FEATURES** Strongly made head, large but in proportion to dog's size; rich, dark hazel eyes; pendulum ears; long, strong and flexible body; rather short tail.

NORFOLK TERRIER

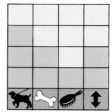

This breed was once classified with, and known as, the Norwich Terrier. The drop-eared Norfolk Terrier and the prick-eared Norwich Terrier originated in the East Anglian area of England and were once very popular with students at Cambridge University. Both little dogs were known as Norwich Terriers from as early as the 1880s. They were probably a mixture of Cairn, Border and Irish Terriers, and their litters contained both the prick-eared and drop-eared varieties.

The only difference between the Norfolk and Norwich Terriers today is still their ears. The writer distinguishes the two breeds by the fact that the ears of the Norfolk are flat like that English county, while those of the Norwich are upright like the spire of Norwich Cathedral. The Norfolk Terrier only gained official recognition as a separate breed from the Kennel Club in Britain in 1964 and, in the United States, it took until 1979 for the varieties to be separated.

Character and care

Despite being among the smallest of the terriers, the Norfolk is described in its breed club standard as being a "demon" for its size. A sociable dog, this hardy, lovable terrier is certainly alert and fearless, but it is good with children, has an equable temperament and makes a fine household pet for those prepared to exercise it. It enjoys a day's rabbiting, and honourable scars are not a drawback in the show ring. It requires daily brushing, and some trimming is all the preparation that is needed for exhibition.

KEY CHARACTERISTICS
● **CLASS** Terrier. **Recognized** AKC, ANKC, CKC, FCI, KC(GB), KUSA.
● **SIZE** Height at withers: about 25.5cm (10in). Weight: 5–5.4kg (11–12lb).
● **COAT** Hard, wiry and straight.
● **COLOUR** All shades of red, wheaten, black and tan, or grizzle; white marks and patches undesirable but permissible.
● **OTHER FEATURES** Broad skull; deep-set, oval-shaped eyes; medium-sized, V-shaped ears, slightly rounded at tip; compact body; tail-docking optional.

The Norfolk Terrier is distinguished by its ears, which drop forward.

NORWICH TERRIER

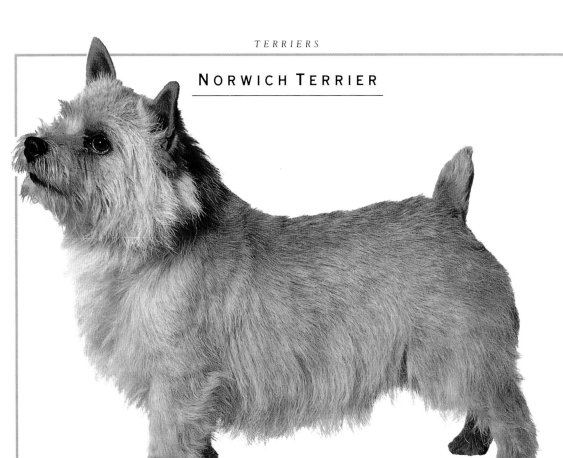

The Norwich is a traditional terrier breed, well suited to hunting small prey in open terrain.

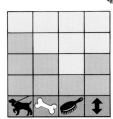

From 1964 in Britain, and from 1979 in the United States, the prick-eared Norwich Terrier has been classified separately from an otherwise identical drop-eared dog now known as the Norfolk Terrier (see page 206). The breed is named after the city of Norwich, which lies in the county of Norfolk in the East Anglian area of eastern England. The Norwich Terrier appears to have originated in East Anglia, and probably includes Cairn, Border and Irish Terrier blood. It was popular with students at Cambridge University, who kept both varieties.

Controversy exists over whether a Colonel Vaughan from Ballybrick in southern Ireland, or a horse dealer named Jodrell Hopkins from the Cambridge area, deserve credit for founding the Norwich Terrier. In the 1860s Colonel Vaughan hunted with a pack of small red terriers, which included many outcrosses and contained terriers with both dropped and pricked ears. There was a tendency to crop the ears of the drop-eared dogs until this practice became illegal. Then the Norwich Terrier Club requested that the breed's standard be amended to include only those terriers with pricked ears. Hopkins's claim lies in his ownership of a bitch, some of whose pups came into the hands of an employee of his, Frank Jones. Jones crossed them with other terriers, including the smaller examples of Irish and Glen of Imaal Terriers. The progeny became known as Trumpington Terriers or Jones Terriers, and a line of Norwich Terriers in existence today claims direct descent from Frank Jones' litters.

Character and care

This hardy and adaptable terrier is usually good with children. It enjoys regular exercise and needs only a daily brushing for its role as housepet and some trimming in preparation for show.

The upright ears of the Norwich Terrier signal its keenness to work.

KEY CHARACTERISTICS
● **CLASS** Terrier. **Recognized** AKC, ANKC, CKC, FCI, KC(GB), KUSA.
● **SIZE** Height at withers: 25.5cm (10in). Weight: 4.5–5.4kg (10–12lb).
● **COAT** Hard, wiry and straight.
● **COLOUR** All shades of red, wheaten, black and tan, or grizzle; white marks and patches undesirable.
● **OTHER FEATURES** Strong, wedge-shaped muzzle; small, dark, oval-shaped eyes; erect ears set well apart on top of skull; short back; docked tail optional.

SCOTTISH TERRIER

A separate breed for more than a century, the "Scottie" has a number of terrier cousins in the Highlands.

Erect ears and prominent eyebrows on a long face give the Scottie a somewhat stern appearance.

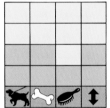

The Scottish Terrier or Scottie was once known as the Aberdeen Terrier, after the Scottish city. Like the Cairn, it was bred with the express purpose of dispelling vermin. The Scottie has existed for many centuries and taken many different forms. Indeed, at the end of the 19th century it was exhibited alongside the Skye, Dandie Dinmont and West Highland White Terrier under the classification, Scotch Terriers. Many people still tend to think that the West Highland White and the Scottish Terriers are one and the same breed. In fact, line breeding of the Scottie began in earnest in around 1800. In 1892, the first Scottish Terrier Club was formed in Scotland and a standard was laid down for the breed.

Character and care

The Scottie tends to be a one- or two-person dog, perhaps at its best as the pampered pet of a childless couple. It has a reliable temperament but does not welcome interlopers and has no interest in anyone outside its own human family. It enjoys walks, loves to play ball games, and is thoroughly sporty, home-loving and independent. The Scottie requires daily brushing. Its beard needs gentle brushing and combing, and its coat should be trimmed twice a year.

KEY CHARACTERISTICS
• **CLASS** Terrier. **Recognized** AKC, ANKC, CKC, FCI, KC(GB), KUSA.
• **SIZE** Height at withers: 25.5–28cm (10–11in). Weight: 8.6–10.4kg (19–23lb).
• **COAT** Sharp, dense and wiry, with a short, dense, soft undercoat.
• **COLOUR** Black, wheaten or brindle of any shade.
• **OTHER FEATURES** Head and skull long without being out of proportion to size of dog; almond-shaped eyes; neat, fine-textured ears; well-moulded ribs flattening to deep chest; moderate-length tail giving general balance to dog.

SEALYHAM TERRIER

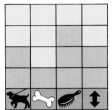

Freeman Lloyd, an authority on the Sealyham Terrier, has traced the breed back to the 15th century, when a family called Tucker is reputed to have imported a small, white, long-backed Flemish terrier into Wales. One of the Tuckers' descendants, the sportsman, Captain Edwardes, wanted dogs that would hunt with hounds and go to ground in the now illegal sport of badger digging. In the 1880s, he developed the Sealyham from various terrier breeds.

The breed took its name from the village of Sealyham near Haverfordwest, Wales, where it was created. The first Sealyham Terrier breed club was formed in 1908 and its founder, Fred Lewis, is said to have done a great deal to perfect the strain. Sealyhams were recognized by the British and American Kennel Clubs in the same year, 1911. Since then, the breed has proved successful in show rings throughout the world. However, the immense rise in popularity of the rather similar West Highland White Terrier over the past decade has resulted in the Sealyham rarely being seen outside the show ring today.

Character and care

The Sealyham makes a fine show dog and family pet. It is good with children, but not averse to a scrap with its fellows. This breed requires regular brushing and must be hand-stripped for the show ring. If intending to exhibit, advice on grooming should be sought from the breeder or some other expert.

KEY CHARACTERISTICS
● **CLASS** Terrier. **Recognized** AKC, ANKC, CKC, FCI, KC(GB), KUSA.
● **SIZE** Maximum height at shoulders: 31cm (12in). Weight: dogs about 9kg (20lb), bitches about 8.2kg (18lb).
● **COAT** Long, hard and wiry, with a weather-resistant undercoat.
● **COLOUR** All white, or white with lemon, brown , blue or badger pied markings on head and ears; much black or heavy ticking undesirable.
● **OTHER FEATURES** Head slightly domed; dark, well-set eyes; medium-sized ears; medium-length body; tail set in line with back and carried erect, customarily docked.

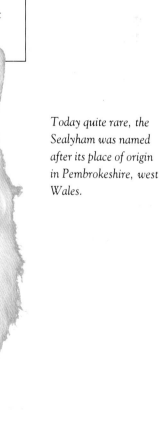

Today quite rare, the Sealyham was named after its place of origin in Pembrokeshire, west Wales.

SKYE TERRIER

The Skye Terrier, which evolved on the island of the same name, used to be known as the Terrier of the Western Islands.

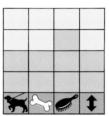

The Skye developed from small dogs kept in the Highlands of Scotland to go to ground after badger, fox, otter and rabbit. The best of these "earth" terriers were said to originate in the Isle of Skye. For a considerable time, the Skye and Cairn Terriers were thought to be one breed, the Cairn being described as a Short-haired Skye. There were also Skyes with drop and pricked ears. These varieties were divided in 1904, and challenge certificates have since been awarded to both drop-eared and prick-eared Skyes. Although the drop-eared variety is still permissible, it is rarely seen in Britain these days, and while it may be more numerous, it is still less common than the prick-eared Skye in the United States.

Probably the most famous Skye Terrier is Greyfriars Bobby, the subject of a romantic tale. In the 1850s, Bobby's master died and was buried in the graveyard of Greyfriars' Church in Edinburgh. Bobby lay on his master's grave for 14 years until his own death, breaking his vigil only to visit the café he had frequented with his late master. A statue to commemorate Bobby's faithfulness still stands, near Greyfriars' Church.

Character and care

The Skye Terrier tends to be suspicious of or uninterested in anyone other than its owner. Its magnificent long coat requires a considerable amount of grooming, particularly as this little dog enjoys country walks.

KEY CHARACTERISTICS
● **CLASS** Terrier. **Recognized** AKC, ANKC, CKC, FCI, KC(GB), KUSA.
● **SIZE** Ideal height at shoulders: dogs 25cm (10in), bitches 24cm (9½in). Weight: about 11.3kg (25lb).
● **COAT** Long, hard, straight, flat and free from curl, with a short, close, soft, woolly undercoat.
● **COLOUR** Black, dark or light grey, fawn or cream, all with black points.
● **OTHER FEATURES** Head and skull long and powerful; brown, preferably dark, eyes; prick or drop ears; long, low body with level back; when tail is hanging, upper part pendulous and lower part thrown back in a curve, when raised looks like extension of the back line.

WEST HIGHLAND WHITE TERRIER

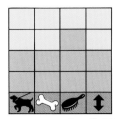

Like other small Scottish terriers, the West Highland White Terrier or Westie was bred to hunt vermin. At one time it was classed along with the Cairn and Skye Terriers as a Small Highland Working Terrier. The Westie has also gone under a number of other names. In the late 1800s, there was a strain of white Scottish Terriers owned by Colonel Malcolm of Poltalloch and known as Poltalloch Terriers. A picture of Colonel Malcolm with his dogs reveals that they were not all that different to the Westie we know today. Dogs of this type were also known as Roseneath Terriers or White Roseneath Terriers, and in a breed supplement published in 1899, they were classified as a sub-variety of the Scottish Terrier.

The first West Highland White Terrier Club was formed in 1905, and the first class for the breed seems to have been held in October 1904 at the Waverley Market in Edinburgh, organized by the Scottish Kennel Club. The Westie was recognized in America and Canada in 1909 and 1911 respectively, but not in Australia until the mid-1960s. Today it is among the most popular of purebred dogs.

Character and care

The Westie is described in its standard as being "possessed of no small amount of self esteem with a varminty appearance". This game and hardy little terrier is easy to train, gets on well with children and is a suitable housepet for people in town as well as in the country. Regular brushing keeps the white coat clean, but stripping and trimming are required for show, and, if it is the intention to exhibit, advice on preparation should be sought from the breeder.

KEY CHARACTERISTICS
• **CLASS** Terrier. **Recognized** AKC, ANKC, CKC, FCI, KC(GB), KUSA.
• **SIZE** Height: dogs about 27.5cm (11in), bitches about 25cm (10in). Weight: 6.8–9.9kg (15–22lb).
• **COAT** Harsh and free from curl, with a short, soft, close furry undercoat.
• **COLOUR** White.
• **OTHER FEATURES** Slightly domed head; eyes set wide apart; small, erect ears, carried firmly; compact body with level back and broad, strong loins; tail 12.5–15cm (5–6in) long.

Undeniably cute with its pricked ears and black button nose, the "Westie" is none the less a game little terrier well able to perform in the field.

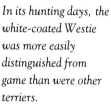

In its hunting days, the white-coated Westie was more easily distinguished from game than were other terriers.

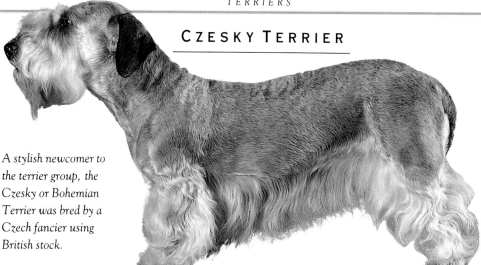

CZESKY TERRIER

A stylish newcomer to the terrier group, the Czesky or Bohemian Terrier was bred by a Czech fancier using British stock.

Still less than half a century old, the breed is well established in blue-grey or light brown versions.

The Czesky or Bohemian Terrier is a short-legged terrier, little known outside its native home of the Czech Republic. It was developed in the middle of this century by crossing the Scottish, Sealyham and possibly other terriers. The result is a tough, sturdy dog that will go to ground after quarry, and is an excellent ratter and guard.

Character and care

As well as being a fine working terrier, the Czesky's equable temperament also makes it a good children's companion. It requires plenty of exercise and expert clipping for the show ring, although pet owners could probably get away with the occasional visit to the grooming parlour and a good daily brushing.

KEY CHARACTERISTICS
● **CLASS** Terrier. **Recognized** FCI, KC(GB).
● **SIZE** Height at shoulders: 28–35.5cm (11–14in). Weight: 5.9–9kg (13–20lb).
● **COAT** Fine and silky, with tendency to curl.
● **COLOUR** Blue-grey or brown with light markings.
● **OTHER FEATURES** Long head; deep-set eyes; pendent ears; sturdy body; tail 17.5–20cm (7–8in) long, carried horizontally when terrier is excited.

KROMFOHRLÄNDER

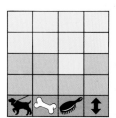

This is a hunting and gundog, and a companion dog, but little known outside its native Germany. It was developed by crossing a Griffon and a terrier. There are three varieties, the rough-coated being far and away the most popular. The others are the long-straight and medium-straight varieties.

It was developed after the Second World War, and was recognized by the German Kennel Club in 1953. Shortly afterwards it was recognized by the FCI.

Character and care

The Kromfohrländer is an intelligent and affectionate companion, and a good guard. It requires plenty of exercise and daily brushing.

KEY CHARACTERISTICS
● **CLASS** Terrier. **Recognized** FCI.
● **SIZE** Height: 38–45.5cm (15–18in). Weight: about 11.8kg (26lb).
● **COAT** Rough and wiry; medium-long and straight; long and straight.
● **COLOUR** White with light to dark brown markings on head and body; head may be brown with white star.
● **OTHER FEATURES** Flat, wedge-shaped skull, little stop; ears set high and U-shaped; tail set high and carried curled to left side of back.

AUSTRALIAN TERRIER

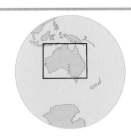

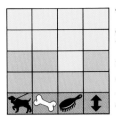

The Australian Terrier is often mistaken for a large Yorkshire Terrier. This is not surprising since it is considered to result from the mating of a Yorkshire Terrier bitch and a dog that resembled a Cairn Terrier. By the time the breed was first exhibited in 1899, it had been in existence for about 20 years and was reputed to be an unsurpassed vermin killer, which could also dispose of a snake.

When the Australian Terrier first arrived in England in 1906, it caused only a ripple of interest. However, it was recognized by the British Kennel Club in 1936 and experienced a boost in popularity when the Duke of Gloucester acquired a breed member following a tour of Australia. The breed was even slower making its mark in the United States, where it was not recognized until 1960.

Character and care

This breed is now proving a popular dog, both in the international show ring and as an alert, hardy and devoted family pet. The Australian needs only a good daily grooming with a bristle brush. Since it has a weather-resistant coat, it may be kennelled out of doors, though most owners do keep them indoors.

KEY CHARACTERISTICS
● **CLASS** Terrier. **Recognized** AKC, ANKC, CKC, FCI, KC(GB), KUSA.
● **SIZE** Height at withers: 25–27.5cm (10–11in). Weight: about 6.3kg (14lb).
● **COAT** Harsh, straight, dense and long, with short, soft undercoat.
● **COLOUR** (A) Blue, steel blue or dark grey-blue with rich tan (not sandy) on face, ears, under body, lower legs and around the vent (puppies excepted); top-knot blue or silver, of a lighter shade than leg colour. (B) Clear sandy or red; smuttiness or dark shadings undesirable; top-knot a lighter shade.
● **OTHER FEATURES** Long head with flat skull and powerful jaw; small eyes; small, erect, pointed ears; body long in proportion to height; tail set on high, customarily docked.

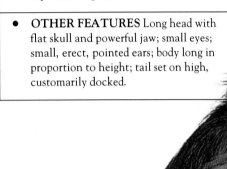

Brought over by settlers, terriers from Scotland and the north of England contributed to the Australian Terrier's make-up.

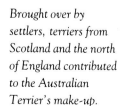

Toy Breeds

COTON DE TULEAR

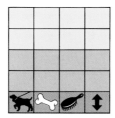

The Coton de Tulear is a member of the bichon family (see page 43). Its ancestors arrived in Madagascar and the nearby islands on trading ships prior to the 17th century, and from these imported dogs arose on Reunion Island, the Coton de Reunion. This dog is now extinct, but its descendants on Madagascar developed through a programme of cross-breeding, including introducing the Maltese. This has produced the breed now known as the Coton de Tulear after the city of Tulear in Madagascar.

The little Coton became known as the "dog of royalty" because it was a favourite of the French nobles who inhabited the islands during colonial times. Indeed, before the 20th century, it was a criminal offence for a commoner to own such a dog, and to this day it is usually only those in the upper strata of Malagasy society who are fortunate enough to own a Tulear. The breed is still comparatively rare although it is gradually becoming established in both Britain and America.

Character and care
The Coton de Tulear is a happy, friendly, intelligent little dog, which is devoted to its owners and likes to be with them. One of its most endearing qualities is its ability to walk on its hind legs. It can adapt to most climates and environments, and requires only daily brushing and average exercise.

KEY CHARACTERISTICS
• **CLASS** Toy. **Recognized** FCI, KC(GB).
• **SIZE** Height: 25.5–30.5cm (10–12in). Weight: 5.5–7kg (12–15lb).
• **COAT** Fluffy, like cotton.
• **COLOUR** White, with or without champagne markings; black and white.
• **OTHER FEATURES** Head carried high; eyes dark and deep-set; tail never docked, carried high and curled gracefully.

AFFENPINSCHER

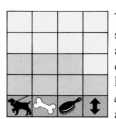

The Affenpinscher is the smallest of the pinschers and schnauzers. Its name comes from its monkey-like face (the German *affen* means "monkeys") and it is also known in its native country as the Zwergaffenpinscher or dwarf pinscher and in France, as the Diabletin Moustache ("the moustached little devil"). It greatly resembles the Griffon Bruxellois, but whether it was the Griffon that contributed to the Affenpinscher or vice versa is debatable. The Affenpinscher was recognized by the American Kennel Club as early as 1938. However, it has made its mark in Britain only within the past 15 years, and was exhibited for the first time at Crufts Dog Show, London, in 1980.

Character and care
This appealing, naturally scruffy-looking toy dog has a keen intelligence and is exceedingly affectionate. It makes a good watchdog and, terrier-like, is not averse to rabbiting. Its thick coat benefits from daily brushing.

KEY CHARACTERISTICS
• **CLASS** Toy. **Recognized** AKC, ANKC, CKC, FCI, KC(GB), KUSA.
• **SIZE** Height: 24–28cm (9½–11in). Weight: 3–4kg (6½–9lb).
• **COAT** Rough and thick.
• **COLOUR** Preferably black, but grey shading permissible.
• **OTHER FEATURES** Slightly undershot jaw; small, high-set ears, preferably erect, but neat drop-ear permissible; round, dark, sparkling eyes; short, straight back; high-set tail, docked in some countries.

BOLOGNESE

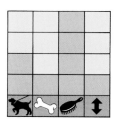

The Bolognese or Bichon Bolognese is a member of the bichon family, all of which are small white dogs from the Mediterranean area. It has been noted that the Bolognese's coat was white and black in the past, but black is now prohibited. The Italians claim that it originated in Bologna and it is recognized as an Italian breed. The Bolognese was a favourite with European royalty centuries ago but is now little seen outside Italy.

Character and care

This companion dog is serious, intelligent, not particularly vivacious, and seeks to please its owner. It requires only a moderate amount of exercise but needs fairly intricate trimming and scissoring for show purposes, and a good daily brush and comb when kept as a pet.

KEY CHARACTERISTICS
• **CLASS** Toy. **Recognized** FCI, KC(GB).
• **SIZE** Height at shoulders: dogs 28–30.5cm (11–12in), bitches 25.5–28cm (10–11in). Weight: 2.5–4.1kg (5½–9lb).
• **COAT** Long, flocked, standing off from body.
• **COLOUR** Pure white without shadings.
• **OTHER FEATURES** Eyes well open, round and large; long, hanging ears set on high; tail well feathered with long, flocked hair, set on at level of croup and carried curved over back.

MALTESE

Much painted and praised, the Maltese is one of the oldest lap dogs, popular with men and women.

In the Maltese a slightly rounded, broad skull is set off by long, silky, snow white fur.

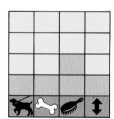

A member of the bichon family, this small, white dog is one of the oldest European breeds. It has existed on the island of Malta for centuries, and also found its way to China and the Philippines via Maltese traders. However, in about AD25, the Greek historian Strabo reported that "There is a town in Sicily called Melita whence are exported many beautiful dogs called Canis Melitei", raising the possibility of Italian origin for the breed.

The Maltese was a favourite in England from Tudor times, and in the reign of Queen Elizabeth I (1558–1603), the early dog historian, Doctor Johannes Caius, wrote, "They are called Meliti, of the Island of Malta . . . they are very small indeed and chiefly sought after for the pleasure and amusement of women who carried them in their arms, their bosoms, and their beds . . .".

The Maltese has been painted by many famous artists, notably Goya, Rubens and Sir Edwin Landseer. It was first exhibited in England in 1864, and a dog named "Leon" was shown in America in 1877 under the title Maltese Lion Dog.

Character and care

The long established Maltese seems to have been overtaken in popularity by other toys, and is now seldom seen outside the show ring. This is unfortunate because it is a happy, healthy, long-lived little dog, which is good with children and makes a lovable pet. It is fairly adaptable as far as exercise is concerned, but requires grooming every day with a bristle brush. Owners are advised to check with the breeder about show preparation.

KEY CHARACTERISTICS
• **CLASS** Toy. **Recognized** AKC, ANKC, CKC, FCI, KC(GB), KUSA.
• **SIZE** Height at withers: not exceeding 25.5cm (10in). Weight: 1.8–2.7kg (4–6lb) not exceeding 3.2kg (7lb).
• **COAT** Long, straight coat, silky texture.
• **COLOUR** White; slight lemon markings on ears permissible.
• **OTHER FEATURES** Slightly rounded, broad skull; well-defined stop; slightly tapered muzzle; long, well-feathered ears; oval eyes; compact body; long, plumed tail carried arched over back.

LÖWCHEN

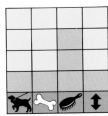

The Löwchen is also known as the Petit Chien Lion (Little Lion Dog) because it was traditionally given a lion clip, similar to that sported by the exhibition poodle. Complete with mane and tufted tail, the Löwchen does look like a lion in miniature.

This breed is a member of the bichon family, and is thought to have originated in the Mediterranean area. It is recognized as a French breed, but has been known in both France and Spain since the late 1500s. The Löwchen is widely believed to be the dog included by the Spanish artist, Francisco de Goya (1746–1828), in a painting of his friend, the Duchess of Alba.

Character and care

The Löwchen is an affectionate, intelligent dog, which is popular in the show ring but rarely seen walking in the park. It enjoys life as a pet given the chance, and is a lively animal, requiring daily brushing. If it is your intention to exhibit your Löwchen, expert advice on clipping should be sought.

KEY CHARACTERISTICS
• **CLASS** Toy. **Recognized** ANKC, FCI, KC(GB), KUSA.
• **SIZE** Height at withers: 25–33cm (10–13in). Weight: 3.6–8.2 kg (8–18 lb).
• **COAT** Moderately long and wavy.
• **COLOUR** Any colour or combination of colours permissible.
• **OTHER FEATURES** Wide, short skull; long pendent ears, well fringed; round, dark eyes with intelligent expression; short, strong body; medium length tail, clipped to resemble a plume.

Established in Spain, France and Germany since the 16th century, the Löwchen, or Little Lion Dog, featured in Goya's portrait of the Duchess of Alba.

BRUSSELS GRIFFON (AND PETIT BRABANCON)

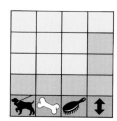

The Brussels Griffon, or Griffon Bruxellois, was first shown at the Brussels Exhibition of 1880. An early example of the breed is depicted in a painting of 1434 by Jan Van Eyck, the Flemish painter. Once kept by hansom cab drivers of 17th-century Brussels to rid their stables of vermin, the Brussels Griffon became a companion breed by virtue of its appealing character.

The smooth-coated Petit Brabançon probably owes its existence to the introduction of pug blood. Other breeds, including the Yorkshire and Irish Terriers, have undoubtedly contributed to the modern griffons. The rough-coated Brussels Griffon and smooth-haired Petit Brabançon are recognized as two distinct breeds in Europe. In America and Britain however, they are exhibited together.

Character and care

This intelligent, cheerful little dog, with its terrier-like disposition, make a fine companion. The Griffon has never suffered from the

The Brussels Griffon has a terrier-like disposition.

YORKSHIRE TERRIER

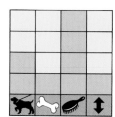

The popularity of the "Yorkie" is quite disproportionate to its small size.

The Yorkshire Terrier or Yorkie is a comparatively recent breed, having been developed in Yorkshire, England, within the last hundred years or so through the crossing of a Skye Terrier and the extinct Black and Tan Terrier, a forerunner of the Manchester Terrier. The Maltese and Dandie Dinmont may also have contributed to its make-up.

It was recognized by the Kennel Club in Britain in 1886. It was introduced into the USA in about 1880 but took some time to become established there. Today, this lively little terrier is one of the most popular toy breeds in the world.

The Yorkie may be seen in so many different sizes that people often think there are two varieties, miniature and standard. In fact, the Yorkshire Terrier should not exceed 3.1kg (7lb) in weight, placing it alongside the Chihuahua as one of the world's smallest dogs. There are, however, many larger specimens which are admirably happy and healthy and make good pets.

over-popularity of some breeds and is a good family choice. The coat of the rough requires a lot of attention, however the coats of pet dogs may be clipped.

KEY CHARACTERISTICS
• **CLASS** Toy. **Recognized** AKC, ANKC, CKC, FCI, KC(GB), KUSA.
• **SIZE** Height: 17.8–20.3cm (7–8in). Weight: 2.2–5kg (5–11lb), most desirable 2.7–4.5kg (6–10lb).
• **COAT** *Brussels Griffon* Harsh, wiry. *Petit Brabançon* Soft, smooth.
• **COLOUR** Red, black or black and rich tan with white markings. FCI classifies the black, black/tan or red/black as Belgian Griffon.
• **OTHER FEATURES** Head, large in comparison to body, rounded, in no way domed, wide between the ears; eyes, black rimmed, very dark; body, short back, level from withers to tail root, neither roaching nor dipping; tail, customarily docked short, carried high.

Character and care

The Yorkie is suited to town or country living and, like most small terriers, is utterly fearless. This bossy, inordinately affectionate and lively little dog makes a fine pet. It is also a first-class show dog for those with the time to spare for intricate grooming.

KEY CHARACTERISTICS
• **CLASS** Toy. **Recognized** AKC, ANKC, CKC, FCI, KC(GB), KUSA.
• **SIZE** Height: about 22cm (9in). Weight: not exceeding 3.1kg (7lb).
• **COAT** Glossy, fine and silky.
• **COLOUR** Dark steel blue (not silver blue) extending from back of head to root of tail, never mingled with fawn, bronze or dark hairs; face, chest and feet rich, bright tan.
• **OTHER FEATURES** Small head, flat on top; medium-sized, dark, sparkling eyes; small V-shaped ears carried erect; compact body; tail usually docked to medium length.

HAVANESE

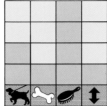

This breed is also known as the Bichon Havanese (Havanais) and as the Havana Silk Dog, because of its long, flowing coat which gives it a somewhat mystical look. It is a member of the bichon family, a group of toy dogs originating in the Mediterranean area and including the Bolognese, Maltese and Bichon Frise. Any of these might be the lesser-known Havanese's ancestor, but legend has it that it is descended from Bolognese dogs taken by some peasants from the Italian region of Emilia to Argentina. There the Bolognese were crossbred with a small poodle, thus creating a new type of bichon. Eventually this dog reached Cuba, where it became popular with the wealthy of Havana.

Character and care

The Havanese is intelligent, serious and calm rather than vivacious, inordinately affectionate and lives to please its owner. It does not require a great deal of exercise but does need considerable brushing and combing, without trimming or coiffing.

KEY CHARACTERISTICS
• **CLASS** Toy. **Recognized** FCI.
• **SIZE** Height: 20–26.5cm (10–10½in). Weight: 3.1–5.4kg (7–12lb).
• **COAT** Long, flat and soft; tufts towards extremities.
• **COLOUR** Beige, havana grey or white; solid or broad markings of these colours.
• **OTHER FEATURES** Black nose; rather pointed ears falling so that they assume a slight fold; quite large eyes, very dark, preferably black; tail carried high, curled, and covered with long, silky hair.

ENGLISH TOY TERRIER

The English Toy Terrier, developed by selective breeding from the smallest specimens of Manchester Terriers, retains many of the bigger dog's working attributes.

A long, narrow head and keenly pricked ears give alertness and dignity to a small dog.

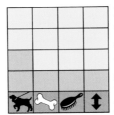

In the United Kingdom, the English Toy Terrier commenced life under that name, was subsequently called the Toy Black and Tan then the Miniature Black and Tan, and reverted to its present title in 1962. In the United States, the breed is known as the Toy Manchester Terrier.

The English Toy Terrier was bred from the Manchester Terrier. This larger but otherwise similar breed was developed from the now extinct rough-haired Black and Tan Terrier and other breeds. The Italian Greyhound and, possibly, the Whippet may also have contributed to the English Toy Terrier. The Manchester Terrier was bred to kill rats in a pit for public entertainment, and its smaller relative is an excellent ratter.

Character and care

Surprisingly rare outside the show ring today, the English Toy Terrier still retains the ability to hunt vermin and makes an affectionate and intelligent companion. It is good with children but tends to be a one-person dog. The English Toy is easy to care for, requiring little more than a daily brushing and a rub-down to give its coat a sheen. It is a reasonably tough little dog and does not have quite the same aversion to rain as its more fastidious Italian Greyhound relatives.

KEY CHARACTERISTICS
● **CLASS** Toy. **Recognized** AKC, ANKC, CKC, FCI, KC(GB), KUSA.
● **SIZE** Height at shoulders: 25–30cm (10–12in). Weight: 2.7–3.6kg (6–9lb).
● **COAT** Thick, close and glossy.
● **COLOUR** Black and tan.
● **OTHER FEATURES** Long, narrow head; dark to black eyes; ears candle flame shaped and slightly pointed at tips; compact body; tail thick at root and tapering to a point.

228

AUSTRALIAN SILKY TERRIER

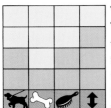

The Australian Silky Terrier, or Silky Terrier, was originally known as the Sydney Silky, and the progeny were registered under that name as recently as 1945. It owes its existence to the cross-breeding of Skye and Yorkshire terriers, and also of the Yorkshire and Australian terriers (the Australian having not only "Yorkie" but Dandie Dinmont, Cairn and Norwich terrier blood in its veins). The first breed standard was not published until 1962 although the breed was "accepted" in America three years earlier.

Character and care

The Australian Silky is a typical terrier in temperament. It is not averse to a spot of vermin hunting but offers its owners much affection. It needs good daily walks to work off its energy and regular brushing and combing – lots of attention to its coat is essential if it is to compete in the show ring.

KEY CHARACTERISTICS
● **CLASS** Toy. **Recognized** AKC, ANKC, CKC, FCI, KC(GB), KUSA.
● **SIZE** Average height: 22.8cm (9in). Weight 3.6–4.5kg (8–10lb).
● **COAT** Straight, fine, glossy.
● **COLOUR** Blue and tan, grey, blue and tan with silver-blue top-knot. Tips of hairs should be darker at roots.
● **OTHER FEATURES** Small, compactly built dog with body slightly longer than height; head medium length; eyes small, dark, round; ears small, V-shaped; tail customarily docked.

The Australian Silky Terrier probably traces its sheen back to the Dandie Dinmont, an early 19th century ancestor which contributed to the line.

Unlike that of the Yorkie (another ancestor), the Silky's coat stops short of the ground, leaving the paws visible.

Originally from China, the Pug is a Mastiff in miniature – sturdy despite its small size.

PUG

comparatively rare in Britain. It was not until 1883 that the breed was standardized and the British Pug Dog Club was formed.

Character and care

This happy intelligent little dog is good with children, and requires only modest exercise, but the Pug should not be exercised in very hot weather. Daily grooming with a brush and a rub-down with a silk handkerchief will make its coat shine.

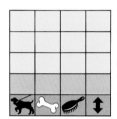

It is likely that the Pug originated in China, and it may be a greatly scaled-down relative of the Tibetan Mastiff. By the 1500s, it had been taken on trading ships to Holland, where it became popular with the royal family of the time, the House of Orange, and is often referred to as the Dutch Pug.

The breed is generally believed to have been introduced into Britain in 1688 by William, Prince of Orange, who became William III of Britain. During William and Mary's reign (1689–94) the Pug is said to have enjoyed unrivalled status. However, by the 1800s when Queen Victoria was building up her kennel, the breed had become

KEY CHARACTERISTICS
• **CLASS** Toy. **Recognized** AKC, ANKC, CKC, FCI, KC(GB), KUSA.
• **SIZE** Height: 25–27.5cm (10–12in). Weight: 6.3–8.1kg (14–18lb).
• **COAT** Fine, smooth, short and glossy.
• **COLOUR** Silver, apricot, fawn or black; black mask and ears and black trace along back.
• **OTHER FEATURES** Ears either "Rose ear" – a small drop ear that folds over and then back – or "Button ear" – the ear flap folds forward with the tip lying close to the head; very large, dark eyes; short, thick-set body; tail set high and tightly curled over the back.

POMERANIAN

This small dog is a member of the spitz family and, like other spitz, originated in the Arctic Circle. The Pomeranian derives from white spitz that existed in Pomerania, northern Germany, from about 1700. They were much larger dogs, weighing about 13.5kg (30lb), and were bred down after being imported into Britain about 100 years ago. By 1896, show classes for the Pomeranian were divided by weight, over and under 3.6kg (8lb). Then in 1915, the British Kennel Club withdrew challenge certificates for the larger variety. The American Pomeranian Club was formed in New York in 1900.

Queen Victoria was much taken with the breed and had a number of the larger variety

in her kennels. This helped to make the breed very popular in Britain, but it was subsequently overtaken there by the Pekingese and today the Pomeranian is not very often seen outside show circles.

Character and care

The Pomeranian seems to have gained the reputation of being an old lady's lap-dog. While it is certainly ideal for that role, adoring lots of attention, it is also a lively, robust little dog which would walk its owners off their feet, if given the chance. This affectionate and faithful dog is good with children and makes a delightful pet. It is also a fine show dog for those with plenty of time on their hands to care for its double coat, which must be groomed with a stiff brush every day and regularly trimmed.

PAPILLON

Britain as "foreign" dogs in 1923, and had to wait another 12 years for official recognition in the United States.

Character and care

The Papillon is intelligent, usually healthy, and has proved an able contender in obedience competitions. It is fairly easy to look after, needing only a daily brushing to keep the coat shining.

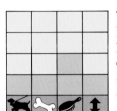

The Papillon is also known as the Épagneul Nain Continental or Continental Toy Spaniel. The name Papillon, which is French for butterfly, comes from the breed's erect ears. An identical drop-eared variety is known as the Phalène or "moth".

The Papillon has often been mistaken for the Long-coated Chihuahua, a variety it helped to produce. In fact, this toy spaniel originated in Spain and is said to be a descendant of the 16th century Dwarf Spaniel. It has been included in paintings by Rubens (1577–1640) and Van Dyke (1599–1641). Papillons were first exhibited in

KEY CHARACTERISTICS
• **CLASS** Toy. **Recognized** AKC, ANKC, CKC, FCI, KC(GB), KUSA.
• **SIZE** Height at withers: 20–28cm (8–11in).
• **COAT** Long, abundant, flowing and silky in texture.
• **COLOUR** White with patches of any colour except liver, tricolours – black and white with tan in spots over eyes and inside ears, on cheeks, and under root of tail.
• **OTHER FEATURES** Head slightly rounded; large, erect ears carried obliquely like spread butterfly wings; fairly long body with level top-line; long, well-fringed tail.

The ears which give the Papillon its name – the word means "butterfly" in French – are balanced at the other end by a gaily plumed tail.

KEY CHARACTERISTICS
• **CLASS** Toy. **Recognized** AKC, ANKC, CKC, KC(GB), KUSA.
• **SIZE** Height: not exceeding 27.5cm (11in). Weight: dogs 1.3–3.1kg (3–7lb).
• **COAT** Long, straight and harsh, with a soft fluffy undercoat.
• **COLOUR** All colours permissible, but free from black or white shadings; whole colours are white, black, brown, light or dark blue.
• **OTHER FEATURES** Head and nose soft in outline; medium-sized eyes; small, erect ears set not too low down or too wide apart; short back and compact body; tail set high, turns over back and is carried flat and straight.

PEKINGESE

By the early 19th century, Pekingese were so prized by the Chinese Imperial court that no commoner was allowed to own one.

Miniature dogs of the Pekingese type have been known in China since the T'ang dynasty of the 8th century.

The origins of the Pekingese may trace back some 1500 years. Believed to be a close relative of the Lhasa Apso and Shih Tzu, they were said to combine the nobility of the lion with the grace and sweetness of the marmoset. Favoured by the 19th-century Chinese Imperial court, they were kept in their thousands in extraordinarily privileged circumstances. The Pekingese first arrived in Europe, and subsequently the United States, when British Army officers raided the Summer Palace in Peking following the Boxer Rebellion of 1860. Five Imperial Pekingese looted from the women's apartments were brought back to England. One of these dogs, appropriately christened "Looty", was presented to Queen Victoria. It lived until 1872.

Character and care

The Pekingese is a thickset, dignified little dog with a mind of its own and is good with adults and children. Intelligent and fearless, it does not mind walking across a muddy field but its ideal role is that of a pampered, sole companion. It requires considerable brushing and combing.

KEY CHARACTERISTICS
• **CLASS** Toy. **Recognized** AKC, ANKC, CKC, FCI, KC(GB), KUSA.
• **SIZE** Weight: dogs, not exceeding 5kg (11lb); bitches not exceeding 5.4kg (12lb).
• **COAT** Long and straight, double-coated with coarse top coat, thick undercoat; profuse mane and feathered tail.
• **COLOUR** All colours and marking are permissible and of equal merit, except albino or liver. Particolours should be evenly broken.
• **OTHER FEATURES** Wide, flat head with shortened muzzle and deep stop; flat face; prominent round eyes; feathered ears carried close to head; thick chest and neck, short body with slightly rolling gait; tail set high and curving over back.

JAPANESE CHIN

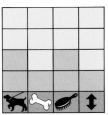

The Japanese Chin probably shares a common ancestor with the Pekingese and the Pug.

There are two theories on the origin of the Japanese Chin or Japanese Spaniel. One is that it derives from Pekingese-like dogs brought to Japan by Zen Buddhist monks in the AD500s, and the other that it descends from a lap-dog sent as a present in AD732 to the Emperor of Japan from Korea. It is not dissimilar to the Pekingese, but is longer in the leg and lighter. Whatever its ancestry, for more than 1000 years this little dog was a favourite of Japanese emperors who decreed that it should be worshipped. It is said that smaller Chins were sometimes kept in hanging cages like pet birds.

Two Japanese Chins were presented to the British Queen Victoria by Commodore Perry, an American naval commander, on his return from the Far East in 1853. The breed first made an appearance in the British show ring in 1862 and, some 20 years later, started being exhibited in the United States.

Character and care
Bearing some resemblance to the King Charles Spaniel, the Chin is a popular show dog but less often kept as a pet. This is attractive and hardy little dog that is good with children. It requires an average amount of exercise and little grooming, except for a daily going over with a pure-bristle brush. Like other flat-nosed breeds, it must not be over-exerted in hot weather lest it should suffer breathing difficulties.

KEY CHARACTERISTICS
● **CLASS** Toy. **Recognized** AKC, ANKC, CKC, FCI, KC(GB), KUSA.
● **SIZE** Weight (ideal): 1.8–3.2kg (4–7lb).
● **COAT** Profuse coat; long, soft and straight.
● **COLOUR** White and black or white and red and white (all shades, including sable, lemon and orange); never tricolour.
● **OTHER FEATURES** Large round head in proportion to size of dog; short muzzle; small ears, set wide apart; large dark eyes square, compact body; well-feathered tail set high and curling over back.

Also once revered by the nobility, the Chin is longer in the leg than the Pekingese, and lighter in colour.

KING CHARLES SPANIEL

This toy breed owes its name to the affection King Charles II developed for its ancestors.

Smaller than the Cavalier, the King Charles has a distinctly domed head and deep stop.

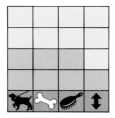

In the United States and Canada, this popular breed is known as the English Toy Spaniel and the name "King Charles" is given to the Black and Tan variety only.

Although the King Charles Spaniel is generally thought of as a British breed, its history traces back to Japan in 2000BC. The slightly larger Cavalier King Charles Spaniel (see page 229), which has the same origin, became very popular at court in 16th century England. Then the fashion came about for short-nosed dogs, and the King Charles Spaniel emerged. It is said that King Charles II (1630–85) was so devoted to these little spaniels that he would frequently interrupt affairs of state in order to fondle and play with them, and there is a law in England, yet to be rescinded, that enables a King Charles Spaniel "to go anywhere".

Character and care

This little spaniel makes a delightful pet, being good with children, full of fun, and able to adapt its exercise requirements to its owner's capabilities. The King Charles should be brushed every day with a bristled brush, and it is advisable to keep the area around its eyes clean with eye wipes.

KEY CHARACTERISTICS
• **CLASS** Toy. **Recognized** AKC, ANKC, CKC, FCI, KC(GB), KUSA.
• **SIZE** Height: about 25cm (10in). Weight: 3.6–6.3kg (8–14lb).
• **COAT** Long, silky, straight coat. Slight waviness permissible.
• **COLOUR** Black and Tan – raven black with bright tan markings above eyes, on cheeks, inside ears, on chest and legs and underside of tail, white marks undesirable. Ruby – solid rich red, white markings undesirable. Blenheim – rich chestnut markings, well broken up, on pearly white ground; markings evenly divided on head, leaving room for lozenge spot between ears. Tricolour – black and white, well spaced and broken up with tan markings over eyes, cheeks, inside ears, inside legs, on underside of tail.
• **OTHER FEATURES** Large domed skull, full over eyes; deep, well defined stop; low-set ears, long and well feathered; wide, deep chest; well feathered tail, carried above level of back (docked in the US).

CAVALIER KING CHARLES SPANIEL

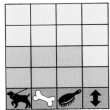

The Cavalier King Charles Spaniel originated in Japan, and there is a resemblance between it and the Japanese Chin or Spaniel. The Cavalier is very similar to the King Charles Spaniel (see page 228), but while the King Charles has an apple domed head, the slightly larger Cavalier is almost flat between the ears and its stop is shallower. Both breeds were named after Charles II (1630–85) and the Cavalier was the original favourite. It was doubtless this breed the famous diarist, Samuel Pepys (1633–1703), was referring to when he complained that King Charles II devoted more time to his dogs than he did to affairs of state.

Today, the Cavalier is one of the most popular pet dogs in Britain and America (although it is not recognized as a separate breed in the United States).

Character and care

This breed is an admirable choice of family pet, being good natured and fond of children. While it is allocated to the toy group, it is among the largest of the toys and enjoys a fair amount of exercise. It should be groomed every day with a bristle brush.

KEY CHARACTERISTICS
● **CLASS** Toy. **Recognized** ANKC, CKC, FCI, KC(GB), KUSA.
● **SIZE** Weight: 5.5–8kg (12–18lb).
● **COAT** Long and silky, free from curl.
● **COLOUR** Black and Tan – black with bright tan marks above eyes, head, chest, legs, underside of tail; white marks undesirable. Ruby – rich red, white markings undesirable. Blenheim – chestnut markings, well broken up, on white ground; markings evenly divided on head, lozenge between ears. Tricolour – black and white, well spaced and broken up, with tan markings over head, inside legs, on underside of tail.
● **OTHER FEATURES** Flattish skull; long ears, set high; large, dark eyes; short-coupled body; long, well feathered tail.

A well tapered muzzle, flat head and shallow stop distinguish this breed from the King Charles Spaniel.

Also a favourite of Charles II, the Cavalier has a fairly flat skull with high ears. The body is long, with a feathered tail.

CHIHUAHUA

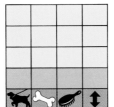

The Chihuahua, the smallest dog in the world, is named after the state of Chihuahua in Mexico and is believed by some to have been a sacred dog of the Aztecs. However, a dog not unlike the Chihuahua may well have existed in Egypt some 3000 years ago. In 1910, a zoologist, K. Haddon, described the mummified remains of a little dog in an Egyptian tomb which had the soft spot in the skull, common in the breed. Chihuahuas have been known in Malta for many centuries, having arrived there from North Africa around 600BC, and a Botticelli fresco (*c.* 1482) in the Sistine Chapel in Rome includes the likeness of a pet that is clearly a Chihuahua. Such early Chihuahuas were slightly larger and had bigger ears than modern ones, which may be the result of a cross with the hairless Chinese Crested Dog.

Character and care
There are two varieties of Chihuahua, the Smooth-coated and Long-coated, the latter having long hair of soft texture, which is either flat or slightly wavy. At one time, it was normal for Long-coated and Smooth-coated to interbreed and both varieties would appear in the same litter, but such interbreeding is no longer permitted. The first Chihuahua to be registered in the United States was "Midget" in 1904, and the breed went on to become enormously popular there. In Britain a Chihuahua was still a comparatively rare sight in the 1950s, but now it draws large entries in show classes.

The Chihuahua is an exceedingly intelligent dog, that is affectionate, possessive, and makes a good watchdog in miniature. Despite being generally thought of as a lap dog, it can walk as far as most owners would wish. Care must be taken on outings that it does not start a fight because it seems to imagine that it is

Although the Chihuahua, the world's smallest dog, is named after the Mexican state, its origins remain uncertain; dogs of this type were known in Egypt 3000 years ago.

At one time the two varieties of Chihuahua – Long-coated and Smooth-coated – were allowed to interbreed, but this is no longer acceptable.

enormous when confronted with other canines. The breed is inexpensive to keep, and both long-haireds and short-haireds are fairly easy to groom, requiring only daily combing and brushing with a soft brush.

KEY CHARACTERISTICS
• **CLASS** Toy. **Recognized** AKC, ANKC, CKC, FCI, KC(GB), KUSA.
• **SIZE** Height: 16–20cm (6.3–7.9in). Weight: up to 2.7kg (6lb)
• **COAT** Long coat: long and soft to touch, slight waviness permissible; smooth coat: short and dense, soft to touch.
• **COLOUR** Any colour or mixture.
• **OTHER FEATURES** Apple-domed head; large flaring ears; large, round eyes that do not protrude; level back; medium length, high set tail, curved over back.

ITALIAN GREYHOUND

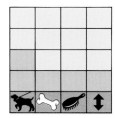

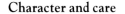

The Italian Greyhound may have been the first breed to have been developed exclusively as a companion or pet.

There is little doubt that the Italian Greyhound (or Piccolo Levriero Italiano) is a descendant of the Greyhound, but there appears to be no record of how and when it was reduced in size. The Greyhound is one of the most ancient breeds in the world, depicted in paintings on the tombs of the Egyptian pharaohs, and there are drawings of smaller Greyhounds dating back to Egyptian and Roman times.

The Italian Greyhound Club has existed in Britain since 1900. At the end of the Second World War, fresh blood was introduced from North America and the Continent, and there are now many excellent examples in the show ring in Europe, USA and Canada.

Character and care

The Italian Greyhound is a delightful and affectionate housepet, which is easy to train, rarely moults and is odourless. Indeed, it was recently publicized as the ideal pet, a statement which caused considerable concern among breeders, who feared that breed members might fall into unsuitable hands. Such concern is justified because this dainty little dog is very sensitive. It feels the cold, can be wounded by harsh words, and its legs are all too easily broken. The breed enjoys a fair amount of exercise, but must have a warm coat in wintry conditions. It is easy to groom, a rub-down with a silk handkerchief making its coat shine.

KEY CHARACTERISTICS
● **CLASS** Toy. **Recognized** AKC, ANKC, CKC, FCI, KC(GB), KUSA.
● **SIZE** Height at withers: 32–38cm (12½–15in). Weight: 2.5–4.5kg (5½–10lb).
● **COAT** Short, fine and glossy.
● **COLOUR** Solid black, blue, cream, fawn, red or white, or any of these colours broken with white; white broken with one of above colours; black or blue with tan markings, or brindle, not acceptable.
● **OTHER FEATURES** Long, flat and narrow skull; slight stop; rose-shaped ears, set well back; large, expressive eyes; hare feet; low-set long tail, carried low.

The Italian Greyhound appears to be delicate, but it enjoys chasing small prey and can leap nimbly to catch a bird in flight. The elegant, finely chiselled head and muzzle of the Italian Greyhound make it an appealing dog to show.

MINIATURE PINSCHER

The Miniature Pinscher is a compact, well-proportioned toy dog, whose self-confidence belies its size.

The broad chest and muscular legs enable the feet to be lifted high in the characteristic hackney gait.

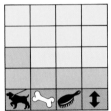

The Miniature Pinscher, or Min Pin as it is commonly called, is known in its native Germany as the Zwergpinscher. It is not, as many believe, a small Doberman, having existed for many centuries. Its ancestor is the German Pinscher to which Italian Greyhound and, it is thought, Dachshund blood was added. A painting, *The Peasant Family*, dated 1640 and currently in the Louvre, Paris, includes the likeness of a dog similar to the Miniature Pinscher.

The breed was officially recognized in Germany in 1870 and has achieved great popularity in a number of European countries. The Miniature Pinscher Club of America was formed in 1929, and the breed still has a much larger following there than in Britain.

Character and care

The Min Pin has an attractive hackney (high-stepping) gait. It makes an ideal pet for town or country, being affectionate and intelligent, and rarely moulting. The breed enjoys obedience work and exercise, often following a scent. It is easy to groom, requiring little more than a daily brush and a rub-down with a silk handkerchief or piece of chamois leather to make its coat shine.

KEY CHARACTERISTICS
• **CLASS** Toy. **Recognized** AKC, ANKC, CKC, FCI, KC(GB), KUSA.
• **SIZE** Height at withers: 25.5–30cm (10–12in). Weight: 4.5kg (10lb).
• **COAT** Hard, smooth, short coat.
• **COLOUR** Black, blue or chocolate, with sharply defined tan markings on cheeks, lips, lower jaw, throat, twin spots above eyes and cheeks, lower half of forelegs, inside of hind legs and vent region, lower portion of nodes and feet.
• **OTHER FEATURES** Tapering narrow skull; small, erect or dropped ears set on high; bright dark eyes; compact, square body; tail set high, level with topline, often docked.

MEXICAN HAIRLESS DOG

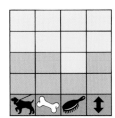

The Mexican Hairless Dog or Xoloitzcuintli is one of the oldest breeds in the world. It was brought to Mexico from north-east Asia by nomadic ancestors of the Aztecs, but possibly originated as far away as Turkey, where there is another naked breed, the Turkish Greyhound. Earlier inhabitants of Mexico, the Toltecs, kept the Chihuahua in their temples for religious purposes. Once the Aztecs had conquered the Toltecs, the Chihuahua and Mexican Hairless lived in the temples side by side and their interbreeding may have produced the Chinese Crested Dog (see right). The Mexican Hairless was also highly valued as a hot-water bottle, having a higher than average body temperature of 38.6°C (101.5°F). It is in danger of extinction, although there are a few breeders in North America. It is recognized by the Mexican Kennel Club and the Canadian Kennel Club but not by those in the USA.

Character and care

This most loving, intelligent dog has a good temperament, and requires only a moderate amount of exercise. Being virtually naked, it needs regular bathing and massaging with baby cream to keep its skin soft and supple. It is a natural vegetarian, but easily converts to a meat diet.

Note: This breed must be protected against sunburn.

KEY CHARACTERISTICS
• **CLASS** Toy. **Recognized** CKC, FCI.
• **SIZE** Height: about 40.5–51cm (16–20in), but may be smaller.
• **COAT** May have tuft of hair on head, tip of tail and between toes, otherwise smooth skin.
• **COLOUR** Skin may be a variety of colours, solid or mottled.
• **OTHER FEATURES** Absence of premolar teeth; sweats through skin; long, tapering tail; hare feet, prehensile leading to endearing habit of gripping owner and objects with its feet.

CHINESE CRESTED DOG

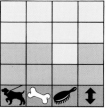

The almost hairless Chinese Crested is said to have originated in China and been taken to South America in Chinese sailing ships many centuries ago. However, there have been hairless dogs in many countries of the world, including Africa and Turkey, and some think the Chinese Crested may be the result of the mating of a Mexican Hairless Dog (Xoloitzcuintli) with the Chihuahua. Certainly the mating of a Chinese Crested with a Chihuahua can produce a completely hairless dog.

Until 1966, an elderly lady in the United States owned the only remaining examples of the Chinese Crested Dog in the world. Four of these were introduced into the United Kingdom and the breed is now thriving in both countries. In Britain it attracts large show entries and received championship show status in the 1970s.

The Chinese Crested has no coat except for a flowing crest or mane, and hair on its feet and gaily carried, plumed tail. However, in almost every litter, there are some haired pups which grow into luxuriantly coated

For show purposes, the hair on the Chinese Crested may be long or short, but a full crest on the head and a full plume on the tail are preferred.

The Powder Puff Chinese Crested Dog takes its name from the silky double coat, which makes its ears drop forward.

adults resembling little sheepdogs. These are known as Powder Puffs and have won the right to be exhibited in the show ring alongside their hairless siblings.

Character and care

This affectionate little dog makes an excellent pet for those who appreciate its loving nature and are not put off by its exuberance. It is frequently hyperactive, playing tirelessly and leaping about in circles in anticipation of the tiniest crumb of food. The Chinese Crested adores food, its body feeling hotter to the touch after it has eaten, and rations should be increased in the winter months. Its paws will grip in an endearing, almost human fashion. Ideally, it should be bathed about every three weeks and have its skin massaged with cream. Whiskers, and any straggly odd hairs, should be removed for the show ring.

This breed can adjust to warm or cold climates but should *never* be kennelled out of doors and must be protected against sunburn.

KEY CHARACTERISTICS
● **CLASS** Toy. **Recognized** AKC, ANKC, CKC, FCI, KC(GB), KUSA.
● **SIZE** Height: dogs 28–33cm (11–13in), bitches 23–30.5cm (9–12in). Weight: not exceeding 5.5kg (12lb).
● **COAT** *Chinese Crested Hairless* Tuft of long, soft hair only on head, feet and tail. *Chinese Crested Powder Puff* Double, long, straight outer coat, soft silky undercoat.
● **COLOUR** Any colour or combination.
● **OTHER FEATURES** Slightly rounded head and skull; low-set erect ears; dark eyes; body may be racy and fine-boned (deer type) or heavier (cobby type); slender tapering tail set high and carried forward over the back in motion.

RARE BREEDS

NON-SPORTING

The **MAJORCAN BULLDOG** is also called the Perro de Presa Mallorquin. This bulldog comes from the island of Majorca in the Spanish Balearic Isles. With the same massive head, "rose" ears and wide chest, it is an obvious relative of the English Bulldog but has a longer neck and its tail is longer and slightly curved. Its colour is brindle with white markings, the less white the better. Like its English counterpart, it was developed for bull-baiting and dog fighting, and became relatively rare when the popularity of these "sports" diminished.

This powerful, courageous dog makes a splendid guard. Like most bulldogs, it is good natured, requires only a daily brushing with a bristle brush, and the minimum of exercise, and is, alas, generally short lived.

WORKING

BROHOLMER, which derives from a Mastiff imported from England, was a favourite of the Danish court from the 16th century. The breed was standardized in 1886 by Count Niels Frederik Sehested of Broholm-Funen, and, as well as being regarded as the national breed, it became a popular working and cattle-droving dog. However, its popularity waned after the First World War and it was feared extinct. A nationwide search was launched in 1974, and, on some isolated farms in the north of the country Broholmers were found which conformed to the standard. The breed was approved by the FCI in 1982 and it can now be shown internationally.

DOGO ARGENTINO or Argentinian Mastiff is used in its native land for hunting puma and other big game, and as a guard. It is a large dog, with a broad skull, deep chest, and loose skin around the neck, characteristic of fighting dogs. It is all white, with a short, smooth coat.

This powerful, loyal, courageous dog is claimed by owners to be trustworthy. However, it is on the British list of potentially dangerous dogs, and requires space, liberal exercise and very knowledgeable handling.

ITALIAN SPITZ is also known as the Volpino Italiano, the Cane de Guirinale and in Tuscany, where it is particularly prevalent, as the Florence Spitz. The Italian Spitz is so similar in appearance to the German Spitz and the Pomeranian that few people other than breed experts can tell them apart. However, the Italian Spitz's eyes are slightly bigger, its ears longer and its skull rounder. It is not known whether the Italian Spitz is a descendant or ancestor of the German Spitz but it has certainly been established in its native land for centuries. It was once a very popular companion dog in Italy, but its numbers have now dwindled.

This loyal, small dog is affectionate towards its owners but somewhat suspicious of strangers and so makes a good watchdog. It is apt to bark a lot, if unchecked. It does not need a great deal of exercise, but its coat requires regular brushing.

KARELIAN BEAR DOG or Karelsk Bjornhund is a member of the spitz family, closely related to the Russian Laika. It is named after the area of Karelia in Russia near the Finnish border. However, its development was mainly carried out in Finland in the 1930s, and it was recognized by that country's Kennel Club in 1935, and by the FCI in 1946. It is a medium-sized breed, and its colouring is black and white. Its tail curls over the back in the characteristic style of the spitz and it has a harsh upper coat and a softer, dense undercoat. It was bred to hunt bear, elk and other large game, and is said to have a flair for locating its quarry and to display great courage when confronting it. It also has a somewhat sullen, quarrelsome nature, preferring its own company and that of its master to canine companions, and so usually hunts singly. This may explain why it is not as popular outside its homeland as other Finnish breeds.

A powerful and temperamental hunter, the Karelian Bear Dog is good at the job for which it was bred, loyal to its master and a fine guard. It can be aggressive towards other dogs, needs firm control and is not suitable as a pet. The breed is generally housed outdoors. It needs considerable exercise and daily brushing. The coat is black and white.

LAIKAS A number of breeds of Laika are recognized in Russia, including the Russian-European, the West Siberian and the Karelian. All are members of the spitz family and are barkers (the name means barking dog). They are used against large and small game and will bark after cornering the quarry to allow the approach of hunters with their guns.

The Laikas may also be kept for purposes other than hunting. The Russian-European Laika, closely related to the Karelian Bear Dog, is probably best known in the West as the dog which was shot into space in Sputnik 2 in 1957. This breed and the West Siberian Laika are both medium-sized dogs and are sometimes used as farm dogs and guards. All three have rough, thick coats, and curled tails. The smaller Karelian Laika, which is found near the Finnish border and resembles the Finnish Spitz, may be used for sledge hauling and herding cattle.

These lively, energetic spitz dogs have a good temperament and may fill a variety of roles, including that of housepet and guard. They need plenty of exercise and food and regular grooming with a brush.

LUNDEHUND is also known as the Norwegian Puffin Dog or Puffin Hound (*lund* is Norwegian for puffin). It is a spitz variety, deriving from the Miniature Elkhound, and has existed for centuries on two islands off the coast of northern Norway. There, its flexible body allowed it to explore the nooks and crevices in the rock where puffins nest. In the past, the dog's task was to retrieve puffins' eggs and the birds themselves, which were eaten by the islanders. The breed has been recognized in Scandinavia since 1943 but is little known outside its native land and few, if any, specimens have been exported. It is a smallish dog with a

The Lundehund is a specialized hunter which can climb steep sea cliffs and reach into narrow crevices to find hidden puffins' nests.

rough, dense coat, and its colour is black, grey or various shades of brown with white. It has five (rather than the usual four) functional toes on each foot. The cartilage in the upper parts of its ears can meet and shut when the ears are partly raised, which may prevent water entering and damaging the ear.

The alert, active Lundehund is a good hunter and is also said to make a faithful companion. It needs daily brushing and plenty of exercise.

PORTUGUESE WATCHDOG is also known as the Cão de Castro Laboreiro. This breed originated in the mountains in the north of Portugal. It is a mastiff-type dog which served as a protector of livestock, even doing battle with wolves. It is now also used as a watchdog and in police work. It is wolf grey, dark fawn or brindle in colour, and has a short, rough coat.

The Portuguese Watchdog is faithful, agile, hardy, intelligent, and makes a splendid guard. It needs considerable exercise but minimal grooming, and does best when given a job to do.

SLOVAKIAN KUVASZ has worked for centuries as a flock guard in the Carpathian mountains in eastern Slovakia, but it is now relatively rare. It is rather similar to the Hungarian Kuvasz (see page 59) and to the ancient **Polish herding breed,** the Polish sheepdog or Owczarek Podhalanski, both of which also occur in the vast Carpathian range which includes the Tatra mountains. Indeed, although their respective countries consider them separate breeds, the three may, in fact, be varieties of the same breed. The Polish and Slovakian types are sometimes called "Tatry" dogs after the mountain range that stretches between both countries.

The Slovakian Kuvasz is quite tall, white or ivory white in colour, and has a straight or wavy medium coarse coat with a fine undercoat. It has a distinctive, perfectly proportioned head, a mane extending to and covering its chest, and a low-set tail.

The Slovakian Kuvasz is a loyal, efficient guard and tends to be kept for that purpose rather than as a domestic pet. It is lively, alert and known to have extremely acute hearing. It needs plenty of exercise and a daily brushing to keep it in good condition.

SWEDISH GREY DOG or Grähund is a medium-sized dog of the spitz type, fox-like in appearance and extremely energetic, with its tail

curled characteristically over its back. It has a moderately long top coat and soft undercoat and occurs in all shades of grey. Like all the spitz breeds, it doubtless originated in the Arctic Circle. The Swedish Grey Dog has been used in its native land for hunting elk, and in America against raccoon and lynx.

This good-natured, lively, confident dog ideally combines the roles of hunter and family pet, provided that it receives a good daily brushing and plenty of exercise. It will not be comfortable in an over-heated house and is usually happiest when kept in an outside kennel.

HERDING

ARMANT This rare breed, also called the Ermenti or Egyptian Sheepdog, is believed to descend from local dogs crossed with French dogs that accompanied Napoleon's army during his Egyptian campaign of 1798. The resultant dog resembles a small collie with a long, rough grey coat, evident moustache and snipey muzzle. Named after the village of Armant (Ermenti), in northern Egypt, it has been used as a herding dog and also as a guard. The Armant is suspicious of strangers and makes an excellent guard but would probably not be suitable as a household pet. It needs regular brushing and exercise.

The breed received some prominence prior to the Second World War when an Armant was brought to Berlin by the Egyptian ambassador. The breed is rarely seen outside Egypt and has yet to appear in the international show ring.

ATLAS DOG Also known as the Aidi or Chien de l'Atlas, this collie-type herding dog is a Moroccan breed about which very little is known. It is prized in its native land as a flock guard protecting against predators, and also works as a drover and watchdog. It has considerable strength and mobility, and a long, thick coat which is said to give it protection against intense heat and cold, and against attackers. The

Atlas Dog is a sensitive, lively, muscular guard which is unlikely to be kept in the home.

BERGER DE BRESSE and **BERGER DE SAVOIE** are robust, reliable, medium-sized working sheepdogs with fairly long bodies and tails curled at the tip. They are light or dark grey, with darker hairs, or are patched blue or brown. Their coat is thick, coarse and short on the head, longer on the body and tail. They have a ruff around the neck. They are named after the regions of eastern France in which they were developed, Bresse being a fertile area east of the Saône River and Savoie lying in the northern Alps.

Like all French sheepdogs, these Bergers are good companions and guards as well as being hardy, reliable workers. There is no reason why they cannot be kept as housepets provided that they are given sufficient exercise and are adequately groomed, but they do benefit from having a task to perform.

BERGER DU LANGUEDOC This entry should really be headed Bergers du Languedoc because, although usually grouped under one name, there are five types of sheepdog from the southern French province of Languedoc. They are also known as the Farou, Berger de la Camargue, Berger de la Grau, Berger des Carrigues and Berger du Larzac. All are small to medium-sized working sheepdogs with a variety of coats. They are fawn or black and fawn.

The Languedoc sheepdogs are strong, hardy, reliable, generally good tempered, and easy to train. They may be kept as companions provided they are given adequate exercise and are not kept in confined quarters. They need regular brushing.

BLUE LACY Little known outside the American South, the Blue Lacy is thought to be the descendant of wild pariah dogs crossed with herding and droving dogs. It is used for herding and driving sheep and cattle, and will also guard most types of farm stock. It is black and tan, tan, yellow, cream and gun-metal grey, its coat carrying the much sought

after "blue" gene. Colours are usually solid, but may be bicolour or tricolour.

This dog is a natural herder, easy to train and makes a tireless worker. Since it is also reliable and has a good temperament, there is no reason why it cannot be kept in the home provided that it is given a job of work to do. It needs regular exercise and grooming.

CATALONIAN SHEPHERD Also known as the Catalan Sheepdog, Perro de Pastor Catalan or Gos d'Atura, this breed is native to the province of Catalonia in Southern Spain. It is probably a descendant of a number of European herding dogs, particularly those of the Pyrenees area. There are two varieties of this sheepdog, differing only in coat: the Gos d'Atura, which has a long slightly wavy coat, and the rarer d'Atura Cerdà, which has a short smooth coat. Its legs and paws are fawn to tan while the rest of its body is black and white. Tan, grey and white marks are not allowed.

The Catalonian Shepherd is popular in its native land, where it is an able herder and inspires confidence in the animals it moves. It has also proved to be a fine army, police and guard, and a stalwart companion.

This intelligent sheepdog of gentle expression is said by some to have a nervous temperament. It makes a good companion and can be kept in

the house, but does best when given a job to do and wide, open spaces. It should have plenty of exercise and needs daily brushing.

CHARPLANINATZ (or Šar Planina), the Yugoslavian Sheepdog, is an ancient breed particularly widespread in the mountainous areas of the Adriatic. It is thought to descend from the dogs which migrated westwards with shepherds in ancient times and then interbred and changed as they adapted to the requirements of work and climate. It may also have links with the ancient Roman Molossus.

The Charplaninatz is sometimes used as a herder or drover, but is kept mainly as a flock guard. It was imported into the US in the 1970s and is now widely used in America and Canada as a stock dog. Devoted to its owners and a dedicated guard, the breed remains principally a working dog and is unlikely to be kept as a domestic pet. The Charplaninatz is courageous and enormously strong. It has something of the wolf about it, with its long, dense iron-grey coat and wolf-like howl.

An energetic herder, the Schapendoes has a roguish, unkempt appearance that belies its steady temperament.

KARST SHEPHERD also known as the Krasky Ovcar, Croatian or Istrian Sheepdog, is a medium-sized, capable flock guard with exceptionally well-developed muscles and a strong constitution. It has a noble head, a medium-length coat with abundant undercoat, and is iron grey in colour. It has worked for centuries in the Karst area, which includes the Istrian peninsula, in the north-west of the former state of Yugoslavia, but is little known outside its country of origin.

This shepherd is courageous, vivacious, loyal and obedient, and makes a fine companion and guard. However, it is not a good choice for the inexperienced dog owner, as it is suspicious of strangers, hard to win over, and ready to defend its owners if it believes them to be under threat. It needs plenty of exercise and food and daily brushing.

PORTUGUESE SHEEPDOG or Cão da Serra de Aires is an ancient breed which comes from the south of Portugal. It is a versatile working dog, which makes a fine guard, but is mainly used for herding and driving livestock. It is a medium-sized, strong dog with a deep chest, long body and tail. It is yellow, brown, grey, fawn, wolf grey or black in colour, and has a long, rough, goat-like coat with a tendency to curl.

This tough, active, intelligent dog is an instinctive herder, devoted to its owners and wary of strangers. It needs plenty of space, considerable exercise, and is best suited to a working life.

RAFEIRO DO ALENTEJO This Portuguese herding dog of ancient lineage originates from the Alentejo province south of Lisbon. It is a mastiff-like dog with a bear-like head, which slightly resembles a light short-haired Saint Bernard. It has a short or medium-length sleek coat, and its colour can be black, grey, brindle, cream or fawn with white markings. It may also be white any of these colour markings. The Rafeiro do Alentejo's job in life has always been to guard flocks and herds from predators. It is little known outside its country of origin

and has yet to make an appearance in the international show ring. This massive, powerful, sober dog is an alert and somewhat aggressive guard. It is readily trained but needs plenty of space and exercise, is rather self-willed and is not suitable as a housepet. It should be groomed with a bristle brush and slicker.

SCHAPENDOES or Dutch Sheepdog (distinct from the Dutch Shepherds, see page 101) closely resembles the Bearded Collie. This is not surprising since this ancient breed is thought to share common ancestry with the Bearded Collie, as well as with the Puli, Bergamasco and Briard. It is an appealing shaggy dog with a long, low-set tail, and a long, harsh coat and a smooth undercoat. The Schapendoes has herded flocks for centuries and is still sometimes used in this role today. However, it is now more widely kept as a household companion and guard in the Netherlands, where it is very popular. The breed has been established since the 1880s and was recognized by the FCI in 1970 but is still little seen outside its country of origin.

This good natured, lively, intelligent dog is easily trained and generally reliable with children. Its coat needs daily brushing, and it should have plenty of exercise.

GUNDOGS

AUVERGNE SETTER or Braque Bleu d'Auvergne comes from the Auvergne province in the south of central France. This tough elegant gundog resembles the English Pointer and the German Short-haired Pointer, both of which are descendants of the Spanish Pointer. The French did produce quite a number of breeds by crossing the Spanish Pointer with various hounds, the short-haired ones becoming known as Braques. However, the Auvergne is often said to be an indigenous breed, or one that evolved through cross-breedings with the old French Setter. Others are convinced that the Braque is descended from dogs

introduced into the Auvergne in 1798 by the Knights of Malta.

This large setter has a white coat with black on the head and ample black ticking to create a blue effect, and has a short, glossy coat.

It is an intelligent and sensitive dog. It requires a lot of exercise, and regular grooming.

CZECH COARSE-HAIRED SETTER seems to have been developed by crossing the rather similar German Wire-haired Pointer or Drahthaar and Wire-haired Pointing (or Korthals) Griffon and breeds, such as the Pudelpointer, with the German Short-haired Pointer.

In all respects other than coat and colour, this breed is like the German Short-haired Pointer. Its coat has three layers, a short, dense undercoat (absent in summer), a close-lying top coat and longer guard hairs.

DRENTSE PARTRIDGE DOG or Drentse Partrijshond originated in the Drentse province of north-east Netherlands, where it has existed for more than 300 years. It is a medium-sized dog with a sleek, close-lying coat that is white with brown or orange markings. It bears some resemblance to the German Long-haired Pointer (Langhaar) but has a shorter head and muzzle. This fine pointer and retriever has keen scenting ability and is used, as its name suggests, for hunting partridge and other birds and small game. It is little known outside its native land, where it is a great favourite as an all-purpose gundog and a competitor in field trials.

Good natured, trustworthy and easy to train, the Drentse Partridge Dog is popular in the Netherlands both with sportsmen and as a family pet. It needs plenty of exercise and a good daily brushing.

OLD DANISH POINTER or Bird Dog is known in its native Denmark as the Gammel Dansk Honsehund. It was bred in the 17th century from Spanish dogs, including the Spanish Pointer, and possibly local dogs. A strong, rugged animal, well suited to the flat terrain of Denmark, it is used as an all-purpose gundog. The breed's popularity waned and it almost became extinct in this century, but fortunately it was revived and was recognized by the Danish Kennel Club in 1962. It is now firmly re-established in its country of origin, but little known elsewhere.

This dog's body is longer than its height at withers, and it has a fairly short head, a well-developed muscular body, a medium-length tail, thick at the root, and a dense, tight coat. Its colour is white with light or dark liver markings.

The Old Danish Pointer is calm and friendly, easy to train, and makes a good, versatile gundog, that can also be kept as a family pet. It needs a regular rub-down with a hound glove and lots of exercise.

PONT-AUDEMER SPANIEL is also known as the Épagneul Pont-Audemer. This spaniel originated in north-west France and is named after a town in Normandy. It is thought to have been developed in the 18th century through the crossing of an old French spaniel and the Irish Water Spaniel. The resultant dog is a fine hunter and swimmer, particularly adept at working in swampy ground. Unfortunately it has become rare, even in its country of origin.

The Pont-Audemer is an attractive dog with dark, amber eyes, a kindly far-seeing expression and a docked tail. Its long coat is slightly wavy and the ears have long, curled fringes which join the dog's topknot to form a curly halo around its short-haired face. It is chestnut with or without grey markings.

This appealing, lively, intelligent dog is known to be an excellent hunter of feathered game over wet and marshy terrain. It happily combines the roles of sportsman's dog and family pet. It needs daily brushing, and handstripping or clipping for a show.

The **SMALL-SIZED FRENCH SETTER**, also known as the Braque Français de Petite Taille, was bred down from the French Setter or Braque Français (see page 133). Thought to originate in Gascony, south-west France, it is an almost perfect scaled-down version of the

The curled tail of the Wetterhoun suggests that this breed descends from Nordic spitz-type stock as well as from the European water dog.

French Setter, but differs slightly in head shape and colour. Like its larger counterpart, it is an ancient breed, which has been used as a hunting and tracking dog in France for centuries. It has considerable powers of endurance and is capable of working over all types of terrain.

The small-sized French Setter is a robust, intelligent, good natured dog, which makes a first-class hunter and retriever, and combines this role admirably with that of family pet. It requires a daily brushing and can cope with limitless exercise.

SPANISH POINTER The modern Spanish Pointer (Burgos Setter, Perdiguero de Burgos), native to northern Spain, is a descendant of the old Spanish Pointer, which is thought to be an ancestor of all pointing dogs. This large, well-built dog will work on any terrain, under any climatic conditions, and can cope with feathered as well as other game. In colour it is white with liver flecks or ticks, or dark liver with white markings, and it has a short, smooth coat.

The Spanish Pointer is a capable, eager and reliable dog of good temperament. In common with other pointers, it will happily combine the role of sporting companion and family pet. It needs plenty of exercise and its short, fine coat requires regular, moderate grooming.

WETTERHOUN or Dutch Water Spaniel originated in the Friesland province of the Netherlands. It was bred from otter-hunting dogs for use against the otter and other water game. It is a fearless hunter with a dense, tightly curled coat, which enables it to withstand harsh climatic conditions. It is medium sized, and occurs in black, brown or blue, with or without white. The Wetterhoun has been known in its native Holland for centuries, but was not recognized by the Dutch Kennel Club until 1942.

This intelligent hunter is a somewhat aggressive animal, widely used as a guard and farm dog in Holland. It needs firm and kindly handling. It needs a lot of exercise and regular grooming, and is best kept kennelled out of doors.

WOOLLY-HAIRED GRIFFON or Long-coated Pointing Griffon or Griffon à Poil Laineux is also referred to as the Boulet Griffon after Emanuel Boulet, a French industrialist who developed the Woolly-haired Griffon in the 19th century with the aid of Leon Vernier. The resultant breed looks like a cross between the Wire-haired Pointing Griffon (Korthals Griffon) and the French Setter or Braque. It is the same size as the Korthals Griffon with the head of a pointer and a coat similar to the Braque's but silkier and softer, like that of the Afghan Hound. Its colour is a dull brown, described as dead-leaf. Boulet's dog and bitch, Marco and Myra, became international champions and are in the pedigrees of most of today's Woolly-haired Griffons.

This gentle, obedient griffon is a good all-purpose gundog with keen scenting ability and great powers of endurance. Its good temperament also makes it a fine household pet. It needs plenty of exercise and daily grooming with a brush and comb.

The Woolly-haired Griffon is a slightly smaller, long-coated version of the Wire-haired Pointing Griffon.

HOUNDS

AUSTRIAN COARSE-HAIRED HOUND or Styrian Rough-haired Mountain Hound is also known as the Steirischer Rauhaarige Hochgebirgs Bracke or Peintinger Bracke. Originating in Styria, a southern province of Austria, it was developed in the late 1800s from the German Hanover Hound and various other Austrian and Istrian coarse-haired breeds. The aim was to produce a dog tough enough to hunt on Austria's high mountains, and this breed is particularly noted for its hardiness. It is a medium-sized, muscular and strongly built hound with drop ears and a curved, sabre-style tail with a small tuft of hair on the tip. It has a rough coat, and occurs in red, pale yellow or fawn; a small white spot on the chest is acceptable. It is kept only for hunting, and is greatly valued as a boar hunter. It has considerable powers of endurance and a magnificent cry.

The good natured, intelligent and appealing Austrian Coarse-haired Hound is readily trained and a popular and willing worker. It is gentle and faithful, but it retains a strong hunting instinct and is not suited to being kept as a household pet. It requires a lot of exercise and the coat needs daily brushing.

The **AUSTRIAN HOUND**, Brandl Bracke or Österreichischer Bracke is a medium-sized dog little known outside its country of origin. In Austria it is highly valued for its ability to follow a cold scent, and is also used to hunt small game. It is thought to be descended from Celtic hounds and to be related to the Jura Hounds and Bloodhound. It is very similar to the Tyrolean Hound, differing only in size, colour and length of coat.

The fine-looking Austrian Hound has a sturdy body, domed skull, long head and tail, and a smooth, glossy coat. It is solid red or black with flame markings, and a small white spot on the chest is permissible.

It is used for hunting all types of game, and is sensible and obedient. It requires a lot of exercise, and regular brushing.

BALKAN HOUND or Balksanski Gonič is a sighthound from the former country of Yugoslavia, bred to suit particular tasks and climate. Its ancestors were brought to Europe by the Phoenicians.

This is a medium-sized breed with a short, coarse, dense coat. It is fox red with a black saddle or mantle extending to the base of the head. It is used to track over rough ground for small and large game, including hare, fox and deer.

This good natured breed is strong and untiring, hard-working, and has a high-pitched voice, making it an excellent tracking dog. It requires a lot of exercise.

BANJARA GREYHOUND This breed is associated with the Banjara people of the state of Rajasthan in north-west India. It is a sighthound, and is used as a hunting and coursing dog. It is rough-coated, muscular, and its colours are brindle, grey, wheaten or sandy.

The Banjara are ancestors of the European Romanies, and their small greyhounds could have contributed to the development of the Lurcher (page 251). Like the Lurcher, the Banjara Greyhound is a mixture, and a pure Banjara would be unique. The breed is not officially recognized, and is not known outside India.

BASSET ARTÉSIEN NORMAND

is a descendant of short-legged hounds once native to the Artois and Normandy in northern France. The hound experts, George Johnston and Maria Ericson, report that there were dwarfed versions of the bicoloured Artois and the tricoloured Normand, and these were interbred, merging over time into the dog we now know as the Basset Artésien Normand. The breed was given its modern name in 1911.

The Basset Artésien Normand is a long-bodied dog, the length of which exceeds its height, making it easier for it to work in thickets. It is either bicolour – orange and white – or tricolour – white with tan head, black back and extremities. The breed is used to hunt rabbits and other small prey and has a keen following throughout much of Europe but is little known in the United Kingdom.

The Basset Artésien Normand retains a strong hunting instinct and still fulfils its traditional role in its native land. It is not suitable as a domestic pet.

BAVARIAN MOUNTAIN DOG

This German breed is also known as the Bavarian Schweisshund or Bayerischer Gebirgsschweisshund. It was bred in the 1900s because the Hanover Hound, although an excellent tracking dog (see page 161), was found to be too heavy to work successfully in the Bavarian mountains. So the Hanover was crossed with the Tyrolean Hound (a relative of the old Bavarian Hound) to produce a lighter, more agile animal, but with the same keen nose.

It has a strong, somewhat fine body and has long pendent ears. It has a thick, rough, close-lying coat, and comes in deep red, red tan, fawn to wheaten, red grizzle or brindle. The Bavarian Mountain Dog is used to hunt deer and to track down wounded game through heavy cover.

This intelligent, lively, muscular dog is suitable for working free, or on a line, in the mountains. It has a calm, steady temperament and is a favourite with deer hunters and gamewardens, and is not kept as a housepet. It should be groomed with a hound glove.

The **BLACK FOREST HOUND** (Slovakian Hound, Slovensky Kopov) is of ancient origin and is the only hound native to Slovakia. It was not a recognized breed until after the Second World War but since then efforts have been made to preserve and perpetuate its characteristics. It is medium-sized, black with tan markings, and has a thick, close-lying coat. The breed has strong hunting instincts, first-class scenting abilities, a well-developed sense of direction, and also makes a good guard. When tracking, it is single-minded and will follow a trail for many hours, barking loudly. It is now used mainly for hunting the European wild boar.

This affectionate hound has a lively personality and immense courage but is extremely independent and needs rigorous training. It is unlikely to be kept as a housepet.

BLUETICK COONHOUND is

similar in appearance to the American Foxhound and is descended from various foxhound types crossed with French hounds such as the Gascony Blue hounds (page 169), the Porcelaine (page 162) and the Saintongeois (page 245). For a time it was registered, along with various other types of hounds, as an English Coonhound, but in 1945 the Bluetick Coonhound was registered as a separate breed in order to resist attempts to make it faster and more like a foxhound.

It is a quite tall hound with a smooth, short, slightly coarse coat. Its colour is white, thickly ticked (spotted) with dark blue, with fawn markings on the head and ears. It is a free tonguer on trail, with a bugle voice when trailing, which may change to a steady chop when running, with a steady, coarse chop at the tree. It is obedient and has great powers of endurance. It should be kennelled out of doors, and given plenty of exercise.

BOSNIAN COARSE-HAIRED

HOUND or Basanski Ostrodlaki Goniči-Barak is a native of Bosnia in the north of the former state of Yugoslavia. This powerful hunter has a thick, tapering tail and a trunk

only slightly longer than its height at withers. It has long, coarse hair over a dense undercoat giving it an appealing shaggy appearance and enabling it to be used over rough ground and in bad weather. It occurs in wheaten yellow, reddish yellow, grey or blackish; bicolour and tricolour are acceptable, as are white areas on the head, dewlap, chest, lower limbs and tail tip.

It has a serious expression, but is said to be both a playful dog and one that is courageous with great powers of endurance. It can be used against all manner of game, but is gentle in the home. It requires a lot of exercise and daily grooming.

BRAZILIAN TRACKER or Rastreador Brasileiro was developed from the American Foxhound and the Coonhounds, the Black and Tan, the Treeing Walker and the Bluetick. The aim was to produce a hardy tracker of the jaguar with great powers of endurance and the ability to work over most types of terrain. The breed has a short, dense coat, quite rough to the touch, a fairly long head, long pendulous ears and dark eyes. It has Foxhound, Treeing

The powerful Basset Artésien Normand is a popular European hunting breed which gave rise to the Basset Hound.

Walker, Bluetick or Black and Tan Coonhound markings – that is, blue merle, white with black or tan patches, or black and tan.

Despite being a keen jaguar hunter and a superb tracking and hunting dog, the Brazilian Tracker is a good natured animal without any history of aggression towards people.

DREVER or Swedish Dachsbracke is one of the most popular dogs in Sweden but is little seen outside its native land. It was developed by mating German Dachshunds with Swedish hunting dogs, and is of moderate size, with a rectangular body shape and expressive eyes. It has a smooth, thick coat, and all colours are acceptable although white should always be well in evidence in front, on the side and behind. The Drever is famed for following fox, hare, deer and even wild boar and, possessing a good voice and keen nose, will drive its prey towards the guns. It began life with the German name, Dachsbracke, and was given its current name when recognition was sought. The breed was recognized by the Swedish Kennel Club in 1949 and by the international body, the FCI, in 1953. It is not, however, recognized by Kennel Clubs in Britain or the United States.

The Drever is a favourite hunting and popular show dog in Sweden. Being intelligent, devoted and of equable temperament, it also makes a splendid family pet provided that it receives plenty of exercise and a good daily brushing.

DUNKER or Norwegian Hound is named after its originator, Wilhelm Dunker, who crossed the Russian Harlequin Hound with other hounds. The resultant dog is renowned for its endurance and staying power rather than its speed, and is used mainly to hunt hare. It has a straight, strong but not too long body and deep chest, a tail reaching to the hocks or a little way beyond, and a close, hard coat. Its colouring is black or blue merle with fawn and white markings. A popular hound in its native Norway and throughout Scandinavia, the breed is little known elsewhere and

is not recognized by the British or American Kennel Clubs.

The Dunker is reputed to be a confident and affectionate dog, which is trustworthy and loyal to its master. This powerful hunting dog is not normally kept as a housepet.

ENGLISH COONHOUND Like other coonhounds, the English Coonhound is descended from English hounds crossed with other hound types. All coonhounds apart from the Black and Tan and Redbone (see page 149), which achieved breed status early on, were originally registered as English Coonhounds. The breed included a variety of types of hounds with both fast and slow, patient styles of hunting. They were used against a variety of game, but particularly fox and raccoon. During the 20th century, types such as the Bluetick (page 244) were classified as separate breeds in order to preserve their distinct qualities.

The modern English Coonhound is a medium-sized dog with a short, hard coat. Its colour is usually redtick – white with red patches and red ticking (specks) in the white areas – although other colours are allowed. It is a fast and efficient hunter, and is popular with sportsmen and in the competition ring. It should be kennelled out of doors, and requires a lot of exercise.

FINNISH HOUND This is also known as the Finnish Stövare and, in its native Finland, as the Suomenajokoira. It is a medium-sized hound with a fairly lean, noble head and a medium-length, thick dense coat. Its colour is black and tan with white markings on the head, neck, chest, feet and tail tip. The breed was created by a Finnish goldsmith named Tammelin who carefully mixed German, Swiss, English and Scandinavian hound blood. The breed has been known since 1700 and became popular in Finland at the end of the 19th century. The Finnish Hound is a popular dog in its native land, where it is famed as a hunter of fox, hare, moose and lynx, but is little known elsewhere.

The Finnish Hound is a good

natured animal but is known to have a mind of its own and has a strong hunting instinct. Although it may be kept indoors outside the hunting season in its native land, it is chosen for its hunting abilities rather than as a household companion. It requires a lot of exercise and a regular grooming with a hound glove.

The **GASCONS-SAINTONGEOIS, GREAT AND SMALL** The Great (Grand) Gascon-Saintongeois is a powerful coursing dog, which is also known as the Virelade after its creator in the 1800s, Baron Joseph de Caryon Latour de Virelade. His aim was to produce a dog that combined the qualities of those fine hunting breeds, the Ariégeois, the Great Gascony Blue and the now extinct wolf-hunter, the Saintongeois. He achieved an animal with a very sensitive nose for tracking, strong enough to hunt large game such as the wolf and the roebuck, and also able to function as a gundog. The Small (Petit) variety was developed in south-west France to hunt hare. Henri de Caryon, Baron de Virelade's nephew, attempted to improve the breed by introducing blood from Bordeaux, but little information is available.

Their short dense coat is predominantly white with black markings. They also have some brown markings on the head, and a grey-brown patch on the thigh.

Today, the Gascons-Saintongeois are rare in France and little seen outside their country of origin.

GREEK GREYHOUND is also known as the Albanian Greyhound. This breed resembles the Saluki (see page 182). It is a hardy coursing dog, which is now extremely rare. It has a short, close coat with fringed ears and tail. It can be any colour.

The Greek Greyhound is a faithful hunting companion, but so rare that it is unlikely to be kept as a housepet. It would require plentiful exercise, and grooming with a soft brush and a brisk rub-down with a towel or hound glove.

HALDENSTÖVARE is named after the town of Halden, in Norway, where it was developed through crossings of local hounds with imported hounds from France, Britain, Germany and, probably, Russia. It is a strong, long-bodied hound of considerable endurance, which can chase game at speed even across snow. It has a medium-sized head, a straight and strong back, broad loins, and a rather thick tail that is carried fairly low. Its colour is white with black markings and brown shading on the head and legs and between the white and black areas. This breed is popular in its native country but little known elsewhere.

The Haldenstövare is a loyal, gentle and affectionate animal. Since it is unusual for Scandinavian hounds to be kept in packs it doubtless generally lives in the home. It requires a lot of exercise and a regular rub-down with a hound glove.

HELLENIC HOUND The Hellenic Hound (Greek Harehound) is a tracking dog of ancient Greek origin. In its native land, it works singly, or in packs, over virtually any type of terrain, often in rocky areas inaccessible to people. It has considerable scenting powers, and a pleasant, resonant bay. It is medium sized, with a short, dense coat, and its colour is black and tan.

This strong, intelligent hound is little known outside Greece and is unlikely to be kept as a housepet there. It requires abundant exercise and grooming with a hound glove.

HYGENHUND This fine Norwegian hunting dog takes its name from a Norwegian breeder Hygen, who developed it in the 1800s. He crossed the German Holsteiner with various other hounds to produce a dog with great staying power, able to hunt over snowy terrain. The Hygenhund was subsequently crossed with the lighter and less regal Dunker, and efforts were made to register the progeny under the name of Norwegian Beagles. These failed, however, and the Hygenhund and Dunker remain separate breeds. The Hygenhund is still used in Norway but is not numerous there and is rarely seen outside Scandinavia. It is a medium-sized dog with a broad

head, dark or hazel-coloured eyes, long, deep chest, and a straight, dense, glossy coat that is slightly rough to the touch. It is chestnut or yellow ochre, with or without black shading, or black and tan. All these colours may be combined with white. It can also be white with tan to yellow markings or spots, or with black and tan markings.

This reliable, affectionate dog is a dedicated hunter with considerable powers of endurance. It requires a lot of exercise and needs a regular rub-down with a hound glove.

ISTRIAN HOUNDS There are two varieties of Istrian Hound or Istrishi Gonič, which differ only in coat. The short-haired (Kratkodlaki) has a short, dense coat, not unlike that of the Pointer, while the Wire- or Rough-haired (Resati) has long, straight, coarse hair over a dense, woolly undercoat. They have a long, narrow head, straight, broad back and medium-length tail. Their colour is snow-white with orange markings on the ears. Markings may also appear on the body, particularly at the root of the tail. Both are ancient breeds native to Istria, a peninsula in the north-west of the former state of Yugoslavia, and are seldom seen outside their land of origin. Possessing a keen sense of smell, the Istrian Hounds locate their quarry by scent and drive it to the guns. They are used to hunt fox and hare, and are also useful tracking dogs.

The Istrian Hounds have great powers of endurance, and are known to be active, friendly and easy to train. They are gentle in the home and happy to combine the roles of sportsman's dog and family pet. The Short-haired should be groomed with a hound glove, the Wire-haired with a wire brush.

KANGAROO HOUND resembles a heavily built Greyhound and is sometimes called the Australian Greyhound. It was developed in the mid-1880s by Australian settlers who wanted a dog that was keen-eyed and fast enough for coursing kangaroos and wallabies, yet powerful enough to hold the quarry when caught. They set about producing such a dog

by crossing the English Greyhound and the Irish Wolfhound. The result was a large, tough sighthound, well able to chase and overpower a kangaroo, with a short, harsh coat, resembling that of the Wolfhound. Its colours are brindle, pied, black, tan and white, or black and tan. However, as its quarry became scarce the Kangaroo Hound dwindled in numbers. Although there are said to be some specimens on remote stations, it appears to be a dying breed and may even be extinct.

LEVESQUE is named after its originator, Rogatien Levesque, who embarked on creating this hound and versatile gundog in 1873. He mated a Great Gascony Blue bitch with a rough-coated Foxhound, and the pups in the two litters produced were crossbred with the Virelade. The resultant progeny were then crossed with the Gascon Saintongeois-Vendéens. There was a considerable stir in Paris when a pack of Levesque was first displayed there. Despite all the crossings, the Levesque now breeds very true to type.

The Levesque is a good-natured hound with light chestnut eyes and an expression which has been described as both sweet and intelligent. It has a smooth, strong, close coat, and occurs in black and white only, although it has a purplish tint on its back. Like all hounds it requires a lot of exercise and regular grooming.

MAJESTIC TREE HOUND This scenthound is used in the American Deep South for hunting big cats and other large game. It was developed recently for this purpose by American enthusiasts, who crossed the Bloodhound with other large hounds. The resultant dog is large, rather ponderous, with an excellent nose, fine voice and great powers of endurance. It has a short, thick, dense coat, loose folds of skin around its face and neck, and can be any colour or combination of colours.

Like its relative, the English Bloodhound, the Majestic Tree Hound is affectionate, good natured and can be kept as a pet by those who have the space to allow it to run and neighbours who do not object to

The Steinbracke (see page 248) can be readily identified by the typical white markings on the head, chest, legs and tip of the tail.

its melodious voice. It should be groomed with a hound glove.

MOUNTAIN CUR This little-known American breed is descended from dogs brought to the United States by European settlers and, possibly, native pariah dogs. It is reminiscent of the now extinct English Drover's dog or Cur, which may have played a part in its ancestry. The Mountain Cur is a strong, stocky hound, able to work over difficult terrain. It is skilled at treeing game and is also a good tracker, which seldom gives tongue, and makes a fine guard.

The Mountain Cur is a tough, courageous dog, capable of doing battle with big game. It does not have a very affable temperament, and is suited to a rugged working life, not the suburban fireside.

PLOTT HOUND The Plott Hound is a medium-sized hound descended from hounds brought to England from Germany by the Plott family in the 18th century, which were crossed with English and other types of hounds. It has bred true in North Carolina for 200 years. It has a short, harsh, close-lying coat, and is tan-

pied with black saddle. It has been used to hunt all types of game, including wolf, puma, coyote, wild cat, red deer, bear, boar and smaller game. It is a tough and persistent hunter, quite able to stand up to its prey. It is best kept kennelled out of doors, and needs plenty of exercise.

POSAVATZ HOUND or Posavski Goriči is a vigorous hound named after the Posavine area around the Sava river in the north of the former state of Yugoslavia. Little known outside its country of origin, it is used there for hunting small game and deer. This medium-sized breed has a thick, dense coat, dark eyes with a "wide awake" expression, and a long, narrow head with pendulous ears rounded at the tips. Its short tail should not reach below the hocks, and the length of the body should be 4–7.5cm (1½–3in) more than the height at withers. It has a short, thick coat, usually reddish. However, it may be wheaten yellow to fawn, but without darkening to deep chocolate brown. White is allowed on the head, chest, feet and tail.

Highly regarded in its native area, the Posavatz is swift, obedient and affectionate towards its owners. It needs lots of exercise, and should be groomed with a hound glove.

RUSSIAN HOUNDS and **ESTONIAN HOUND** There are three breeds of hound recognized in Russia: the Russian (Drab Yellow) Hound, the Russian Particolour (Harlequin or

Piebald) Hound and the Estonian Hound. The Drab Yellow, which was standardized early in this century, is an indigenous Russian breed. Fox-hound blood was added to the Russian Hound to produce the Particolour which is tan, sometimes with a black saddle, and with white or yellowish markings. Both these hounds are used for hunting fox, hare and sometimes badger, and are extremely popular in their native land.

The Estonian Hound, which is black with fawn markings, has a more elongated body and longer ears then the Russian Hounds and is comparatively rare. The two Russian Hounds are medium sized and similar in conformation, except that the ears and tail of the Particolour are shorter. The Estonian's body is twice as long as its height, and it looks rather Basset-like. All three have short, dense coats.

These are fine scenthounds, being of good temperament with keen noses and great endurance. They will hunt in a pack or singly and require abundant exercise. They should be groomed with a hound glove.

SCHILLER HOUND or Schiller-stövare is named after the Swedish breeder, Per Schiller. He developed it in the late 1880s using local Swedish dogs crossed with hounds from Austria, Germany and Switzerland. The resultant Schiller Hound is believed to be the fastest of the Scandinavian hounds. This powerful, medium-sized dog has a short coat, and is black with reddish brown or yellow markings. Sturdy as well as swift, it is hunted singly and is also used as a tracking dog. The breed was recognized in 1952, and is now one of the most popular hunting dogs in Sweden.

This is an excellent hunting dog and faithful to its owner, but is not suitable for keeping as a housepet. It requires abundant exercise and grooming with a hound glove.

The **SMALL BLUE GASCONY GRIFFON** or Petit Griffon Bleu de Gascogne combines the qualities of both the Griffon – or rough-coated hound – and the Small Gascony Blue from which it was bred. It is a rustic looking, solidly built, low-slung

French hound which is similar in appearance to the Small Gascony Blue apart from its smaller size, shorter muzzle and ears, and a dry coat that is harsh to the touch. Its coat is white with black markings and specific tan markings. The Small Blue Gascony Griffon is now extremely rare.

It is a hard-working, tireless hunter with a good nose, and is used for hunting hare. It is not suitable for a family pet. Like all hounds, it requires a lot of exercise. It needs daily grooming with brush and comb to prevent its coat matting.

The **SMÅLAND HOUND** or Smålandstövare is indigenous to Sweden and named after the densely forested southern Swedish province of Småland. There and elsewhere it is used singly to hunt game, mainly fox and rabbit. The Småland is a light, medium-sized dog with a keen sense of smell. Although an ancient breed, it was not recognized until 1921 and the standard was revised in 1952. It is a powerful, medium-sized breed, has a short smooth coat, and is black with tan markings. It can be born with either a long or short tail.

The breed is calm and reliable, and devoted to its master. It is not suitable as a housepet. The Småland needs abundant exercise and should be groomed with a hound glove.

SMALL GASCONY BLUE or Petit Bleu de Gascogne was bred down from the Great Gascony Blue to hunt smaller game. Its ancestor is one of the most ancient hunting dogs in France. The Small Gascony Blue differs from its larger relative only in size and in having a finer head and thicker ears than those of the Great Gascony Blue. The Small has a keen sense of smell and is used mainly against hare, but is now rarely seen outside its native south-west France.

SPANISH HOUNDS There are two varieties of Spanish Hound or Sabueos Español, the Large (de Monte) and Small (Lebrero), which differ only in size and colour. Both are descended from hounds brought by the Celtic people in the 1st millennium BC. These long-bodied, short-legged dogs have keen noses. They have long heads and wrinkled foreheads, and a fine coat. The Large is white with patches of black or deep orange. The Small is the same except that patches may cover almost the entire body excepting the neck, chest, feet and muzzle. At one time they were used in packs for tracing game and, later, also drove quarry towards the gun. Today they are still used for tracking, but mainly by the police, and as guard dogs.

These fine hounds have considerable endurance and perseverance on the trail, but can be self-willed and need firm training. They require a lot of exercise, and should be groomed with a hound glove.

STEINBRACKE is a medium-sized German hunting and tracking dog that is used against small game. Less common than other breeds within the bracke group, it is one of a number of old hounds of similar type that once existed in Germany. The German hound club produced a brief standard for the Steinbracke in 1955 which was accepted by the FCI. The breed bears some resemblance to the Westphalian Dachsbracke, but is much longer in the leg and squarer in outline. It has a long, very dense,

The Tawny Brittany Griffon is an ancient European breed which was developed to guard flocks from predators.

hard coat, and is always tricolour.

The Steinbracke is a lively, friendly dog requiring plenty of exercise and grooming with a hound glove.

STEPHENS' STOCK, one of five varieties of mountain cur found in the Deep South of the United States, is similar in type to but smaller than the Mountain Cur. Also known as "Little Black", this hound was developed to hunt small game by the Stephens family in the mid to late 1800s. It was not until 1970, after 100 years or so of breeding true, that it was described, and it is not yet recognized by any kennel club. It is fairly small with a strung-up, sinewy appearance, a small head with narrow muzzle and rat's tail. It is black and has a short coat.

Stephens' Stock is essentially a working dog and is greatly favoured by hunters, being quick, courageous and fairly easy to train. It may be kept in the home provided that it has adequate space, plentiful exercise and, above all, is used for the job for which it was intended.

TAWNY BRITTANY GRIFFON or Griffon Fauve de Bretagne is a medium-sized, muscular, well-boned hound, with a rustic appearance, hard, fawn-coloured coat, expressive eyes, pendulous ears and a very coarse coat. This ancient breed was reputedly used for wolf hunting in the Middle Ages. Tawny Griffon packs were disbanded in the breed's native Brittany after 1885 when their quarry had become extinct. It

was saved from extinction itself by a few breeders and is now used in its native land to hunt wild boar and fox but is still comparatively rare.

TRANSYLVANIAN HOUND

The Transylvanian Hound (Hungarian Hound, Erdeliy Kopo) traces back to hounds brought by the Magyars when they invaded the Carpathian region in the 9th century. It originated through the crossing of the Magyar hounds with local dogs and thereafter with Polish dogs. The result was a versatile hunting dog able to cope with the dense forests and extremes of climate in the Carpathian mountains. It was once used by Hungarian royalty to hunt wolves and bears. Today there are two varieties, the Large being used to hunt wild boar, deer and lynx, and the Small, fox and hare. The Large is a medium-sized dog, with a medium-length, straight, dense coat, black with tan markings. The Small is slightly smaller, with a short, straight, dense coat, brown-red, with slightly lighter markings towards the belly. Both have fairly long bodies, nearly square in outline, and long tails set on low.

The Transylvanian is a tireless, obedient hound which is brave and easy to train. It requires boundless exercise and should be groomed with a hound glove.

The **TREEING TENNESSEE BRINDLE** This smaller coonhound was, like the other coonhounds, bred from crosses between English and other types of hounds. It is an excellent tracker, fearless and fast, and is used against game such as raccoon and squirrel. It is also intelligent and affectionate and makes a good hunting companion. It should be kennelled out of doors, and needs plenty of exercise.

The **TREEING WALKER COON-HOUND** is of definite foxhound type, descending from the English Foxhound (page 176) crossed with other hounds. This medium-sized hound has a good treeing ability, and although it is used for hunting all types of game it is particularly suited to raccoon and opossum. Its short,

smooth, harsh coat occurs in a variety of colours – black, brown, red, white, black and white, red and white or other combinations. It preferably has a clear, ringing, bugle voice on a cold trail, changing to a chop or turkey mount on a running trail. It has a deep, throaty, loud chop mouth at the tree. It is persistent and obedient, and is popular for use in field trials. It should be kennelled out of doors, and needs plenty of exercise.

Another coonhound breed, the Trigg Hound, is very similar to the Treeing Walker Coonhound.

TYROLEAN HOUND

TYROLEAN HOUND or Tiroler Bracke was bred by hunters in the Tyrol province of Austria from a number of local hounds. It is a long-headed dog with a long, slightly curved tail, a smooth or wiry short coat and an expression similar to that of the Austrian Coarse-haired Hound. It can be black, red or fawn yellow, or tricolour (black and tan with white markings). There are two varieties of the breed, which are identical except for size and are often described as Standard and Miniature. Both are used against fox and other game in the Tyrol's high mountains. Possessing an excellent nose, the Tyrolean Hound locates quarry for the hunters and is particularly good at tracking wounded game in dense cover.

This versatile hunter is well adapted to harsh mountain climate and terrain, and is capable of great endurance. It is an intelligent, trustworthy, and obedient dog. It is usually kept kennelled out of doors. It needs considerable exercise and does best in the role of hunting companion. It should be groomed with a hound glove.

WALKER HOUND

WALKER HOUND was bred from the American Foxhound (page 177) and crossed with hounds imported from England. It is used as a pack hound after various types of game. It is a medium-sized hound with a short, hard, close coat, and is usually black with tan spots above the eyes, but it may be any foxhound colour.

YUGOSLAVIAN MOUNTAIN HOUND

YUGOSLAVIAN MOUNTAIN HOUND (Planinski Gonič) and the Tricolour Hound (Tribarvni Gonič) occur in the southern mountainous part of the former state of Yugoslavia. Similar in size with rectangular bodies, the Tricolour is slighter than the Mountain Hound. The Tricolour is black or yellowish black, pale yellow to tan and white, and has a short, dense, glossy coat. The Mountain Hound is black with rust-coloured markings, and has a thick, flat, slightly coarse coat with an abundant undercoat. Both are used to hunt hare, fox, deer and other game and are untiring and diligent in pursuit. They are little known outside their country of origin where they are uncommon.

These strong, compact, attractive-looking hounds are calm, gentle and of good temperament. They require plenty of exercise and daily grooming with a hound glove.

TERRIER

AMERICAN STAFFORDSHIRE TERRIER

AMERICAN STAFFORDSHIRE TERRIER (Pit Bull Terrier, Yankee Terrier) is descended from the English Staffordshire Bull Terrier, which is the result of a mating between the Old English Bulldog and an English Terrier. This strong dog had reached the United States by 1870, where it was used, as in Britain, to fight other dogs in pits. It was recognized by the American Kennel Club as the Staffordshire Terrier in 1935, the name being revised in 1972 to American Staffordshire Terrier. By this time, the "sport" of dog fighting had long since waned, and the breed had been developed into a companion dog.

The American Kennel Club did, at one time, allow the American Staffordshire Terrier and the Staffordshire Bull Terrier to be exhibited together and even crossbred. However, the American Staffordshire was bred to be a larger, heavier dog than its English relative and it is now a quite different breed. The ears on its massive head may be cropped.

An American Staffordshire from a reputable breeder should, like its

Sturdy and fearless, the American Staffordshire Terrier rewards firm handling with unswerving loyalty.

English relative, be affectionate and trustworthy towards its owner and a fine guard. Owing to its ancestry, it is likely to be aggressive to other dogs and to need firm control. However, some irresponsible breeders and owners have encouraged the dog's aggressive tendencies, making this breed widely feared. There are very strict laws on the keeping of American Staffordshires in the United Kingdom, and it is forbidden to breed them there. It needs a lot of exercise and regular grooming.

AUSTRIAN SHORT-HAIRED PINSCHER Also known as the Österreichischer Kurzhaariger Pinscher, this terrier is an old breed native to Austria. It is little known elsewhere and there appears to be some confusion about what constitutes a good specimen. However, it is generally a medium-sized dog with a short neck, sturdy broad-chested body and short, smooth coat. The tail is short and curled up over the back or docked, and the ears on the pear-shaped head may be erect, semi-erect or dropped. It has

a short coat, and is fawn, golden, red, or black and tan, sometimes with brindle markings; white markings are common. It is said to be a fearless hunter and, in true terrier fashion, will readily go to ground after quarry.

This brave, vivacious and noisy dog makes a good guard but is best suited to an active country life and to being kennelled outside. It needs plenty of exercise and grooming with a bristle brush.

Toy

PERUVIAN INCA ORCHID or Moonflower Dog is an ancient hairless breed native to Peru. Prized by Inca nobility, this deer-like dog is still kept as a pet in Peru and has been exported to North America, Europe and other parts of the world. In common with most other hairless breeds, it also exists as a coated variety, which may occur in litters of hairless parents. It may have a tuft of hair on its head, but otherwise it has smooth skin. The coated variety has long silky hair. It can be pale pink, cream or white, solid or mottled in any colour. It has a high body temperature, an absence of premolar teeth, and prehensile hare feet that can grip objects.

The Peruvian Inca Orchid is a calm, sensitive dog and makes a loving, devoted companion. It needs only a moderate amount of exercise, and its skin should be massaged with cream or oil to keep it supple. This breed must be protected against the cold and against sunburn.

Unclassified

CAROLINA DOG Occurring in the Deep South of the United States, this dog is a descendant of Pariah-type dogs (see p. 8), which probably migrated from Asia to North America thousands of years ago. It is a medium-sized, lightly built animal with a yellow coat that has earned it the nickname "Old Yeller". It is doubtful whether anyone outside the Deep South would ever have seen the Carolina Dog had it not starred in the Walt Disney film *Old Yeller*, made in 1957.

The Carolina Dog tends to be slightly more friendly than many Pariah-type dogs and some are kept as companions and have even been trained to the gun. However, it is really a wild dog, which must be reared carefully by humans from a very early age if it is to be domesticated and trained, and so it is not the ideal choice of pet.

DINGO The Australian Dingo is a Pariah-type dog which, according to the late Dr Erich Schneider-Leyer, occupies a position between ancestral dogs and the Pariahs. It is thought to have migrated to Australia with Aborigines over 20,000 years ago. The Aborigines tamed some and used them as hunting dogs but most remained wild. Operating singly or in packs, the Dingo is an efficient hunter and, when Europeans arrived, it started preying on rabbits, sheep and other imported livestock as well as native animals. So it was killed on sight and continues to be persecuted but still survives. It is medium sized, with a short, thick coat, and is usually reddish to pale fawn, sometimes with black on the back. Black, white or cream, solid or patched, can also occur.

The Dingo is a naturally suspicious, alert and extraordinarily intelligent animal. It can be reared by humans from a young age and trained gently but it basically remains a wild dog.

JINDO or Korean Dog is an excellent runner, able to bring down a rabbit or other quarry at amazing speed. It is named after Jindo island in Korea, where in the past this ancient breed was used in the hunting season against small animals and wild boar. At other times of the year it earned its keep as a watch dog. It is powerfully built, has a straight coat, and is usually red-brown in colour with light markings. It is something of a wild dog and, although the occasional litter has made its way overseas, the breed is not recognized by the FCI.

This beautiful dog is, unfortunately, proud, dominant and fairly difficult to train, the bitch being slightly more amenable.

LURCHER The English Lurcher is not a purebred dog but is of definite type, usually having a member of the greyhound family as one of its parents. It is thought to have been developed because, at one time in England, only those of noble blood were permitted to own a Greyhound. So Greyhound crosses were made to produce an efficient hunting companion for commoners and a popular poacher's dog. Possibly the best Lurchers result from a Greyhound/working Collie cross. Saluki, Deerhounds, Afghan Hounds and Borzoi are a few of the other members of the Greyhound family used. Its coat can be rough or smooth and it should look like a relative of the Deerhound or Greyhound.

The Lurcher is generally an obedient dog, which makes an excellent coursing hound and hunter, and will combine this role with that of a faithful and affectionate family pet. It needs plenty of exercise and a daily brushing.

NEW GUINEA SINGING DOG is a wild dog native to the large island of Papua New Guinea near Australia. Probably descended from early domesticated dogs of the southern hemisphere, it is a medium-sized Pariah, similar in type to the Dingo and named after the surprisingly melodious sound of its howl. It has a broad head, a short, smooth coat with plumed tail, and is red, with or without white markings. It existed in the wild state mainly in mountainous areas of its island home but is becoming increasingly rare there and, to the writer's knowledge, most surviving specimens are to be found in zoological parks.

This tough, efficient hunter may be approached and, on occasions, handled by humans. However, like the Dingo, it is a wary dog of uncertain temperament and must always return to the wild.

TELOMIAN This is a smallish Pariah dog, indigenous to Malaysia. It bears some resemblance to the

The Lurcher may have originated in Ireland. It is an excellent poacher's dog, able to run down prey swiftly and silently.

Basenji (see page 148), with which it shares a number of characteristics, including facial wrinkles and a yodelling rather than barking vocalization. It is medium-size with a short, smooth coat, and is sable with areas of white, sometimes speckled. The Telomian has been kept for centuries by the native inhabitants of Malaysia. They often lived in houses on stilts and the dog is said to have climbed a ladder to reach its human family's home at night. It hunted small game and otherwise existed on a mainly vegetarian diet. Perhaps because of a change in diet, specimens are now believed to be attaining a greater height.

The Telomian is gradually becoming known in Europe and North America, but has yet to be recognized by any kennel club.

Although the Telomian is intelligent, courageous, and basically of good temperament, and has lived with humans in Malaysia, it remains a semi-wild dog and so may not be a good choice of family pet. It must be reared by humans from an early age and carefully handled, if it is to be a companion, and does not like to be confined.

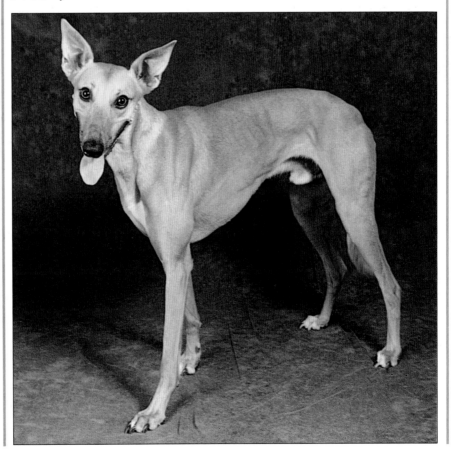

DAILY CARE

OBTAINING A DOG

Puppies are available from a number of sources: from pet stores, through advertisements, direct from a breeder or from welfare organizations – finding a suitable dog is a complex business.

Right: Basenjis are unusual dogs in several respects, not least because they do not bark in the normal way. For this reason, they make an unsuitable choice for those who are looking for a guard dog. Their short coats do not need too much grooming, however, and they have lively, affectionate natures.

DOGS ARE AMONG the most demanding animals to keep in a domestic environment, a fact that is sadly illustrated by the thousands of dogs abandoned by their owners every year. Before undertaking the responsibility of caring for a dog – a commitment that may well last for 15 years – it is essential to consider your own resources and preferences very carefully.

Taking care of any dog can be expensive and time-consuming, but breeds vary so widely in size, appearance and temperament that it is possible to select one which will fit your own circumstances. Age and gender are other factors to bear in mind: puppies settle easily and females may be more manageable. Whatever disruption or inconvenience they may cause in the household, however, dogs truly become part of the family.

Age
In the long term, puppies are easier to manage than most older dogs, which may have had a number of different owners. Puppies demand a great deal of patience until they are fully trained, but can settle more quickly in new surroundings than adult dogs. The

BASIC CONSIDERATIONS

are naturally quieter than others, which can be an important consideration if there are neighbors close by. Chihuahuas, despite their size, can bark persistently, often for no apparent reason. But once all these factors have been taken into account, certain breeds will undoubtedly appeal more than others for very personal reasons and it is on this basis that the final choice will probably be made.

As individual breeds have been developed to conform as closely as possible to prescribed standards, specified by the governing canine authority of the country concerned, certain features are actively encouraged, or altered artificially. The tails of certain breeds, such as the Boxer, are docked shortly after birth and the double dew claws on the hind legs of others, such as the Briard, are retained.

Unfortunately, as some features have been emphasized, weaknesses have also been introduced and some are actually encouraged by the breed standard. For example, Dachshunds, which have quite elongated bodies, often suffer from inter-vertebral disc problems. The folds of skin on the face of the Bloodhound can become a site of infection and interfere with vision. The huge size of the head of the Bulldog means that bitches can encounter difficulties giving birth, and puppies

Left: Big dogs, such as Irish Wolfhounds are relatively expensive to feed and require spacious surroundings and plenty of exercise.

Below: Toy breeds, such as the Yorkshire Terrier (below, with a Great Dane), by contrast, are cheaper and easier to care for and may even be content with living in an apartment.

temperament of a puppy is likely to be trustworthy, whereas an older dog may be nervous, even aggressive. Adult dogs that have spent most of their lives in kennels will not be house-trained, and it often proves extremely difficult to correct this fault, even if they are otherwise obedient. It will also take time for an older dog to respond to a new name or to trust a new owner.

Breed

Breeds of dog vary considerably in appearance, size and, to a certain extent, temperament. Choosing a breed involves considering a number of factors, ranging from issues of personal taste to more practical questions. In general, dogs with long coats or hair that requires constant trimming will need more care than short-haired breeds, and may create more mess around the home during periods of molting. Larger dogs need more space, more food and usually more exercise. Dogs that have been bred for their working characteristics, whatever their size, are less easy to manage in a domestic environment. Indeed, some working breeds, such as working sheepdogs, should never be kept as pets. Certain breeds

Puppies are very appealing, whichever breed they are, but it should be remembered that even small puppies may grow into big dogs. To assess the future size of a mongrel puppy, look at its feet; if they are relatively big, the dog will probably grow to a fairly large size. In the case of pedigrees, a much more accurate assessment can be made from studying the breed standards. The Jack Russell (above) will grow to only a small size, while the Staffordshire Bull Terrier (right) is a medium-sized dog.

often have to be removed by Caesarean section. Efforts are being made to modify the breed standards in cases where these are responsible for such problems. A significant proportion of the abnormalities that are associated with some particular breeds are, however, inherited, and are not directly related to show points. One disorder of this type is collie eye anomaly, which causes impaired vision and, in severe cases, even blindness. The British Veterinary Association and the Kennel Club have initiated a joint scheme to check breeding stock for such defects. Certificates are issued if the dogs show no signs of the condition.

Certain disorders are more commonly encountered in particular breeds. Great Danes can suffer from a narrowing of the vertebral canal in the neck region, causing pressure on the spinal cord and affecting movement. Such dogs become unsteady on their feet and are described as "wobblers". Surgery may help, but the treatment is complex and expensive.

Although many individual dogs may never suffer from such difficulties, potential breed weaknesses must be thoroughly considered before a final choice is made. Even relatively minor flaws can be distressing. One such example is the noisy, snuffling breathing of brachycephalic dogs, such as the Pekingese, which is due to their compressed faces and nasal passages. Deafness, typically associated with white Bull Terriers, also requires understanding from the owner.

Many mongrel dogs are also chosen as pets and some people do prefer them to pedigrees. It is untrue, however, that mongrels will not succumb to the same illnesses as pedigree dogs, although mongrels are certainly less likely to suffer from some of the hereditary disorders outlined above. Mongrels do still need just as much care and attention as other dogs do. They are much cheaper to acquire than pedigree dogs, but their temperaments are generally less easy to predict unless their ancestry is known. Before buying a mongrel puppy, it would be advisable to visit the litter if at all possible.

Size

Size is a crucial factor when selecting a dog. Although big dogs may deter intruders, they are more expensive to keep and require larger surroundings. It is easier to predict the size of a pedigree breed than that of a mongrel, whose parentage may be unknown. But although it is hard to know how large a mongrel puppy will grow, the size of the feet should give some guidance. Puppies with large feet are almost certain to grow into biggish dogs. By four months, a dog should be about two-thirds of its final height. The size of the bark is not a good indicator of a dog's size, as some small breeds, such as the Beagle, have a powerful voice.

Training is particularly important with large dogs, as they are invariably strong. If they are not controllable, they can prove a liability for older people and children, and a nuisance in the home. Sight hounds, such as the Afghan, can be very difficult to train to return once they are off the lead. Large breeds kept as guard dogs, such as the Doberman, need firm handling from an early age, as they possess determined, sometimes aggressive, natures, and are certainly not suitable for a home with young children. The smaller toy dogs are often ideal companions where space is limited, but it would be inadvisable to have them where there are children, as they can be easily hurt or injured by rough handling and this, in turn, can cause the dogs to become distrustful, making them liable to bite. As a general rule, the life expectancy of a small breed is longer than that of one of the giant breeds.

Left: A Great Dane puppy will grow into one of the tallest dogs in the world.

Gender

The sex of the dog is another factor that must be considered prior to deciding on a particular individual. Male dogs are supposed to be less demanding than bitches, but this is not always the case. They are certainly more prone to wandering, particularly if there is a bitch on heat in the neighbourhood, and they may prove harder to train, as they possess more dominant natures than bitches. Bitches are preferred as guide dogs for these reasons.

The major drawback of owning a female dog is the two periods of heat which are likely to occur every year through to old age, and the accompanying discharge from the vagina can cause problems around the home, and the bitch may need to be closely supervised to prevent uncontrolled mating.

After a period of heat, an additional problem may arise in certain bitches – especially those of the toy breeds – known as false or pseudo pregnancy. This state, as its name suggests, resembles a genuine pregnancy to the extent that milk can be produced, although the bitch was never mated during the preceding heat. Pseudo pregnancies can become a persistent complaint in some cases, and affected bitches prove rather temperamental, and possibly even aggressive at such times. Neutering is one option which can be considered under these circumstances, but the cost of this surgery in a bitch is likely to be twice as much as for a dog.

There are various ways of controlling the sexual behavior of dogs of both sexes. If, however, the dog is required for showing, a bitch, which could later be used for breeding, should be chosen, rather than a male dog.

Sources

Puppies are available from a variety of sources but not all are suitable. Certain pet stores stock mongrel and even pedigree puppies, and there are also large suppliers, who may advertise a range of breeds in newspapers. In neither case are the puppies likely to have been bred on the premises, so such sources are usually best avoided and should always been investigated with caution. The puppies will almost certainly be stressed, after having been moved from a breeding unit and mixed with other dogs in an environment that may not be ideal. Stress has been shown to be a major predisposing factor to parvovirus infection.

Below: The Komondor has an unusual coat that requires meticulous grooming.

Above: Direct contact with a reputable breeder is always the best way to obtain a pedigree dog.

Right: Always choose an inquisitive and confident puppy. The timid one is likely to grow into a nervous dog.

Many people prefer to acquire mongrels from animal welfare organizations. Addresses of these societies can be found in telephone directories, or obtained from a veterinarian. Litters of mongrel puppies are frequently given to these organizations, and make delightful pets. If new homes are not found for these puppies, they often have to be destroyed.

Obtaining an adult dog from this source is more risky, however, especially if the temperament and background of the dog are unknown. No organization will knowingly try seek a home for a vicious dog, but an individual may prove relatively withdrawn and nervous after maltreatment by previous owners. Due allowance must be made for such behavior, especially at first, but, even when warned beforehand, people still accept such dogs only to return them a few days later. Ill-treated dogs require considerable patience and may never completely regain their trust in humans. Those closest to them will probably be accepted eventually. Homes with small children are not ideal environments for dogs of this type, because any teasing, particularly with food, can have serious consequences.

Increasing numbers of pedigree dogs are also passing into the care of welfare organizations, often because their owners can no longer afford to keep them as pets. Before allowing pedigree dogs to go to new homes, many societies will want to be assured that the dog will not be used for breeding, and will often retain the dog's pedigree for this reason when a new home is found. Some insist on neutering, and the new owners will probably be interviewed to establish whether they will provide a good permanent home for the dog. Enquiries of this type, and even home visits, are not unusual, and should not be taken as a personal slight. The society is probably trying to ensure that the dog has a stable future.

Animal welfare organizations are rarely wealthy. Feeding and other expenses mean that costs often run alarmingly high, with no guarantee of income. When accepting a dog from an organization of this type, a donation should always be made to their funds, to help their work to continue.

Greyhounds which have been retired from the track – certainly by the age of five years and often younger if they have not proved fast enough – are sometimes offered as pets. As these dogs have been kept in kennels for their entire lives, it is not easy to adapt them to a domestic environment. Such dogs will not be housetrained, will take time to settle down satisfactorily, and other pets, such as cats, may be at risk. However, it can be possible for them to adapt, and various specialist greyhound homing groups now exist to train them for this purpose. Organizations of this type can be contacted through a local track.

When seeking a particular breed of dog, it is strongly recommended to contact a breeder directly to discuss specific requirements. The vast majority of breeders are genuine enthusiasts and, although they cannot keep all the dogs they breed, they will have an interest in ensuring their subsequent welfare. There are various means of

discovering the addresses of such people, depending partly on the breed required and the purpose for which the dog is intended.

Local newspapers often run advertisements from breeders in the immediate vicinity, but, for more unusual breeds, traveling further afield will probably be necessary. Annual directories published in many countries, list breeders under breed headings and may be available in libraries. Specialist papers and periodicals will provide details of breeders and reports of shows, revealing which bloodlines are winning consistently. Those seeking a potential show dog should visit shows. Veterinarians may also be prepared to pass on addresses of breeders known to them. Lastly, direct contact with the canine governing authority of the country concerned may yield results.

Breeders will, if requested, notify a prospective owner when a litter becomes available. The price paid for a pedigree dog depends to some extent on the breed, the bloodline, and the qualities of the individual dog. Rarity value can often be significant; Shar-Pei puppies, for example, currently fetch about $2,000 each in the United States (£3,800 in Britain). Although breeding dogs on a small scale is rarely a profitable enterprise, a breeder recognized for breeding prize-winning pedigrees will charge high prices for stock. Pedigree and type will be important factors for an intending exhibitor but not for someone seeking a pet dog.

If one puppy in a litter has an insignificant fault, such as incorrect coloration or markings, that renders it of little value for show purposes, a breeder may be pleased to find a good home for it, usually at a reduced price. Such bargains must be viewed sceptically, however, as, if the dog has a real deformity, this could prove a costly source of trouble later. It is well worth asking about any examination the breeding stock may have undergone, for hip dysplasia for example, or congenital diseases. Breeders should readily volunteer such information.

Left: Dogs that have spent much of their lives outside in kennels rarely adapt very well to a domestic environment. They will not be housetrained and may be shy and withdrawn.

CHOOSING AN INDIVIDUAL

Below: If possible, it is worthwhile observing a group of puppies for a time to attempt to assess something of their character in terms of fearfulness, friendliness, alertness, activity and dominance.

Aside from health considerations, visiting a litter before choosing a puppy can be very useful for assessing behavioral characteristics. A breeder will be more interested in specific show points, while a pet owner will be more concerned about general temperament. Observing a litter at first-hand provides an ideal opportunity to pick an individual that suits particular requirements, although there is more likely to be variation from litter to litter than from puppy to puppy. It can be best to avoid the most submissive or nervous puppy and the most aggressive: in later life, these may be unpredictable and difficult to manage. A puppy displaying a lively, outgoing temperament may merely reflect the fact that it has been given more attention, but it is likely to settle better in a new home, and prove more acceptable and more responsive to training.

Puppies will not be fully independent and able to go to a new home until they are at least eight-weeks old, but breeders are generally happy for litters to be seen earlier – around five weeks after birth. The environment where the puppies are being kept is significant. Their surroundings should be relatively clean; any loose or runny motions in the pen might indicate a digestive disturbance. A litter reared close to people, rather than being kept isolated in a kennel, is likely to prove more amenable

to human company, and the puppies will probably settle more quickly into a new home.

Puppies at this age naturally sleep for long periods, and then become very active for short spells. Bearing this in mind, dominant individuals can most easily be spotted at feeding time. These more pugnacious puppies, as well as the most submissive and the smallest, are best avoided, in case these traits become emphasized in later life. There should be no signs of lameness or any limb deformities. The bitch may appear slightly thin at this stage, having nourished her offspring for over a month, but this is no cause for concern.

Being able to recognize a healthy puppy in a pet show is particularly important, as the staff are unlikely to be as knowledgeable as breeders. Look for signs of general good care – a healthy coat, for instance – and be wary of indications of poor health – particular thinness, for instance, may indicate undernourishment. In any case, a closer examination should always be carried out, with the owner's permission. The skin of a puppy is quite pliable, and should be loose to the touch. It is worth feeling the skin underneath the puppy, in the midline, to see if there is a swelling under the skin, which could indicate an umbilical hernia. This is not usually a serious complaint, but it could require surgical correction later. Herniation elsewhere on the abdomen is less common. The eyes must be clear and bright, while the ears should not reveal any sign of discharge or unpleasant smells. There should be no hint of lameness when the puppy walks.

It is best to acquire a puppy when the weather is mild enough for training outside. Dogs should never be obtained before the new owner goes away on holiday. Apart from the

disturbing effect on the animal, most kennels will not take puppies, as often they do not settle well away from home. Dogs should never be obtained at Christmas either, as the household will probably be in temporary chaos.

A conscientious breeder may well ask prospective owners various questions, to ensure that they appreciate the responsibility of owning a puppy, and will be able to care for it. There is now a trend toward waiting until the puppy is about nine weeks old before moving it to a new environment. The actual phase of social development in puppies is concentrated largely in the 4- to 12-week period after birth. Individuals are at their most impressionable at this time and start to relate to their littermates and other creatures, including humans. Puppies begin to learn the sensation of fear at about eight weeks of age and so moving a puppy at this stage will serve to emphasize the traumatic experience of isolation from its dam and littermates. Research has revealed that if puppies have not experienced human attention by the age of three months, they are likely to be withdrawn, and subsequently prove unresponsive to training. Individuals isolated too soon from other puppies show the reverse effect, being disadvantaged in later life when meeting other dogs, and bitches may even refuse to mate for this reason.

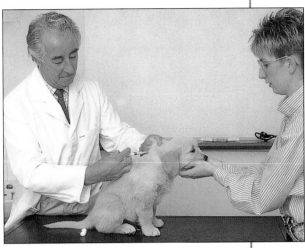

Above: Inoculation against common canine diseases is vital.

SIGNS OF HEALTH

● You should make sure that the puppy of your choice is healthy before finalizing your purchase. Pick up the puppy to check that it does not object or show signs of pain; its body should be firm and relaxed (1). Lift the ear flap and check that the ear canal is dry and clean (2). Open the mouth and gently check that the tongue and gums are pink (3). The eyes should be clear and bright and there should be no signs of discharge (4). Run your hand against the grain of the coat to check for sores and the black dust caused by fleas (5). Check under the tail that there is no staining, which would indicate diarrhea (6).

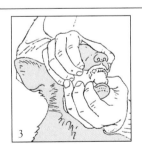

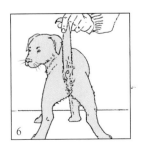

SETTLING IN

Essential equipment

It will be necessary to obtain various items for the dog prior to its arrival. A vast range of pet equipment is now available, but only certain items will be essential at the outset. Feeding and drinking bowls are obviously necessary, and various types are stocked by most pet stores. Plastic generally is not to be recommended, as most bowls made of this material are easily chewed or scratched, and prove difficult to clean thoroughly as a result. Stainless-steel containers are relatively expensive, but are much more hygienic, although they can be tipped over quite easily. The traditional glazed earthenware bowl is easy to clean and stable.

A bed is an important part of the puppy's world and the puppy must be taught to recognize it as its own particular territory. Initially, the bed need not be expensive or elaborate: a clean cardboard box will suffice, with the front cut away for easy access. The bottom of the box should be lined with newspaper, and a blanket placed on top. As the puppy grows, the box can be replaced with another of a larger size. Once the deciduous teeth are lost, and the accompanying chewing phase is passed, a permanent basket can be obtained. A large number of types are currently produced, but it is important to select one for its functional rather than decorative value. The main criterion must be to ensure that the basket can be easily and thoroughly washed, to prevent fleas.

During recent years, bean bags manufactured for dogs have gained greatly in popularity. Available in a variety of sizes, these are filled with polystyrene beads and, apart from providing somewhere to sleep, they can also serve as a play area. The outer covering should be removable and washable, and must also be tough enough to withstand any chewing or scratching. The dog can snuggle down, displacing the beads in the bag, to find the most comfortable sleeping position. Some designs have fire-retardant properties.

Special pens can also be bought to restrict a puppy's domain. These are made up of wire mesh panels that can be clipped together; stored flat when not in use; or fitted into the back of a car to make a traveling cage.

A puppy should get used to wearing a thin collar around the home, although it should not be taken out on a lead until after its course of vaccinations is completed. Most collars are still made of leather. Nylon collars are also popular, being easily washed and strong, without causing damage to the fur. Plastic

Right: A wide range of beds and bedding is available, including:
1 & 2. plastic beds
3. a vet bed
4. china bowls
5. a plastic bowl
6. a metal bowl
7. a padded bed

collars are not as durable as nylon or leather. Some collars cannot be altered in size, while others are adjustable, which is useful for a growing dog. Broader collars are recommended for bigger dogs.

An identity medallion of some kind is a legal requirement in various countries, including the United States and Britain. These should give the dog's home address, and a telephone number if possible. Some countries require other information to be included, such as a license number and details of rabies vaccination. Plastic capsules, containing this information written in indelible ink on a piece of paper, are an alternative. Some dogs, such as racing greyhounds, are tattooed with a number on the inside of the ear but this is an unusual method of identification.

Many dog toys are now available, but the least elaborate are generally preferable. Care must always be taken to avoid those which could be chewed into sharp fragments or inadvertently swallowed: small balls, for instance, can prove lethal. A large, lightweight plastic football is better. Various hide chews also provide good, safe exercise.

The new puppy

It is always best to collect a puppy during the morning if possible, so that it will have time to settle into its new surroundings before nightfall. If you are driving, take a secure container to put the puppy in, or let it travel on a passenger's lap, which should be protected with an old blanket. The unfamiliar sensations of the journey may make a young dog sick, and paper towelling may be needed for clearing up.

For a pure-bred puppy, it will be necessary to obtain its pedigree from the vendor. This document gives details of all direct ancestors extending back over at least four generations. The prefix "Ch." indicates that a particular dog was recognised as a champion, and suggests that the puppy itself may eventually do well in the show ring. Registration papers or the correct form to show transfer of ownership to the registration body, will also be needed.

A vaccination certificate, giving details of past vaccinations is an important document for future reference, and this applies to any dog, not just a pedigree puppy. A two-month-old dog will probably have received its first set of vaccinations; another set will be required about a month later to complete the protection and enable the dog to be taken out safely. A diet sheet must also be obtained from the breeder, to show what the puppy has been eating and the frequency of feeding. For the first week, it is sensible to follow this closely, to minimise the risk of digestive disturbances.

Changes in feeding should be introduced only gradually, over a period of time.

After the journey, the puppy will want to relieve itself, and should be encouraged from the start to do this outside, supervised, so that it cannot run away. If the weather is bad, the puppy should be taught to use a dirt box filled with cat litter, placed on newspaper in the house, or in a suitable adjoining outbuilding.

Above: Feeding and drinking bowls are essential equipment. They are marketed in a variety of materials – stainless steel is among the most hygienic.

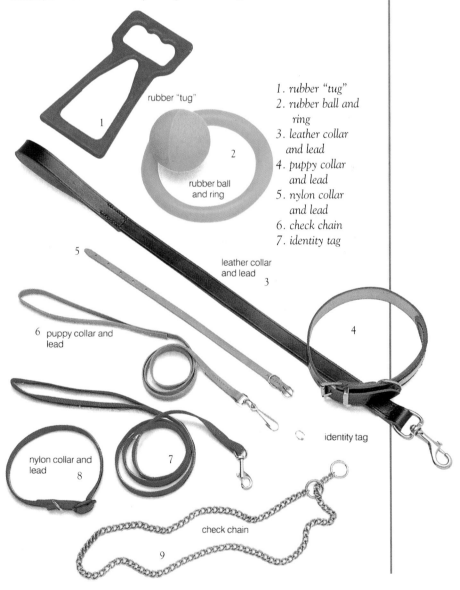

1. rubber "tug"
2. rubber ball and ring
3. leather collar and lead
4. puppy collar and lead
5. nylon collar and lead
6. check chain
7. identity tag

rubber "tug"

rubber ball and ring

leather collar and lead

puppy collar and lead

nylon collar and lead

identity tag

check chain

The puppy will take time to adjust to its new environment and may not eat heartily at first. The puppy should be offered food and then left alone with its bowl for about a quarter of an hour. Any food remaining after this period should be removed, but a fresh supply of water must always be made available. After the food there might be a brief period of play, and then the young dog can be placed in its bed and will probably go to sleep.

It is likely that the puppy will be restless on its first night, after being separated from its fellows and finding itself in strange surroundings. Some owners decide to put the basket in their bedrooms, with a pen around it, for perhaps a fortnight until the puppy feels more secure. Left on its own, the young dog is almost certain to cry and howl for a while, but must not be punished, particularly during these early days, when every effort should be made to forge a strong bond between puppy and owner.

The older dog

How well an older dog settles into a household will depend very much on its previous history. If it has been trained, and is used to living in a

Above: Puppies are always playful and sometimes quite disruptive, but they do like to integrate and become part of the family.

Right: Contact with other animals must not be forced by the owner, but some surprising alliances can be formed if circumstances are right.

Left: When there is already an established dog at home, the introduction of a new puppy must be carefully controlled, particularly once the younger dog has grown more assertive. Fighting is particularly likely to break out over food. Dogs should always be given their food in separate rooms, out of each other's way. Introduce two adult dogs on neutral territory, such as a local park, rather than on home ground, where the newcomer is more likely to be viewed as a challenger.

house, then it will probably adapt quite quickly, unlike one that has spent its life in kennels. If its vaccinations are up to date, there will be no need to restrict an adult dog to the garden, and it can be taken out on a lead for exercise. This is particularly useful if two dogs have to be introduced, as their first meeting can take place on neutral territory, such as a park.

Introductions to other pets

Two puppies of similar age kept together are often less of a problem than a single individual, as they will provide company for each other and will play together. Dogs, being pack animals, are very social creatures and so should not be left on their own for long periods every day. In some circumstances, a dog already established in a household may well resent a newcomer, unless the introduction is carefully controlled.

Trouble is particularly likely to arise if the new dog is younger and receives much more attention. The older individual, who would normally be the dominant member of the pair, is likely to feel that its position is being challenged and resent the newcomer. It is important to ensure that the established dog receives equal, or preferably more, attention than the puppy, to reinforce its dominance. The situation may alter subtly over a period of years, however, as the younger dog assumes the dominant role from its ageing companion. Two bitches normally live most contentedly together, particularly if they have been brought up together. Feeding times are always especially likely to lead to disagreements, and

the two should be fed separately, well out of reach of each other, and preferably in separate rooms.

In the case of older dogs, careful supervision will be required to prevent them fighting to decide an order of dominance. Once again, the established dog should receive adequate attention from the owner, to emphasize its dominant position and lessen the risk of subsequent disputes.

Where there are other pets already in a household, like cats, a similar method of introduction should prevent difficulties arising It is possible that the cat might resent the puppy for a few days and disappear for longer periods than usual. It will take several weeks for a dog and a cat to accept each other fully but they may then become devoted companions.

Above: The critical period for socialization is between five and twelve weeks of age, after this time puppies will have difficulty accepting human company. A single puppy may pine for a while after it has been moved to a new home.

BASIC DAILY CARE

*Pets are not able to look after themselves and dogs are no exception;
they are considerably more dependent on their owners than cats are.
A balanced diet and regular exercise are really the essence of daily
care. Different breeds require different amount of exercise,
but all dogs need supervised walks or runs outside every day,
and all dogs appreciate an organized feeding routine.*

*Below: Dog food
comes in a variety of
forms:*
1. *semi-moist meat*
2. *tinned meat*
3. *complete dried food*
4. *fresh meat*
5. *dog biscuits*
6. *chew sticks*
7. *vitamin treats*
8. *raw hide chew*
9. *puppy mixer
   meal*

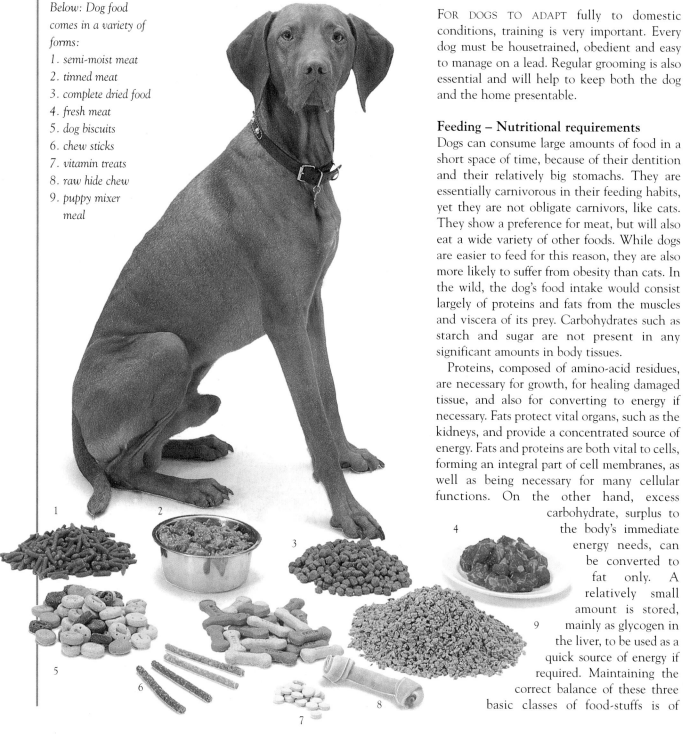

FOR DOGS TO ADAPT fully to domestic conditions, training is very important. Every dog must be housetrained, obedient and easy to manage on a lead. Regular grooming is also essential and will help to keep both the dog and the home presentable.

Feeding – Nutritional requirements
Dogs can consume large amounts of food in a short space of time, because of their dentition and their relatively big stomachs. They are essentially carnivorous in their feeding habits, yet they are not obligate carnivors, like cats. They show a preference for meat, but will also eat a wide variety of other foods. While dogs are easier to feed for this reason, they are also more likely to suffer from obesity than cats. In the wild, the dog's food intake would consist largely of proteins and fats from the muscles and viscera of its prey. Carbohydrates such as starch and sugar are not present in any significant amounts in body tissues.

Proteins, composed of amino-acid residues, are necessary for growth, for healing damaged tissue, and also for converting to energy if necessary. Fats protect vital organs, such as the kidneys, and provide a concentrated source of energy. Fats and proteins are both vital to cells, forming an integral part of cell membranes, as well as being necessary for many cellular functions. On the other hand, excess carbohydrate, surplus to the body's immediate energy needs, can be converted to fat only. A relatively small amount is stored, mainly as glycogen in the liver, to be used as a quick source of energy if required. Maintaining the correct balance of these three basic classes of food-stuffs is of considerable importance in keeping a dog both healthy and well nourished.

Vitamins and minerals must also be present in the diet, in relatively minute quantities. Vitamin D is especially important, as it is ultimately responsible for good bone development; as are the minerals calcium and phosphorus. Vitamin A is one of the fat-soluble group of vitamins stored in the liver. It helps to ensure good eyesight and prevent infections. Vitamin C, while important for preventing infections, is less vital in a dog's diet, as most can manufacture this vitamin in their bodies. About one dog in every 1,000 is unable to carry out this process, however, and will require dietary supplementation: 100 mg of ascorbic acid for every 55 lb (25 kg) of body weight. Vitamin C is a relatively unstable compound, and can deteriorate quite rapidly. For this reason, it should not be stored for long periods before use.

A small amount of roughage, such as bran, is also beneficial. Although indigestible, and thus not of nutritional value, it provides bulk and assists the movement of food through the intestinal tract. It is possible that dogs consume grass in order to provide themselves with roughage. Grass may also act as an emetic; young puppies suffering from roundworms often eat grass and then vomit both grass and worms in an apparent attempt to purge themselves. In view of such behavior, it is unwise to treat areas of rough grass with chemicals: these areas, rather than lawns, are favored for this purpose.

Types of food

Prepared food – The manufacture of dog food is a major industry today and much study and research has been carried out to ensue that such products conform to dogs' nutritional requirements. Canned foods are still the most popular and palatable of all the commercial dog foods, and most of those on offer provide a complete, balanced diet. However, the label should always be checked – a few brands contain only meat, with no added vitamins or minerals.

Canned foods can contain a high level of water – sometimes more than 80 percent. If the water content is high, the dog will need to eat more to satisfy its nutritional requirements. The price of canned dog foods can vary widely

Above: Young puppies have voracious appetites. Their growth rate is at its peak during the first six months of life, so a sufficient intake of food is essential to produce the energy required for healthy development.

Left: If a puppy is reluctant to feed at first, some supervision – perhaps hand-feeding by offering food on a finger – may help.

Above: Dogs guard their food jealously. However, aggressive behavior towards humans over the dinner bowl should not be tolerated.

according to the instructions on the pack, as an excessive intake will lead to obesity.

Manufacturers have recently started to produce more specialized foods. Many ranges now include canned foods designed for puppies, containing a relatively high level of protein to assist growth. Small cans are also marked for fussy eaters or delicate dogs, notably some toy breeds. Canned cat food can be fed to dogs and is generally higher in protein, which may tempt fastidious eaters. (Cats should not be fed dog food, however, as cats require the amino acid taurine in their food.)

All canned foods can be kept, unopened, for over a year. Once opened, however, even if stored in a refrigerator as recommended, they will not stay fresh for more than a few days.

Semi-moist dog foods are often prepared to resemble raw chunks of meat but in fact contain relatively little meat. Soya bean meal is a common ingredient, providing part of the protein value of the foodstuff. The water content of semi-moist foods may be as little as 25 per cent; various chemicals are added to prevent the food from drying out or spoiling. Sucrose is often added for these reasons, and to improve the palatability of the food. These products are sold in sealed foil packets and, unlike canned foods, do not need to be refrigerated, but must be used within three months or so.

from brand to brand, usually reflecting differences in the amount of cereal included. Cheaper brands contain more carbohydrate in this form, whereas more expensive canned foods contain actual chunks of meat in a gravy. Manufacturers often suggest supplementing canned food with a biscuit meal, especially if the brand contains a relatively high proportion of meat. This helps to reduce the overall cost, as the biscuit is used to provide the energy content of the diet, while the meat contributes protein. It is important to feed the biscuit meal

FIRST 12 MONTHS FEED CHART			
NUMBER OF MEALS PER DAY AT AGE IN MONTHS	WEANING 0–3	3–6	6–12
TOY (less than 4.5 kg /10 lb)	90–150 g (3–5 oz)	200–600 g (7–21 oz)	300–800 g (11–28 oz)
SMALL (4.5–9 kg /10–20 lb)	200–350 g (7–12 oz)	350–800 g (12–280 oz)	750–950 g (26–33 oz)
MEDIUM (9–22 kg /20–50 lb)	350–600 g (12–21 oz)	700–1 kg (25–350 oz)	850–1.6 kg (30–56 oz)
LARGE (22–34 kg /50–75 lb)	600–850 g (21–30 oz)	800–1.6 kg (28–56 oz)	1.6–2 kg (56–70 oz)

Dried dog foods are marketed in various forms, such as pellets, flakes, meal and expanded chunks. Heat is used in the manufacturing process, and serves to make the starch component more digestible, but also destroys certain vitamins, particularly Vitamin A and members of the Vitamin B group. To compensate for this loss, vitamins are added in proportionately larger amounts at the start of the process, or included in the fat that is sprayed onto the foodstuff to improve its palatability after the water has been removed. Dried dog foods do contain some water – normally about 10 percent – and can be stored without refrigeration. They can also be kept for long periods without losing their vitamin content, although most manufacturers specify an expiry date on the packaging.

There are certain advantages in feeding dry food. Relatively little in terms of weight is required, and dry food is also supposed to reduce the risk of accumulations of tartar on the teeth. Manufacturers usually recommend soaking dry food when first introducing it to the diet, and there is no reason for not continuing this preparation, except that, once soaked, any food left uneaten at the end of the day will need to be discarded, or it will turn moldy, particularly in damp weather. A dog that eats dried food will need to drink more water to compensate.

Various meat products are also available, sold in blocks or tubes in many pet stores. Most need to be kept refrigerated, especially once opened, and contain no additional vitamins or minerals, or even cereal in some cases. These foods do not provide a balanced diet on their own and must be mixed with biscuit meal to ensure that vital nutrients are obtained.

Fresh food – Although there is no need to keep changing a diet when commercially prepared foods are given, variety is important if the diet consists of fresh food. It is not adequate to feed just meat on its own, as this is deficient in various vitamins such as A, D and E, as well as minerals such as iodine. In addition, the ratio between calcium and phosphorus – which should be of the order of 1.2 to 1 – is seriously imbalanced in meat, where the tissues contain excessive amounts of phosphorus. This will cause skeletal abnormalities, particularly in young dogs. In severe cases, bones may fracture easily, and the dog may become reluctant to walk.

As well as from meat from body tissues, internal organs or offal can be given. Heart, kidneys, "melts" (spleens), "lights" (lungs), and tripe (from the stomachs of herbivores), are all sold cheaply by butchers for pet food. In kennels, tripe is sometimes fed raw, not dressed as it would be for human consumption, and, although favored by many dogs, it smells extremely unpleasant in this state.

While there is certainly no truth in the story that raw meat makes dogs aggressive, various parasites and infections can be transmitted by this means; to kill these, it is always advisable to cook meat before feeding it to the dog. The meat should be cooked for about 20 minutes; any longer and excessive loss of vitamins will occur. Allow the meat to cool to prevent burning the dog's mouth, but slightly warm food is more palatable than cold, and may tempt a dog with a poor appetite to start eating again. It is often easier to cook a relatively large quantity of fresh food at one time – perhaps a week's supply – and then freeze some for later use. All frozen food must be completely thawed before being given to the dog, to prevent digestive disturbances.

Fresh food must be mixed with a biscuit meal supplemented by vitamins and minerals. Approximately equal quantities of fresh food and biscuit should provide an adequate balance. Some dogs are allergic to gluten – a component of protein that is present in flour. In this case, they cannot be fed biscuits or meal. Potatoes that have been well boiled, or boiled rice, can be given as alternatives, with a vitamin and mineral supplement.

Vegetables are of no direct benefit to dogs, as they are relatively indigestible. Some, such as boiled cabbage, tend to precipitate flatulence. Their only value lies in the fact that they add bulk to the diet without significantly increasing the calorific value of the meal, and thus they help satisfy the appetite without causing weight gain. Some dogs like raw carrot, which provides carotene that is converted in the body to Vitamin A.

Bread can sometimes be harmful to dogs. Flour used to contain a bleaching agent to emphasize the color of white bread and the chemical used for this purpose, nitrogen trichloride, caused fits in dogs. In time, its effects were realized and the use of this chemical has now been banned in most countries. Both brown and white bread are safe in the United States and Britain.

A practical diet – How much a dog is fed and how often will depend on the type, size and age of the dog and on its general state of health. Young, pregnant or lactating dogs require more food than normal adults and will probably need to be fed more frequently. Active, or working dogs, especially those spending much of their time outside – hunting hounds, for instance – require more food than pets. Overweight individuals, or those suffering from specific ailments, will need a modified diet.

Above: Puppies generally learn fairly quickly to eat from a plate or bowl, typically picking up this skill from their mothers.

The manufacturers' recommendations given on the labels of canned and prepared foods can be followed with confidence. Most guidelines are in the form of a weight (or volume) of food to weight of dog ratio, specifying, for example that a 15 oz (430 g) can daily will be adequate for dogs weighing about 30 lb (3.6 kg). If your dog is a particular breed, it will be easy to establish how much it should weight by consulting either the breed standard or a reference book. If there is any uncertainty, or if the dog is a mongrel, weighing is a simple procedure. Weight your dog by subtracting your weight from the weight shown on the scales when you are holding them.

Dogs are usually fed once a day, or in half-rations morning and evening. Recent studies suggest that either is satisfactory. Feeding a dog immediately before the rest of the household has its meal, can ensure that it is less likely to become a nuisance at the table. Dogs should never be fed late at night either, because they will probably want to relieve themselves afterwards, since food in the stomach stimulates intestinal movement.

Only dry food can be left in the feeding bowl during the day. Any left over the following day can be placed on top of the new supply, or simply discarded. This method of feeding is not recommended for young dogs, however. Other types of food will attract flies and spoil

if left for long in warm weather. In any case, dogs usually bolt their food within minutes. After the dog has finished, its bowl should be washed using detergent – separately from the utensils used for humans – and then rinsed.

Dogs appreciate a routine and, once a feeding pattern is established, it is best not to alter it. Dogs do not seem to get bored with the same food every day, but some owners still offer fresh food once or twice a week.

Water

The volume of water a dog consumes will depend partly on its diet, as dogs fed on canned rations drink less than those given dried foods. More water will be drunk in warm weather and after periods of exercise. Abnormal thirst can indicate various medical conditions; if a disorder of this type is suspected, the amount of water drunk each day should be recorded to help the veterinarian make a diagnosis. It is always dangerous to withhold or restrict water from a dog, even if it is proving incontinent.

Many dogs like to drink from puddles, but this should be discouraged because of the danger of disease. They must also be prevented from drinking from toilet bowls, both for hygiene reasons and because of the risk of ingesting harmful substances such as bleach. This behavior can be avoided by ensuring that the lid of the toilet is always kept down.

Right: This chart illustrates the age–weight relationship of different breeds – their growth curves. While these are broadly similar, certain breeds take longer to reach their optimum weight.

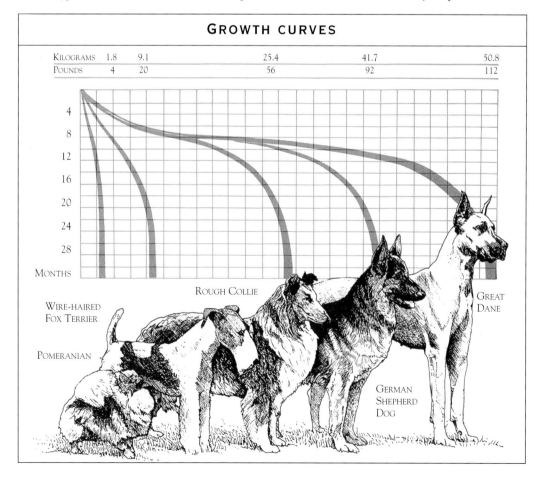

GROWTH CURVES

Kilograms	1.8	9.1		25.4	41.7	50.8
Pounds	4	20		56	92	112

ROUGH COLLIE

WIRE-HAIRED FOX TERRIER

GREAT DANE

POMERANIAN

GERMAN SHEPHERD DOG

Left: Loss of appetite can be the result of feeding tidbits between meals. Human treats – such as ice cream – are best avoided.

Treats

Chocolate drops are manufactured especially for dogs and can be particularly valuable for use as rewards in training. They must never be fed above the recommended level, however, as this can be harmful. Other sweets are of no value and will probably lead to tooth decay. Excessive sugar may well result in diarrhea. Yeast-based tablets of various kinds are highly palatable, and can act as a valuable source of B vitamins. It should be remembered that dogs are very much creatures of habit, however, and giving treats between meals will cause repeated pestering – it is best to set and maintain a regular time for giving treats, such as late evening.

Bones are again not essential from a nutritional viewpoint, but dogs undoubtedly appreciate being able to gnaw on a bone. It is possible that this lessens the likelihood that the dog will try to damage furniture or carpeting by chewing them. It is also understood to help prevent a build-up of tartar on the teeth. Great care must be taken, however, not to give bones that can splinter, or be swallowed and become lodged in the mouth or throat. Big marrow bones, obtainable from butchers, are most suitable, providing the cut ends show no signs of flaking. Bones from poultry and rabbits are among the most dangerous, and should never be given; make sure none are left lying around where dogs could steal them.

Milk is not essential either for dogs, and is indigestible for many. Greyhounds, for instance, lack the enzyme lactase, necessary to break down the sugar that is present in milk. The sugar is then converted by bacteria in the gut into lactic acid, and this causes diarrhea. Other beverages are also not recommended, although some dogs will drink cold tea, especially if it contains sugar, but they do not like saccharin.

Loss of appetite

Some dogs can be fussy eaters – easily put off their food by the presence of strangers or by alterations in their surroundings. This applies particularly to the smaller breeds, although the problem is rare. Because loss of appetite can be a symptom of various diseases, some of which are serious, it is always best to have a dog checked by a veterinarian if such behavior does occur. If there is a bitch in heat nearby, then a male dog may be distracted from its food. Dogs may also appear to lose their appetites if they are scavenging elsewhere.

Feeding tidbits between meals is likely to spoil the dog's appetite, and, on a regular basis, will lead to obesity and other harmful effects. If a dog is genuinely fastidious about food, it is possible to improve palatability by smearing margarine or some other type of fat over the surface. Canned or fresh foods are generally more acceptable than dried diets.

TRAINING

*Below: Simple
commands, such as
"Sit" and "Stay" will
be learned first.*

Training is a vital part of dog ownership: it ensures both a greater degree of safety for the dog, and the development of a good bond between an owner and their pet. An untrained adult dog is a liability in every sense. If it has never had to adopt a submissive role, it may regard itself as dominant to its owner and prove aggressive. Basic training is not difficult

Right: The first stage of house-training is to teach a puppy to use newspaper.

Far right: Accustomizing the puppy to a new bed is another important step in early training.

to accomplish, but must be carried out regularly to a fixed routine. Much can be achieved by varying the tone of the voice – to express displeasure for example – and physical punishment should only be used in the very last resort: a sharp tap from a rolled-up newspaper is more than adequate. Praise and affection greatly stimulate good behavior.

Housetraining

A small area of garden should be set aside for the dog's use. Scent plays a very important part in the dog's selection of a site for urination and defecation. Dogs are naturally clean animals and, once introduced to a correct routine, will normally attempt to follow it after a short period of time.

After meals, and last thing at night, the puppy should be placed on the designated spot. Repeated use of a phrase such as "Clean dog" will help to ensure that it learns to associate this sound with the required response. Best results are likely if the puppy is monitored during this activity, rather than being allowed to wander off, or follow its owner back to the door. Once it has performed, it should be praised. Good training relies on repetition of words or actions.

A dirt box, low-sided to permit easy access,

should be provided for young puppies if the weather is bad. A large plastic tray, filled with cat litter, is ideal for this purpose. The tray should be lined with newspaper, and sheets should also be spread around the floor nearby, in case of accidents. Make sure that the underlying surface is also easy to wash off and disinfect if required.

If an accident does occur, there is no point punishing the puppy unless it is caught in the act. Dogs are not capable of associating harsh treatment with a past transgression and rubbing a dog's nose in its excrement would be both useless and unpleasant. Once the area is cleaned up, it should be washed thoroughly with one of the commercially available de-scenting preparations, or with vinegar, to remove the puppy's scent from

Left: When you are fairly confident your puppy has performed outside, open the door, let it in and praise it lavishly.

the spot. Certain pine disinfectants that are available are now believed to reinforce scents rather than disguise them. If any trace is left, the puppy will be attracted back to the site for the same purpose. It is also possible to buy chemicals specifically designed to attract a puppy to a certain spot. These can certainly be useful if the puppy cannot be let out for any reason; for example when it is very young and still unvaccinated.

It is very important to ensure that dog feces are removed as soon as possible, because of the accompanying health risks – especially where young children are present. One means of disposal now available is a bucket-type container with slits in the side which can be buried in a corner of the garden and covered with a lid. The feces are deposited inside the container with a shovel, and chemicals break down the excrement. This process will not guarantee to destroy parasitic worm eggs – such as those of *Toxocara canis* which can present a serious danger to human health – but they are a good idea if children are present as they will provide some degree of protection for them.

It will take about three months to train a puppy to ask to go out when it needs to and slightly longer before it performs on demand. In unfamiliar surroundings, such as in a veterinarian's surgery when a urine sample is required, the latter command may be ignored, particularly in bitches. Whereas a puppy might relieve itself as many as six times in the course of one day, an adult dog will only defecate once or twice and has much better control over its bladder. Letting a dog out last thing at night and early in the morning should ensure that there is no soiling indoors. When the dog is asleep, urine production falls naturally in any case.

Male dogs urinate much more frequently than bitches. This is because their urine also acts partly as a territorial scent marker. When out on its walk, a dog often sniffs at lampposts and trees, before lifting its leg and urinating to leave its scent. On the other hand, a bitch invariably squats when urinating, as does a young male before puberty.

In public places such as parks, specific areas are sometimes set aside for dogs, and these should be used whenever possible. Much of the unpopularity of dogs in city areas stems from the soiling of walkways. If an accident does occur the owner should always clear up the resulting mess. Under no circumstances whatsoever should dogs be allowed to use children's sandpits or play areas because of the risk of transmitting disease from their excrement.

A breakdown in toilet training may occur in elderly or sick dogs and the introduction of a new dog to the household may cause an established male to lose its sense of housetraining. The dog is only emphasizing that it is already settled in the territory and it should return to its old habits once it has accepted the presence of the intruder.

Obedience training

Various commands must be taught to ensure obedience. A combination of patience and firmness achieves the best results; it is counter-productive to punish a puppy harshly if it fails to respond correctly every time, especially at the beginning.

At mealtimes, dogs will be more receptive to teaching. A young dog will soon learn to come if its name is called when food is offered. It can be taught to sit before being given its dinner, but must it is important never to tease a dog with food as this is likely to lead to serious problems later. Sitting is a normal posture for a dog and this command is often easily mastered. At first, it may be necessary to exert gentle pressure over the hindquarters to encourage the puppy to adopt the required posture.

It is important to teach a puppy to "stay" on command, to enable it to be controlled off the lead and in city areas. After play, the puppy can be placed in its bed, and told to "stay." It might remain there if it is tired, but if not, it may leap up again and should be put back, and the command repeated.

After the commands of "sit" and "stay" have been learned, more complex lessons can then be taught. Next, the puppy can be taught to "lie down." This is more difficult because young dogs are normally especially active and will not wish to stay in any one position for very long. Once again, it may be necessary to put your puppy into the required posture initially, remembering always to praise it when it obeys.

Another important command is "drop." This command is vital for retrievers, in particular. In the home, a dog that has not been taught to give up an item readily is likely to be both very possessive and possibly will develop aggressive tendencies in later life. Care must be taken when trying to train older dogs of uncertain temperament, as they may bite if someone attempts to take what they believe is their property away from them. Gently prize the jaws apart to retrieve an item from a puppy, while repeating the command. This also accustoms the dog to having its mouth opened, useful for veterinary examinations.

Far left: Training a dog by reward is always the best policy.

Lead training

The first step is to accustom the puppy to wearing its collar – at first, it may well attempt to pull it off. The collar should fit comfortably, neither excessively tight, causing it to rub on the neck, nor so loose that it slides forward toward the head. The size needs to be adjusted as the puppy grows.

There are various types of lead or leash, some of which are only used in certain situations, such as the show ring. For general purposes, the most important feature of a lead is that is must include a secure means of attachment to the collar. Leather leads are more traditional and easier on the hand if the dog is untrained, but nylon is also increasingly available. Harnesses are used for guide dogs, and recommended for breeds such as Dachshunds, which can often suffer from disc problems in the neck region. A harness also makes it easier to pick up a small dog, as the straps will support its weight.

The puppy should be accustomed to a lead before it is actually taken outside the garden. Walking puppy along a fence or similar barrier ensures it cannot pull away in all directions. The puppy will instinctively try to go ahead and this should be gently, but firmly, corrected using the word "heel". Short periods of exercise, lasting a maximum of ten minutes, are sufficient at this stage, and greatest benefit will be gained if they are repeated once or twice daily.

For older dogs, choke or check chains are often employed to facilitate lead training but these are not necessary and a lead and collar can be used in a similar way. It is vital to ensure that the correct size of chain is chosen and that it fits properly; otherwise, a variety of injuries can be inflicted. The size required can be calculated by taking the measurement around

the base of the throat and up over the ears, and adding an extra 2 inches (5 cm). Chains with large links are less likely to cause physical injury. When pressure from the lead is lessened, the chain should slacken, rather than remain tight. The dog should be walked on the handler's left side, with the lead held in the handler's right hand. If the dog starts to pull ahead, the command "heel" should be given. If this is ignored, the command should be followed by a quick, sharp jerk on the lead, and the instruction repeated. This will cause the chain to grip tightly around the dog's throat, creating an unpleasant feeling. When the dog learns to walk at the right pace, it should be praised.

Dogs should not be allowed off the lead in towns for their own safety; bylaws often prohibit this in any case. If the dog is going to be allowed off its lead, choose a spot well away from traffic, people and other dogs. By this stage, the dog must be trained to respond to its name, stay reliably and come when called. Whistles can be useful if the dog disappears off into the distance. A number of blasts on a high-frequency whistle, which will be almost inaudible to the human ear, will help the dog locate its owner from a long way away.

Above: A well-trained dog will observe the rules of the road.

Left: Dog collars should always be adjustable and properly fitted, ensuring that the dog cannot be caught up by its collar and injured.

Right: Dogs are
capable of performing
quite complex tasks.
They can be trained
for a variety of police
and military work,
such as attacking and
chasing suspects,
crowd control,
detection of narcotics
and explosives, and
tracking.

Professional training

Dog obedience classes are held in many areas, under the guidance of an experienced dog handler, and can be valuable for overcoming specific problems with an individual dog. Advanced classes are also often available, once basic training has been mastered. Details of such courses can be obtained from a veterinarian or a local library or information bureau; the cost is usually nominal. It is also possible to send a dog to a professional trainer, at much greater expense. The outcome is less likely to be satisfactory because, although the dog may respond to the trainer, it will not subsequently take commands from its owner as readily. Personal involvement is a prerequisite for successful training.

One particularly severe method of training, which is sometimes advised for difficult cases, but which should not generally be attempted, is the use of a shock collar. There are various types on the market; some are notoriously unreliable and potentially very dangerous. The mild electric shock, triggered by the trainer when the dog fails to respond, may cause physical injury if water is present on the coat. Certain models, which are activated by barking, can be set off by other dogs, and simply serve to confuse the dog who is wearing the collar.

Common behavioral problems

When puppies reach the age of six months they will be teething and, to try to relieve the irritation, are likely to chew anything within reach. This is a natural tendency, the effects of which can be made less devastating by providing hide chews and by ensuring that shoes and similar items are not left lying around. In older dogs, destructive chewing often occurs when the owner is out for long periods. It may indicate a lack of security or inadequate exercise. The remedy lies essentially with the owner, who must compensate for the deficiency and give the dog more attention. A pregnant bitch may also chew or scratch in an attempt to make a nest. This is normal breeding behavior, and may even occur in pseudo pregnancies. The phase will pass, although treatment of the pseudo pregnancy may be required.

Dogs that jump up at people are annoying. It is a habit that stems from inadequate training or may be a sign of exuberance, but either way it must be treated firmly. The dog's front legs should be put back on the floor, with the command "No". The dog should then be ignored for a few minutes.

Dogs often bark at the approach of strangers or at sudden, unexpected noises, but prolonged periods of barking must be discouraged, if only for the neighbors' sakes. Again, such behavior often stems from excitement and is generally encountered more in small breeds, such as the

Right: Other
specialized working
dogs include guide
dogs for the blind and
"hearing" dogs for the
deaf. Certain breeds
are particularly well
suited to this role: for
instance: German
Shepherds and
Labradors.

COMMUNICATION

● The dog communicates through a variety of body positions and facial expressions. The consecutive changes from normal stance to submission are shown here.

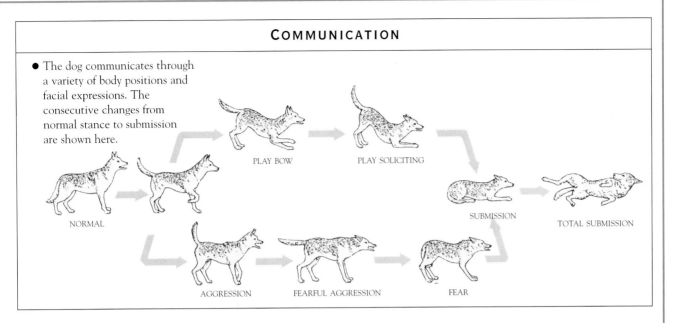

NORMAL

PLAY BOW

PLAY SOLICITING

SUBMISSION

TOTAL SUBMISSION

AGGRESSION

FEARFUL AGGRESSION

FEAR

Chihuahua, rather than bigger dogs. Barking can also be unintentionally encouraged by an owner: for example, if a dog barks when it wants to come inside and the door is opened at once, the dog will associate barking with the door being opened, and carry on until it is let into the house. Leaving a dog alone for a long period may also cause it to bark. If a dog barks persistently when people are present, spraying a jet of water at its head, avoiding the eyes, may discourage it. A muting operation (ventriculocordectomy) is not advisable, although in special circumstances, such as wartime, dogs have been muted so that they could not betray their position.

Wandering is more common in some breeds than others; Beagles, are particularly bad in this respect. Prevention is the easiest solution.

Ensure that all gates are kept closed and fences around the property are well maintained. An urge to wander can result from lack of exercise or from sexual instincts, especially in the case of male dogs when there is a bitch in heat nearby. Neutering has been shown to prevent most males from wandering. If a dog does escape and causes a road accident, its owner may be sued for damages. Insurance against this eventuality is strongly recommended, and is available at very moderate cost, often as part of a health insurance scheme.

One of the most unpleasant behavioral problems is coprophagia, when dogs eat their motions. It has been suggested that a Vitamin B deficiency may predispose to such behavior, but there is often no obvious explanation. Coprophagia is a relatively common vice of dogs that have been kept kenneled in unsanitary surroundings for much of their life. Breaking the habit can be difficult, but if temptation is removed as soon as possible, this will help to overcome the problem.

Far left: The German Shepherd Dog combines high intelligence, slightly aggressive tendencies and acute scenting abilities, making it perfect for training as a guard dog.

Left: Sometimes a court of law may order a dog to be muzzled if it has a proven record of ferocity.

EXERCISE

Above: A dog's vision in daylight is thought to be inferior to that of a man. A dog sees color, static shapes and details very poorly, although it is very sensitive to moving objects and can see a hand waving up to a mile away.

Exercise

The amount of exercise a dog requires depends, to some extent, on the breed. Toy breeds are often quite content with a walk of about half a mile (1 km) every day, but larger dogs, especially those with a working ancestry, need up to 8 miles (13 km). Size can be deceptive, however, when assessing a dog's exercise requirements.

Regular daily exercise is important; rather than marathon sessions at the weekend. If the dog does not settle down when it returns form its walk, the walk was probably not long enough. Where the dog can be let off the lead, encourage it to run back and forth chasing a ball or toy; in this way, it will cover two or three times as much ground. Never allow dogs to run free close to livestock, especially sheep. Dogs can inflict hideous injuries on sheep, especially at lambing time, and farmers are legally entitled to shoot to protect their flocks or herds. For the dog's own safety, running free off the lead should also be curtailed in urban areas. In some cities, this is banned by law.

Sometimes, exercise must be restricted. Young puppies of giant breeds, such as Wolfhounds, must not be exercised excessively before they are skeletally mature, as this can cause problems later with their joints. Old dogs, especially those with heart complaints, and pregnant bitches will also need less exercise. Dogs should not be taken out during the hottest part of the day in summer. During warm weather, Pekingese, Boxers and similar flat-faced breeds may become distressed and start to breathe very noisily.

Right: The Greyhound has a gait that is distinct from that of any other dog. Its galloping movement consists of a series of bounding leaps, leaving the dog airborne for considerable periods of time and using up large amounts of energy.

Left: Dogs can see much better than humans in poor light conditions, because of the predominance of rod receptors in a dog's eyes.

Right: Exercise needs vary considerably. A "Westie", for example, enjoys a good walk, whereas a Chihuahua needs only a short stroll each day. Surprisingly, a Greyhound does not require nearly as long a walk as a Labrador; a working dog needing good, solid exercise every day. Bigger dogs need a substantial daily outing, although puppies must avoid lengthy walks as these can affect bone and muscle development. A dog will run to and fro, and cover at least twice as much ground as its owner.

Dogs can also be exercised in the garden, on a running chain which can be attached to a stake fixed firmly in the ground. This enables the dog to cover quite a large area without actually being free. Shelter must be available from the sun and the elements, and water must always be within easy reach. Dogs do seem to resent being tethered for any length of time, however, and they may try to escape in these circumstances. Tethering can also encourage aggressive tendencies.

CHIHUAHUA
Average daily walk: 0.5 mile (0.8 km)

WEST HIGHLAND WHITE TERRIER
Average daily walk: 1 mile (1.6 km)

GREYHOUND
Average daily walk: 3 miles (4.8 km)

LABRADOR RETRIEVER
Average daily walk: 8 miles (12.9 km)

IRISH WOLFHOUND
Average daily walk: 9 miles (14.5 km)

GREAT DANE
Average daily walk: 6 miles (9.6 km)

GROOMING

It is best to accustom a dog to grooming at an early age, even if it is a short-haired breed. As well as improving the dog's appearance, grooming provides an opportunity to look for fleas and other parasites which may have attached themselves to the body. Frequent short periods of grooming are preferable; if carried out regularly, there is little risk of mats forming in the coats of long-haired breeds. These, aside from being unsightly, can be difficult, and even painful, to remove.

If matting does occur, it may just be possible to tease the hairs apart. In bad cases, the hair will have to be cut off and allowed to re-grow. Special de-matting combs are available but can cause considerable pain, and it is often kinder to take the dog to a veterinarian or a grooming parlor; and some degree of sedation may be required.

Brushing and combing

For normal brushing, a brush comprised of pig bristles is best; nylon brushes create static electricity and may damage the hair. Wire brushes can also be harmful if used excessively, but can remove dead hair from breeds, such as poodles, that do not molt in the conventional sense. A rubber brush with a strap that fits over the hand is ideal for grooming a smooth-coated dog. A studded hound glove will also help to give the coat a good lustre. Soft brushes are best for puppies.

Plastic combs can be used for fine-coated breeds, but steel combs, with rounded teeth to prevent damage to the skin, are best for long-haired dogs, as the teeth will not break off easily. A comb mounted on a handle is preferable, and a relatively broad gap between the individual teeth is recommended for general purposes. A fine-toothed comb can be used on the head and for finishing touches. Certain breeds may require specific grooming tools – Afghans, for example, are prepared with a pig-bristle brush and a plastic comb.

To brush or comb a dog, stand it on a flat surface, such as an old table. Brushing should begin on the head and run in the direction of the fur. Particular parts of the body require special attention in some breeds, such as the ears of spaniels, and the so-called "feathers" or fine hair at the backs of the legs of dogs such as Irish Setters; in general, these need careful combing. A thorough combing is generally recommended after brushing; this will have removed most of the loose hair. The amount lost will increase noticeably at certain times of the year, when the dog is molting. Usually, the undercoat is largely shed in spring.

It is sensible, when you buy a puppy, to discuss with the breeder the basic equipment you will need, which might include at least some of the items shown here:
1. *ear wipes and eye wipes*
2. *chamois sponge*
3. *wire comb*
4. *plastic comb*
5. *nail clippers*
6. *soft brush*
7. *rubber brush*
8. *hound glove*
9. *wire brush*
10. *toothbrush and paste*

Clipping

Most dogs molt naturally and their coats do not need clipping. In certain conditions, however, such as very hot weather, breeds with profuse coats, like the Old English Sheepdog, may be more comfortable if they are trimmed. Medical disorders can also be a reason for clipping. In elderly dogs, especially long-haired breeds, the coat around the anus may become soiled. Clipping will help keep this area clean and decrease the likelihood of fly strike. The inside of the spaniels' ears may need to be trimmed to reduce the risk of ear infections, or to facilitate treatment of such conditions. The long hair between the toes of dogs such as Golden Retrievers should be cut if an infestation occurs.

Those breeds that do not shed their coats must be clipped at intervals of six weeks. Various types of trim are recognized for exhibition dogs; for show poodles, the clip recognized by the country concerned must be adopted. As poodles have very sensitive skins, the coat is trimmed more often with scissors than mechanical clippers, and then thinned with specially designed scissors.

Many people prefer to have their dogs trimmed at a grooming parlor; some of these operate a home visiting service. For the serious exhibitor, there are courses where such skills can be learned. For maximum efficiency and minimum discomfort for the dog, the clippers must be well maintained. The cutter-heads of electric clippers, which should be interchangeable, should be oiled regularly. Magnetic-type clippers are probably best for the home groomer, however, as they are simple to operate.

Bathing

Bathing is not as essential as brushing and general grooming, although it is an important part of show preparation for certain breeds, notably the Yorkshire Terrier. Try to accustom the dog to bathing from an early age; sudden introduction to it later on may cause resentment. Pets will need to be bathed if their coats become soiled, but otherwise a bath every two or three months should be adequate, and will prevent them from smelling. Shampoo will remove some of the coat's natural grease, which normally acts as a waterproofing agent, but this is soon replaced. Excessive bathing, however, will make the coat dull and less attractive.

Wash the dog outside if the weather permits, using a tub or even an inflatable bathtub. The water should be lukewarm. The shampoo you choose should depend on the state of the coat. Some dog shampoos are suitable for all breeds;

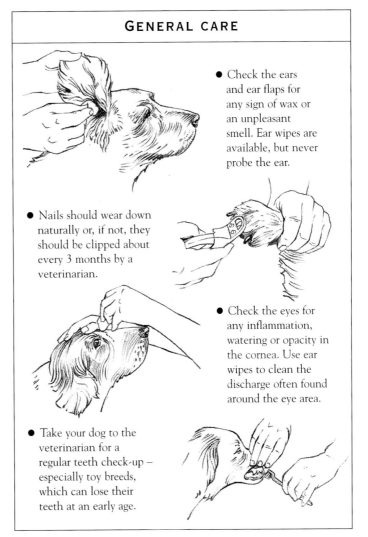

GENERAL CARE

● Check the ears and ear flaps for any sign of wax or an unpleasant smell. Ear wipes are available, but never probe the ear.

● Nails should wear down naturally or, if not, they should be clipped about every 3 months by a veterinarian.

● Check the eyes for any inflammation, watering or opacity in the cornea. Use ear wipes to clean the discharge often found around the eye area.

● Take your dog to the veterinarian for a regular teeth check-up – especially toy breeds, which can lose their teeth at an early age.

others specifically help to prevent tangles and are recommended for long-haired dogs. Shampoos that highlight particular colors are available, and some are formulated for puppies and dogs with delicate skins, such as poodles. Baby shampoo is also suitable as an alternative. Medicated shampoos should only be used under veterinary advice; any insecticidal preparations, for controlling fleas for example, must be mixed and used strictly in accordance with the manufacturer's instructions.

It is advisable to wear some type of protective clothing when bathing dogs. Half fill the bath and then, if necessary, lift the dog into the water. Using a jug, or even a milk bottle, wet the back and hindquarters first, moving up the body gradually. The shampoo should be applied and rubbed into a lather. Be sure to shampoo between the toes where the eccrine sweat glands are. Rinse the coat with clean water; certain medicated shampoos, however, may have to be left on the coat for a while before rinsing.

Below: Considerable time may need to be spent on grooming certain breeds. This "before and after" picture shows how much work is required on the Bichon Frise.

The head should be washed last. Great care must be taken to ensure that shampoo does not enter the dog's eyes. Once the head is wet, the dog will probably shake itself, spraying water everywhere, and it should then be lifted out of the bath as soon as possible. It can be rubbed down with an old towel and dried off with either an electric hair-dryer or one of the dryers used in grooming parlors. The dryer must be moved back and forth over the body to prevent the hair and skin from being scorched by the heat. Separating the wet fur with a brush will also help it to dry more quickly, and, used with a towel, may be the only way of drying the fur of a dog that is disturbed by the noise of a hair-dryer.

After the dog has been bathed, make sure it does not immediately run away to roll in earth or manure: its body scent will have been largely removed by washing and it might try to reinstate it by such behavior. Dry shampoo is sometimes used as an alternative to ordinary shampoo, especially for a show, and will not degrease the coat like wet washing. It is useful in cases where wet shampooing is inadvisable, for example, if the dog is elderly. The powder is rubbed in, left for a period, and then brushed out again. Dry shampoo will not clean a very dirty coat, and traces will show up on dark fur. Considerable brushing may be required to remove the shampoo and this, in turn, may cause a build-up of static electricity, preventing the coat from settling down properly. Powders also lead to runny eyes and sneezing if they are applied indiscriminately around the head. Talcum powder is one of the main ingredients of dry shampoo, and is also used to improve the appearance of white breeds such as the Bichon Frise.

Various commercial preparations, designed to improve the appearance of the coat, are also available, either in the form of aerosols that are sprayed onto the coat to make it shiny, or as quick-drying liquids to be rubbed in. As rubbing in must be done evenly, aerosols are often easier to use. The value of such products is debatable, although they may be useful for giving finishing touches before a show.

BOARDING KENNELS

It is not always possible to take the dog with you on vacation, particularly when going abroad. If kenneling is necessary, the arrangements should be made as far as possible before the date of departure. Satisfied clients will take their dogs to the same kennels every year, and it is often difficult to find a vacancy at peak holiday times, especially in a well-run establishment. A kennel should be chosen on recommendation, either from a breeder or

Right: It is important to make all kenneling arrangements well ahead of time, as the best kennels in any area are usually booked well before the peak holiday season.

veterinarian; otherwise, a visit to the kennels under consideration should be arranged, as this will give an opportunity to inspect the premises. Much can be gathered from simply seeing the surroundings and meeting the people who care for the dogs. The kennels and outside runs ought to be clean, with no signs of overcrowding. The occupants should look alert and well. The interiors of the kennels should be dry and snug, and the water bowls should be filled and clean.

In most countries, reputable kennel owners will ask to see certificates of vaccination against lepospirosis, canine infectious hepatitis, distemper and parvovirus. For additional protection, vaccination against Bordetella bronchoseptica, a bacterium which is partly responsible for the so-called kennel cough syndrome, is now available. This disease is normally relatively minor, but spreads rapidly among dogs in kennels at holiday time. It is important to inform the kennel staff of any significant medical condition, such as a

Left: Although most dogs settle well into kennels, it may be unwise to board an old or chronically sick dog, even for a relatively short time.

heart complaint, and to supply the correct treatment, together with the name, address and number of the dog's veterinarian. A vet may be prepared to take a chronically sick dog, such as a diabetic, for a holiday period.

Although a few do not adapt readily to kennel life, particularly if it is their first time, most dogs settle well. Older dogs are more likely to pine.

Below: Boarding kennels may appear rather formidable places, surrounded by fences, yet most dogs settle in to a well-run establishment within a few days.

TRAVELING

Right: It is dangerous to allow a dog to ride in a car with its head out of the window.

At some point, most dogs will have to be transported by car and will probably adapt fairly quickly to the experience. Throughout the journey, the dog must always be kept properly restrained so that it will not distract the driver, or damage the upholstery. If a dog is allowed to travel free in the car, it should always be accompanied by a passenger who can restrain it if necessary in the back seat. Traveling cages that fit into the back of an estate car or station wagon are one solution but another option is to install a dog guard.

These guards can be acquired from motor accessory stores and, depending on the make and model of your car, either may need to be fitted to the body shell or may need to be held in place by suction pads attaching to the roof or floor. With fine-nosed breeds such as greyhounds, square or rectangular meshes are essential, as it is otherwise possible for the dog to push its head through horizontal bars and get stuck.

Many dogs look forward to going out in a car and get into a state of great excitement

Right: Most breeders transport their dogs in special carrying pens or behind fitted dog guards.

because it means they will be having a walk. Making a fuss over the dog will make it believe that you want to encourage excitable behaviour. If the dog persists in leaping about and barking while in the car, give a firm command for it to be quiet and, if this fails, park the car and disappear for a few moments. The delay in reaching the site for the walk means the dog will not have achieved its aims and, in time, will come to realize that not every trip in the car will end in a walk or run – particularly if an owner travels a lot with a dog.

A dog must never be allowed to ride with its head out of a window. Apart from the obvious risk of colliding fatally with another object at speed, the velocity of the air is likely to lead to conjunctivitis, and small particles of gravel may also enter the eyes.

Never leave a dog alone in a car with the windows closed, especially during the summer months. If leaving a dog in a car is unavoidable for a short period of time, always ensure that windows are left partially open. The interior of a car can heat up very quickly and, without ventilation, a dog can be killed in a frighteningly short space of time.

Always keep a dog on a lead when traveling with them on public transport. Small dogs can be held on the lap, while larger dogs should be kept under close control, always well out of the way of other passengers. If, for any reason, a dog has to be transported by air, special shippers can be contacted to organize both the necessary paperwork and the crating. Various health tests will also be required for dogs that are being sent abroad.

Left: While farm dogs ride happily in the back of open vehicles, this type of transport cannot be recommended for most dogs, which are liable to be distracted by a scent or another animal.

Left: A dog that is allowed to travel free in a car should be accompanied by a passenger who can restrain it if necessary in the back seat.

HEALTH CARE

GENERAL HEALTH CARE

Providing a sensible diet, regular exercise and ensuring frequent and careful grooming will help a dog remain healthy, lively and alert. Early check-ups at the veterinarian will help aid speedy recovery from many illnesses.

MODERN ADVANCES IN CANINE HEALTH care have meant that it is now possible for the occurrence of the major fatal canine diseases to be almost entirely prevented by means of regular inoculations. Safe anesthetics and sophisticated equipment also mean that surgical procedures can be undertaken with minimum risk; so the dog's life expectancy is probably greater than ever before. There are significant dangers for a dog however, both in the home and on the road. Every year, many dogs die from collisions with vehicles. Good training and supervision on the part of a dog's owner are therefore vital to an effective health-care program, as well as direct involvement from a veterinarian.

Right: It is important to look after a dog's paws. Overgrown nails should be clipped by a veterinarian, using a pair of specially designed clippers.

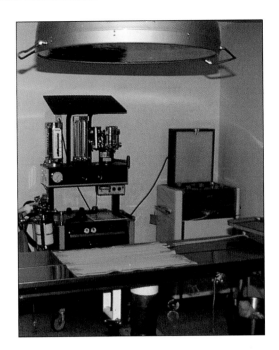

Your vet

It is not difficult to find a veterinarian in most areas, and soon after a new dog is acquired, it is a good idea to visit the local surgery, so inoculations can be given if necessary, and a checkup carried out.

How can I tell if my dog is ill and in need of veterinary attention?

The key indicators to a dog's general state of health are likely to be the its appetite and drinking habits, as well as its general alertness and desire to exercise. When you take your dog to a veterinarian, be sure to go with a written note of the symptoms that are worrying you and the length of time they have lasted. The veterinarian may also want to know how long you have had the dog and if it has been inoculated. You will need to provide the date of a bitch's last heat and whether she has been neutered. Some of this information may be available to the veterinarian if you have made previous visits, but have it on hand in case it is needed. Your veterinarian will probably ask you questions before carrying out an examination of the dog. This is sometimes referred to as "taking the history of the case". Be as precise as possible. If your dog has been drinking more water than usual, specify the amount by saying that it now consumes X quarts over the course of a day. It is unreasonable to expect a veterinarian to be able to gain a meaningful impression of your dog's health if you say, for instance, that it empties two bowls, without defining the volume of the bowls concerned! Keep a watch on your dog when it relieves itself. You will then be able to say whether or not it is having difficulty urinating or defecating.

Does it matter whether I go to the same veterinarian every time?

In cities, many veterinary practices comprise a group of veterinarians rather than a single one. There are obvious advantages to this system. Duty hours can be rotated, and veterinarians with particular interests can act as specialists in specific areas. It may even be possible to reduce costs this way, for a more efficient practice. Nevertheless, it does mean that you may not be able to see the same veterinarian on every visit. This is not a problem, however, as your dog's records will be on the premises and can be used by any member of the team.

This does not apply if you change your practice. To go from one practice to another without giving due notification means that the dog's previous medical history and laboratory test results will not be available to the new veterinarian. This can make his or her work more difficult, and can be dangerous for your dog and more expensive for you if tests have to be repeated. If you are unhappy with treatment you receive, you can arrange to transfer to

Left: Veterinarian practices are well equipped for diagnosis and treatment of canine ailments.

Below: The eyes, nose, mouth and ears are all good indicators of the general state of the health of your dog.

another veterinary practice in advance. Simply telephone and say you are changing to another veterinarian, or write if you prefer. This will also be necessary if you move away from an area, but your new veterinarian can refer back to previous treatment.

Is it possible for my veterinarian to give me advice over the telephone?

Most veterinary practices are busy and receive a large number of calls during the day. Some are likely to be emergencies. It is very difficult for a veterinarian to get a clear picture of a case without actually carrying out an examination. Be prepared, therefore, to take your dog to the office initially and, once treatment has begun, you can make quick calls for advice if necessary. Remember that a charge may be made for telephone advice, depending on the circumstances. Do not expect to be able to speak to your veterinarian automatically, especially if you haven't pre-arranged your call. The veterinarian may be tied up in a consultation, or may be operating when you

telephone. His staff will be able to deal with your query, referring to the veterinarian when this is necessary and as soon as possible.

Will my veterinarian visit my dog at home?

As a rule, take your dog to the veterinarian's office, where specialist help and equipment are available. Home visits are extremely time-consuming, and therefore expensive for the client. In an emergency, such as when a bitch encounters difficulties in giving birth, a veterinarian may visit. Most dogs tend to be easier to handle out of their own territory, which is another reason for taking your dog to the vet's office if possible.

My dog seems fine, but should he be checked regularly by the veterinarian?

Providing your dog appears healthy, there is probably little point visiting your veterinarian. Be sure de-worming and inoculations are kept up to date. This will involve a visit once or twice a year, when your veterinarian can examine your dog to check its state of health.

GENERAL NURSING

Below: A raised bowl can encourage good posture.

If a dog becomes ill, or is injured in an accident, veterinary advice is likely to be required without delay. However, an owner can do much to assist the recovery process.

My dog has to be anesthetized, and I have to leave it with the veterinarian overnight. Is this routine?

Yes, as a general rule it is routine to leave the dog with the veterinarian overnight, but it depends on individual circumstances. It is important that your dog receives nothing to eat or drink for a period beforehand. Under the effects of the anesthetic, vomiting can occur, food or fluid can pass down into the lungs and, as the dog will not be able to cough normally at this time, this could be fatal. A full stomach may also interfere with breathing when the dog is unconscious. If you suspect your dog has scavenged something during the period when nothing should be consumed, notify your veterinarian: it may be possible for him to reschedule your dog's operation.

The risk of administering an anesthetic to a dog is normally low. If the veterinarian is especially concerned, he will discuss the relevant factors with you. Obviously, old or obese dogs face a higher risk than young, healthy dogs. Complications are more likely to arise with certain breeds. In the case of the Greyhound, for example, there is little body fat to absorb the barbiturate anesthetic administered by injection. If this is used, the dose will have to be adjusted accordingly. Such factors can also influence the recovery time. It is quite usual for a veterinarian to keep the dog under close supervision until it has recovered from the immediate effects of the anesthetic, as well as from the operation itself, for your dog's sake.

My veterinarian prescribed a course of pills. How should I give these to my dog?

The simplest method is to disguise the pills in food, as long as they do not have to be given at a separate time from meals. The best way is to conceal the pill in a suitable piece of meat, as dogs readily detect the presence of an inedible object in their food. If you have more than one dog, make sure the correct dog consumes the pills and actually swallows them.

It may be necessary in some cases to administer the pill directly. This is not difficult with a dog that is used to being handled, but it is a procedure that needs to be carried out carefully. There are also automatic dispensers that can be used. Try to give the pill on the first attempt. The dog is likely to become increasingly restless if the process proves protracted.

How should I administer liquid medicine to my dog?

Probably the easiest means of giving liquid to a dog is with a syringe. The required quantity can be measured precisely, and the syringe placed at the back of the dog's mouth from the right side, and its contents emptied with steady pressure from the right hand. The left hand is used to open the mouth sufficiently to allow the syringe to be placed within the dog's mouth while restraining both jaws. (The may be reversed for a left-handed person.) In both cases, it is helpful to have someone else available to restrain the dog for you. If you run the medicine in slowly, the dog should not attempt to choke. If it does, let the head down without relinquishing your grip. The head needs to be positioned at an angle of about 45° from the horizontal. Tilting it too far back, though, will lead to coughing as fluid enters the larynx.

It is harder to administer liquid medicine to a dog by means of a spoon, especially if you must give a specific amount. Avoid filling a spoon fully, as it will spill much more easily. Dosing will be easier if the dog is at a reasonable height off the ground – stand it on a table, for example, protecting the surface from the dog's claws and any spilled medicine.

Afterwards, wash the syringe or spoon thoroughly. Do not forget to show affection to the dog and give it a tidbit if it has been well-behaved. Try to open a puppy's mouth regularly, so that in later life, it will let you administer treatments via the mouth when required.

GIVING A PILL

● First hold your dog's muzzle with one hand and tilt the nose up a little; put your thumb in the space between the canine tooth and the first molar and press it against the roof of the mouth – this will force the dog to keep its mouth open. With your other hand, drop the medication as far back in the dog's mouth as you can, making sure the pill is on top of the tongue, not under it. Then hold the mouth closed and gently massage the throat until you feel the dog swallow the pill. It may help to persuade your dog to swallow a pill by camouflaging it with a favorite snack.

The medication may have a sugar or similar coating; it is vital that you do not break pills of this type because they may then have an extremely bitter and unpleasant taste and may also cause the dog to salivate profusely. The dog will probably resent any future attempts to give it pills. If you need help to restrain the dog, get someone else to restrain the neck with an arm so that the dog cannot slip away from you.

Initial dosing may lead to a noticeable improvement in the dog's condition, and it may appear as healthy as ever before the course of pills is completed. Nevertheless, always be sure to give all the pills prescribed by your veterinarian following precisely the strict directions given on the packaging. Failure to give a full course of antibiotics may not only cause the condition to reappear but can also lead to bacterial resistance to further treatment by the drug concerned. Antibiotics have altered the face of veterinary medicine, but they are not of value in every instance.

How critical are the dosage directions that my veterinarian has given for my dog's medicine?

You should always try to follow directions as closely as possible. Certainly, if the directions say to administer medicine before a meal, this is important. Some drugs, such as tetracyclines, are not absorbed well from the intestinal tract in the presence of food; calcium combines with this group of antibiotics leaving lower quantities to be absorbed. Its effectiveness in fighting infection is correspondingly reduced.

With regard to times of dosage, it is also important to adhere to these as far as possible. This will insure that a therapeutically active level of the drug is retained within the body at all times during the course of treatment. The required dose will be specified by your veterinarian and will vary according to the size and weight of your dog. If the pills need to be given twice daily, give them at, say, 8.00 am, and at the same time at night. The precise time is not as important as the interval between doses, during which the level of the drug in the body declines. Do not give the dog one or two pills then stop. To be effective, they must be administered regularly for at least five days. In certain circumstances, as with eye infections where the tear fluid is constantly washing the medication away, more treatment will be needed during the course of a day.

How can I keep my dog warm? Are there any dangers attached to using a hot water bottle in his basket?

The methods used to keep young puppies warm are equally applicable for sick dogs. An infra-red heater placed out of the dog's reach above the sleeping area is probably most satisfactory, providing that there is also a cooler spot accessible for the dog. A heating pad can be used in the basket, and a hot water bottle is also suitable, as long as you make sure that the dog cannot burn itself accidentally. This applies especially in the case of a dog that is in a semi-comatose state and unable to move easily. The most important factor is to use warm water only, as boiling water can burn the skin. Wrap the hot water bottle in a thick towel as an additional precaution. Rubber bottles are preferable to those of stone which are uncomfortable for the dog to lie on. Make sure the top is fitted properly, and that the rubber is in good condition because otherwise water will saturate the dog's bed rapidly.

How can I find my dog's heartbeat in an emergency?

Flex the elbow joint on the left-side of the body to its maximum extent. This will give you the approximate position of the heart. It should be possible to feel the heartbeat, particularly after exercise, as long as the dog is not excessively overweight.

What care does a paraplegic dog require?

A dog that is unable to walk (usually because of spinal injury) needs considerable care. If it lies in the same position over a long period, it may develop pressure sores, particularly on bony parts of the body. Bigger, heavier dogs run the greatest risk. Pressure sores should not be confused with the thickening skin commonly seen on the elbows of healthy dogs of the large breeds, although the case is similar.

Caring for a paraplegic dog is a considerable undertaking. It can be made easier by making a foam bed with removable covers, or by encouraging the dog to lie on a bean-bag. Do not allow the dog to remain in the same position for more than a couple of hours, and if any sores appear and form ulcers, contact your veterinarian. An additional problem is that such dogs are likely to be incontinent, so their surroundings must be easy to clean thoroughly.

Will I ever have to give my dog an injection? Needles worry me!

The only circumstance in which you are likely to have to administer injections to your dog is if it becomes diabetic. Your veterinarian will show you how to carry out the necessary injection of insulin, and if you are concerned, you can practice using an orange as a substitute for the skin. The insulin will have to be administered subcutaneously (that is, under the skin rather than into a vein) which makes the process easier. Having filled the syringe, scruff

Below: A wet nose is general accepted to indicate good health in a dog.

the loose skin on the back of the dog's neck and insert the needle through the skin. Draw back slightly to insure that no blood appears in the syringe (this would indicate that you have struck a blood vessel) and if all is well, push the plunger firmly and then withdraw the needle. It is important to use a new needle each time, not only on grounds of hygiene but also because they blunt rapidly. Dog's skin is surprisingly tough, and a blunt needle makes the process more difficult. Dispose of your old needles carefully by placing the protective covers back on them and returning them to your veterinarian. These injections will probably have to be administered on a daily basis.

Is it true that a dog's nose will feel wet if it is healthy?

This is generally accepted as a sign of good health; the moisture is produced largely in the lateral nasal glands in the nose. However, dogs that are dehydrated but otherwise healthy will have dry noses because the body responds by reducing fluid output via urine and even in the nasal glands. A dog that has been sitting in a warm spot may also have a temporarily dry nose. In addition, a dog that has recovered from distemper at an early age may be left with a nose that is permanently dry.

What constitutes an emergency situation in which I should contact my veterinarian without delay?

Conditions requiring rapid veterinary attention are normally those of sudden onset. If your dog collapses, appears unable to breathe, loses consciousness or starts having convulsions, then contact your veterinarian without delay. Injuries from accidents can also be life-threatening. As well as giving immediate first-aid, you should contact a veterinarian at once. Serious hemorrhaging, obvious fracture, poisoning, drowning or scalding are cases in point. Also, any problems during whelping are likely to require urgent veterinary attention.

How do I know when to contact my veterinarian?

If you are concerned for any aspect of your dog's health, seek professional advice without delay. Some cases are less urgent than others, however, and if you do not feel that it is an emergency, arrange an appointment at a convenient time. A veterinarian will always see a genuine emergency at any time of the day or night but will not welcome being called out in a case where the dog has been ill for two weeks and you have chosen to do nothing until late on a Sunday night.

INFECTIOUS DISEASES

The majority of these are positively life-threatening, yet the threat can be overcome successfully by means of preventative inoculations. All dogs should be protected against these killer diseases.

Is distemper the same disease as hard pad?

Hard pad is one form of distemper, in which a virus attacks the outer layer of the skin of the dog's foot pads and nose, causing callus-like pads to form on the feet and thick horny-like skin to form on the nose. The disease is caused by a virus, and apart from its immediate effects, distemper can lead to very serious long-term complications. It is spread by close contact between dogs – often from urine – and first invades the tonsils and neighboring lymph nodes. In some cases, where antibodies are produced by the dog's defense system at this stage, it is possible for them to overcome the infection: for some time the dog feels ill, but it recovers uneventfully.

It may be possible to recognize a dog in later life that was afflicted with distemper as a puppy by examining its teeth. The virus causes the surface layer to take on a rough brownish appearance if the enamel had not been fully developed at the time of the infection. Other signs are a dry, cracked nose and the thickened foot pads in some cases. The symptoms of distemper are variable in severity, but any dog suffering from a generalized infection will appear seriously ill.

Is it possible to protect against distemper? And can the human measles vaccine be of use for this purpose?

Every owner should have their dog inoculated against this highly unpleasant disease. However, many forget or simply do not bother until an epidemic occurs. The infection can be spread by wild canids including foxes, racoons, badgers and ferrets. Young dogs run a particular risk since, without inoculation, they possess no immunity to the disease from about 12 weeks of age on. It is important to maintain inoculation cover because older dogs can succumb, especially if they have spent much of their lives in an area where there were few dogs and they were unlikely to encounter the virus. An inoculated dog in an urban area is almost certain to be exposed to the infection (which has a worldwide incidence) but, being protected, will not develop clinical signs. A subsequent challenge boosts the antibody level still further and improves the dog's immunity.

The distemper virus belongs to the same group as the measles virus, but the disease cannot be spread to humans. Nevertheless, the measles vaccine can indeed protect young puppies against distemper in a specific situation where the traditional distemper vaccine would be ineffective. Dogs less than eight weeks old cannot be inoculated against distemper because the antibodies in the mother's milk will overcome the vaccine.

The measles vaccine is unaffected by maternal antibodies. It can be used to build up the puppy's immune system, giving it early protection in a situation where it could be at grave risk. For example, the measles vaccine might be used in a welfare kennel where a bitch whose history is unknown gives birth during a distemper outbreak among other dogs in the same environment. Should you feel that puppies need the measles vaccine, refer to your veterinarian, not your doctor.

Is it true that there are two different forms of canine adenovirus which have widely differing effects?
Yes. Canine adenovirus type 1, abbreviated to CAV-1 results in infectious canine hepatitis

(ICH), also known as Rubarth's Disease. The route of transmission is highly significant. When taken into the body via the mouth, its effects will be on the liver. If inhaled, a less severe disease affecting the respiratory tract is likely to occur. Some dogs overcome the infection in the early stages and few clinical symptoms appear. Young dogs again run the greatest risk of infection. Prevention is straightforward and entails inoculation early in life with annual boosters. There is a slight danger that live vaccine may give rise to blue eye – Afghan Hounds are most susceptible to this symptom.

In contrast, the second form of adenovirus, CAV-2, tends to localize in the respiratory tract and is one of the causes of kennel cough. A vaccine is also available to protect against this form of adenovirus. Kennel cough is normally mild but can lead to pneumonia if it goes untreated: it is a disease that is contagious and spreads as fast as 'flu. However, it can be treated by antibiotics.

Parvovirus infection of dogs received widespread publicity several years ago. Is it still a threat?
Yes, but inoculation has helped reduce the incidence of this disease. It first appeared during the late 1970s, and soon spread worldwide. The reasons for its onset are not

TRANSMISSION OF A VIRUS

● Diseases are more likely to spread where there is a high density of dogs, for example, at a show or in boarding kennels. Kennel cough is spread by airborne viruses (1). Some of the more resistant viruses may either simply be transmitted directly on contact (2), or from contaminated items such as bedding, grooming implements and feeding bowls. Scavenging dogs are susceptible to disease by ingesting contaminated foods (3). Other kinds of virus can be spread by animal vectors – bites from insects such as ticks or, in the case of rabies, bites from other mammals (4). Open cuts or wounds are another danger, as viruses are often carried in the bloodstream (5). A particular danger to developing puppies is that some viruses are small enough to pass across the placenta or contaminate the mother's milk and so infect puppies either before or soon after they are born (6).

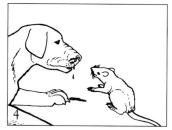

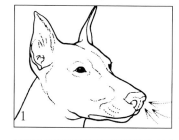
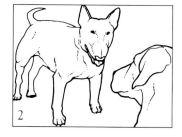
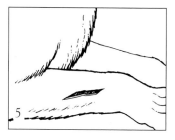

fully understood yet. It may well have been a mutant form of the feline panleukopenia virus which is also a parvovirus, "parvo" means small and refers to the size of the individual virus particles.

The virus itself is very durable and can exist outside the body for at least a year. It is also resistant to many disinfectants. It can be spread by clothes and shoes as well as through more obvious routes such as feeding bowls. After an outbreak, the premises should be washed thoroughly with sodium hypochlorite (bleach). Protective footwear which can be immersed in a solution of bleach should be worn to minimize the risk of spreading the disease to uninoculated dogs.

Does inoculation provide an absolute guarantee that my dog will be safe from serious diseases such as parvovirus?

Unfortunately, there is no such guarantee, but, correctly administered, the vaccine should, apart from in rare cases, provide full protection against the diseases concerned. To work, a vaccine must activate the body's immune system. If this does not happen (if maternal antibodies neutralize the vaccine in a young puppy, for example), then there will be little or no protection later in life. This is why inoculations are repeated in a young dog. The immune system in a tiny minority of dogs may be unable to respond after the influence of maternal antibodies wears off. It is possible to measure the antibody response to a vaccine, but this test is not carried out routinely because it tends to be expensive, and vaccines are usually found to be extremely efficient. There is certainly no valid reason for not having a dog inoculated on the grounds that the vaccine will be ineffective.

Manufacturers are spending vast sums of money on research and development of vaccines for dogs and are constantly monitoring their effectiveness. It is known that certain drugs – notably corticosteroids – depress the body's immune response. Therefore, to give inoculations when a dog is receiving such treatments is not recommended. Similarly, if a bitch is pregnant, she must not receive a live vaccine because this could cause harm to the developing puppies. As a dog gets older, it is less able to produce antibodies, and regular inoculations thus assume increasing importance towards the end of a dog's life.

Will our dog be at risk from leptospirosis when we stay on a farm for a few days?

Two forms of this bacterial disease are recognized; they are caused by Leptospira icterohaemorrhagiae and Leptospira canicola. The former serotype is linked with rats, and dogs such as terriers can run a risk in agricultural areas where they may come into contact with the bacterium via urine. A dog that has recovered from the bacterium and remains on the farm could also be a source of infection as it too will be continuing to excrete the bacteria in its urine.

Infection with the serotype Leptospira icterohaemorrhagiae usually leads to jaundice. Early symptoms are also likely to include diarrhea, vomiting and a fever. Antibiotics are of value in combating this disease. In the later stages, the body temperature falls significantly, and the dog may experience difficulty in breathing and drink at every opportunity.

Below: Care should be taken in any situation where a dog comes into contact with other animals, such as on a farm. It is also worth remembering that a pet dog visiting a farm may chase sheep or other animals and cause a considerable nuisance itself.

IMMUNITY TO DISEASE

● When foreign organisms such as bacteria or viruses enter the body, they stimulate the host to produce antibodies that attach to the organisms and neutralize them (1). These antibodies are produced both at the site of entry – the nose or intestines – and in the bloodstream by white blood cells, the lymphocytes (2). Once neutralized the organisms can be engulfed by other white cells in the blood, the macrophages, and broken down (3). A vaccine stimulates the body to produce antibodies so that it can respond more quickly to future infection (4).

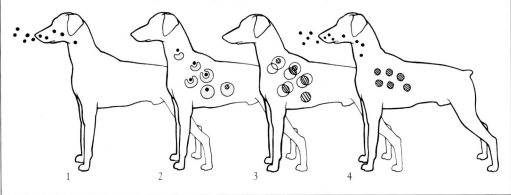

Below: Regular inoculations will protect your dog against many serious or fatal infectious diseases.

How safe are vaccines?

The likelihood of adverse reactions occurring in a dog that has been vaccinated is extremely small. If there were to be a reaction, symptoms are likely to appear within minutes of the vaccine's administration and can normally be reversed by an injection of adrenalin. There is virtually no risk of your dog developing the disease when it is given a live vaccine. If it does succumb to distemper within a few days, for example, this is likely to be due to the fact that it was already incubating the disease before it was inoculated. In other words, the vaccine could not evoke its normal protective response simply because the infection was already present in the body.

Is it possible to inoculate orphaned puppies?

These run a great risk if they have not received any protective colostrum, especially in kennel surroundings where other dogs are present. In these cases, it is preferable to give a hyperimmune serum because the puppy's own immune system cannot manufacture antibodies from birth when challenged by the vaccine. The puppy can be vaccinated for the first time approximately one month after the administration of the serum.

Should my dog be inoculated against rabies?

Rabies or hydrophobia (fear of water) is one of the most dangerous viral infections, fatal to unimmunized dogs. Because this disease is also dangerous to humans, any suspicion of rabies must be reported to public health authorities. If you or your dog have come into contact with a dog suspected of being rabid, your dog must be quarantined and you must submit to complete medical treatment. Immunization can protect your dog from this fatal disease.

How does rabies spread?

In North America, before 1951, all cases of human rabies were caused by either cat or dog bites. But, following extensive vaccination campaigns, dog-borne rabies has been virtually unknown in the United States since 1951. However, a growing number of wild animals such as foxes, rabbits, bats, skunks and racoons have been reported as carriers in the United States and it is unlikely that the disease will ever be totally eliminated.

What emergency action should I take if I am bitten by a rabid dog?

You do not have to be bitten by a rabid dog to succumb to rabies. The virus can be transmitted in saliva just before clinical symptoms appear, entering the body through a cut on the hand, for instance. If you are bitten by a dog that could have rabies, wash the cut immediately using alcohol, if available, or rinse under running water and treat the wound with iodine. Contact your doctor without delay so that appropriate medical treatment can be arranged immediately. This should ensure that the disease does not develop Once symptoms become apparent, the likelihood of recovery is virtually zero. In areas where the disease is endemic, supervise children closely, especially if they are unfamiliar with this disease. Some wild animals suffering from rabies can seem friendly and are therefore extremely dangerous. Although the symptoms of the disease are most fearsome in carnivores, rabies is equally lethal for herbivores such as cattle. The major source of infection for humans, however, is dog bites.

Is there any other disease that could be confused with rabies?

It is possible that Aujeszky's Disease, a viral disease usually associated with pigs, can produce similar symptoms; it is called pseudo-rabies. Dogs living on pig farms or those which have gained access to contaminated uncooked pork run the greatest risk of infection.

Can my dog get kennel cough in the home?

It is possible but less likely than at kennels or shows, where air space can be limited and ventilation poor. There is no single organism responsible for kennel cough (or infectious tracheobronchitis). The bacterium Bordetella bronchoseptica can be isolated in the majority of cases, leading to a cough that occurs whenever the throat region over the trachea is touched.

Kennel cough tends to be self-limiting and is not often a life-threatening disease although it is very unpleasant for the dog. Complications such as a pneumonia are likely to arise in the older dog. The symptoms should routinely disappear within about three weeks, but recurrent cases in kenneled dogs are not unusual because immunity tends to be transient. In any event, an effective vaccine against all the main causes of kennel cough is now available, and its use is to be recommended in dogs that are being kenneled or attending shows regularly. This vaccine may be given intra-nasally (sprayed up the nostrils) in some cases rather than being injected as it usually is with young puppies.

ANIMAL VECTORS OF RABIES

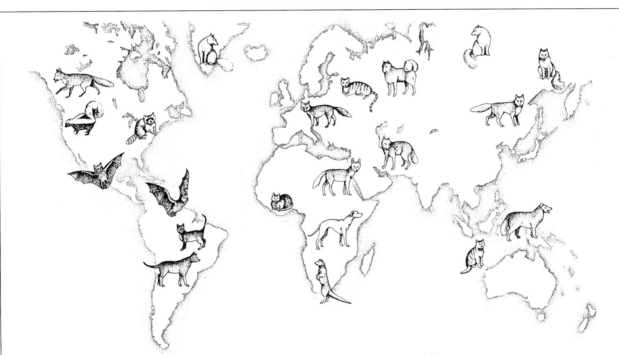

● The distribution of rabies is world-wide and in places where the disease occurs regularly there is usually a "reservoir" of the infection in wild animals – foxes in Western Europe, skunks and racoons in the United States, mongooses in South Africa, India and the Caribbean and vampire bats in Central and South America, Australia, the United Kingdom, Antarctica and Hawaii are the few rabies-free places in the world – thanks to their isolation by water and extremely strict import controls.

PROBLEMS DOWN BELOW

Incontinence is disturbing for both dog and owner, as dogs do appreciate that they should not soil carpets in the home. Bitches are often more prone to urinary problems, after spaying.

What are the causes of diarrhea? How serious is it?

Diarrhea is not a disease but a symptom associated with various conditions, some of which are infectious. Bacterial diseases, such as salmonellosis, and viruses already mentioned can all cause diarrhea. Parasites, such as Coccidia, a unicellular organism described as a protozoa, may also be implicated in some cases. Non-infectious causes include malabsorption of certain foodstuffs, which may be caused, for example, by pancreatic insufficiency.

Veterinary advice may be needed, especially when puppies are affected, as they can rapidly become dehydrated. In an older dog, withholding food for 24 hours and then offering a small bland meal of chicken and rice, for example, can resolve the problem assuming the dog basically healthy. Diarrhea can result from scavenging unsuitable or old food.

Any trace of fresh blood in your dog's stools suggests that there is a digestive disorder in the lower part of the digestive tract. Inflammation of the large bowel, known as colitis, is a typical condition which causes such symptoms. The feces are almost jelly-like in appearance because of their high mucous content. If the source of the blood loss is the small intestine, there will be no fresh blood in the feces because the blood will have been partially digested as it moved through the gut and will have taken on a reddish-brown appearance.

What are the anal glands? My veterinarian says that my dog has blocked anal sacs that need emptying.

The anal glands are really sacs that produce a secretion that is deposited on the feces and can be recognized by other dogs. The first sign of a blockage is likely to be the dog rubbing its rear quarters along the ground in a bid to overcome the irritation. Such behavior is sometimes described as "scooting." The anal area becomes very tender and causes the dog considerable discomfort. It may try to bite itself. It is important to get the sacs emptied before defecation proves painful, and the area becomes infected. In severe cases, open channels (fistulae), may develop around the anal ring. These can be difficult to heal successfully and may require cryosurgery.

Your veterinarian may be able to empty the sacs manually, but in more severe cases, the dog will have to be anesthetized. It will then be possible to wash the sacs out, and hopefully prevent a recurrence. Actual removal of the sacs may be necessary in chronic cases, but try adding bran to the dog's food, as this improves the roughage level of the diet and can help to resolve the problem. Most dogs have outlived the use of these glands.

Is it true that bitches are more prone to urinary infections than male dogs?

Yes, because their urethras are shorter than those of male dogs. Ascending infections result in cystitis, inflammation of the bladder. Cystitis causes frequent urination and requires antibiotic treatment. In turn, an infection can be a predisposing factor in the development of bladder stones, known technically as calculi. The symptoms will depend on the part of the tract where the blockage has occurred. Difficulty in urinating will certainly be present, as will pain. It will probably be necessary for the veterinarian to examine the dog using a special contrast media X-ray technique to find the site of the problem. There are various options for treatment available, depending on the individual case. Some calculi may be washed through the tract or dislodged by means of a cannula, but recurrences in susceptible individuals are relatively common. A course of antibiotics may help cure an underlying infection, but there can be a genetic susceptibility to urinary calculi, as in the case of the Dalmatian, because of metabolic defects. Other breeds prone calculi are the Dachshunds, Corgis and Basset hounds.

ANATOMY OF A DOG

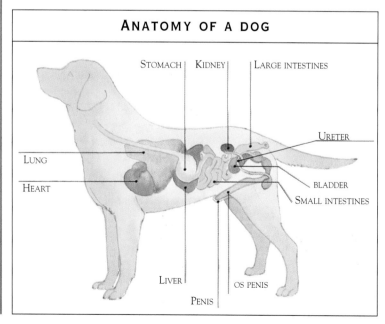

STOMACH KIDNEY LARGE INTESTINES

LUNG

HEART

URETER

BLADDER

SMALL INTESTINES

LIVER OS PENIS

PENIS

EAR AND EYE PROBLEMS

Selective breeding has created some undesirable characteristics – such as the heavy ears of Spaniels that are ideal sites for infections, and hereditary eye disorders that may need surgical correction.

What are the common eye disorders in dogs?

The most significant inherited weakness is progressive retinal atrophy (PRA), a progressive deterioration of the cells of the retina at the back of the eye where the image impinges. Early symptoms will include poor night vision. The condition can be generalized extending over the whole retina or be confined to the central area as in Collies, Labradors and Briards. Dogs afflicted with generalized PRA include the various breeds of Poodle. Sadly, there is no treatment available. The characteristic changes can be seen, however, by using an ophthalmoscope to view the retina directly. If you suspect your dog is having difficulty in seeing, causing it to bump into objects around the home, consult your veterinarian.

Injury of the eye can result when a dog walks through undergrowth and a sharp twig or a similar object hits the eye. If there are signs of blood, emergency treatment will be necessary. There are occasions when the surface of the eye is damaged, causing a condition known as keratitis, which is usually painful. An ulcer can form at the site, if the infection is left untreated, and this will be difficult to heal successfully. Breeds with relatively prominent eyes, such as the Pekingese and the Pug, are most likely to be affected.

Where is the dog's third eyelid? Are eyelid problems common in dogs?

The third eyelid is rarely seen in a healthy dog. When the eye is closed, this fleshy membrane extends across the surface of the eye beneath the external eyelids. If, however, the dog is sick and has lost weight, the fat behind the eyeball is reduced, and the eye sinks slightly in its socket, revealing the third eyelid. It can be damaged and may even become inflamed.

The incidence of eyelid disorders varies somewhat according to the breed of dog concerned. It is possible for the eyelids to be abnormally inverted so they rub on the surface of the eyeball and cause a condition known as entropion. This is relatively common in the St Bernard, Chow, Labrador and Golden Retriever, as well as in various Setters. The reverse situation, in which the lower eyelid is

direction away from the eye, is described as ectropion and often occurs in the Bloodhound and breeds of Spaniel. Surgical correction is required in many instances.

Another condition which may require surgery is the narrowing of tear ducts. This impairs drainage of fluid from the eye so the dog appears to be crying. It occurs in such breeds as the Poodle and Pekingese. The actual marks staining the face can be wiped away with cotton.

Are some dogs more at risk from ear infections than others? What is the likelihood of a cure?

Any breed that has long floppy ears with a thick covering of hair is likely to be susceptible because the ear canal is occluded, enabling bacteria and other potentially harmful micro-organisms to colonize the region. Regular, gentle cleaning of the ears can be particularly advisable in dogs such as Spaniels to help prevent infections of this type. Use a damp cotton swab for the purpose, taking care not to probe deeply within the ear but making sure the canal is free of dirt and wax.

A dog that scratches and rubs its ears repeatedly is likely to be suffering from an ear infection. There may also be an unpleasant odor associated with the ears. If the dog paws its ears repeatedly, it may injure the tissue on the earflap and cause blood to build up within, leading to a swelling called a hematoma. It may be necessary for a veterinarian to correct the hematoma by surgical means.

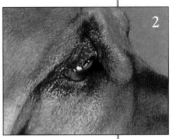

Above: Some of the range of dogs' eye shapes: the German Shepherd Dog (1), the Bloodhound (2), and the Chihuahua (3).

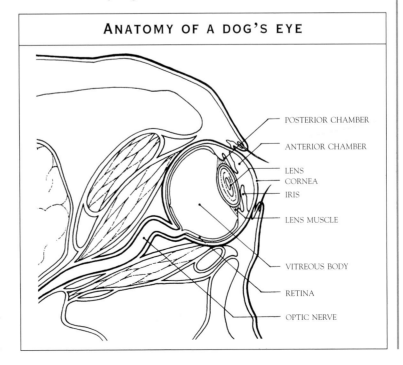

ANATOMY OF A DOG'S EYE

POSTERIOR CHAMBER
ANTERIOR CHAMBER
LENS
CORNEA
IRIS
LENS MUSCLE
VITREOUS BODY
RETINA
OPTIC NERVE

LOOKING AFTER EYES AND EARS

● To clean the eyes use cotton wool moistened with warm water and wipe the eye gently (1). Apply drops of ointment directly to the cornea (2).

● To clean the ears and remove wax, use moist cotton buds (3), but be careful never to prove deeply into the ear, as this can cause damage. Turn the dog's head to one side to apply drops (4) and then massage behind the ears.

The major problem in curing ear infections is that the cause is not straightforward. Bacteria, fungi and sometimes ear mites can all be involved, and frequent use of medication tends to lead to antibiotic resistance. In addition, treatment usually needs to be maintained for a relatively long period of time to prevent recurrence. When there is no improvement, surgery will probably be the only solution.

In an operation called an aural resection, the vertical part of the ear canal is opened permanently. This opening will not be noticeable when the ear flap is in its usual position. If a dog suddenly appears to have great pain in its ear, the cause is likely to be a grass seed or a similar foreign body, not an infection. In most cases of this type veterinary advice should be sought.

How should I administer eye medication?

This usually comes in the form of drops or an ointment. Check that the dog's head is adequately restrained and then cautiously apply the fluid as close as possible to the eye without actually touching the surface. If necessary, pull the lids apart gently, bearing in mind that the dog will probably blink when the medication makes contact with the eye itself. Ointment is perhaps easier to apply since there is no risk of it being washed away with a blink, but restrain the dog for a few moments following application so that it does not wipe off the medication.

ANATOMY OF A DOG'S EAR

PINNA

CRANIAL CAVITY

EAR CANAL

VESTIBULE

OPENING LEADING TO
INNER EAR CANALS

INCUS

MALLEUS

STAPES

COCHLEA WINDOW

MIDDLE EAR CAVITY

METABOLIC DISORDERS

Metabolic disorders can sometimes be of acute onset – for example, in the case of milk fever in a suckling bitch. However, generally, these conditions tend to be more insidious and can be rather variable in their effects on the body.

My veterinary has suggested my dog may have pancreatic insufficiency. What is this, and is treatment possible?

If a dog loses weight over a period of time but maintains a healthy appetite, then this could indicate pancreatic insufficiency. The pancreas

Below: Any changes in a dog's appetite should be monitored closely.

*Above: Unusual
tiredness in a dog
could be a symptom
of a thyroid disorder.*

is a vital organ, producing hormones, such as insulin, as well as enzymes to help digest the food in the small intestine. In a case of pancreatic insufficiency, there is an inadequate output of enzymes, leading to an incomplete breakdown of food for absorption into the body. Pancreatic insufficiency can be confirmed by laboratory tests.

Treatment consists of providing sufficient enzymes via the food itself, usually in the form of capsules or powders, to compensate for the deficiency. It may also help to add ox sweetbread (pancreas) to the diet, and some formulated rations are of particular value for dogs suffering from this complaint. Alternatively, increase the level of protein relative to the levels of carbohydrate and fat in the dog's diet. Unfortunately, although some degree of supplementation can improve the digestive process, dogs suffering from pancreatic insufficiency may remain thin, rather than putting on a great deal of weight. While it is not difficult to cope with a dog suffering from pancreatic insufficiency compared to one suffering from diabetes mellitus, many owners find the prospect depressing and have their dog put to sleep.

Are there two different forms of diabetes recognized in the dog?

Yes. The most common type is known as diabetes mellitus (also known as sugar diabetes). This is a condition that results from a deficiency of the hormone insulin which is produced by the pancreas and which stimulates cells to take up glucose present in the blood stream. In the case of diabetes mellitus, the sugar accumulates in the bloodstream and the cells are deprived of this vital nutrient. Once a critical level is reached, glucose passes into the urine, giving it an unusually sweet and sickly smell, and increasing volumes of urine are passed. Body tissues then begin to be broken down to meet the body's energy requirement, and this leads to weakness.

Diabetes mellitus is more likely to affect middle-aged dogs and is much more likely to be found in bitches. Once diagnosed, regular injections of insulin on a daily basis will probably be required, and the dog's condition will have to be closely monitored through regular urine samples.

The urine is also significant in the case of diabetes insipidus. A shortage of the anti-diuretic hormone (ADH) leads to a greatly increased output of urine, because water normally reabsorbed during its passage through the kidney is lost. As a result, the dog has a prodigious thirst to compensate for the

increased water loss. Diabetes insipidus is a relatively rare condition, much less commonly seen than chronic renal failure which can produce similar symptoms. It is likely to be caused by a brain tumor. A synthetic form of the hormone can be administered to alleviate symptoms even if the actual source of the complaint cannot be corrected. As in its human form, diabetes is a disease that can only be controlled rather than cured. The main signs of the disease, are excessive water intake, obesity and sweet-scented breath.

What disorders can arise from a malfunction of the adrenal cortex? Will effects be seen throughout the body?

The adrenal glands are located close to the kidneys. The outer zone of these glands, known as the cortex, produce two hormones. Although relatively small, the adrenal glands have widespread effects, and any disorder has far-reaching consequences. The two hormones of significance are cortisol and aldosterone. If the level of output is relatively low, the condition known as Addison's Disease results. This is more often seen in bitches than in male dogs, and the symptoms are particularly apparent after exercise. Vomiting and a loss of appetite result from a deficiency of cortisol, while a shortage of aldosterone leads to dehydration. It is possible, once the condition has been diagnosed, to provide synthetic replacements keeping the dog in good health. The reverse situation, an excessive production of these hormones, results in Cushing's syndrome. Characteristic changes include uneven loss of hair on either side of the body and a weakness of the abdominal muscles, leading to a pot-bellied appearance. Although this, again, is a serious condition, some degree of treatment may be possible.

Could my dog be suffering from a thyroid gland disorder? It seems very inactive.

The thyroid glands are important in regulating overall body activity. If the output of hormones from a dog's thyroid is depressed, it is likely to appear listless, although such behavior doesn't necessarily indicate that the dog has a thyroid disorder. Other symptoms of a thyroid disorder can include weight gain, greasy skin and a noticeable aversion to cold surroundings. Pills given regularly to a dog suffering from these symptoms will lead to a distinct improvement. A shortage of iodine in the diet may also cause similar symptoms, and for this reason, some breeders use kelp (seaweed) powder as a general tonic. Basenjis appear to have an unusually high requirement for iodine.

EXTERNAL PARASITES

While fleas are a well-known external parasite, others can also be encountered on dogs, some of which, such as *Demodex* mites, can have very infectious and serious consequences.

How will I know if my dog has fleas, and how can I overcome this problem?

Keep a close watch on the coat of your dog, especially during grooming. You may not immediately see fleas, but you are likely to spot their characteristic dark reddish-brown specks of dirt. These are the remains of the blood that fleas remove from their hosts. If placed on a piece of wet tissue or blotting paper, the dirt will tend to dissolve and create reddish rings. One of the major problems in combating fleas is that they spend relatively little time on their hosts but remain hidden in the environment for long periods. You might see a flea rushing through the hair of the dog around the base of the tail, a favored site on the body. Special flea combs are available, but such is the athleticism of fleas that even when detected, they are extremely difficult to catch. If you have an empty small container, fill it with water before you start grooming the dog (preferably outside) and keep it close at hand. If you should discover a flea, try to transfer it to the water from which it should be unable to escape. Alternatively, squeeze it firmly between the thumb and index finger using your fingernail on its rear end to kill it.

The dog should be treated by means of a powder or an aerosol intended for this purpose. Be careful when applying these potentially toxic preparations; always read the directions carefully beforehand, especially if you buy one of the brands available through pet stores, because not all are safe for young dogs. When using powder, brush it in against the natural lie of the coat. Use an aerosol in a similar manner, taking particular care around the head to avoid the eyes. It is likely that the dog will attempt to lick some of the chemical out of its coat. To deter this, take your dog out for a walk immediately after applying the treatment. Do not be surprised if your dog is frightened by the noise of the aerosol. It is often preferable to opt for a powder for this reason.

In addition to dealing with the dog, it is vital to treat its surroundings also. The bed will need to be washed, powdered or sprayed as well as any bedding. The flea's life cycle takes about five weeks to complete, and the minute eggs are likely to be scattered around the floor. Any that escape into the environment are likely to hatch later, precipitating a new epidemic of scratching in your dog. Repeat treatments as necessary, always following the directions on the product.

In severe cases, you may need to call in a professional firm to treat your house so that no stages in the life cycle can remain viable. The chemicals used may have a residual action so that no other fleas will be able to establish themselves for a period of time. Do not forget to remove from the room any other pets, such as fish, that may be affected by chemical treatment, before the work starts. It is quite possible for dogs to transfer fleas to cats, and vice versa, so any felines in the house must also be treated. Bear in mind that they are likely to be even more susceptible to the effects of such chemicals than dogs.

LIFE CYCLE OF A FLEA

● The female dog flea (1) lays her eggs either on the floor (2) or in bedding and in about a week they hatch into larvae (3) which spin cocoons, inside which the pupae (4) develop into adults within two or three weeks. The dog flea acts as an intermediate host for the larvae of the common tapeworm, *Dipylidium caninum*, which makes it even more vital that flea infestations should be controlled. Also, dog fleas can bite the owner and, in fact, the human flea, *Pulex irritans*, often lives on dogs and vice versa.

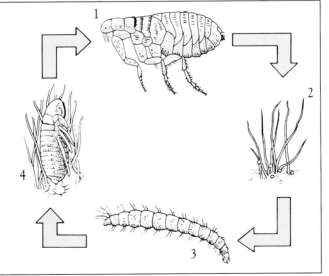

Above: Cats can transfer fleas to dogs and vice versa, so both must be treated at the same time. Beware, though, that certain preparations are not safe for use with cats.

Precautions

As a precaution against fleas, some owners use flea collars for their pets, but these must be fitted strictly in accordance with the manufacturer's direction if they are to be effective and safe. If your dog has a naturally sensitive skin, check regularly to be sure there is no adverse reaction to the impregnated strip forming the collar.

Flea infestations build up during the summer months in temperate climates. Some owners prefer to bathe their dogs with an insecticidal shampoo to deter fleas and other external parasites. This should be mixed with a specified volume of water and is rinsed out of the coat. Other means of combating such parasites include pills and injections. The concentration of the drug in the blood kills the flea when it feeds but offers no protection to the dog's owner, who may also be bitten by these parasites. Thus, the environment must also be treated.

Are fleas harmful to dogs?

Yes. Even in only mild cases, the presence of fleas can cause not only scratching but also severe irritation, which leads the dog to bite itself. In certain instances, dogs become allergic to the flea saliva which is injected in minute quantities when the flea bites. This will result in a very bad reaction following a single contact with flea saliva. There are also various diseases and canine parasites that can be spread by fleas including the tapeworm

Dipylidium caninum. Puppies that are bitten by fleas may suffer from anemia.

What are the common mites that may afflict my dog?

This will depend partly on the area where you live, but the mites described below are all relatively common on dogs. The skin irritation caused by any of these mites is described as mange, and it can prove difficult to treat successfully. The mite *Demodex canis* lives deep in the hair follicles and is usually associated with short-coated breeds, especially Dachshunds. It can cause hair loss, and thickening of the skin, and bacteria may invade the damaged tissue leading to the formation of pustules; the dog can become very sick. *Demodex* spreads from a bitch to her puppies although the symptoms may not be immediately apparent. Confirmation of the presence of *Demodex* requires skin scrapings viewed under the microscope to find the parasite. The condition is often difficult to treat. Infected bitches should not be mated to prevent the transmission of these mites to puppies.

Sarcoptes scabiei is found on the skin, and the first indication of its presence will probably be red patches on the inner surface of the thighs. The whole life cycle takes place on the dog and causes considerable irritation. Diagnosis is made in the same way as for *Demodex*, and treatment may need to be prolonged. If these mites are suspected, take precautions to see that they do not spread to humans, especially children. Another skin mite that commonly afflicts puppies, but which is also present in older dogs, is *Cheyletiella yasguri*. This mite leads to an excessive build-up of scurf in the coat, which is, in part, the mites themselves, as they are white in color.

The ear mite, known as *Otodectes cynotis*, lives within the ears. These mites cause irritation by invading the sensitive tissue, and they will contribute to an existing infection. It is possible to see them in situ by means of an auroscope, but, more simply, an accumulation of reddish-brown wax in the ear canal itself is indicative of their presence, especially if the dog paws repeatedly at its ears. Obtain treatment from your veterinarian.

Most species of mite normally live on the dog's body throughout their life cycle. The exception is the harvest mite *Trombicula autumnalis*. In this particular case, only the larval stage in the life cycle is likely to be parasitic. The adults appear as small, free-living spidery creatures, reddish in color. The larvae are found in vegetation and usually attach to the dog's paws between the pads and cause severe irritation. The dog will chew at its feet. A careful inspection will reveal the tiny groups of larvae responsible. The related North American chigger (*Eutrombicula alfreddugesi*) produces identical symptoms. Washing the feet by dipping them in a solution of insecticidal shampoo will kill the larvae.

What other external parasites may afflict my dog?

Lice are most likely to be seen on puppies; they are usually spread by direct contact or via grooming equipment. Typically, they congregate around the head where their egg-cases cling to individual hairs. In most instances, repeated treatment will be necessary to clear the infestation. Ticks, in comparison, live on dogs for only a short period in their life cycles, often dropping off after feeding on the dog's blood. Rather than trying to pull a tick out, and risk breaking off its head and leaving it embedded in the skin to act as the source of an infection, simply smear its body with petroleum jelly. With its respiratory pore blocked, the tick will be unable to breathe and will drop off intact.

In tropical areas especially, ticks can transmit serious blood-borne protozoal infections. One of the most widespread is babesiosis, in which the protozoan *Babesia canis* is linked to the brown dog tick *Rhipicephalus sanguineus*. The resulting illness is described as redwater because an acute anemia leads to reddish urine being produced. Blood transfusions as well as drugs are likely to be required if treatment is to be successful. Moving a dog to an area where such ticks are endemic carriers of babesiosis is hazardous, and the dog should be watched closely. The protozoa are easily detected in a blood smear, stained in an appropriate manner for microscopic examination.

Certain flies can also parasitize dogs. The flies are usually attracted to fecal deposits, where they lay their eggs. The eggs give rise to maggots which attack the skin and produce a toxin that enters the blood stream and can prove fatal. The fly larvae should be removed at the earliest opportunity and the affected area cleaned up, using antibiotics if necessary. In parts of the United States, dogs can be attacked by the maggots of the fly *Cuterebra maculata*. These invade the skin when the dog is walking over ground where the eggs from which the larvae hatch were originally laid. Thick-coated breeds are most likely to be attacked, and maggots will have to be removed by surgery.

Dietary methods can help to control external parasites. Large amounts of vitamin B generate an odor in the skin of dogs that is repellent to biting insects.

EXTERNAL PARASITES

● A variety of external parasites can afflict dogs and these include: *Cheyletiella*, fur mite (1), *Trombicula*, harvest mite (**2**), *Demodex*, demodectic mite (3), *Ixodes*, sheep tick (4).

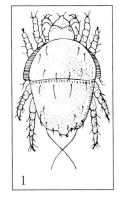 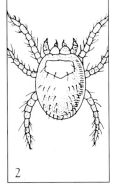 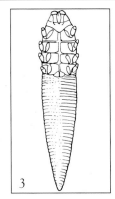 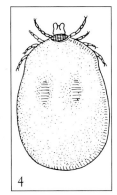

1   2   3   4

INTERNAL PARASITES

Dealing with the majority of these is usually a straightforward procedure, as there are a number of effective drugs available. Internal parasites can be spread in several ways.

How can I recognize tapeworms?

Tapeworms are named after their flattish appearance. They resemble a piece of whitish tape, becoming broader away from the head end. They anchor in the gut by their heads, and the segments of their bodies become mature towards the tail. Pieces break off and are passed out with feces. The segments are not directly infectious for other dogs however because they require an intermediate host. This, in the case of the tapeworm *Dipylidium caninum*, can be lice or fleas. The dog acquires the infection by consuming an external parasite that has been parasitized by the immature tapeworm. It may be possible to spot tapeworm segments around the dog's anus; they resemble rice grains in appearance and sometimes appear to move.

Other tapeworms use herbivores as intermediate hosts. Dogs acquire infection by eating raw meat containing the tapeworm cyst. One particular species, *Echinococcus granulosus*, is commonly associated with sheep, but can also be spread to humans. If a human ingests the eggs, cysts about 6 inches across may develop in the body with disastrous consequences. The adult tapeworm in this instance is remarkably small, reaching a maximum size of no more than one fifth of an inch, and does not cause obvious harm to the dog, even when there is a heavy burden present. In order to combat the risk posed by *Echinococcus*, the New Zealand government has made it compulsory to deworm dogs regularly, and this controls the problem effectively.

Below: Puppies may be born infected with some forms of parasite, or may subsequently ingest them.

Are roundworms important parasites in the dog?

Considerable media attention has been focused on the slight but nevertheless real risk to human health posed by the canine roundworm known as *Toxocara canis*. Puppies are frequently born infected with this parasite, having acquired it from the bitch before birth. These roundworms may cause diarrhea, vomiting and a pot-bellied appearance. Repeated treatment through the pregnancy and following birth, as directed by a veterinarian, will eliminate the danger posed to human health. In fact, the eggs of *Toxocara canis*, when present in the feces, are not immediately infectious but must remain outside the body for some time before the larval stage can develop. Once primed, however, and ingested accidentally by a child, for example, the eggs will hatch in the gut and the larvae will migrate through the body, a process known as *visceral larval migrans*. If the larvae develop in the eye, blindness can result. They may also invade the brain, with serious consequences.

Heartworm

Other roundworms may be more localized in their distribution. The heartworm (*Dirofilaria immitis*) occurs in the warmer parts of the world. It is transmitted when biting insects remove immature heartworms (called *microfilariae*) from the circulation of an infected animal and introduce them to another host when they feed again. The adult heartworm finally localizes in the blood vessels close to the heart making treatment very difficult. As a result, medication is given regularly to prevent the microfilariae from developing to the final stage in the life cycle, thus avoiding this problem.

Lungworm and whipworm

Dogs in kennels run the greatest risk of acquiring parasites, including certain roundworms. Coughing after exercise in the case of Greyhounds suggests a lungworm (*Filaroides osleri*) infection. The parasites may be seen at the bifurcation of the trachea into the lungs with a fiber-optic endoscope. Whipworms (*Trichuris vulpis*) are also quite often encountered in greyhounds, they localize in the appendix and cause intermittent diarrhea.

Hookworms are also a danger in kennels because they enter the dog's body via its feet. Those of the Ancylostoma species then move

LIFE CYCLE OF THE ROUNDWORM

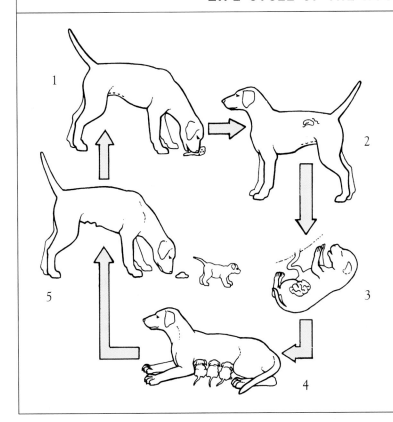

● The embryonated infective eggs or larvae of the dog roundworm, *Toxocara canis* are ingested by the dog (1) and migrate to the body tissues (2) such as the kidneys. Unfortunately, the larvae usually enter the tissues of developing fetuses (3) and localize in their intestines, being activated by pregnancy. After the birth of the puppies the larvae can also migrate into the puppies' system and infect them through the mother's milk (4). The worms mature, passing eggs in the puppies' feces which are consumed by the mother and can reinfect her (5). Alternatively, larvae which fail to establish themselves and are passed out in the feces, may find another host and begin producing eggs. The eggs are not immediately infective, but need a short period outside the body to mature.

to the intestines and may result in a severe anemia. Other hookworms, such as *Uncinaria*, tend to have less serious effects.

Kidney worm

A rather peculiar nematode seen in certain parts of the world is the giant kidney worm (*Dioctophyma renale*). In the majority of cases, it tends to localize in the right kidney. The only treatment available is to remove the affected organ. This nematode is usually spread from raw fish, and females can grow up to 40 inches in total length. A dog will need rest after this treatment.

Dioctophyma renale is endemic in parts of the United States and elsewhere. Although found in some parts of Europe, the kidney worm does not occur in the United Kingdom or Australia.

Other parasites

Various other parasitic worms can be spread to dogs, but they tend to be regional in distribution, especially if they are associated with the wildlife of an area. One parasite which resembles a worm in appearance, but is in fact a mite, is *Linguatula serrata*, popularly known as the tongue worm. It has a life cycle that requires an intermediate host such as a rabbit. A dog consuming the uncooked flesh of an infected herbivore can acquire these mites. They localize in the nasal chambers and cause a runny nose and impaired breathing. The dog

may sneeze repeatedly, trying to dislodge the parasites, but they have to be removed by a veterinarian.

Should I deworm my dog on a regular basis?

Yes, this is vital, especially in a home with young children. Deworming is carried out against roundworms such as *Toxocara*, which can be spread directly, as well as against tapeworms. Different medication may be required for the latter. Half-yearly dosing is recommended for adult dogs, but young puppies and dogs will need more frequent treatment. Treatment for tapeworms also requires control of the intermediate hosts when these are fleas or lice. In sheep farming areas, particular care is recommended because of the threat posed by the tapeworm disease *Hydatidosis*.

Check with your veterinarian on the recommended regimen for your area. It is probably preferable to obtain deworming pills from your veterinarian too, although products can be purchased elsewhere – possibly more cheaply – without prescription. However, i you do buy other than from your veterinarian, be sure to follow directions on dosage. The newer, less toxic compounds tend to be restricted to veterinary outlets, and you can be sure that you will receive sound advice and the correct medication for your dog there.

YOUR HEALTH AND YOUR DOG

As with all animals, there are diseases that the dog can spread to humans. Many parasites can be overcome by regular deworming.

How serious are the risks to human health by dogs? How can I minimize them?

Various diseases spread from dogs to humans, and these are termed zoonoses. In the vast majority of cases, there is no significant risk, especially if the dogs are dewormed regularly and their feces removed from the environment. Indeed, very many dogs are kept by families with children, and the benefits of ownership far outweigh the small, but significant, risk from zoonoses. Teach your children to wash their hands if they have handled the dog, especially prior to a meal time, and do not encourage a dog to lick their faces. If you or your family are bitten, clean the wound and see your doctor about inoculation. A dog bite may lead to tetanus; the bacteria are introduced via the deep puncture wounds caused by the canine teeth. The risk of rabies has been mentioned previously.

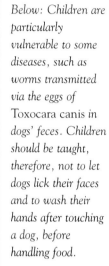

Below: Children are particularly vulnerable to some diseases, such as worms transmitted via the eggs of Toxocara canis in dogs' feces. Children should be taught, therefore, not to let dogs lick their faces and to wash their hands after touching a dog, before handling food.

The use of prepared or cooked food will minimize the threat of diseases such as salmonellosis affecting your dog and being transmitted to other members of the family.

There is potentially a much greater risk of zoonosic disease being acquired outside the home, as some dog owners are not fastidious about deworming. Toxocara eggs, for example, remain viable for a long time once established in the environment. The only means of destroying them is by intense heat on a hard surface such as concrete. In soil, they can survive for over two years. Stray dogs clearly represent a major source of infection, as they are less likely to have been regularly dewormed than a house pet. Young children are most susceptible to Toxocara and should be supervised when out in public places such as parks so they do not come into contact with feces. If regular deworming was required by law, as in New Zealand, the threat from Toxocara could be reduced even further; a move of this type would have the support of all concerned dog owners.

What is ringworm, and how can I recognize it on my dog?

Ringworm is not a parasitic disorder, but a fungal disease that affects the skin and hair. Various fungi can lead to the characteristic circular bald patches with hair breaking off around the circumference of the site. The disease can often be confirmed by means of a Wood's light, which shows the fungus up as fluorescent green in a darkened room. Alternatively, cultures can be grown from skin scrapings, but the results may take several weeks, as fungal growth can be slow, even in special cultural media. Specific antibiotic therapy using griseofulvin will be necessary, but this cannot be given safely to pregnant bitches for fear of causing fetal damage.

It is important to realize that the fungal spores will almost certainly have contaminated the dog's environment, especially its bed and grooming tools. If you have a cat in the house, have it tested as well because ringworm can be transmitted from dog to cat and vice versa, and the signs of infection are not generally as obvious in cats. Alcohol or disinfectants of the iodoform type are effective against spores, and every effort should be made to clean the environment thoroughly because ringworm is one of the diseases that can be spread from dogs to humans. If you develop reddish, circular lesions on your arms or elsewhere on your body, see your doctor.

FIRST AID PROCEDURES

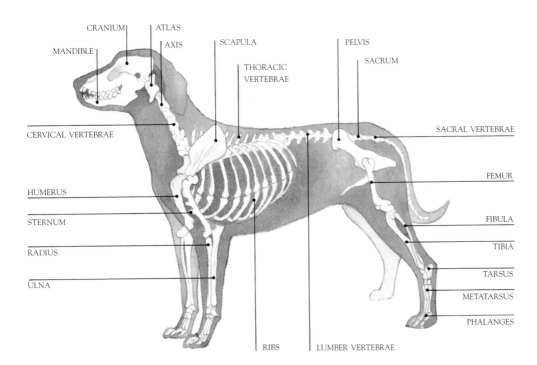

CRANIUM | ATLAS

MANDIBLE | AXIS | SCAPULA | PELVIS

THORACIC VERTEBRAE | SACRUM

CERVICAL VERTEBRAE

SACRAL VERTEBRAE

HUMERUS

FEMUR

STERNUM

FIBULA

RADIUS

TIBIA

ULNA

TARSUS

METATARSUS

PHALANGES

RIBS | LUMBER VERTEBRAE

The basic steps rely on commonsense, and are an extension of those techniques practiced on humans. There is always a risk that a dog may become involved in an accident, and the owner can help.

How should I handle a dog that has been involved in a traffic accident?

A dog that has been hit by a vehicle is likely to be in pain and distress. Always approach it with caution because it may well bite. Rather than attempt to grasp the neck and attach a lead, restrain the dog by means of a noose. Loop the bottom of the lead through the handle, slip the noose over the head and then tighten, making sure that your hands are out of the dog's reach throughout. In an emergency, you may be able to use a belt in this way. Always try to catch the dog with minimum disturbance and guard yourself, too, from passing traffic. Talk quietly to the dog and reassure it as far as possible. If it is very aggressive, a temporary muzzle may be required. Again, create a noose using a belt or tie. Loop it over the jaws, pull tight and knot the material behind the ears. Be sure that it is placed well back so it will not slip off accidentally. Muzzling short-nosed breeds can be particularly difficult.

When a dog is lying flat, move it very carefully, especially if you suspect it may have serious internal injuries. And remember, it may attempt to snap. If there is a blanket available, gently transfer the dog to it, taking care not to tip it. With assistance, the dog can

then be carried from the road in the blanket. Take the dog to a veterinarian immediately for a full examination.

What should I do if the dog is bleeding badly?

You may not be aware of a serious internal hemorrhage, although the mucous membranes such as the gums will appear abnormally pale and the color will not return readily if the area is touched with a finger. The superficial scruffing and grazing often seen following a road traffic accident may be accompanied by bleeding, but this is usually self-limiting because the blood should clot readily. If an artery has been severed, however, blood will spurt from the site of the injury. In this case your action may be vital in attempting to save the dog's life. Wrap clean material around the apparent site of the hemorrhage and hold it tightly in place. This should help stimulate the formation of a blood clot. Get someone to telephone the nearest veterinarian. Move the dog cautiously to minimize the blood loss. Tourniquets are dangerous if used for any length of time and should be avoided if possible.

What are the signs of shock in a dog?

There are many causes of shock besides blood loss, including poisoning, fractures and burns. The symptoms are unmistakable. The dog becomes weak, and color disappears from the extremities. It appears cold, often shaking, and may be reluctant to stand. The heart beat is noticeably raised, while the respiratory rate tends to be shallow and rapid. Keep the dog warm (not excessively hot) and quiet and take whatever steps are necessary to counter the underlying cause of the symptoms of shock. If you have to take the dog to the veterinarian, wrap it carefully in a blanket and make it as comfortable as possible for the journey. Do not give alcohol because this is likely to prove counterproductive.

What should I do if my puppy burns itself?

Cool the burned area with cold water immediately to reduce the inflammation and then seek veterinary assistance. Burns, although superficial, may be serious and are likely to be slow to heal. Shock is inevitable, and a further complication may be bacterial infection.

What should I do if my puppy electrocutes itself?

Avoid this situation by never leaving an appliance plugged in and turned on in a room where there is a teething puppy that may choose to chew the wire. Never touch a dog that has been electrocuted until the source of the current has been switched off. This applies

especially in the case of a dog on a railway line as it could prove fatal.

Is it possible to distinguish between a fracture and a dislocation? What treatment will be necessary?

A fracture is a clear break in a bone, whereas a dislocation involves damage to a joint when one of the component bones is dislocated. In the case of a fracture, there will be no restraint on movement, but an audible grating sound (*crepitus*) is likely to accompany it. Avoid unnecessary handling as this will be painful for the dog. By way of contrast, a dislocation inhibits free movement. The swelling is confined to the region of the joint only, and the bone does not penetrate the skin.

The first aid you should provide is similar in either instance. Bearing in mind that the dog is in pain, try to restrain it. Confine it to a small area to encourage it to lie down and take the weight off the affected part of its body. Leave the treatment of the condition to the veterinarian. He may take X-rays to assess the state of the damage.

There is a congenital tendency in some breeds to develop luxating patellae (knee-caps). If the problem persists, surgical correction may be necessary. In the case of a

---

BANDAGING A DOG

● Any bandage must be securely tied to prevent the dog removing it. In an emergency – such as a cut pad, which will bleed profusely – binding a bandage tightly around the foot is the best way to stem blood loss. Bandages will also be necessary for other injuries, such as broken limbs.

EAR: Cover affected ear with bandage, leaving other ear free as anchor.

ABDOMEN: Bandages may be secured along the spine or at the tail.

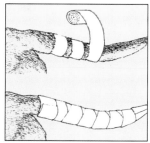

TAIL: Prevent slippage by including hair; anchor with adhesive tape.

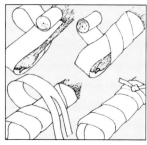

LEG OR FOOT: Wrap the bandage down the back and up the front of the paw, then across the leg. Tie ends securely or finish with adhesive tape.

TORNIQUET: Use a handkerchief twisted above injury. Loosen often.

SPLINT: Two flat pieces of wood secured with tape can support a fracture.

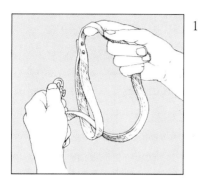

Above and right: A dog that has been injured, for example, in a traffic accident, may need to be restrained in some way so that it cannot bite or cause itself further harm. A simple noose can be made by looping the end of the lead through its handle and slipping it over the neck of the dog (1). If the dog has been knocked over, a blanket makes an ideal stretcher (2).

fracture, the veterinarian can opt to fix it, for example, internally by means of screws and plates or externally by placing the leg in a cast. The decision will depend on the site and type of fracture – cases where a bone penetrates the skin are more serious than clean breaks.

A temporary muzzle

Rarely, as a form of restraint, an improvised muzzle, made of a length of bandage is useful. A loop is placed over both jaws, with the knot at the top of the nasal region. The free ends of the bandage are brought round under the jaw and then crossed and tied behind the ears.

There may be times, after a road accident for example, when it will be necessary to catch a stray dog. If a dog appears aggressive, always remember the possibility that it could be afflicted with rabies, and avoid touching it directly. Loop a belt or lead to form a noose and slip this over the dog's neck.

My dog collapsed when we were coming back from a walk. He did recover, but could it happen again?

This is an alarming situation, and you must seek veterinary advice. There could be a number of causes, and the problem could recur. Epilepsy is not unknown in dogs, especially in Cocker Spaniels, and can lead to a sudden collapse. The dog appears to lose all control of its body functions during a seizure and may defecate as well as urinate. It will paddle with its legs while lying on its side. The cause is unknown, but treatment is available to control the seizures.

Another cause of collapse, especially in such brachycephalic breeds as the Bulldog, is a malformation in which the soft palate is longer than normal. This in turn may affect the larynx and prevent the dog from breathing normally at times. When this happens, pull the tongue forward at once and, if necessary, open the jaws to make sure there is no obstruction. If there is no response, artificial respiration must be given without delay.

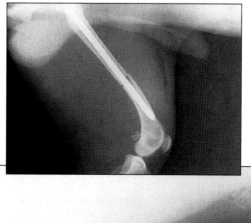

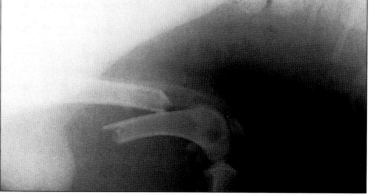

Below and left: A serious fracture of a dog's thigh bone is apparent using X-ray facilities. A metal pin may be used to help repair the break and the bone should knit together perfectly.

My dog has a grass seed lodged in its paw. What can be done to remove it?

Grass seeds are a relatively common "foreign body" that can injure a dog if they penetrate the skin. A sudden onset of lameness, with the dog licking persistently at its paws may indicate the presence of a grass seed. If you can see the seed, try to pull it out with a pair of tweezers; you may need someone else to restrain the dog for you. Unfortunately, in many instances nothing will be visible because the grass seed will have tracked further up the leg. A veterinary examination using special forceps will be necessary. But even with these, it is not always possible to discover the seed responsible for the irritation.

Other foreign bodies such as glass, needles and pins can also be dangerous for your dog. Needles, for example, may be ingested accidentally and can become stuck in the mouth. Do not attempt to remove an object from the mouth yourself, if possible, because the tongue is a very vascular organ and profuse bleeding may result. The symptoms of the presence of a foreign body will depend very much on where the object has become lodged. Gagging and pawing at the face can be expected in this instance.

How should I treat my dog if it requires artificial respiration?

If the dog is unable to breathe, the oxygen supply to the brain will be impaired, and the brain could be permanently damaged. Before giving artificial respiration, first check and make sure that the tongue does not block the entrance to the airway at the back of the mouth by pulling it forward. Then, with the dog on its right side, press gently and repeatedly on the rib cage with both hands at intervals of about five to ten seconds. If the chest wall has been punctured, by a deep wound for example, the usual pressure gradient will be lost, and you will have to adopt a different approach. Keeping the dog's jaws firmly closed, blow forcefully up the nostrils, with a few seconds gap between each breath. At the same time, check the heartbeat. Direct mouth-to-mouth resuscitation is of little value in the case of the dog.

Treating shock

An accidental injury may give rise to shock, the response to which should be geared according to the particular problem. Keep the dog in a warm environment and seek professional advice.

Below: In hot weather, particularly, dry grass seeds easily attach themselves to a dog's coat and can work their way inwards, penetrating the skin or becoming buried in the ear cavity.

ARTIFICIAL RESPIRATION

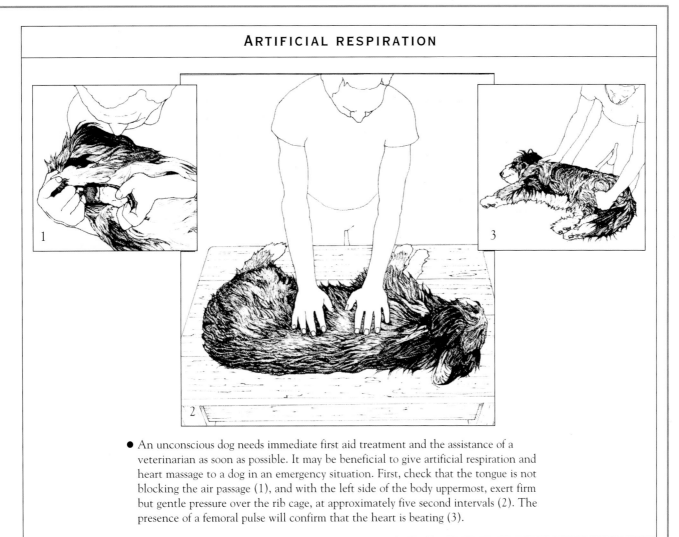

● An unconscious dog needs immediate first aid treatment and the assistance of a veterinarian as soon as possible. It may be beneficial to give artificial respiration and heart massage to a dog in an emergency situation. First, check that the tongue is not blocking the air passage (1), and with the left side of the body uppermost, exert firm but gentle pressure over the rib cage, at approximately five second intervals (2). The presence of a femoral pulse will confirm that the heart is beating (3).

We live in a hot climate. Should we take any special care with our dog?

Try to prevent your dog from going outside when the sun is at its hottest, particularly if there is any sign of reddening on its skin. This is likely to indicate sunburn and is especially common in the nasal region of collies and similar breeds. Repeated burning of sensitive areas can lead to skin cancer. To prevent burning, use a suitable barrier cream; it is even possible, and can be effective, to darken white areas with shoe polish.

It is not just dogs left in unventilated cars that die from heatstroke. In hot weather, dogs that are kept in outdoor kennels or in doghouses that have poor ventilation are also greatly at risk from overheating.

If your dog is suffering from heatstroke, first cool it down as quickly as possible with water, until the rectal temperature is 1°F above normal. This temperature should then fall to normal without further application of water. If it falls excessively, there is a danger that the dog may succumb to hypothermia. Have drinking water readily available, and massage the dog's legs to improve the circulation at this critical time.

Below: Heatstroke is very dangerous because the only way dogs can control their body temperature is by panting – causing heat loss from the body by evaporation of water – or through the pores between their toes and on the inside of the ears. Therefore, it is vital for a dog to have access to a cool spot and plenty of water, particularly in hot climates.

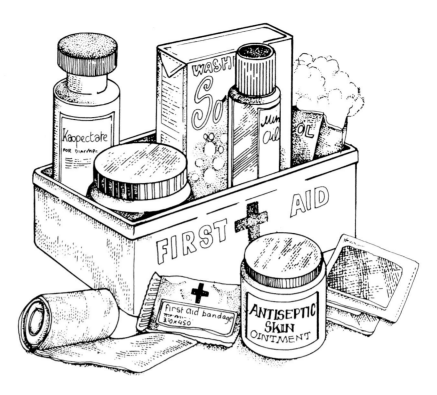

What are the most common poisons that dogs encounter?

Among common household products, there are poisonous substances that have a fatal attraction for dogs. Anti-freeze for example, contains ethylene glycol, which has a sweet flavor that dogs like. In the body, however, it converts to oxalic acid and is deadly: only 1 ounce proving fatal for a dog of 15 pounds in weight. Metaldehyde, often combined with arsenic and used in slug baits, is also appealing to dogs and should be carefully monitored.

It may be possible to reverse the effects, depending on the substance involved, and the speed of diagnosis, but it is vital to give as much information as possible to your veterinarian. You may not realize a dog has eaten poison. Certain preservatives and lead paint, for example, are likely to prove fatal if your dog chews woodwork. Some house plants and outdoor plants are poisonous too. The incidence of poisoning is higher in young dogs because of their natural curiosity and chewing instincts, and the risk is greatest for those that lack proper supervision. In case of emergency, call your local veterinary hospital or ask for information from the Poison Control Center.

How do I deal with insect and snake bites?

Many dogs are stung by insects such as wasps, usually on the head. In the case of a bee, the ruptured sting will be left behind and should be removed with tweezers. It will resemble a fine splinter partially protruding from the skin. The swelling will soon subside in most cases. If the dog was stung on its tongue, the tongue will become inflamed and may block the opening to the trachea making breathing difficult. Call your veterinarian if this occurs. Most dogs rapidly learn to distinguish stinging insects, but snakes are a different proposition. Try to remember what the snake looked like even if you cannot identify it. In the United States there are several poisonous snakes, such as the colorful coral snake and the rattlesnake, as well as poisonous lizards and a species of poisonous toad. Deadly poisonous insects also occur in some parts of the world such as Australia. A close examination of a snake bite may help you to determine whether poison was released into the wound. If there is a large swelling with two holes in the center, it is likely that this was the case.

Often, a snake bite occurs when you are well away from a vehicle, and the availability of a veterinarian with anti-venom at hand is unlikely. If the bit is on the leg, tie a tourniquet around it to restrict the spread of the poison to the rest of the body. It should not be too tight; leave it loose enough so you can slip a finger under it when it is in place. An ice pack, created with ice cubes in a sock and applied to the site of the bite, will also be of assistance. Carry the dog if possible back to your vehicle and contact a veterinarian as soon as possible for further advice.

While it is feasible in dire emergencies to cut into the wound and suck out the poison, this is difficult in practice. Make a small cut between the two fang marks to reach the fluid, suck the wound and then spit the poison out. Finally, rinse your mouth out thoroughly.

AILMENT	SYMPTOM	ACTION
Anal glands	Dog will rub hindquarters on the ground, showing obvious signs of irritation.	Dogs have little scent glands on each side of the anus. If they become overfilled they cause irritation and, if not relieved, abscesses may develop. The task of emptying the anal glands can be undertaken by the dog's owner once the veterinarian has demonstrated the correct procedure.
Aujeszky's Disease	Dog will paw and scratch its face and show no signs of aggression. An initial phase of excitement leads to other neurological symptoms and finally to a coma about two weeks after infection.	No treatment is available. The disease presents no threat to human health.
Bad breath	*see* Worms (could be stomach disorder).	Tablets available.
Broken leg	–	Call the veterinarian without delay. Do not give anything by mouth. Move the dog as little as possible and try to immobilize the broken limb by, for instance, tying it to its partner on the opposite side of the body.
Canker	Continuous shaking of head and rubbing against floor and furniture.	Canker is the name usually applied to all types of canine ear infection stemming from an accumulation of wax due to dirt or mites. It is sometimes detected by an accompanying unpleasant smell. There are any number of preparations available, but first ascertain the cause of the trouble by consulting your veterinarian. Warm olive oil acts as a cleansing agent. It could well clear up the trouble.
Choking	Dog may try to vomit or tear at mouth with paw.	Endeavour to open the dog's mouth and remove the foreign body – a piece of bone or a chew could have become wedged across the roof of its mouth. In some cases, a general anesthetic may be needed, so check with your veterinarian.
Collapse	Dog will lie on its stomach and refuse to rise. May be breathing heavily.	Summon veterinary advice as soon as possible. Meanwhile, transfer patient onto a suitable mattress or blanket and keep warm. Bathe the mouth with glucose, or sugar in water. Do not force the dog to swallow. The dog should not be allowed to lie on one side for more than 20 minutes.
Cushing's syndrome	Dog loses hair evenly on both sides of the body, and gains a pot-bellied appearance.	This condition results from an abnormality in the adrenal glands, positioned close to the kidneys. Seek veterinary advice.
Cut foot	Sudden bleeding from foot, with or without lameness. This often occurs on beaches, and when dogs swim in ponds where there is broken glass. Similar symptoms may be shown when a claw is broken near its base.	If bleeding is profuse, wrap foot in lint or cotton wool and apply firm roller bandage with even pressure round the foot. Be careful not to bend a broken claw. Take the dog to a veterinarian for whatever treatment is necessary. Never use an elastic band or other constricting material.
Diabetes	Increased thirst and appetite, with associated weight loss.	Contact your veterinarian. You may have to learn how to give your dog daily injections of insulin.
Diarrhea (acute)	Very loose motions that may contain blood; can be accompanied by vomiting and weakness in the hind legs.	Starve the dog and keep it warm. Bathe the mouth and gums with a warm solution of glucose or sugar in 1 pint of water. Phone for veterinary advice.
Distemper	Symptoms range from a high temperature to diarrhea, vomiting and serious neurological signs, including twitching of the facial muscles, fits and even paralysis.	Consult a veterinarian immediately. Although treatable to a certain extent, the effects of distemper are extremely unpleasant and can affect a dog for the rest of its life. A decision may be made to put a dog to sleep on humanitarian grounds.
Earache	The dog will scratch its ear, or ears, and may hold its head on one side and shake it.	There may a grass seed in the ear. Contact your veterinarian. Meanwhile, do not put anything in the ear. It is easy for owners to make the wrong diagnosis, so it is best to wait for professional treatment.

AILMENT	SYMPTOM	ACTION
Eczema	Can be wet or dry. An angry patch appears on the dog's coat causing it to bite and scratch.	Causes range from diet deficiency to a hormone disorder. The veterinarian may try several treatments, from cream application to a course of injections, before the trouble is cleared up.
Fits	Sudden uncontrolled spasmodic movements, often with champing of the jaws: usually accompanied by salvation. The dog may fall onto its side. The muscles across the top of the head and down the neck may twitch violently.	Remove collar, if tight. Make sure that the dog cannot injure itself, for instance in a fireplace. Make sure that it can breathe by holding the head and neck, extended if necessary. Keep in a darkened, quiet room until you can get help, and prevent all sudden noises, door bells, slamming doors, etc. Most fits are over quite quickly. Seek veterinary advice as soon as possible.
Fleas	Scratching. Poor coat condition.	There are four common types of external parasites; lice, and their eggs (nits), which are found mainly in the dog's head; and fleas, ticks and mites, which may be found on its body. Treatment is available in the form of special shampoos, dusting powders and aerosols. Fleas are brownish and easily detectable in a dog's coat. They leave their droppings not their eggs, in the dog's coat.
Grass seeds	*see* Earache.	The seed may work its way through into the ear canal, and should be removed by a veterinarian. Check that grass seeds – and items like chewing gum – do not become lodged in the paws.
Heart attack	Usually self-evident. Often occurs in hot weather following exercise, particularly in the case of older – and flat-nosed – dogs.	Lay the dog on its right side with the head and neck extended. Open doors and windows to obtain as much fresh air as possible. If the tongue becomes blue, or breathing stops, massage the heart vigorously. Obtain veterinary help immediately.
Heat stroke	Panting and obvious distress.	Owners of flat-nosed breeds that are particularly susceptible to heat stroke should never travel without pre-soaked towelling dog coats and a supply of icy water. The latter should be applied to the dog's head. WARNING: Never leave a dog in a car without lots of ventilation.
Hepatitis (or CAV-1)	Jaundice, swollen lymph nodes, hemorrhages, weight loss.	Seek urgent veterinarian help. Infected dogs may die suddenly without necessarily appearing very ill beforehand. The virus may localize in the kidneys and be excreted in the urine for a considerable period of time, during which it can be transmitted to other dogs. There is evidence to suggest that infection with CAV-1 can create permanent kidney damage, and that it may be a contributory cause of chronic renal failure in old age.
Incontinence	The dog is unable to refrain from relieving itself for a normal period of time.	This is usually a sign of kidney failure as the dog approaches old age. The condition can be helped with medication.
Injured eye	One eye appears very sore, or is kept closed.	Look for, and carefully remove, any obvious foreign body, such as grass seeds. To do this, flush it out using clean, warm water. Keeping the dog in semi-darkness, take it to the veterinarian for treatment if possible. If not, put a drop of medicinal paraffin or olive oil in the eye as an emergency measure and prevent the dog from rubbing the affected eye with its paws, or on the furnishings.
Kennel cough	Persistent cough usually after a spell in boarding kennels.	Rarely serious. Prevention is better than cure as it is possible to vaccinate the dog by intranasal administration of a small doze of Intrac, using a specially designed applicator. Antibiotics should help existing sufferers.

AILMENT	SYMPTOM	ACTION
Limp	–	This could be the result of something embedded in a paw, a cut, a torn muscle or ligament; or even in the case of an older animal, arthritis or rheumatism. Restrict the animal until the veterinarian has examined it.
Mange	Unsightly bare patches.	Varieties of mange include: sarcoptic, demodectic, and otodectic (affecting the ears). Caused by an infestation of mites, which burrow in the roots of a dog's coat, it is highly contagious and can be transferred not only from dog to dog, but also to humans. The need to wash one's hand thoroughly after applying ointment cannot be over-emphasized. Consult your veterinarian, who will recommend appropriate treatment.
Misalliance	Obvious: your bitch has accidentally been mated.	Your veterinarian can give an injection within 48 hours, but preferably within 24 hours, to prevent your bitch having puppies.
Pancreatic Insufficiency	Dog will excrete food in a relatively undigested state in pale-colored, loose feces with a highly unpleasant odor. Weight loss will appear over a period of time.	Consult your veterinarian.
Parvovirus	Vomiting, blood-stained diarrhea, dehydration, severe weight loss.	Consult your veterinarian about inoculating your puppy against this potentially fatal virus. If symptoms appear, seek urgent veterinary attention.
Poisoning	There may be sudden acute sickness, prostration or violent muscular movements.	If the dog is seen to swallow a known poison, induce vomiting by pushing a solution of salt (a teaspoonful in a tumbler of water for an average-sized dog) down the throat. Give milk if the substance swallowed is at all corrosive. Never do this more than once. Seek your veterinarian's advice quickly, taking with you the remainder of the poisonous agent, if known.
Rabies	Unpredictable moods, irritability, hypersensitivity to noise and light. Possibly, the dog will attempt to eat indigestible objects, like stones, but refuse normal food. Running amok, attacking and biting, difficulties in swallowing, and excessive drooling may follow.	Seek immediate veterinarian attention.
Road accident	You may witness the accident, or your dog may return lame.	Restrain your dog if necessary to prevent further injury and get it and bystanders away from the road. Be careful with injured limbs. Put a cold compress using wet cotton wool or lint on any obvious bleeding points, but, above all, keep the dog warm and comfortable. Contact your veterinarian as quickly as possible. Don't leave your dog lying in the road.
Shock	Depending on the cause: weakness, severe drop in temperature, shivering, inability or reluctance to stand, shallow breathing, unconsciousness.	Get the patient to a veterinarian as quickly as possible. Never give anything by mouth to an unconscious dog – it could choke and die.
Temperature	The best means of taking your dog's temperature is to insert the thermometer about 2 in (5 cm) into the rectum. The normal temperature is 38.9°C (101.5°F).	A low temperature in dogs is serious – call your veterinarian.
Worms	Bad breath, poor coat, ravenous appetite, pot belly.	There are a number of types of worms: roundworms, tapeworms, hookworms, whipworms and, in some countries, heartworms. However, the most common is the roundworm (*Toxocara canis*), which is most prevalent in puppies and in bitches before and after whelping. At such times worming is often recommended by veterinarians at 2-weekly intervals. Normally, however, worming is recommended every 3 to 6 months. Many veterinarians will offer a wormer whenever a dog is presented for a booster injection.

NUTRITION AND GROOMING

CHOOSING A PUPPY

Choosing a pup is almost certainly the most important decision regarding his pet, that an owner ever makes; the individual that is selected will be his responsibility for many years to come.

MANY CONSIDERATIONS WILL AFFECT an owner's choice os a puppy, including the size of the home and the garden, the size of the dog, and the facilities that exist for exercise, both at home and in the surrounding area. There are also likely to be personal preferences regarding breeds and perhaps limited availability of puppies at the time when one is being sought. The health and behavior of the available puppies will almost certainly affect the choice, as will the decision to opt for either a pedigree or a non-pedigree dog or to choose between puppies of either sex. It is a very important decision and one that deserves a great deal of careful thought.

Many of these decisions are matters of commonsense. For example, it would be foolish to choose a large dog where there is only limited room available to house and exercise it. Indeed, a surprising number of owners make mistakes of this type, leading to the regrettable need for welfare organizations to take in and look after animals that have been abandoned once the mistake has been realized too late.

The puppy's behavior is vitally important, and here there are a number of considerations, which often pass unnoticed by even the most considerate of owners.

The temperament of a dog is crucial and depends on many factors. One of these is certainly its parentage, so before making any choice, it is wise to try to see at least the mother, and if possible the father, in order to assess their temperament. The future behavior of any dog is also likely to be strongly influenced by the age at which it is purchased and brought into the owner's home. It would be difficult to over-stress the importance of the socialization period, and it is clear that around seven or eight weeks is the best age at which to obtain a new puppy. Certainly it would be inadvisable to purchase a puppy that is either under six weeks or over thirteen weeks of age. The puppy will then become fully socialized towards its new owner, and sufficiently – but not too greatly – towards other dogs as well. Any puppy kept with other dogs for more than its first thirteen weeks is most likely to be virtually untrainable as a pet.

CARING FOR YOUR DOG

• The choice of the right puppy for the owner's circumstances is vital, if a happy relationship between man and dog is to be created. The dog will be part of the household for many years, and the owner must take responsibility for the things which help keep a dog happy and healthy – grooming, exercise and correct nutrition. Like any human, the dog requires a changing diet as it grows from puppyhood to maturity, has a tendency to put on weight if overfed, and needs

It is important to try to purchase a puppy at an early age, as it is less likely to be disturbed by the sudden changes to its surroundings. Puppies become gradually more familiar with surroundings as they get older. For example, being moved from a kennel into a house where there are lots of children may be very traumatic for an older puppy, while a younger one would merely wish to explore and show interest.

Once you have found a suitable litter of pups from which to make your choice, it is best to try to consider the various puppies as individuals, and look for evidence of different personalities. The first decision to make is whether to purchase a bitch or a dog. In general, a dog is likely to be more assertive and need firmer handling than a bitch, and it is a little more likely that you might have to deal with problems such as straying, or urination indoors. A bitch, on the other hand, will come into heat twice a year and so will need special attention at these times. In addition, it is important to consider the risk of unwanted puppies with a bitch.

Standing out in a crowd
As well as the sex differences, an examination of all members of the litter is likely to reveal that some puppies in it are very different from

Far left and above: There is unlikely to be any one best dog in a litter. Rather, there will be significant differences between them which should be carefully observed and noted. Ask the owner's permission to carry out a routine health check before making your final choice.

others. Some may be more pugnacious and come forward to meet you interestedly, or perhaps start play fighting with another puppy, while others may appear rather quiet or fearful and stay away from you in their box.

There is unlikely to be one best dog in any litter, as differences in human personality mean that different dogs appeal to, and suit, different people. For example, a bold assertive dog would not suit a quiet, elderly person living alone; similarly a quiet bitch might not suit an outgoing person with a forceful personality.

It is advisable to try to judge the potential character and degree of dominance of a young puppy, and then to relate this to your own character, or to the characters of anyone else who may share the household where the dog will be living. It is obviously difficult to make judgements of this kind for either party, but it is certainly worthwhile studying a group of puppies for a time and attempting to assess something of their character in terms of fearfulness, friendliness, alertness, activity and dominance.

CARE AND ATTENTION

Any potential owner takes on a considerable responsibility when acquiring a dog. Therefore it is vital to give careful and thorough consideration to what is involved: the care that the dog will require, the substantial costs you will incur in keeping it, the restrictions you will come to face when planning future holidays, the plans you will need to make when absent from home, and the length of the commitment you are taking on; that is, the likely lifespan of your dog.

Unlike most purchases, which can be resold or discarded, it must be considered that a dog will form part of your family for at least ten years. During that time, of course, it will give back to you unquestioning love and devotion in return for all the care you lavish on it.

The first few days after you bring a puppy – or an older dog – into your home are of immense importance, because this is the foundation on which its future happiness will

be based. Think carefully and make appropriate plans and necessary arrangements well before its arrival, so that all is ready in good time. Any new puppy away from its mother, littermates and familiar surroundings for the first time is bound to be frightened. It should be given a dark box or basket in which it can shelter, a toy to chew on, and as little fuss should be made of it as possible, in case it becomes frightened.

A dog is for life
It is a mistake to bring a puppy into the house at Christmas time. There will be much more activity than usual, less time to devote to the puppy, and the child for whom the pup may have been bought will have too many other distractions. The puppy is much more likely at this time to be considered as a short-term toy than a living animal that will need care and attention for many years.

Below: Puppies generally learn fairly quickly to eat from a plate or a bowl.

Planning for vaccinations

Vaccinations are necessary at about the time a puppy first enters the home. When the puppy is twelve-weeks old, or possibly earlier, you must ensure vaccinations are given against four major diseases: distemper, hepatitis, jaundice and nephritis. It is important that you find out the history of a puppy's vaccinations when making your purchase, as it is possible that some of these may have been given while the puppy was with the breeder. A worming preparation should also be given at this time. Puppies, even more so than adult dogs, are liable to pass worms in the feces, but worming should be continued, even when they are older, and it is especially important for the pregnant bitch.

In most countries of the world – the United Kingdom is an exception because the disease is not endemic there – dogs are given rabies vaccinations annually, and this is usually compulsory by law. The disease can be passed on to humans by an infected dog, and, unless treated quickly, can cause death. It is therefore inadvisable to play with a strange dog in an infected country because, while the classic view of a rabid dog is that it is mad and foaming at the mouth, the disease more frequently manifests itself in a quieter form.

There are numerous other diseases that can affect dogs. You should make an appointment for a consultation with your veterinary surgeon as soon as your dog appears unwell; any delay may make the condition worse, and perhaps more expensive to cure. The cost of treatment

is an important consideration for potential dog owners, as almost all dogs come to require medical attention at some point.

Above: A retriever demands energetic play times of its owner.

EXERCISE AND GROOMING

Unlike cats, which manage to gain enough exercise simply through their own endeavours, dogs usually need to be exercised by their owners. By nature, dogs are built for stamina and traveling long distances and, as a species, they have a tendency towards obesity. Cats, on the other hand, are designed for short, fast bursts of movement and they regulate their own body weight, therefore, quite effectively. In humans, a lack of sufficient exercise is widely thought to contribute to diseases of the heart and arteries, and it is much the same where dogs are concerned.

Some dogs are able to get sufficient exercise without troubling their owners, if they have a large enough garden to run around in. By themselves, they are unlikely to run enough, but the presence of another dog will lead to play and chasing games which will give both dogs plenty of exercise.

For most dogs, however, a walk with its owner is the principal source of exercise. The length of the walk that is required will depends very much on the breed (see p. 59), but a useful rough calculation is to work out the requirement roughly in proportion to the size of the dog. For an owner, the walk need not be particularly long, if the dog can be exercised off the lead, which will depend both on the walking area, and the training the dog has received. A dog that can rush around on its own will probably cover three times the distance its owner will walk. A hard run uses up several times more energy than a slow walk over the same distance, so it is difficult to say exactly how far a dog needs to go each day. Even the smallest toy breeds need at least half a mile or so each day, but, for the largest breeds, several miles is probably ideal. As a dog grows old, less walking is needed but exercise should never stop.

Grooming

Apart from exercise and feeding, dogs should have their coats groomed regularly. For short-haired dogs, daily grooming is not necessary, but occasional grooming does improve the appearance of the coat. Daily grooming may well be best, however, for the long-haired breeds. This should begin when the dog is still a puppy, so that it becomes part of a standard routine to which the dog will not object.

Grooming helps to prevent the coat matting, gives it a shine, and also removes excess hair, reducing the amount shed on furniture and carpets. The length and type of coat will determine which combs and brushes should be used. While grooming a dog, it is a good idea to look out for parasites, such as fleas and lice, so that immediate treatment can be given.

Dogs need to be bathed and shampooed at least occasionally. Again, it is sensible to introduce the idea of bathing while the dog is still a young puppy, so that it is not frightened as an adult.

A dog's claws, which are really part of the skin, grow in the same way as hair does and may therefore need regular treatment. Trimming is best done little and often; if the dew claw has not been removed, it will need a lot of trimming because it will not wear down as it grows, unlike the other claws.

CARING FOR YOUR DOG

- All dogs should be groomed to keep the coat in a good, healthy condition. Some dogs, such as the poodle, need special clipping every 6–8 weeks, as they do not molt. Scissors or electric clippers can be used for this.

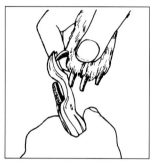

- Long nails should be carefully trimmed.

- Long hair needs grooming daily, to avoid matting.

- Ears should be inspected and wiped, but not probed.

- Calculus may build up on teeth and need to be cleaned.

- When bathing the dog, avoid getting soap in eyes and ears.

- Dry with a large towel after the dog has shaken itself.

Far right: All dogs enjoy periods of play and regular exercise, which benefits them both physically and psychologically.

CARS AND KENNELS

Most dogs are likely to travel fairly frequently in cars. The vaccinations already mentioned will necessitate a visit to the veterinarian, and in many cases this will be by car. Unfortunately, treatment at the veterinarian's will almost always give some discomfort to the dog, and this can make any visit after the first one a fairly traumatic event, once the dog senses where it is going. If the dog's first car journey is to the vet, this may make it frightened of all car travel by a process of association. It is therefore worth thinking ahead, and perhaps giving the puppy a brief ride to a place it will like, such as a park, before the first visit to the vet

Some dogs dislike car journeys for other reasons. Travel sickness affects some dogs, as it does some people, and for the same reason: the influence of the car's movements on the balance organs. On the other hand, many dogs enjoy car rides immensely, regarding the car as an extension of their home territory, and they may bark at any strange person that approaches when they are left alone in a car.

Traveling by car

It is not good for the dog to stick its head out of the window while the car is moving. Not only is there a danger of it hitting something, but also the fast flow of air can dry out the eyes, causing irritation. When the car is parked and the dog is left inside, it should be in the shade and a window should be left open a few inches to provide air (see pp. 64–6).

Dogs are very dependent animals, and are unhappy even when their owners are absent

Below: A caged pet will not chew furniture and will rarely soil its bed. Indoor kennels are a boon for house training and for times when you want to leave it for short periods – but don't keep it shut up too long.

Right: Adequate ventilation and, in hot weather, water and shade, should be provided for a dog left in a car.

for short periods. Any potential owner who is at work daily with no one else in the house should think carefully before buying a dog. When left alone, dogs become bored, distressed and sometimes destructive.

Boarding kennels

If you are to be away from home for a period of days or weeks, you may need to consider taking your dog to be boarded in a kennel. Here it will not suffer from loneliness in one sense, because it will at least be in the company of other dogs. Nevertheless, the change in surroundings, the low level of human contact, and the absence of its owner can have a psychological effect on any dog. Most dogs can cope with a kennel for two or three weeks very well, although it is probably a good idea to leave a familiar toy at the kennels and, if possible, the dog's normal food, even though it may eat less than usual.

Some kennels are not just for boarding, but act as sanctuaries for stray and unwanted dogs as well. Many people prefer to purchase their pet from one of these instead of buying a young puppy, as these unfortunate dogs are in great need of a home and being able to provide a caring home can be very rewarding. Dogs of this kind are likely to present more problems than a puppy because their characters are already formed. Also they may have been mistreated, and being older are less adaptable and less easy to train. (See p. 36.) However, with love and patience, many such dogs can become excellent house pets – no different from those reared in one home since they were puppies. The quiet, planned introduction into the new home, and the necessary basic training should be just the same as for any younger dog. However, it may well take longer for the dog to become a fully socialized member of the family.

THE AGING PROCESS

Right: It may be preferable to feed the puppies individually to ensure that they all have an adequate share and that there are no squabbles among the siblings.

It is often said that one year of a person's life is equivalent to about seven of a dog's. This is rather misleading, however, as a few dogs will live to 15 or even 20 years, the "equivalent" of which no human ever reaches. On the other hand, certain breeds such as the Great Dane and the Irish Wolfhound have a comparatively short average lifespan, perhaps only six or seven years. No one is certain why dogs age so much more quickly than people, and one of the questions that puzzles biologists is why the various diseases of senility should occur so much earlier in dogs.

The commonest causes of death are not quite the same for dogs as for people. Dogs show a much higher susceptibility to accidents, particularly road accidents. This is because dogs never learn as well as people how to respond to traffic, and they are more likely to be distracted and suddenly rush into danger.

As dogs get older, a number of changes take place. Their stamina is reduced and they start to exercise less. This, combined with a general reduction in metabolic rate, means that they need less food. This should be watched carefully, and rations should be reduced as soon as an elderly dog shows signs of putting on weight. The protein requirement will also fall, and those dogs that develop kidney problems may need a special low-protein diet.

In many ways the diseases of dogs in old age are similar to those of humans. They can develop cancers; may have heart trouble or other problems of the circulatory system, and they may also suffer from a range of other age-related diseases. Especially common are problems with the eyes and with the joints. The latter seem particularly severe, because a disabled dog is an especially sad sight. Some joint problems – in particular patellar luxation which affects the forelimbs, and hip dysplasia which attacks the hind-limbs – are proportionately more common in certain breeds. These diseases seem to have a strong genetic component, as do some other afflictions, including eye problems and even some behavioral illnesses, such as epilepsy.

Of course it cannot be possible to halt old age in a dog, but a great deal can be done to keep the dog happy as it grows old. The continuing of established routines can be very beneficial, and it should be remembered that in old age some behavior problems can be triggered by a sudden change in circumstances, such as moving house or being introduced to active young children.

Two of the most difficult things to face are the question of when it is kindest to put a dog down, and then the period of bereavement that follows. The death may be especially difficult for children but, despite the sadness, this can help to teach them about death, and in turn will help them cope later with the death of a relative. If a well-loved pet is replaced by a young puppy, this helps to demonstrate the continuity of life and bring happiness back to the household. The love for the former dog will quickly be transferred, and this is true not just for children but for adults too, because replacement of a favorite dog at a later date is always more difficult. (See pp. 180–1.)

Right: As a companion for an elderly person, a dog may be ideal. But the choice needs to be considered carefully – obviously a large, boisterous puppy would probably be unsuitable.

HIDE AND SEEK

The feeding habits of dogs are as varied as those of humans. Some dogs will eat almost anything they can get hold of; some are extremely particular about what they eat; and some may have very strange individual preferences but generally will eat quite normally.

Compared to its wild relatives, the domestic dog has an easy time finding its food. The wild members of the family are essentially carnivores, eating principally mammals, ranging from mice up to large deer, although, in suburbs of English towns, the red fox may subsist largely on earthworms at certain times of the year. Also, during times of hardship, several wild canid species will turn to vegetable matter and, if times are especially bad, this can become their main source of food.

Most large carnivores are thought to eat only intermittently, and gorge themselves when they do catch something, but this does not apply to all members of the dog family. Those that eat small animals catch their prey and eat at intervals throughout the day, and even those that feed on large animals often return to eat at intervals after the initial killing.

Dogs can certainly thrive quite happily being fed only once a day, but dogs that are given continuous access to food, eat between about 8 and 25 small meals per day, depending on the individual. On this type of regime many dogs will eat only the food they require; others may get fat, although these are the ones that are likely to get fat on any regime.

If dogs do not eat all their food at once, they may cache what is left over; both wild and domestic dogs do this and the most common example of it is bone-burying. Any food surplus to immediate requirements may be hidden where the dog can easily find it again.

Foxes have often been observed caching their food, carefully carrying it to a chosen spot where they dig a shallow hole, which is then neatly covered with soil.

Although the dog is primarily a carnivore, it should strictly be classified as an omnivore, because it can, and often does, eat vegetable matter. It is this ability to be omnivorous that creates the big range of preferred diets among dogs. It also explains why dogs are much less particular about what they will eat than cats, which are true carnivores, eating only meat.

Above: Like the fox, and other species of wild dog, the domestic pet is often observed caching its surplus food. A dog will return to these hiding places in time and chew on the old bones.

FEEDING HABITS OF THE FOX

- Foxes will carry the food to be cached to a selected spot.

- The fox holds the food in its mouth while it digs a shallow hole.

- The fox then replace soil from the cache by long sweeps of its nose.

OVERFEEDING

One of the commonest dietary problems in dogs is obesity, due to overeating; most estimates find that between 20 and 30 per cent of pet dogs suffer in this way. The likelihood of obesity varies from breed to breed; the Labrador and Cocker Spaniel, for instance, are commonly affected, while others, like the Red Setter and most of the Terriers, are much less susceptible.

Many factors can affect a dog's weight, but the simplest solution to obesity is to feed the dog less and make sure it is not getting food elsewhere. Sometimes there are medical causes, and if there is any suspicion of this, a veterinary surgeon should be consulted before a weight reduction program is started.

Causes of obesity

It is interesting to speculate as to why dogs should show such a high susceptibility to obesity. One theory is that it is directly linked to the palatability of the food. Certainly a dog is likely to eat more than usual if it is given an especially tasty meal. However, in the long-term most dogs cease to respond in this way and regulate their intake as before.

Another related factor is the social side of eating; what psychologists call social facilitation. Studies have revealed that puppies eat more if they feed in a group than they do if they are left alone. This may still apply to adult dogs, for whom the owner's mere presence may encourage the dog to consume more. However, in the majority of cases of obesity, it is almost certainly a result of the dog's own weight-control mechanism rather than these external factors. For one thing, all breeds would show the same tendency to obesity if external factors were wholly to blame. On the whole, the breeds that are most particular about their food – often the smaller ones – have fewer weight problems than the larger, often less choosy, breeds. It is also well established that the spaying of bitches and the castration of dogs both tend to increase the likelihood of obesity. It appears that the hormonal changes resulting from these operations in some way alter the mechanisms which regulate weight.

Age, exercise and the seasons also play a part; older dogs need less food than growing dogs or active young adults, and cold weather increases appetite so that some dogs may need more food than others.

A balanced diet

A method of regulating a dog's weight that is often effective is to maintain the bulk of the diet while reducing the calories (the same principle is used with some human diet foods). Balanced diets of this kind can be obtained from veterinary surgeons. This is unlikely to fool the dog for long, because dogs, like humans, regulate their food intake by calories rather than bulk. This is also why a range of diets, from complete dry and semi-moist to canned meat and fresh food, are all acceptable to most dogs.

Far left: Dogs should never be allowed to eat from dishes used for human food, because of the risk of transmitting disease.

SUGGESTED FEEDING GUIDE FOR ADULT DOGS

● As they contain little or no carbohydrate, meaty foods are not designed to be a complete food for dogs. To obtain a properly balanced diet and retain the palatability of meaty foods, they should be mixed with biscuits in equal parts by volume. This is best for smaller breeds. Larger dogs, or active dogs with large appetites, can be fed two-parts biscuit to one-part meaty food, by volume. The chart below shows the proportion of a large can 376–411 kg (13–142 oz) to be fed per day. (All quantities are approximate.)

	COMPLETE FOOD	SEMI MOIST	MEATY FOOD
● TOY BREEDS 2–4.5 kg (5–10 lbs) Pomeranians Pekingese Yorkshire Terriers			
● SMALL 4.5–9 kg (5–10 lbs) Bostons Dachshunds Small Terriers Fox Terrriers Scotties			
● MEDIUM 9–23 kg (20–50 lbs) Beagles Spaniels Bull Dogs Chow Chows Poodles			
● LARGE 23–60 kg (50–130 lbs) Collies Labradors Setters German Shepherds Great Danes			

GROWTH AND NUTRITION

Dogs have certainly been reported to eat, and apparently enjoy, a huge range of foods, some of which seem rather bizarre. Dogs are commonly seen eating grass; it is unlikely that they obtain more than a tiny amount of nutritional value from this because their digestive system is not equipped to cope with it. Nor is it likely that dogs eat grass for vitamins, since, unlike humans, they do not have to take in vitamin C because they make it in their body. Most frequently dogs eat grass

because it acts as an emetic, making them vomit; this is desirable if, for example, the stomach contains indigestible fur or bones.

The partially omnivorous nature of the dog's diet is probably why the dog needs less protein in its diet than the cat. Like all other animals the dog requires a mixture of carbohydrates, fats and proteins. These all supply energy, and protein is also required for body building. Certain important minerals, such as calcium for bones and salt for body fluids, are also

THE AGE–WEIGHT RELATIONSHIP

● Puppies are of a relatively similar size at birth, but clearly from the graph it can be seen that they will grow into dogs of very different sizes and reach their optimum weight at different ages. As a general rule, a smaller dog will reach its adult size quicker than one of the bigger breeds. Conversely, however, smaller dogs often obtain their permanent set of teeth relatively late, compared with their large counterparts.

Pomeranians · Pekingese · Boston Terriers · Fox Terriers · Cockers · Poodles · Collies

MONTHS									
30									
28									
26									
24									
22									
20									
18									
16									
14									
12									
10									
8									
6									
4	1 week old pup								
2	ONE WEEK OLD								
0									

KILOGRAMS	1.8	3.6	5.	7.3	9.1	10.9	16.3	21.8	25.4
POUNDS	4	8	12	16	20	24	36	48	56

required. Other minerals and vitamins are necessary for specialized functions within the body; for example, the red blood cells depend on iron.

Wild dogs obtain all these substances from their naturally varied diet. Pet dogs can be given the right nourishment in a number of ways. Most convenient are specially prepared pet foods which are carefully balanced by the manufacturers to provide the right nutrients in the correct proportions. Cooked meat or offal with biscuits is also quite satisfactory, but it is all too easy to supply insufficient calcium. Lean meat by itself contains almost no calcium, unlike the dog's natural diet which would contain some bone. If prepared foods are used, whether canned, dry or semi-moist, the instructions should be followed carefully.

Another major question is whether a dog should have variety in its diet or if a standard diet is sufficient. There is ample evidence that dogs can live quite satisfactorily and be perfectly healthy for a lifetime on an unvarying diet, provided this is complete nutritionally; undoubtedly the dog's wild relatives may at times eat a similar diet for long periods of time. However, this approach to feeding takes no account of the possible pleasures of eating, and there is evidence that dogs do enjoy variety in their diet. It is generally found that most dogs prefer a novel food to a familiar one provided the two are comparably palatable. This suggests that dogs are rather like humans and appreciate variety.

Left: When using any types of prepared foods the instructions should be followed carefully.

Great Danes

German Shepherd Dogs

Setters

| 9.0 | 32.7 | 34.5 | 41.7 | 50.8 | 58.1 |
| 4 | 72 | 76 | 92 | 112 | 128 |

Above: Two of the three main forms of pet foods: dry and semi-moist.

Above: Tinned foods are balanced to provide the correct nutrients.

THE ADULT DOG AND FEEDING

The daily care of a dog is straightforward, although initially, it may be difficult to decide between the wide array of foods and other equipment that are available today. Soon, however, a routine will develop, covering all aspects of the dog's care, ranging from feeding and grooming to exercise requirements. Dogs have adaptable natures, but usually prove themselves to be creatures of habit, preferring set daily schedules. They will soon come to identify mealtimes, and the time of day when they can expect to be taken for a walk. Some variation, within reason, is to be commended however, otherwise the owner can become a slave to their pet!

Ice creams or sweets are of no nutritional value and will probably lead the dog to develop tooth decay; also, excessive sugar may well result in diarrhea.

Below: Various options now exist for feeding dogs and, recently, dry and semi-moist commercially produced foods have gained in popularity, at the expense of canned rations These are complete foods, offering all the essential nutrients that a dog requires, although some canned diets are comprised of meat only.

Feeding

Today it is easier than ever before to offer dogs a sound, balanced diet. The adverse effects of nutritional excesses (not deficiencies) are most commonly seen: obesity and over-supplement of vitamins being increasing problems.

As dogs are carnivores, should they be fed on meat only?

No. In fact, dogs are less dependent on meat as the basis of their diet than cats are. A wide range of foods will keep your dog in good health; the main ingredients are the same as those that should be present in a human diet. Protein, comprised of various individual amino acids can be derived from either plant or animal sources. The protein of plants lacks certain so-called essential amino acids, which should be present in the diet if a deficiency is to be avoided. Protein is necessary for growth, and has other specific functions, including a vital role in the cell membrane of the body. The healing of tissues also requires protein.

Carbohydrates in the diet are used essentially to meet the body's energy requirement, and are frequently provided in the form of biscuit meal, rice or bread. These ingredients of the diet are relatively cheap and are often used to bulk up a ration. The third major category of foodstuffs is fat, a highly concentrated energy source. Indeed, surplus carbohydrate is stored in the body as fat, and can be broken down later for use as an insulator against the cold, and to protect the vital organs – such as the kidneys – from trauma. There is an essential fatty acid, known as linoleic acid, which must be included in your dog's diet.

Vitamins, minerals and trace elements, although required in only minute amounts, are vital to the well-being of your dog. Vitamin D for example, controls the calcium stores of the body, and this mineral, in conjunction with phosphorus, is essential for a healthy skeletal structure.

Is it possible for us to maintain our dog on a vegetarian diet?

It certainly is feasible but will require extra work, and your efforts may not be appreciated by the dog, especially if it has been used to a meat-based diet. It may be possible to wean a puppy onto such a diet successfully, but it will certainly be harder with an adult dog. As plant protein is not as balanced in terms of its amino-acid content as meat, opt for soya protein, which is the best form available. Unfortunately, amounts above 1 ounce per 12 pounds of the dog's weight tend to cause diarrhea. The carbohydrate content of the diet is easy to provide, but fat can be more of a problem. Eggs and high-fat cheese will be necessary, along with corn oil to act as a source of linoleic acid. Vitamins and minerals can be provided by way of a suitable preparation

Below: Dogs can
reciprocate care and
love and integrate well
into a human family.

Right: Natural foods, such as apples or carrots, can be given occasionally and will not lead to tooth decay.

sprinkled over the food, and specific food items, such as carrots, can be used as additional sources on a regular basis. Apart from being more time-consuming, it may also prove more expensive to feed a dog on a vegetarian diet. While it may appeal to you, it is probably not in the dog's best interests.

My mother is convinced that dogs do better when fed home-made rather than commercially prepared foods. Is she right?
Generally no, and indeed, the reverse could be true. The major problem with preparing a dog's diet oneself is making sure that it is suitably balanced, with adequate variety present. Indeed, feeding prime steak over a period of time will be harmful, as it is low in vitamins A, D and E, and the ratio of calcium to phosphorus is seriously imbalanced, which, coupled with a deficiency of vitamin D, could give rise to skeletal abnormalities. The high protein level of such a diet would also be a waste of money, as the protein would be broken down to provide energy when there are much cheaper alternative sources, such as potatoes, available. It could also prove harmful in a dog that was already affected with kidney failure.

Various meats sold cheaply by butchers for pet food includes lungs and spleens, as well as tripe. All are valuable sources of protein, but the latter, being the stomach of ruminants, smells highly unpleasant unless "dressed." Ground meat invariably has a high fat content, especially when it is sold specifically for pets. In order to provide a balanced diet, the meat component should be mixed with a suitable biscuit meal, or with dog biscuits. Check that the brand you use is supplemented with the vitamins and minerals likely to be low in the meat content of the diet. It may be necessary, particularly for dogs that have sensitive teeth, to soak the biscuits for a few minutes before feeding, in order to make them more palatable.

Should such meats be cooked before feeding?
Yes, it is highly recommended that you cook all such foodstuffs if they are purchased raw, to minimize the risk of disease to your dog. There are several parasites that can be transmitted via raw meat, including Toxoplasma gondii, as well as bacteria such as Salmonella, which is a frequent contaminant of raw poultry carcasses. Cooking also serves to improve the palatability of the food – boiled potatoes for example, are readily eaten by dogs while their raw counterparts are not. It may also be easier to feed a particular item once it has been cooked – eggs are a case in point, and hard-boiled eggs are a valuable source of protein. A fussy eater can often be persuaded to take warm food which has been cooked previously and allowed to cool, but distinctly cold food is less popular. If you discover your dog has eaten some raw meat by accident, it may have a digestive upset, but it will not become vicious, as some people suggest.

Any frozen or refrigerated foods should be allowed to warm up before being fed to your dog; otherwise they may cause a digestive disturbance. It is possible to cook a relatively large quantity of meats, for example, and deep-freeze them, weighing and packing them, as required into plastic bags. By this method, it is quite possible to prepare a full week's meals individually at one time, leaving you simply to take the packs out of the freezer each evening for feeding on the following day, after thawing out at room temperature overnight.

I want to feed my dog a commercially prepared diet. What types are available?
The huge size of the market for prepared pet foods means that manufacturers have spent a great deal of money researching in this area, not only to provide truly balanced convenience diets, but also to ensure that pet foods are as palatable as possible for the dogs themselves. It is not only easier, but also safer to use a complete diet because these eliminate the risk of nutritional deficiencies.

The canned diets are the main prepared food on the market at present. It is a complete food that meets all of your dog's nutritional requirements. It contains a mixture of muscle meat, stomach, heart, liver, lung, vegetable matter, vitamins and minerals. Some canned foods have a higher level of carbohydrate than others. For foods with the lower carbohydrate level, add one part cereal flakes, cooked rice or corn meal to two parts canned food. The cans can be stored for long periods of time without deteriorating but, when opened, they should be kept in a refrigerator

Left: Specialized lines of canned foods can now be found on the shelves of supermarkets and pet stores for puppies and for the more fussy eaters.

DRIED FOOD

● Recently, the market for semi-moist dog foods has been expanding. Although designed to resemble succulent chunks of meat, these foods often contain relatively high levels of soya and have a lower water content – about 25 per cent – compared with their canned rivals. They are usually sold in foil-wrapped sachets in boxes, and they may feature other ingredients, such as sucrose, which serve to preserve the food and improve palatability. Bear this in mind if your dog is diabetic.

● Dried dog foods contain only about 10 per cent water. There are various types of dried food, such as flakes, meal, pellets and expanded chunks. They can be kept without refrigeration and, unlike other foods, will not sour if left dry in a bowl for several days. Most manufacturers recommend immersing the dry food in water, or even gravy, at first to encourage the dog to take this unfamiliar foodstuff. If you follow this procedure, remember that the food, once moistened, will sour rapidly. As dogs normally obtain a proportion of their fluid requirement from their food, a dry diet will encourage an increased water intake compared with a diet based on canned food.

Right: The storage of dog food will vary according to its ingredients. Fresh items need to be kept refrigerated and, if deep-frozen for any reason, they must be allowed to thaw and warm up before being fed to your dog. Canned items, once opened, must also be kept refrigerated. Foil packaging maintains a product's freshness and so, although there is no need to store them in a refrigerator, such items should be used up as soon as possible, after the package has been opened. Dried foods, with a very low water content, can be kept for a considerable period of time, although the vitamin content will decline, and the product should be used by the date recommended on its packaging. Once water or other fluid is added to a dried ration, it should then be treated as fresh food, and, if not eaten, disposed of within a day.

and used as soon as possible. There is some evidence to suggest that the unused contents of a can should be transferred to a plastic container and the can itself discarded because of the oxidization of the interior of the can when it is exposed to air.

The price of a canned diet is variable, and is usually a reflection of the amount of carbohydrate present, as it is this that reduces the cost. The use of a corn meal with a canned food is a good idea in the case of the more ·expensive cans that have a higher level of meat. It is false economy to sue protein as an energy source. Always follow the manufacturer's recommended feeding directions – the amounts suggested are likely to be on the generous side in any event.

The excessive use of dog biscuits or corn meal is certainly to be discouraged as this will lead to obesity, particularly in a dog that is not working. Various specialized lines of canned foods can now be found on the shelves of supermarkets and pet stores for puppies and for the more fussy eaters. In the latter instance, however, cat food may prove a cheaper alternative. It has a higher protein content than dog food, as a general rule, and this can increase its palatability.

A few canned dog foods may not be complete, but contain only meat of a particular type. If in any doubt, check the ingredients shown on the can's label.

How do I decide how much food I should give my dog?

Feeding directions will accompany the convenience diets. Remember that less dried food will be required with such food, because it contains a reduced amount of water. As a general rule, only 1 ounce of dry food is required for every 2.2 pounds of the dog's weight. This is in contrast to the 3.5 ounces of a complete canned food that will be necessary for the same dog. As a general rule, smaller dogs tend to eat relatively more than their large counterparts because a dog's food requirement is much more a reflection of its surface area than of its body weight.

There are various other factors that are involved in assessing a dog's nutritional requirement. The level of activity of the individual will have a bearing on its feeding needs: a working dog, for instance, will need considerably more food than a small and comparatively passive pet dog. Age is also a significant factor; an older dog will tend to need less food and will naturally come to eat less and less. Another reason for a noticable change in appetite is pregnancy. In the latter stages of pregnancy, a bitch's appetite will increase considerably. Puppies, not surprisingly, also have a relatively high feed requirement in order to support their rate of growth, which requires considerable energy.

It is hardest to estimate the amount of home-cooked meat and biscuit that should be provided, as there will be no obvious guidelines available. Mix the biscuit on an equal weight basis with the cooked meat and feed 1 ounce per 2 pounds of body weight for a dog of average size.

WEIGHTWATCHING

- The easiest way to weigh a dog is to use an ordinary bathroom scale. Stand on the scale, holding the dog, and then subtract your known weight from the final weight. Regular weighing may help to detect chronic illness reflected by a loss in weight. Clearly the dog must be used to being picked up. Some individuals may sit contentedly on the scales, but this is perhaps not very hygienic.

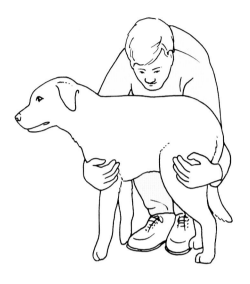

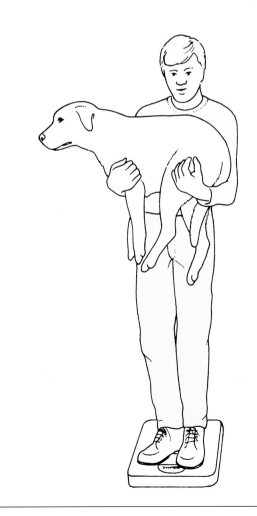

I am worried that my dog may be becoming overweight. How can I check this?

It is a good idea to weigh your dog on a regular basis and to keep a record of the results so you can see clearly if it is gaining weight.

With a small or medium-sized dog, the simplest way to weight it is to lift it up and hold it in your arms while you stand on a bathroom scale. Then put the dog down and weigh yourself. Subtract the second figure from the first and you are left with the weight of the dog only. Larger dogs can be rather more of a problem unless they can be coaxed onto the scale. In many instances, the correct – or recommended – weight for a pedigree dog can be found by referring to the breed standard, where the ideal weight will be specified. In certain cases, two figures are given, with bitches usually being lighter than their male

Above: Most dogs will commonly eat rapidly, and loss of appetite can be an early sign of illness. Certain individuals do prove fussy eaters however, and may need to be coaxed to eat their food.

counterparts. Breeds can vary considerably in weight; Pomeranians can sometimes be as light as 4 pounds, while Mastiffs may tip the scales at as much as 190 pounds.

How many meals a day should I give my dog?

It is advisable to follow the breeder's instructions at first with a puppy to establish how many meals it needs a day. A puppy needs much more frequent feeding than an adult dog. By the age of about nine months, most dogs are receiving either one large meal – usually in the early evening – or two smaller meals given in the morning and the evening. This latter regimen is most applicable to smaller dogs as they will simply not be able to manage a single larger portion of food as well as a bigger dog can. The main point, however, is to develop a system that suits you, as well as your dog. It would be foolish, for example, to feed your dog at noon for several weeks and then suddenly to change the time significantly, as this will cause upset and confusion. Dogs are essentially creatures of habit; they should receive their full daily ration at fixed mealtimes every day, as far as possible.

In the United States, it is fairly common practice to leave a dog with food throughout the day so that it can help itself. It is important that only dry food should be offered in this way, as meat products will tend to sour, bacteria will develop rapidly, and flies are likely to be attracted, especially during the warmer months of the year.

Studies have revealed that dogs transferred to this system may eat more than usual at first, but the vast majority then tend to regulate their food intake in accordance with their energy expenditure so that they do not put on excessive weight.

Under normal circumstances, with canned food for example, dogs will bolt their meal down within minutes of its being provided. This is quite normal behavior and need not be a cause for concern. Occasionally a dog, particularly a bitch with puppies, will vomit the food back up almost immediately. Such behavior may appear particularly unsavory or cause alarm, but it originates from when a bitch in the wild would start feeding her offspring in this way to wean them on to solid foods. The feeding routine during pregnancy, as well as subsequently, during the rearing phase, will need to be altered (see p. 171). By the age of five months, most puppies should be receiving two, or possibly three meals each day. It is inadvisable to put them onto the free-feeding system described above until they are nearly adult.

There is absolutely no benefit to be gained by starving a dog for one day a week – a practice sometimes thought to be beneficial for the dog's health. This idea comes from the behavior of wild dogs – they undergo periods of fasting when they cannot make a kill. In the domestic dog, however, such action is more likely to encourage undesirable vices, such as stealing food, or possibly aggression towards members of the family.

Is it acceptable to feed our dog table scraps?

Yes, in moderation, but it is best to try to avoid feeding it while you are actually eating. It may not be easy to stop your children from doing this, however, but you must try. Otherwise, dogs will soon come to expect food every time other members of the family are eating. In addition to encouraging obesity over a period of time, this will cause the dog to pester everyone and even howl if ignored. It may also make it rather unpopular with members of the family or visitors! A dog that is not fed from the table is unlikely to develop these undesirable traits and will leave its owners to enjoy their meal without a battle of wills taking place.

Dogs will eat a wide range of typical human foods – some will even eat fruit, especially apples. Avoid hot spicy foods or excessively fatty items. Green vegetables will also be consumed by dogs, but tend to cause flatulence. Potatoes should be cooked, as the starch will otherwise be fairly indigestible. Dogs can eat either brown or white bread, and loaves with extra fiber are perhaps beneficial. Some owners add a small amount of bran to their dog's diet to increase the level of fiber.

Should I buy a vitamin and mineral supplement for my dog?

This depends to some extent on what you are feeding; in the case of a home-prepared diet, it may be advisable, especially if you are not using a corn meal with essential chemicals added during manufacture. Today, such is the craze for vitamins and minerals, however, that instead of showing signs of deficiency, dogs are now afflicted with problems resulting from overdosage with these chemicals. It is certainly not true in this case that, if a little is good, a lot must be better. Always follow the directions given on the package. The young, growing dog is most at risk from excessive supplementation, and large breeds are the most susceptible as they normally develop more slowly than smaller breeds. Various abnormalities in the growth of their skeletal system and possibly other symptoms such as lameness may result.

On a balanced diet, it is unlikely that supplementation will be necessary, although under certain circumstances, it may be recommended. A dog with kidney failure, for example, may need a vitamin B supplement because excessive levels of this group of vitamins may be lost from its body. Perhaps one in a thousand dogs is incapable of making its own vitamin C, and in such instances, specific supplementation in order to prevent scurvy from developing will be essential. This can be achieved by adding a tablet to its food. Allow 1 gram for a dog weighing 55 pounds. This vitamin deteriorates rapidly; do not purchase a large quantity and always keep it stored in the dark.

A shortage of vitamin D is unlikely because this vitamin is made by the action of sunlight falling on the dog's coat. It is stored in the liver along with the other so-called fat-soluble vitamins, A, E and K. There are specific instances when a vitamin K deficiency could occur, notably as a result of certain types of poisoning or excessive antibiotic therapy.

Below: Feeding tidbits should be avoided as this will lead to obesity over a period of time. In addition, if dogs are fed from the table, they tend to pester the family and guests at mealtimes, which can prove very troublesome.

FEEDING BEHAVIOUR

Dogs can prove great scavengers and will also thieve food intended for human consumption. A combination of firm training and thoughtfulness will prevent such conflicts.

Does a dog become bored by being fed the same food each day? My dog tends to be a rather fussy eater.

There is no convincing evidence to confirm that dogs get bored when given the same food every day. Provided they are receiving a balanced diet, there is no need to be concerned. By all means, vary the diet somewhat if you wish; some cooked meat and corn meal occasionally instead of a convenience food is perfectly acceptable. There is unlikely to be a link between the food you are offering and the dog's fussy eating habits. The root of the problem is almost certainly elsewhere. Do you feed a lot of tidbits between meals? This can depress appetite, particularly if the meal is less palatable than the snacks, although more nutritious. Do you get very concerned if your pet refuses to eat a meal? Some dogs soon come to realize that self-deprivation can bring rewards from their owners, either in the form of extra affection or more appealing food. Such behavior is most often seen in the toy breeds.

Try to be firm. Cut out all additional food of any type offered between meals. Leave the dish of food available for an hour in the usual spot where the dog is fed, and then remove it if none has been eaten. Repeat this procedure at the next meal time. The dog will soon come to recognize that it must eat what is being offered or else it will lose out. It will not starve to death, even if it eats nothing for a couple of days. Do make sure that the food you are providing is as appealing as possible. You could add a little margarine over the surface of canned food, soak corn meal in warm gravy and make sure that the dog will not be disturbed more than necessary while the food is available. You may want to encourage him to eat by offering food from your hand.

A number of medical reasons exist for loss of appetite. If a dog suddenly refuses to eat and shows other symptoms, such as lack of interest in other activities like going out, then it is advisable to contact a veterinarian without delay. Or if your dog plays with its food, particularly corn meal, it may have a painful tooth or gum infection. Studies suggest that male dogs tend to be fussier about their food than bitches. This may be a throwback to their wild ancestry, when the dominant male in a pack had preference at the kill.

Right: Performing tricks – such as standing on hind legs in return – for tidbits should be discouraged, as food between meals may spoil your dog's appetite and, eventually, could lead to obesity.

Can I offer my dog chocolate drops?

Chocolate is very palatable to dogs and can be given occasionally. It is available in the form of special treats at some pet stores. Do not give large quantities and do not give chocolate other than that specifically made for dogs. This may affect the dog's appetite in the short-term and can result in other problems such as dental decay, obesity and possibly diabetes mellitus. Excessive amounts of chocolate can also give rise to diarrhea, so always take care to place boxes of sweets well out of a dog's eager reach.

There are other, healthier tidbits that can be used as rewards during training and at other times. Raw carrots cut into small pieces appeal to many dogs to the extent in some cases that they may attempt to dig up carrots growing in a garden once they acquire a taste for them. Yeast tablets are also very palatable to dogs and provide a source of vitamin B. Always restrict the amounts of such items that you give, so the dog does not come to view them as an extension to meals rather than a reward for good behavior.

Should I let my dog chew bones?

From a strictly nutritional viewpoint, there is probably no need to provide bones, provided your dog is being fed correctly. Yet dogs certainly enjoy having bones to gnaw, and this activity may help to keep their teeth clean. There are potential dangers, however, some dogs become extremely possessive about bones and need to be trained to relinquish them readily when told to do so. This can be carried out more easily with a young dog. Be careful when dealing with a strange dog, as you cannot be sure how it will react to being deprived of its bone.

Provide only large marrow bones which will not cause a possible obstruction in the digestive tract by being accidentally swallowed. Chicken and rabbit bones, being light, are particularly dangerous; they splinter readily, often in the mouth, where they can become embedded in the tissue. Larger bones, such as those from chops, may be inadvertently swallowed and become stuck in the throat. Try to be sure that the edge of the bones you provide are not rough, as fragments may break off and cause problems.

If, in the light of the above, you feel it is too risky to provide a bone for your dog to chew, consider one of the chew toys available at most pet stores.

Right: A combination of firm training and thoughtfulness will ensure good behavior in a dog, and prevent its natural inclination to scavenge or thieve food intended for human consumption.

My dog is a persistent scavenger. What is the reason for this behavior, and how can I prevent it?

Unfortunately, all dogs, to a greater or lesser extent, are scavengers by nature and will steal food if a suitable item presents itself. In certain instances, they may be driven by a medical reason. Pancreatic insufficiency, for example, often causes an increase in appetite (see pp. 81–2); the dog will steal food at every opportunity while continuing to lose weight. Veterinary help must be obtained if a condition of this type is suspected. Otherwise, try to prevent a dog scavenging by placing food out of reach, and keep a close watch when you are out walking in case the dog finds the discarded remains of a picnic such as a chicken carcass. It is always possible that digestive troubles such as vomiting or diarrhea or a combination of these symptoms will follow scavenging.

My dog insists on eating grass. Is he lacing anything in his diet?

Probably not, but you could try increasing the level of fiber, especially if the dog is prone to constipation. Eating grass seems to be natural behavior; it is often followed by vomiting, presumably in order to relieve some of the irritation. Puppies may vomit roundworms by this means. Check that your dog is not eating grass that has been treated with chemical sprays. Most dogs prefer thickish stems to ordinary lawn grass so this behavior is more likely to occur when you are walking close to an area of long grass.

A few dogs develop abnormal appetites for other, more harmful, things. If you take your dog to the beach, make sure as far as possible that it does not attempt to swallow pebbles.

While the canine digestive tract is fairly tolerant of foreign bodies, pebbles can become stuck, with far more serious consequences.

I believe that my dog has a food allergy. Is this likely?

Such problems are not unknown, but relatively little study has been carried out in to this area. Now that a link between hyperexcitability in children and certain ingredients in prepared foodstuffs has been found, similar links in dogs may no longer be considered implausible. It is important not to confuse an allergy with the virtually immediate reaction to eating indigestible food. In the case of a dog that cannot digest the lactose in milk, for example, the resulting diarrhea does not come from an allergy to lactose, but from the inability of the body to digest it. Skin rashes often result from an allergy. A wide range of foods may be

OBESITY

- Obesity is more likely to affect middle-aged dogs and the risk of obesity increases with age, as the level of activity declines and food intake remains constant. The side effects are especially noticeable in warm weather, when the dog will pant excessively. The Labrador Retriever is a breed that is particularly prone to becoming overweight when kept in a domestic environment. Interestingly, studies have shown that the majority of obese dogs also have overweight

Left: Young puppies typically display an uncontrollable urge to chew, as their first set of teeth is shed and replaced by 42 permanent teeth.

Below: When you are out walking, keep a close watch in case the dog finds the discarded remains of a picnic too tempting to resist.

Right: A healthy dog – in this case a Cavalier King Charles Spaniel, crossed with a whippet – is totally dependent on its owner to provide nutritious, regular food, and plenty of exercise.

Above: Eating grass is fairly common in dogs – it may act as a natural emetic or add fiber to the diet.

implicated, and it can be a time-consuming task to track down the most likely cause. Various items have to be removed from the diet in a strict sequence, to see when the irritation disappears. An immediate improvement is unlikely to be apparent. It will probably take several days.

How harmful is obesity in a dog?

It has been suggested that no fewer than 30 per cent of the dogs in the United States are obese, and this figure is mirrored in other countries, such as the United Kingdom. Certain breeds are more likely to become overweight than others – Beagles and Labrador Retrievers are especially susceptible. But the problem also affects small breeds, such as the Dachshund. In this latter instance, obesity may well lead to intervertebral disk problems, to which Beagles can also be prone. Obesity more often affects bitches than male dogs, and neutered dogs are most at risk from becoming overweight. Obesity often becomes a problem in middle-age when a dog's level of activity declines.

How should I reduce my dog's weight?

First decide on the correct weight for your dog. If it is not a pedigree animal, aim to reduce its weight to the level where its ribs can be clearly felt but not seen beneath the skin as a rough guide. Special obesity diets can be obtained from your veterinarian and should help to lower your dog's weight. Otherwise reduce the overall amount of food you offer to it by about 40 per cent. Keep a check on your dog's weight on a weekly basis. Weight loss in the smaller breeds should work out to about a quarter of a pound weekly and will be about treble this figure in the case of big dogs.

The majority of obese dogs are overweight because they are being given too much food by their owners. It is vital to cut out all snacks while the dog is on its diet, and to make sure that no food is being scavenged from neighbors during this period. Studies suggest that dogs fed on home-prepared rations are most likely to become overweight. The dog is receiving surplus carbohydrate which is not being used on energy expenditure and is thus converted to fat. On a diet, part of the body's fat reserves are burned to meet the energy demands, and they are therefore gradually reduced leading to a corresponding loss of weight.

Once you have succeeded in slimming your dog down to a better weight, try to insure that it does not become fat again. Increase the amount of food offered by about 20 per cent so that it is receiving just 80 per cent of its previous food intake. Obesity does not always result from excessive feeding, but hormonal changes with a similar effect are quite rare in dogs. In severe cases of obesity, a veterinarian may recommend hospitalization so the dog can be placed on a crash diet, with only water being provided.

How much water should my dog drink? At times, it drinks more than usual.

Always make sure that your dog has a clean bowl of drinking water available; change the contents every day. There is no fixed amount that a dog will drink during a day. The quantity consumed will vary, depending on such factors as its diet, temperature and the amount of exercise it receives. Typically, dogs fed on a dry diet will drink more to compensate for the relatively low amount of fluid in their food. And in hot weather and following exercise, the dog's thirst will be increased. You may not even know how much the dog is actually drinking, as water bowls alone are not a reliable indicator. Unfortunately dogs will often drink from other sources such as puddles, when out for a walk, and toilet bowls at home. The latter is particularly dangerous, especially if there are chemicals such as bleach in the water. Keep the bathroom door closed and the lid of the toilet down at all times.

Measure the amount of fluid that your dog is drinking by filling the bowl with a fixed quantity and noting how much is left at the same time the following day. There are various medical problems which may encourage a dog to drink more than usual. If you are concerned, see your veterinarian. As a guide, a dog about the weight of a Cocker Spaniel should consume an average of one point when kept on a canned diet. Never withhold water from your dog, even if it is incontinent. This could be fatal as a dog needs to make up the excessive water loss from its body. The only circumstance in which it may be best to prevent your dog drinking water freely is when it is vomiting, as drinking water can precipitate further vomiting and further loss of vital body salts. Provide only a small quantity after vomiting appears to have ceased and seek veterinary advice. Conversely, there may be occasions when you need to encourage your dog to drink. This is usually when it has an infection of the urinary tract, or has deposits such as bladder stones in the tract.

Your dog's water intake may be reduced if you are providing milk for it to drink. Remember that milk is not essential and cannot be digested properly by all dogs. Some individuals get a taste for tea, but this is probably because of its milk content and any sugar that may be present. Do not encourage your dog to drink any form of alcohol; this is potentially harmful, and dogs, like humans, can become addicted to alcohol, with similar consequences. If you are going to the beach for the day in the summer, take a supply of fresh water and a bowl for your dog. Otherwise, in hot weather especially, a dog may resort to drinking sea water, and this can prove fatal in any quantity because of salt-poisoning.

I was horrified that my friend's dog eats its own feces. Why is this?

Such behavior, known as coprophagia, is quite common in various mammals including not only dogs but also chimpanzees! Various reasons have been suggested for such behavior in dogs. It could be that the dog is suffering from a digestive problem, notably a deficiency

Left: The majority of obese dogs are overweight because they are being given too much food, or too many tidbits, by their owners.

Right: The water intake of dogs varies according to their diet and the prevailing environmental conditions. Excessive thirst, however, can be indicative of certain diseases and is often linked with urinary incontinence.

Above: Swimming is a useful form of exercise for dogs, but be careful not to let your dog swim in water that is badly polluted, as some of it may well be ingested.

of certain B vitamins or vitamin K which are normally manufactured in the gut by bacteria. By consuming its feces, it obtains these essential elements which otherwise would be lost in large quantities from the body. It may be worth supplementing these vitamins to see if this overcomes the problem. Yet such behavior appears to be addictive and is often seen in dogs that have been kenneled under fairly unsanitary conditions for part of their life. A bitch will frequently eat the stools of her puppies, and they may consume hers early in life. It may be that this helps to establish the beneficial vitamin-producing bacteria in their intestinal tracts.

If a dog is suffering from a malabsorption disease, part of the food will pass through the digestive tract unaltered, and re-emerge in the feces. These are attractive to the dogs because of the undigested foodstuff present in them. A condition of this type requires veterinary attention; the behavior can be corrected by appropriate therapy for the original problem.

Nevertheless, in many cases there is no clear-cut explanation for coprophagia. Always try to clear up the feces as soon as possible after they are expelled from the body so the dog has no opportunity to eat them. It is also possible to lace the stools with a foul-tasting substance such as curry powder. Other treatment involves the use of a drug called Cythioate, normally used to control fleas, which will taint the feces and cause them to taste bad when eaten. In bad cases, it may be necessary for apomorphine (which induces vomiting) to be administered as soon as possible after the dog eats its feces. Shortly afterwards, the adverse effects of the drug will become apparent, and the dog will feel ill for a couple of hours or so. It then comes to associate the feeling of nausea with eating its own feces and should then desist from this practice. Obviously such a drastic remedy must be discussed beforehand with your veterinarian.

Some dogs show no interest in their own excrement but are attracted to that of cattle and horses in particular. The dog may eat the feces or (perhaps worse from the owner's viewpoint) roll in them, with cow dung being especially favored. While the eating of such excrement is carried out for basically the same reasons as given previously, the deliberate soiling of the coat probably results from a totally different cause. Two schools of thought exist: one maintains that the scent from the herbivore's feces disguise the strong canine odor and helps hunting dogs conceal their presence from potential prey; the other believes the smell may act to reinforce the dog's body odor.

The latter explanation seems more feasible in practice as dogs that have recently been washed often have the maddening habit of seeking out the excrement of herbivores to roll in at the first opportunity when out on a walk. Because a bath removes the usual canine odor, the dog may be seeking to reinforce its social status because it has been deprived of its natural means of doing so. Nevertheless, another bath will be necessary and the dog's access to such sources of feces will have to be restricted as far as possible.

Left: Dogs enjoy drinking water from alternative sources to their feeding bowls. They also have a tendency to roll around in mud as soon as possible after a bath, to restore their body scent.

GENERAL HYGIENE

Regular grooming is recommended to remove dead hair from a dog's coat, and to spot signs of external parasites. Your dog will need to be washed periodically.

How should I wash my dog?
It is best to perform this task out of doors, particularly during the summer months, because it tends to be a messy procedure. Wear a protective plastic apron or some other waterproof clothing for the purpose. A suitable tub of metal or plastic should be half-filled with tepid water. Remember that a dog's claws are sharp and can puncture inflatable pools and scratch the enamel on a bathtub. If a dog is dirty, the only cleaning necessary is to stand it in a plastic tub or your bathtub or sink and rinse its legs and belly off with lukewarm water (without soap). It is important to rub it down with a towel or use a hair-drier until it is dry.

For a general washing, use a mild baby shampoo or a suitable canine shampoo available from your pet store. There are various types available. Some are useful under special circumstances – to emphasize the coat color of a poodle, for example. If your dog is very dirty, with oil on its coat, for example, use one of the special detergent gels produced for this purpose. Otherwise avoid detergents, dishwashing compounds, and medicated soaps as these are likely to have an adverse reaction on the skin.

A dog that is used to being bathed from an early age will not resent the process nearly as much as one that has never been near the tub. First place the dog gently in the water, and then, with a clean bottle or pitcher, pour the water over him carefully, starting at the hindquarters and progressing forwards. Apply the shampoo as directed and work it into a lather. The head should be washed last, taking particular care not to let any shampoo run into the eyes. By this time the dog is likely to have shaken itself, spraying water everywhere. It

WASHING YOUR DOG

● Outdoors is the best place to wash your dog. For hygienic reasons, it is preferable not to use the bathtub – although to new dog owners, it may seem the obvious place. Begin at the hindquarters and gently massage your dog. Insure all the shampoo is thoroughly rinsed and then dry the dog with an old towel. Dogs tend to shake themselves vigorously as well to remove most of the excess water, so wear a protective overall.

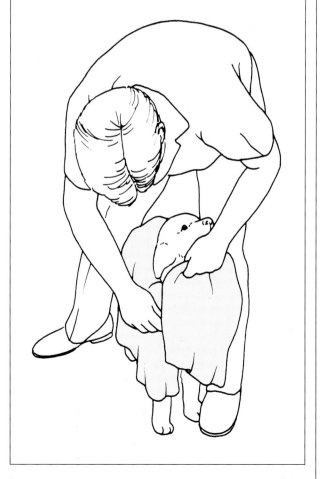

Left: Adequate preparations should be made before bathing a dog because it will not remain in the container of his own accord. It is a good idea to have plenty of tepid water at hand before beginning the washing operation.

can be lifted out of the bath, and the dirty water poured out. Before the process is repeated, rinse the shampoo thoroughly out of the coat. Indeed, a hose can be used cautiously for this purpose, out of doors. It is then a matter of drying the hair after your dog has shaken off most of the remaining water from its coat. An old clean towel can be used initially for drying, followed by a hair-drier of some type for the final stage. The dog may be frightened by this apparatus at first so try to introduce it gradually and run it at a low temperature from the outset so as not to burn the skin. A brush used in conjunction with the hair-drier will speed up the process by serving to separate the hairs.

How often should I bathe my dog?

If your dog's coat becomes soiled with the excrement of other animals, it will need to be washed immediately. But it may not be necessary to give a full bath. Excessive washing of the coat is not to be recommended, as it removes the natural waterproofing agents and tends to make the appearance of the fur rather dull. Mud on the coat can be allowed to dry and then brushed out. A bath every three months on average will prevent the typical pungent "doggy" odor from becoming overpowering. It may be necessary to wash your dog before an important show, however, to create a good appearance for the judge. The use of hair conditioner is recommended by some owners to settle the coat after washing. This is because the coat carries static electricity after repeated grooming, and the negative charges involved tend to repel the individual hairs. A conditioner should help to neutralize them.

Above: Hairdriers will help to dry your dog's coat thoroughly after a bath, but be gentle because the noise and unfamiliar sensation of warm air may initially frighten some dogs.

Left: Drying your dog with a towel after a swim is a good idea, not only to remove excess water, but also as a means of reinforcing the bond between dog and owner.

GROOMING ROUTINE

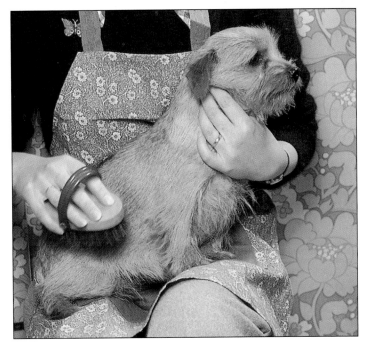

Above: Grooming techniques do vary according to the breed concerned, but for the smaller breeds it is easiest to sit the dog on your lap and use a dandy brush to disentangle the matted fur.

Right: Red Setters and other long-haired breeds are relatively more demanding as far as grooming is concerned and the job is easier if you stand your dog on an old table outdoors.

Besides keeping your dog's coat clean and healthy looking, brushing and combing can give mutual pleasure and so cement the emotional bond between the dog and owner.

How should I go about grooming my dog?

If you have a young puppy, get it used to the sensations of the comb and brush. More serious grooming can begin later, and the dog will then not be frightened of the procedure. The long-coated breeds need grooming on a daily basis. It is much better to spend a short time

each day on grooming your dog than to neglect this task and then have to deal with mats. This will be painful for the dog, and it will come actively to resent the process. With a strange dog that seems not to like being groomed, place a temporary muzzle on it for safety's sake. If your dog has a heavily matted coat, take it to a veterinarian. He or she will be able to give a sedative and save the dog any further distress while the matted areas of the coat are removed.

In addition to improving the appearance of your dog, grooming provides a valuable means of detecting fleas and other parasites which may be present on the skin. Sharp burrs that could have become entangled in the coat while the dog was walking through undergrowth can be removed before they cause physical injury, and any superficial growths can be detected at an early stage. Dogs generally appear to find grooming pleasant once they are used to the process. And grooming helps to massage the skin.

When grooming, start at the head and run the brush or comb down the body in the direction of the fur. It is important that the dog stands on a firm surface at a comfortable height for the groomer. For the larger breeds, the task will probably have to be carried out with the dog on the floor. Smooth-coated breeds like the Beagle can be groomed with a hand glove. Dogs lose some of their hair throughout the year, but in the spring, the thicker winter coat will be shed. Another heavy shed will occur during the following autumn. At these times of year, grooming will take longer but it will prevent dead hair from being deposited around the home. A comb can be used on the finer points such as the so-called feathering, most noticeable at the

The Yorkshire Terrier is one breed that needs daily grooming to keep it looking its best.

GROOMING YOUR DOG

- Begin with the stomach, using a brush and working with firm short strokes, brushing the hairs upwards, right from the roots. Also, try and loosen any tangled or dead hair.

- Then brush the "trousers" on both the fore- and hindlimbs, holding the tail to one side while you brush each hind leg down, gently but firmly (3). After the legs, brush the tail thoroughly, working from the root to the tip.

- Using a comb rather than a brush repeat the procedure to remove any other remaining tangles.

- To groom the rest of the body, start from the dog's back, working from the tail end, towards the head.

- The neck and ears should also be brushed, carefully holding each ear while grooming the area beneath it and teasing out any tangles with your fingers, keeping the brush away from the dog's face.

- The well-groomed Pomeranian is displayed showing its soft bushy undercoat, long straight topcoat and abundant fluffed-up fur around the neck.

GROOMING THE HEAD

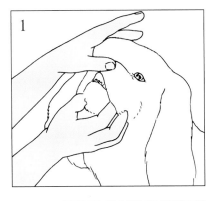

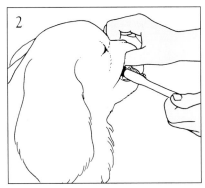

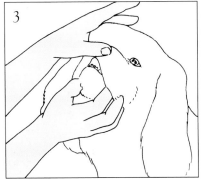

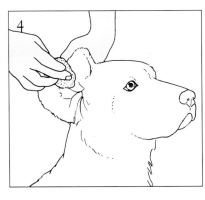

- To open the mouth of an obstinate dog hold the lower jaw firmly with one hand, at the same time block the nostrils; inspect the teeth with special attention to the molars (1).

- Using a toothbrush may hurt the dog's gums if they are sensitive and so it is best to use a damp cotton ball to remove superficial debris. Special dog toothpastes are available (2).

- Any tear staining, loose hairs or eyelashes can be cleaned away using a moistened cotton ball; use a fresh one for each eye (3).

- The ears should also be groomed thoroughly and inspected for any signs of infection (4). Dogs with long heavy ears that hang down, such as Spaniels, are most at risk.

Right: Inspecting and cleaning a dog's teeth, usually by wiping them, should be routine but, as many dogs are reluctant to open their mouths, it is important to encourage puppies from an early age to do this.

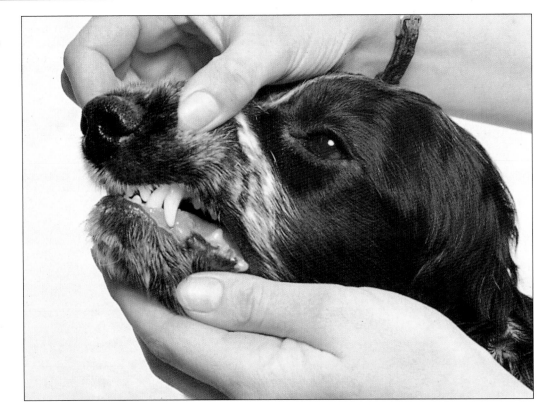

back of the legs of breeds such as the Irish Setter. A comb avoids the need to brush around the eyes and other sensitive parts of the body. An overall grooming with a comb after a thorough brushing will remove any surplus dead hair and will insure there are no remaining clumps.

What is dry shampooing? Will I not have to bathe my dog in the winter if I use this?
Unfortunately, dry shampooing – used main in show circles – is no real substitute for a thorough bath. A powder, which removes surplus grease and dirt from the coat, is applied over the body and rubbed in well. A short time

later, the shampoo is brushed out. The white color of the powder makes it unsuitable for use on dark-colored dogs, and it may cause the dog to sneeze when applied close to the head. The considerable brushing required to remove all traces of the powder from the coat can generate static electricity which makes it difficult to settle the hair down (a nylon-bristle brush will make this worse). Dry shampooing, therefore, has only limited applications and certainly will not remove heavy dirt from the coat. It may help to improve the appearance of dogs with pale coats without having to wet them thoroughly.

LOOKING AFTER THE PAWS

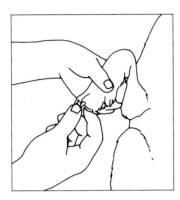 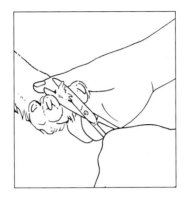 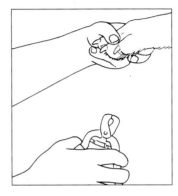

- The space between the toes should be examined carefully for grit and small stones. If there is a grass seed in the dog's foot, it can be removed using a pair of tweezers but it is probably preferable to seek veterinary advice. Inspect the undersides of the foot pad in the same way and remove any embedded mud with a moist cotton ball.

- Excess fur between the toes can be carefully trimmed away with round-tipped scissors, so as to minimize the risk of any infection.

- Overgrown nails should be clipped with a stout pair of clippers, specially designed for the purpose. It is safest simply to trim off the sharpest points – never cut too short or near the quick.

Left: The Yorkshire Terrier has a very fine, silky coat, which requires a great deal of attention for show purposes, and much shampooing and combing is needed. To prevent the dog's coat from spoiling during the journey to a show, it is often tied up in curl papers or "crackers".

POODLE PARLOURS

Above: Tidying and neatening up the shaggy and profuse coats of Old English Sheepdogs prior to a dog show is in fact part of the general daily routine and care of this breed. Their coats are left shaggy for show purposes but sometimes clipping of their coats is advisable, especially in warm climates.

The help and experience of professional groomers are essential for most people who wish to show their dogs. Groomers also assist with other tasks, such as general clipping.

What is actually involved in the work of a professional groomer?

One part of a professional groomer's work is to wash dogs brought to them. Certain breeds with long, silky coats may develop mats, and in severe cases, these will have to be cut away. Prior to bathing, the groomer will concentrate on removing the mats and combing the hair. Never bathe a dog with mats in its coat as these will then be even harder to extract afterwards, and the process will be more painful for the dog.

A large proportion of the breeds taken to grooming parlors are those whose hair needs to be clipped properly. This procedure is also carried out prior to washing, if required. The frequency of clipping varies somewhat according to the breed concerned. Poodles, for example, need clipping quite often – at least every two months, as do other dogs that do not shed their hair. Various types of clip are recognized, with the so-called "lamb" clip finding favor with many poodle owners. For this, the coat is trimmed to a uniform length, either short or long. The "Dutch" clip is slightly more ornate with short body hair contrasting with longer hair on the legs. The

most elaborate clip, known as the "lion" clip, is usually seen only on show dogs as it is time-consuming and, therefore, expensive.

Other breeds may also be clipped, depending upon the time of year. Old English Sheepdogs may well need to have their thick coats cut short during the warmer months. Spaniels are also clipped – usually about every two or three months. This provides an opportunity to remove some of the hair on the ears, and helps to reduce the likelihood of ear infections, to which these dogs are prone. It is also not unusual to remove hair from between the toes. This is where the so-called eccrine sweat glands are, and the fur can become a source of irritation as well as a hiding place for harvest mites, which have a similar effect. Clipping may also be required for medical reasons such as diarrhea, which would otherwise soil the coat around the anus and attract flies to lay their eggs amidst the matted fur, giving rise to the condition known as fly-strike.

The majority of wire-coated terriers will need to be stripped twice a year. This can be painstakingly carried out by hand using a tool known as a stripping knife. But even when undertaken by an expert, this is a slow and therefore particularly costly process. As a result, the showing of such breeds as the Airedale Terrier requires considerable dedication as, for exhibition purposes, there is no acceptable alternative to hand-

stripping. Most pet terriers, including the smaller Scottish Terriers and West Highland White Terriers, are simply clipped, with surplus coat being removed by means of thinning scissors.

At what stage should I have my poodle clipped?

The clipping of a poodle can begin as early as 12 weeks of age. It is important to get them used to the sound and sensation produced by electric clippers while they are still young so

they will not resent the process later in life. Young poodles are usually given the "puppy" trim at first. This is fairly basic and resembles the "lamb" trim. If you are interested in learning to clip your own dog, join one of the grooming courses that are organized in various regions. These are often advertised in dog magazines. In some countries clipping can prove a worthwhile career for someone who is keen to work with dogs but who lives in an urban area where there are few opportunities for kennel workers.

Above: Poodles as a breed are available in three sizes: standard, miniature and toy. As they do not shed hair, they are frequently clipped in order to prevent matting of their coats, and this has become an accepted part of keeping many dogs besides show poodles, with regular visits to a grooming parlor being required every

POODLE CLIPS

- Styles of clip vary. The Lion or English Saddle style is favored by the British Kennel Club whereas the American Kennel Club does not discriminate between the Puppy, English Saddle or Continental styles. Poodle parlors will be able to advise on this aspect of show preparation.

TRAINING AND BEHAVIOUR

TRAINING AND BEHAVIOR

Experiments by the Russian scientist Pavlov led to theories of conditioning that were to form the basis of modern training methods and theories. The poorly-trained dog may exhibit a variety of behavioral problems, from destructive or aggressive tendencies, to jealousy towards other pet dogs and attempts to dominate its owner.

Below: This well-trained dog is walking to heel at its owner's side.

HOUSE TRAINING

- A young puppy will prefer to urinate on newspaper, not the floor.

- Move the paper progressively closer to the door.

- Begin to place the paper outside and, eventually, dispense with it altogether.

- After a meal, the puppy will show signs of wanting to relieve himself.

- The puppy should be gently lifted up and taken outside.

The Pavlovian dog

A dog's training can progress from simple toilet training through the basic commands such as "heel," "sit," "wait," "come," "down" and "stay," to the complex training of dogs who compete in championship obedience classes. The essential principles used in training are similar whatever is being taught, and it is these that owners should try to understand. By the application of these principles, any dog can be taught at least the basic commands, and most much more than that.

Some breeds tend to be more responsive to advanced training than others, and it is noticeable that the majority of dogs compete in obedience championships are border collies. When dogs fail to learn even basic training it is almost always owing to the training itself, or lack of it, rather than the dog. Nevertheless, a tiny majority of dogs have genuine mental or behavioral problems as a result of their genetic background or severe distress early in life.

The process of training a dog is essentially that of conditioning it to perform a particular action from a repertoire at a specific moment. In order to train a dog successfully, it is helpful to understand how conditioning works in the dog's mind.

Two kinds of conditioning are recognized by scientists. Classical conditioning was discovered by the Russian scientist Pavlov early this century while he was working with dogs. In his now famous experiments, Pavlov noticed that his dogs always salivated when they smelt their food on its way. When he introduced the sound of a bell just prior to the dogs' meal time, the dogs came to associate the sound of the bell with the anticipation of their food and, in time, began to salivate at the sound of the bell itself, regardless of whether food was being offered.

Pavlovian conditioning is useful for house training. Whenever a puppy shows signs of wanting to relive itself, which will probably be on awakening or just after a large meal, it should be gently lifted up and taken outside. If the puppy is taken outside sufficiently often in this way, an association will be established between the act of going outside and the act of relieving itself, in much the same way as Pavlov's dogs made a connection between a bell and food. Puppies generally prefer to relieve themselves out of doors anyway, which facilitates this training. The same principle of conditioning can be applied to the newspaper method of house training.

Far left: This well-trained dog is walking to heel at its owner's side.

REWARD AND PUNISHMENT

The second type of conditioning is easier to understand because it is based on giving a reward whenever the dog does something that pleases the owner. The principle of this type of conditioning is simply that if a dog is rewarded for behaving well, the good behavior is likely to be repeated. Similarly, if a dog is scolded or punished for doing something, the undesired behavior is also likely to be repeated.

Most dog owners will be able to think of several occasions when these techniques have apparently been unsuccessful. Commonly, this is because a dog gets confused by what appears to be a lack of consistency in its owner's behavior. A dog can only relate a reward or reprimand to its most recent behavior.

Right: A dog will not be able to understand illogical behavior on the part of its owner.

Although a human understands that a puppy is being scolded because it wet the carpet while the owner was out, it is quite unreasonable to expect the puppy to associate the two actions unless one follows immediately after the other. A delayed scolding will always cause confusion in a dog's mind. The dog will associate the punishment with whatever it is doing at the time, and this may be something the dog is usually rewarded or praised for.

Although there is a place for both reward and punishment in the upbringing of a dog, as a general rule, reward is always the best policy. Punishment is normally used to stop a dog doing something, or as a reprimand for a misdemeanor, but it only works if the dog is caught in the act. For example, if a dog has chewed up a pair of shoes while his owner is away, and on his return the owner punishes the dog as they enter the room where the shoes

are, the dog will see this as a reprimand for going into that room. The dog may then be afraid of going into the room, but he will continue to chew up shoes.

When a dog is actually caught in the act, some consideration should be given as to just how the punishment should be administered. Physical reprimand should never be too severe, and a slap on the rump or a shaking by the scruff of the neck is quite sufficient. As with reward training, it is useful to associate punishment with a verbal command such as "bad dog," so that, later on, the command alone will stop the dog from behaving badly.

Punishment can have both beneficial and detrimental effects on the general behavior of a dog. A certain amount of well-judged punishment reminds the dog that the owner is the boss, and so reduces the likelihood of the dog asserting himself too strongly. On the other hand, the use of too much punishment can detract from the ideal dog-to-owner relationship of loving obedience. A dog that is frequently punished can become very confused by receiving both punishment and care and love from the same source.

It must also be remembered that punishment will not always be interpreted by the dog as having the meaning the owner intended. To some dogs, the physical contact involved in most forms of punishment also acts as a positive stimulus. While a slap may hurt momentarily, the fact that the owner is interacting with him physically may be seen by the dog as part of a game. If a dog sees punishment as partly rewarding, its effectiveness is obviously greatly reduced.

Some people have attempted to solve these problems associated with punishment by making and advocating the use of electric shock collars. These administer a very small but punishing shock to the dog by remote control. Clearly, these remove the problem of the owner's being directly associated with the punishment, and make it easier to catch the dog in the act, but they have caused a number of problems in practice and are generally considered unacceptable. For example, if a dog is given a shock during a fight with another dog in the hope of stopping it from fighting, the dog is likely to fight more furiously than ever because of the pain it has received. As conventional training methods are perfectly satisfactory and sufficient, and electric shocks are as unpleasant to dogs as they are to humans, there are really no grounds whatever for the use of these shock punishments.

LEARNING OBEDIENCE

Puppies vary considerably in the rate at which they mature, but informal training – especially house training – should start as soon as they are moving around independently. This is the time to teach a puppy its name and then a few basic commands. It is best to choose a short name that can be spoken clearly, it will be quickly learned by the puppy, and will not be embarrassing to shout out in public.

Formal training at registered training clubs does not start until puppies are six months old, and it can be completed in about three months. However, informal training should certainly begin much earlier than this, otherwise bad habits will develop. Some of these may not become apparent until later in life, and a particularly common example is the dog that jumps up. In a small puppy this presents no problems, and indeed many owners may enjoy your puppy playing in this way. However, when dogs grow larger, it can become undesirable, irritating, or even dangerous in extreme cases, such as if a St Bernard were to jump up and place its paws on a small child.

It is useful to consider why a dog starts to jump up in the first place. If jumping gains the attention of the owner and results in play or affection, this is taken by the dog as a reward for the act of jumping. A reward for a dog can take many forms. At tidbit of food is one of the most common rewards used to encourage a good dog, or one that has done what the owner wanted.

If food was the only possible reward, a dog would very likely overeat excessively during a formal training session. An alternative is to associate in the dog's mind a phrase such as "good boy" by saying it each time a reward is given. "Good boy" will then come to be considered as a reward in itself, just as the bell caused Pavlov's dogs to salivate. The other great alternative to food is affection; dogs are particularly easy to reward in this way, and withheld affection is a common cause of jumping up.

One of the simplest ways to eradicate an undesirable habit, such as jumping up, is simply to stop rewarding it. For example, each time a dog jumps up, the owner should walk away and ignore him. The dog should get the message fairly quickly unless the habit is too well established. It is also a good idea to reward the dog with affection when it behaves in the desired manner, such as standing quietly.

An alternative to ignoring the dog and hoping that undesirable or awkward behavior will stop, is to use punishment, say a slap on the rump (never on the nose because this is very delicate). Punishment is sometimes unlikely to help but this is invariably because the dog is confused. If a dog usually receives a reward in return for certain behaviour and then receives punishment immediately after what is, to the dog, the very same act, this is interpreted as being both illogical and disturbing. In time, it will probably lead to other behavior problems.

Left: Dogs should not be allowed to develop the habit of jumping up, or being allowed to occupy a certain favorite chair against an owner's wishes. Consistency is vital from the start, as established behavior is almost impossible to change.

THE WELL-TRAINED DOG

The commands that are generally taught at basic training are "heel," "sit," "wait," "come," "down" and "stay." Although the formal lessons at training schools are not usually offered to puppies under six months old, it should be possible to go some way towards teaching these commands before that time. With a young puppy, and also even with an older dog, it is particularly important to give training in a large number of short lessons rather than marathon sessions during which the dog will quickly get tired. Most dogs will naturally enjoy their training and this should be encouraged as much as possible by giving plenty of attention both during the sessions and afterwards.

The way the basic commands are taught is based upon the methods of conditioning, reward and punishment already described. There is no fixed order in which the commands should be learnt, but a dog is often trained to walk to heel before anything else. The dog should walk steadily at the pace of the owner, close to his or her leg, but not in front of it; it is customary for the dog to be taught to walk on the left hand side.

Normally the puppy or dog will try to rush off ahead from time to time, particularly when it smells or sees another dog. When this happens, check the dog with a sharp jerk on the lead, and at the same time the command "heel" should be given. The dog should learn that it is more comfortable to walk in the correct way, and it will also associate the command with the action. Once the dog is well trained to walk to this command, it should continue to do so even when it is off the lead; this should first be attempted in a quiet open space.

When the dog has learned to "heel", the command "sit" is often taught next. This can be done in a number of ways, with or without the use of a food reward. Begin by pushing the hindquarters of the dog down into the sitting position at the same time as the command "sit" is given. Again, the dog will learn the command by associating the word with the act. This can be further reinforced by speaking the word when the dog moves into the sit position of its own accord.

However, as an alternative, it can be a good idea to teach the command entirely or in part by using a food reward. It is well worthwhile teaching a family dog to sit quietly when he is about to be fed, instead of pestering the person preparing his meal, or worse still a group of people sitting around a dinner table.

Right: Walking to heel is one of the first things a dog learns – not to rush ahead, but to walk with the owner even when off the lead.

LEAD TRAINING

Be careful putting on the lead, so as not to frighten the pup.

The dog may be playful or nervous during the first lessons.

Hold the lead in the right hand, reassure or admonish with the left.

The lead should be slack, with the pup walking at the owner's pace.

To teach "sit" with the use of food rewards, begin with a small food reward and give it to the dog so that it takes it gently, but only as soon as it has gone into a sitting position. The word "sit" should be spoken at the same time. The dog is more likely to sit automatically if it is backing away from you up against a wall, so it is a good idea to engineer such a situation to help the process along. If this technique is used repeatedly, the dog will come to associate the sitting both with being fed and the command "sit." Once this has been established, it is a relatively simple next step to get the dog to sit quietly while its food is being prepared. The meal itself will then act as a further reward for the act of sitting.

The dog that pesters people for tidbits at a dinner table may be amusing sometimes, but, as a rule, this is an undesirable habit, and should never be allowed to start. It usually begins with a waste scrap from the side of a plate which the dog immediately accepts. The problem is that the dog quickly comes to expect a scrap at every meal, and only quietens down when he gets it; he has now trained the owner. Once allowed, it will be almost impossible stop. If the dog is trained to sit or lie down during meals, and is never rewarded with scraps, the habit will never begin.

SIT TRAINING

Push the dog's hindquarters down, to reinforce the command to sit.

Teaching the dog to sit against a wall may help the learning process.

HIS MASTER'S VOICE

The traditional way to train a dog to stay is to start by doing repeated exercises with the dog on the lead. The lead must either be long, or else extended by attaching a cord, to allow for an increasing distance between the dog and owner. Extendable and retractable leads can be bought, which are ideal for this stage of training in particular. The dog is put in a sitting position and the owner then moves slowly away, repeating the word "stay." Some people also find it useful to use a hand signal to reinforce the verbal command.

At first the owner should only back up a short distance and then return and praise the dog if it has not moved. If the dog moves, the owner should say "bad dog" and put it back in its original position. The distance between the owner and the dog should then be slowly increased so that the dog continues to stay still on the majority of occasions. When the dog

responds successfully to the stay command the owner should return, rather than allow the dog to come towards him thinking all is over, because this will hinder the learning process.

Once the dog has learned to stay while the owner moves several yards away, it is time to move on and teach the dog to come when called. The lesson should again begin with the dog on a long lead. The dog should be told to stay and when the owner is some distance away, he should tug gently on the lead and say "come" at the same time. The dog should learn this command quickly because he will be much happier to come up to the owner and be petted rather than be left sitting alone. However, this is a very important command for the dog to learn well, as it is essential for the owner to be able to call a dog to him, for example, when the dog is loose with other dogs in a park, or is about to rush away across a road. Once a dog has been trained in this way on the lead, it should be given training off the lead.

A whole range of other commands can be taught using similar methods to those already described, all of which depend on the conditioning techniques of rewarding a dog with food or affection, or repeatedly associating a command with a particular act.

The most useful commands to teach next are "down" and "fetch." "Down" can be taught in a similar way to "sit," with the frontquarters of the dog being pushed if necessary. Most dogs will fetch readily and therefore limited teaching may be required, but a problem can arise if the dog fails to let go of the object it has fetched. For this reason, an occasional food reward may help, because the dog will have to release the object to get the food. The reward can be given first when the dog is holding an object, say a stick, in its mouth. He will then start to come with the stick hoping for a reward. The reward can then be given less often, and the word "fetch" used each time the dog goes to pick up an object, perhaps one that has been thrown.

It is important that dogs learn to urinate on command; they can be taught this quite successfully so that they can be given the instruction only when they are in a suitable place. The method used for teaching is similar to other training with a command such as "clean boy" being given each time the puppy has relieved itself. The puppy will quickly learn to associate the two. That this method can be successful has been demonstrated by the British guide dogs for the blind, all of which are taught in this way.

Below: By teaching a dog the "sit" or "stay" command, you could, for instance, prevent it from rushing across a road and having an accident or, indeed, causing one.

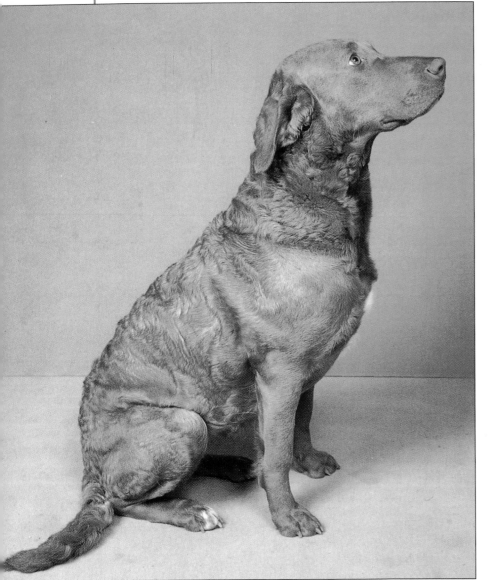

TRAINING

- When lead training (1), have the dog walking on your left. Hold the end of the lead in your right hand and take up most of the slack in your left hand. Give the command you are going to use, such as "heel", and walk on. Every time the dog pulls away from you, give a small jerk on the lead with your left hand, but release it again as soon as the dog returns to the correct position.

- There are several ways in which to teach a dog to "sit". One of the easiest, (2), is to walk with the dog on your left, holding the lead up with your right hand and, with your left hand, firmly pressing down the dog's hindquarters. At the same time, firmly utter the command "sit". Do this repeatedly during your walk until the dog gets the idea of what is required.

- The command to "stay" is a progression from "sit". Put the dog in the "sit" position, then move in front of it, saying "sit" then "stay" very firmly, jerking on the lead if it attempts to move (3). If it does, you must start again.

- Tremendous patience is called for in dog training. Once the dog knows how to "sit and "stay", you can begin using the command "stay" as you gradually move further and further away from it (4 & 5).

- The command to "come" (the recall command) is a progression from the puppy-lead training, when you first drew the bewildered pup towards you. Adopt the same procedure now, uttering the command "come" once the dog is in the "sit-stay" position, and making a great fuss of it when it obeys, so that it associates the command with a pleasing experience.

THE LEADER OF THE PACK

Dogs can develop what appear to be psychological problems, although in reality, these are much more likely to be social problems. A common behavior problem arises from a dog's instincts as a pack animal. It may consider itself to be an ideal candidate for leadership, and attempt to establish itself in this position. Usually, it will regard its owner as the pack leader, but it may try to achieve for itself the position of dominance. This problem is greater with larger breeds.

If a dog dominates the family, it can cause all sorts of difficulties. It will refuse to obey orders, be uncontrollable on walks, "defend" its owner against visitors and aggressively reserve its right to occupy the best armchair. In some cases, the dog may seek to dominate the whole family. In other instances, it may simply decide that one particular member of the household deserves a lower position than itself in the social structure. Either way, these problems can be solved only with difficulty.

The best time to correct a dog's behavior is when it first tries to assert its dominance, probably when it is quite a young puppy. Holding it down by the scruff of the neck if it ever becomes assertive should be effective.

If the problem already exists in an adult dog, or starts to appear, such treatment may not be successful. However, in all but the worst cases, the application of suitable psychology should be of some help.

However dominant the dog may be, it must still look to its owner for food. It will also still enjoy a little play and affection from time to time. The owner can therefore use food and affection as a reward in the re-training of the dog. The dog must be taught by conditioning that these rewards can be obtained only from the person whom it has previously tried to dominate, and so learn to associate this need with good behavior.

To succeed, the technique must be used slowly and gradually, and the dog must not be provoked to aggression. The person, or people, who are most dominated by the dog should take complete care of it. In particular, they should handle all those activities which give pleasure to the dog. When the dog indicates an inclination to obey, they should use the food reward in an effort to engage it in basic training: to sit or stay, for example. Other family members should ignore the dog except on unpleasant occasions such as a visit to the vet.

Far left: The dominated owner will have great problems with the dog, being unable to control it on walks and being victimised by it in the house. He or she must re-train it, gradually, to be dependent and obey orders.

Left: Food, play and affection are the best combination to re-train a dominant dog

DOGS ON THE LOOSE

Male dogs may cause their owners more problems than female dogs. There are three reasons for this. Firstly, male dogs are much more likely to try to assert dominance, and, as we have seen, this can result in a number of difficulties (see p. 149). Secondly, male dogs tend to be much more strongly motivated sexually, and this can lead to a range of problems in that area. Thirdly, there are a number of behavior traits that are characteristic of male dogs, which are almost never displayed by bitches.

Right: A potentially aggressive encounter between two Border Collies will usually end without a serious fight. The subordinate dog, with its tail down, usually retreats.

The first of these traits is that of roaming, or straying. It is quite common for some male dogs to disappear for hours, days or even weeks, before returning home. Sometimes they may be in good condition suggesting that they could have been found and looked after; other times they may be extremely disheveled. It is not known why dogs should roam in this way, although, interestingly, male cats have this very same tendency. It is only possible to speculate that the males of both species may, at certain times, be affected by an instinctive urge to investigate a wider area than their normal home range. It is known that males of some species closely related to the dog, such as the fox, often have a surrounding range of several square miles, which makes the range of most dogs very small.

A male dog is also very likely to stray when he detects a bitch on heat and he may then try to stay close to her throughout the duration.

Roaming is not only confined almost entirely to males in both dogs and cats, but it also seems to be directly linked to the male sex hormones they possess. In a study by Drs. Hopkins, Schubert and Hart from the University of California it was demonstrated that, following castration, almost 95 per cent of the animals that had previously roamed habitually, subsequently lost the habit, either rapidly or gradually.

The same study also investigated a second behavior problem, confined almost entirely to male dogs, that of urine-marking in the home. This is, of course, normal outside the house, but dogs are trained as puppies not to do it indoors. Nevertheless, its function is essentially that of territorial marking, and the tendency to mark indoors sometimes reappears in adult male dogs, which were previously housetrained as puppies. This may be one of the many indications that, for a dog that is dominant within the household, the urine marking is being used to establish its territory beyond dispute.

The treatment for this can be the same as that already recommended for the dominant dog (see p. 149). An alternative, more drastic solution, is castration, or possibly a hormonal treatment that can be obtained from a veterinary surgeon.

Dogs of this kind have not gone wild, but they do tend to behave as packs in many distinct and easily observable ways. For example, it is frequently obvious that a dominance hierarchy exists between dogs in a pack. If the pack moves from one area to another, it is very often the same dog that leads the way each time.

Packs such as these are very much temporary as they only exist for short periods each day. Also they tend to have a different membership from day to day. Partly because of this, they are likely to interact with each other in a range of different ways, since they cannot achieve the high level of understanding between individuals that seems to exist in, for example, a wolf pack, or indeed in a pack of the second type of stray dogs – the feral dogs.

Feral dogs differ from free-ranging dogs both in that they have no permanent homes, and they support themselves quite independently from humans. Occasionally, there are odd times when they may be left some scraps, but generally they remain independent. Within the developed world, the feral dog is found in noticeable numbers only in the United States. Here, they represent a particular problem in some areas, and therefore some detailed studies of them have been made.

Feral dogs are generally distinguished by being in very poor condition and often emaciated. They do not allow humans to come near, and they become aggressive if they are made to feel threatened or cornered. Interestingly they live as individuals, rather than in packs. The packs that do exist are usually small, made up of only two or three dogs. This is probably not so much owing to their behaving inherently differently from other dogs, but rather to the pressures of the environment in which they live. They usually find it difficult to obtain adequate food, and if they lived in large groups this would obviously be an even greater problem. They are also often threatened by dog-catching agencies, which are more likely to chase a group of dogs than an individual.

Studies have shown that feral dogs rarely manage to rear their own puppies. This apparent inability means that their continuing existence is dependent to a large extent on recruitment from tame and free-ranging dogs, and is therefore, in effect, entirely in the hands of the dog-owning public.

Above: The feral dog lives as a scavenger, raiding rubbish bins in city areas in search of food.

THE CANINE VANDAL

Whatever training it is given, a dog will nevertheless retain its own personality. That it does so is dependent on many factors, including its genetic background, its early socialization with people, the way its owner interacts with it, and the quality and effectiveness of its early training.

Behavior that causes problems for the owner can arise from any one of these factors, and for a few other reasons as well. One particular

difficulty is destructive behavior. This can take a number of forms, including scratching at doors or furniture, or knocking over valuable items, but the most common is the chewing of clothes, shoes, carpets or furniture while the owner is out.

It is best to begin a definite program to avoid any destructive behaviour when the dog is first

acquired. The dog should be left in one room while the owner stays quietly in another for increasing lengths of time. If the dog is quiet for a few minutes, the owner should go back in and praise this good performance. If the dog is heard to make destructive noises, the owner should either leave it until it is quiet and then reward it with praise, or else give some sort of punishment while the destructive behaviour is still in progress. Probably the best sort of punishment is a scolding through the door. If the owner goes and punishes the dog physically, the pleasure of the owner's company may outweigh the pain of the slap, thereby actually encouraging the dog to be destructive.

If an early training of this kind is not undertaken, there is an ever-present danger of the dog either destroying something, or barking persistently while the owner is out. These activities are similar, as both probably arise as a result of boredom when the dog is left on its own. It is very easy for the owner to encourage accidentally, or reinforce, this type of behavior when on returning. If the dog is scolded, it will associate this with the his behavior immediately preceding the scolding. More than likely, the dog will have heard his owner returning and will therefore have stopped barking or chewing the carpet some time before his owner reaches him. It is therefore possible for destructive behavior or barking to become conditioned accidentally, making the habit doubly difficult to break.

If a punishment is necessary, it is very important never to delay it once the undesired behaviour has ceased, as the dog will not be able to connect the punishment with the cause unless the two occur successively (see p. 142).

Bad habits are most effectively dealt with by trying to condition the dog to good behavior instead. One approach is to give the dog a ball, ring or some other toy to chew when it is alone. If dog and owner play games with this toy, the dog will develop an attachment to it, and can be given it each time the owner goes out. A training program can then begin, starting with short departures and slowly lengthening the time. The departures should be made as realistic as possible, with all the usual noises and actions associated with leaving the house. If the dog has chewed the wrong thing, or if it has barked persistently, it should be ignored by the "returning" owner so that this behavior is discouraged. As the program continues, the dog will gradually come to associate quiet, good behavior while alone with a subsequent happy, playful reunion with its owner.

Left: When left alone in the house or car, the pup should be provided with its own toys, such as a leather bone – like the one in this picture – to avoid destructive behavior which may damage furniture or clothes.

AGGRESSIVE BEHAVIOR

Above: Aggressive encounters between dogs are rare, as the subordinate individual usually backs down.

Below: Dogs use their sense of smell to recognize each other and may leave their scent to establish their dominance.

It is quite natural for dogs to exhibit many forms of aggression, and these have already been described. Displays of aggression that pose problems for owners therefore have many different causes and several potential cures.

The dog that bites the mailman is giving vent to his territorial aggression, but it is, of course, the same type of aggression that makes him attack a burglar. It is almost impossible to train a dog to differentiate between such intruders, and it is therefore extremely difficult to stop a dog threatening a mailman. The best solution is for responsible owners to prevent the dog making unwanted territorial attacks, by keeping it indoors at times of routine visits by the mailman.

Territorial aggression may also be practised on visiting friends or relations, but this is less common because the presence of the owner ought to inhibit the dog's feeling of aggression. However, if a dog comes to dominate the owner in the manner already outlined, its territorial aggression may well be more freely exhibited. If this is the case, re-training should be tackled to lessen the dog's dominance (see. p. 149), as this is the underlying cause of the aggressive behavior.

If the aggression is entirely territorial in nature, a different type of training is required. Physical punishment is never a good solution for aggression, so a less severe punishment should be given. For example, put the dog alone in a room for a short period each time it barks or growls at visitors.

Aggression that arises as a result of fear is also very common, and the relatively high incidence of minor dog bites can most probably be attributed to fear of strangers, along with some kind of territorial component. Aggression of this kind is revealed in the dog's facial expression and body posture (see p. 151). It can usually be cured by a program of socializing the dog more fully with a wide range of people, including the type that the dog particularly tends to threaten.

The best technique is a process called desensitization: gradually introducing the dog to their fear in small steps of increasing intensity. The dog should first be approached by someone it knows and fears. The person should begin by keeping at a distance so as to minimize the likelihood of frightening the dog. The dog should be rewarded with affection, praise or food if he shows no fear. It is crucial, though, that on no account should the dog be rewarded if he responds with any measure of aggression. The person should then come gradually closer to the dog on successive occasions, but this should not be attempted too quickly because the learning will then be less strong. Once the dog responds satisfactorily to someone he knows, the same process can be undertaken with a stranger. The whole sequence should be repeated, and then perhaps reinforced once again with the type of person that previously provoked most aggression, say an adult man or a playful child.

Cures of this kind are slow and can never be absolutely certain to work. To ensure the greatest success, it is best that they are undertaken without delay when the dog first exhibits anti-social aggression, and not when the behavior has become firmly established.

SEXUAL PROBLEMS

Some of the most common and persistent problems for dog owners arise from their dog's sexuality. These difficulties range from the dog that appears completely uninterested in other dogs when the owner wants it to breed, to the dog who frequently attempts to mount the legs of people instead of dogs. As many dogs spend their lives surrounded by people, it is not really surprising that dogs sometimes get confused as to whether they are dogs or people when it comes to reproductive behavior.

Most of a puppy's socialization occurs when it is between five and fourteen weeks old. During this period, dogs learn their social response towards dogs, humans and any other animals with which they have contact. It is also likely that a dog develops its future sexual preferences during this period.

Therefore a dog that is removed from its parents at a very early age, say about five weeks, and is then brought up only with people, may become so strongly socialized towards people that it believes these, rather than other dogs, are its potential sexual partners. This belief can reveal itself in more than one way. It is quite common for dogs, male or female, to refuse to mate with other dogs. Sometimes the dog is put off by what it regards as an unpleasant experience, but frequently such dogs do not appear even to recognize other dogs as potential partners.

A more awkward problem is when the dog or bitch displays apparently aberrant sexual behavior towards people. A dog that tries to mount a person's leg can cause a great deal of embarrassment. Mounting of this kind is sometimes practiced by bitches as well. This may seem unnatural, but it is almost certainly the result of a frustrated response on behalf of a bitch who is not sufficiently socialized towards her own species to accept advances from a male dog.

This sort of behavior tends to be persistent, even in the face of disappointment, and difficult to cure because it comes naturally to the dog, who therefore may not readily respond to punishment. Even when attempts are made to avoid situations where the dog can behave in this way, the tendency is not extinguished, but lies latent until the right stimulus presents itself.

These factors make sexual problems more difficult than most other kinds of problem, but conditioning may sometimes succeed. An alternative is to consult a veterinary surgeon who may be able to help in one of two ways: either by castrating a male, after which sexual behavior will decline rapidly; or by prescribing a hormone preparation, although this may be a temporary rather than a permanent solution.

The option with the best long-term chance of success may well be to try and help by bringing the dog into contact with others of its own species. Most sexual problems occur with single pet dogs; greatly increased contact with other dogs may help to heighten a dog's – even an older dog's – awareness of his own species, and so may cure or alleviate the problem.

Left: Unlike these puppies, single pet dogs are more likely to develop sexual problems and regard the humans they live with as potential sexual partners.

DOG IN A MANGER

Right: When two dogs share the same home, they will come to develop a dominance relationship between themselves and should get on well. Play can turn to fighting between pets when an established relationship changes, perhaps through illness or when a younger dog grows to assert itself.

When two pet dogs have been brought up together from puppyhood, they generally very likely to get on together extremely well. Problems are more likely to arise when a dog is brought into a house where another dog is already in residence. More often than not, no conflict will occur at all that the owner will notice and, when it does, it will generally be resolved without too much difficulty.

When there are two or more pet dogs in the same home, they will always develop a dominance relationship among themselves, which may or may not be readily apparent to the owner. If there is a stable dominance relationship, the two or more dogs will all live peaceably together. However, any change in this relationship – caused, for example, as a result of illness in an older dog or a younger puppy's increased assertiveness – will almost always result in conflict between the dogs. Sometimes they owner will not even notice this, because it will all be over very quickly, perhaps in one brief encounter. At other times there may be a long power struggle with frequent fighting.

A change in dominance relationship can occur for many reasons. Where there is an older dog already in residence and a new puppy of a larger breed is brought in, a problem will very likely arise when the younger dog grows up, because at some stage it will almost certainly try to take over the top position. This is likely to be resisted by the previous top dog, and there can be a prolonged canine equivalent to a power struggle, with frequent fighting, growling, or competition over food and prized objects.

If a top dog suffers a minor illness or injury then there could be a change in dominance between it and other dogs, but this may not even be apparent to the owner, although it will be extremely clear to the underdog.

A natural dominance relationship between two dogs can easily be upset by the attitude of the owner. The owner may seem to favor the older dog rather than the newcomer, or the smaller dog rather than the larger. Showing any such preference often takes the form of favoring the underdog.

Unfortunately, dogs do not view things in this way because, in their hierarchy, the upper dog should always have precedence over the lower one and should always receive more attention from the individual ranking above it, namely the owner. If the owner favors the underdog when the top dog is present, the latter will view this as "insubordination" on the part of the underdog, and may well threaten, or even attack him in the owner's presence. Many owners misunderstand such behavior and may attempt to resolve the situation by protecting the underdog or scolding the dominant dog, but this in fact does not have the result that the owner intends. If this occurs, the dominant dog is likely to feel compelled to attack the other dog to maintain its dominance, even when the owner is there and the other dog knows it is being protected.

Below: Where only one dog is kept as a pet, it may try to assert itself against people or other pets – although the relationship may be very playful, as here.

PACK ORDER

● The owner may be unaware of the established pack order between pet dogs, favoring the underdog – the smaller, older or weaker.

● This will upset the natural order, causing the dominant dog to defend its position by attacking the favorite.

● The owner should show affection to the dominant dog. The position of both dogs will be defined, the hierarchy accepted.

It is indeed difficult for owners, but in these circumstances they should try to reassure, and show affection for, the dominant dog rather than the underdog. This is, in fact, best for both dogs because otherwise the fighting may continue almost indefinitely. Also, by emphasizing the dominance hierarchy of the owner, dominant dog and underdog, a situation is established which all, especially the dogs, can readily accept. Even the underdog will be happier to know exactly what it can, or cannot, do, instead of having to rely on the protection of the owner or to be left in uncertainty. Confusion in the underdog, if left unchecked, may well lead to further behavioral problems in the longer term.

THE EARLY STAGES

Dogs, like babies, are creatures of routine, and like to establish a fixed pattern for mealtimes and other activities, that reassures them in their new home and lifestyle.

What sort of training will my puppy need?
Training is often seen as a rather one-sided activity; that of imposing the owner's will on that of a dog. In fact, training can be valuable to both dog and owner. A dog that will stay on command is less likely than an untrained dog to dash wildly across the road into the path of oncoming traffic. It will not harass animals in a field when out for a walk and is therefore unlikely to be shot by a farmer. Training also serves to emphasize the relationship between the parties involved. Dogs, being pack animals, look to their leader, and firm training, particularly of the more dominant breeds, will prevent behavioral problems later in life as the dog will have learned to recognize its subordinate role and not challenge its owner's position. To get maximum enjoyment from dog ownership, therefore, you must train your dog well from the outset. Young dogs are most responsive to training; this can begin as soon as the puppy enters the home.

There are certain basic behavioral requirements that the dog must learn. It must obviously be housebroken and should be taught to ask to go outside when it wants to relieve itself. Within the home, it must learn not to damage furnishings or jump on beds. The young dog must respond to its name and allow items such as bones to be taken away without any form of resentment being shown. It must come to recognize other members of the family and show no aggression toward them or toward welcomed visitors.

Out of doors, the young dog must return when called, walk properly on a leash without pulling, and stay and sit when told to do so. It should not jump up on people, go into fields where there are other animals, especially sheep, or foul sidewalks. Overall, training will have been successful only if the dog responds without hesitation.

What basic training should I give my puppy?
Successful training depends to a large extent on repetition and praise when a command is carried out correctly. To start with, call the puppy by its name at mealtimes, and occasionally at other times of the day, rewarding it first with a piece of food when it comes. The young dog soon associates the sound of its name with either food or affection, and responds accordingly. Never tease the puppy with food if it fails to act as requested. This particularly applies to the command "sit." The sitting posture is a relatively natural position, and the puppy, having responded to its name, can then be encouraged to sit and stay while the food bowl is placed in front of it.

The most important basic training during the early stages of the puppy's life is housebreaking. Dogs are naturally clean animals and do not soil their quarters as a general rule. They tend to relieve themselves in specific areas delineated by scent. This can lead to conflict in the domestic environment, however, because a puppy, having soiled a rug once, will then be attracted by its scent and return. It is vital that an area that has been dirtied be both cleaned up thoroughly and left completely free of scent. Various preparations for this purpose are sold in pet stores. White vinegar is also useful, as is bleach on a suitable floor (though it must be appropriately diluted). Accidents can be prevented by watching the puppy for the tell-tale signs, which are often apparent after a meal or when the young dog awakes. It will search for a suitable spot, sniffing the floor beforehand.

Always take the puppy outdoors into the yard, in good weather, or to a tray or box. Choose an area outside which will not become excessively muddy and is not part of the lawn, as the acidity in canine urine can kill grass over a period of time. If an accident does occur inside, there is no point in punishing the puppy unless it is actually caught in the act. It will not comprehend the reason for such treatment later. When the puppy is seen soiling a rug, speak to it harshly and smack it with the hand on its hindquarters firmly but not excessively hard. Never hit a dog around the head; this can cause physical injury and will encourage the dog to bite.

When training a dog, always be firm and consistent. This will give the best results because the dog will soon come to understand what it can and cannot do. Do not allow it to jump and sleep on chairs as a young dog, for example, and then attempt to prevent it clambering on the furniture when it has grown up. Try to be positive in your approach, encouraging your pet as far as possible, rather than scolding it if it fails to respond or disobeys. Dogs are usually keen to please their owners, and this trait should be uppermost in the trainer's mind. If a puppy starts jumping on you, place it firmly on the ground and say "no."

After a short period, it will realize that such behavior is not permitted, and stop doing it.

I realize that I can't take my puppy outside into public places until it has been fully inoculated, but should I begin leash training beforehand?

It is certainly useful to start such training early so that the puppy is used to walking on the leash before being taken out for the first time. Choose a suitable collar and leash and begin walking the dog up and down along a fence so that it is effectively sandwiched between you and the barrier. This will prevent the puppy pulling away and encourage it to walk in a straight line. The puppy may nevertheless try to pull ahead. If so, encourage it to adopt the correct position by stopping, saying "heel" and placing it in the correct position. These early sessions should be quite short, about ten minutes or so in length, and simply serve to get the puppy used to the restraining effect of the lead. Variations can also be introduced. Encourage the puppy to "sit" while on the leash, and to "stay," giving the commands clearly with the dog's name attached so it will learn to associate these commands with itself. Try to make training sessions fun for the dog. Do not get annoyed if it fails to respond immediately as it will probably be confused. Remember, that a happy dog will become a receptive, responsive and affectionate dog.

LEAD TRAINING

- Walking to heel is taught by holding a light lead in your right hand, with the puppy on your left-hand side (1). Call the puppy if it tries to pull ahead, using an authoritative, consistent command such as "heel". If he continues to pull forward, jerk the lead firmly back (2).

- Sit and stay training is the next stage. First, make your puppy sit in one spot, raise the lead above its head and circle him slowly, repeating the "stay" command (3). Then walk away, just a lead length, and if the puppy stays in the same position, return to it and give plenty of praise. If it disobeys, return him to the original sitting spot, push him into the sit position, and give the "stay" command (4) repeatedly until he learns to obey.

- A puppy learns to be recalled by hearing its name followed by a vocal "come" command, from the sit position, while still on the lead. If it doesn't respond or hesitates, jerk the leash simultaneously to your command (5). If the puppy rushes up to you and jumps up, push it away, and begin again (6).

- Profuse praise is important at the end of each training session. Remember that your puppy's powers of concentration will begin to wane after about ten minutes or so. Having learned these basic commands instantly, go on to teaching your puppy to respond in the same way without the lead.

DOGS' DENTITION

• The jaw shape of dogs is quite variable, but the pattern of dentition tends to be constant. In breeds with narrow muzzles, there is a tendency for the incisors to become squashed together, whereas in broad-muzzled dogs like the Bulldog, there may be an undesirable gap between these teeth. The characteristic sharp and pointed canines are used for seizing and killing prey in wild dogs. They also assist in tearing meat into pieces, which tend to be swallowed whole rather than chewed, which is why, dogs appear to bolt their food. This is usual behavior and need not be a cause for concern.

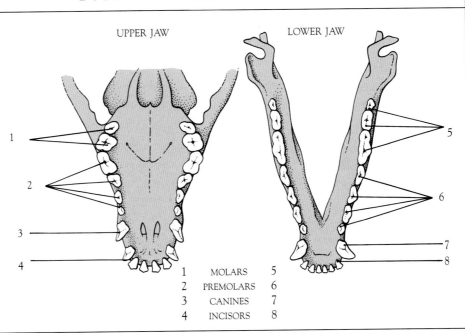

UPPER JAW   LOWER JAW

1	MOLARS	5
2	PREMOLARS	6
3	CANINES	7
4	INCISORS	8

I'm not sure how to choose my veterinarian. How should I set about this?

If you are obtaining your puppy locally, the breeder concerned may recommend his own veterinarian. Or ask dog-owning friends whom they use. The other option is simply to choose the veterinary practice nearest your home. This can be most convenient, particularly in an urban area where the practice is almost certainly going to have a "small animal" bias as distinct from veterinarians who treat mainly farmstock and horses, popularly regarded as "large animals". As all veterinarians undergo comprehensive training, there is no need to worry about their competence with dogs, even if you have to call upon a large animal practice in an emergency. Nevertheless, it is likely that small animal clinicians will have more specialized equipment at their disposal, and this will save the need for a referral in some instances to another veterinarian. Veterinary hospitals may have additional facilities, but all practices are able to hospitalize patients in their care, even if an initial consultation takes place at a branch office.

Always telephone ahead, if possible, to find out details of office hours, and make an appointment if required, making sure to tell the receptionist that you are a new client. Be sure to arrive promptly, and be tolerant if you are kept waiting. Emergencies do happen, and these can delay appointments in even the most efficient practices. An early check-up, at the time of the puppy's inoculation, or before if you are concerned for any reason, is to be recommended. A veterinarian will be able to give your puppy a basic clinical examination and may discover a problem that both you and the breeder were not aware of, such as a congenital heart defect. Although rare, a disorder of this type is clearly best detected early in life before later signs become apparent. It is also a useful time to ask any questions that are worrying you about your new pet. Do not hesitate to write them down beforehand; in the heat of the moment, they can be easily forgotten.

Medical insurance for animals is available, and some veterinarians have proposal forms available. Details can also be obtained via the various dog periodicals – usually in the advertisement columns. As the cost of treatment for a dog involved in a road traffic accident can be high, it may well be worth taking out insurance. But, as always, read the small print carefully and pay particular attention to the various exclusions. Routine veterinary care, such as inoculations and neutering, are not covered. An additional bonus of some schemes is that they also afford cover against third party claims, which is well worth considering. It is possible for the owner of a dog to be sued if, for example, the dog causes an accident or bites a visitor, and clearly, under certain circumstances, damages could be very high.

My puppy is now six months old, and chewing ferociously. How much longer will it be before the teething phase is passed?

Dogs have a full set of permanent teeth by the age of seven months, so you should be through the worst of it by now! The upper incisors are pushed out at about 14 weeks of age, as the permanent teeth erupt. The lower incisors are changed several weeks later, and the canines also at about 18 weeks. There are normally 28 deciduous teeth, and 42 permanent teeth. If you have a dog of one of the brachycephalic or "short-haired" breeds, such as the Bulldog, you may notice that the teeth are rather tightly spaced in the reduced dimensions of the jaw. In some dogs such as Chihuahuas the deciduous teeth are not always shed properly and may remain in the jaw alongside permanent teeth. If this appears to be the case, consult a veterinarian. He or she will be able to remove the deciduous teeth, under an anesthetic if necessary.

I am concerned about inoculations for my puppy. What vaccines will it need?

The vaccinations most often given are for rabies, leptospirosis, distemper, infectious hepatitis, kennel cough and parvovirus. These are all serious diseases, and the protection afforded by inoculation is highly recommended.

Many vaccines now available offer protection against a number of these diseases in a single injection. In the case of puppies, it is usual to give two injections at the ages of eight and twelve weeks followed by annual "boosters" to maintain immunity. This system follows the protection provided to puppies early in life by their mother's milk, specifically the portion known as colostrum which is produced for a short period immediately after the birth of the puppies. In the human child, protective antibodies against infections early in life are passed via the placental connection before birth. But this route is of very little significance in the dog, and antibodies are passed via the colostrum. These specific proteins are not digested but absorbed into the young dog's body.

It is difficult to know precisely when the maternal antibodies have disappeared. As the puppy's own immune system starts to function to protect it from infection, so the level of the antibodies from the colostrum declines. In some cases – depending on the quantity of colostrum consumed by the individual puppies – the maternal antibodies may have disappeared even before eight weeks of age (the usual time of the first injections), but this is generally the shortest time they will be effective.

KINDS OF BITE

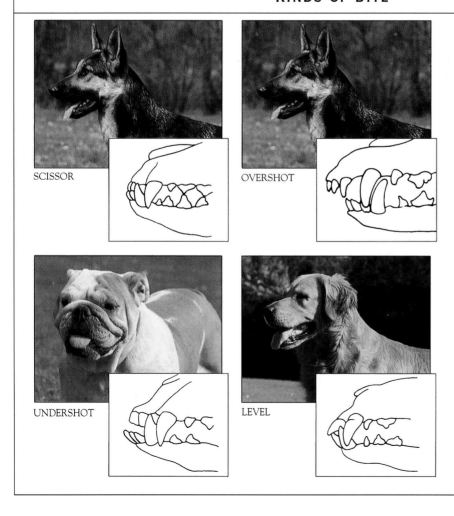

SCISSOR

OVERSHOT

UNDERSHOT

LEVEL

- Selective breeding for looks has tended to emphasize differences in the arrangement of the upper and lower jaws and has resulted in much less effective jaws and teeth in some dogs. The German Shepherd Dog has been bred to ideally have a scissor-like bite (1) and a slightly longer, overshot jaw (2). An undershot jaw in this breed is considered a serious fault, leading to disqualification in the show ring. In the Bulldog, Pekingese and other short-faced breeds, the jaws have become so squashed that there may be no room for some of the teeth and the bite is referred to as undershot (3). In fact, some Bulldogs cannot hunt at all because their bite has become so distorted. The show standard for the Golden Retriever demands a level bite (4). Clearly, any pronounced abnormalities can give rise to difficulty in eating.

BREEDING DOGS

BREEDING DOGS

Breeding dogs must never be undertaken haphazardly or irresponsibly. There are many factors to be considered and complex procedures to be followed.

Right: Dogs readily detect a bitch in heat and will congregate around her, even if she is not in the receptive phase of the cycle – oestrus. During the pro-oestrus part of the cycle, the vulva swells and there is a bloody discharge from the vagina. This normally lasts about nine days.

THE REPRODUCTIVE CYCLE

Male

The onset of maturity, known as puberty, occurs form the age of six months onwards in male dogs, although this varies to some extent from breed to breed. As a general rule, males attain puberty at a slightly later age than bitches of the same breed, with certain exceptions in whom such as the Beagle, the situation is reversed. This delay is usually a matter of weeks, but can extend to months in a few breeds such as the Saluki and Chow Chow.

Dogs should only be allowed to breed after the age of one year, to ensure maximum fertility. They can mate all the year round and will remain sexually competent though progressively less fertile. Stud dogs should not be mated too frequently, as this will cause a temporary decline in fertility.

Female

The bitch has distinct sexual cycles, resulting in periods of oestrus. These "seasons" or "heats" may be noticed from the age of six months onwards, but certain breeds are much slower to mature, and may not begin their cycles until the age of 18 months. Oestrus occurs every seven or eight months on average, but intervals anywhere between two and 18 months are not unknown. The size of the dog has no particular effect on the length of oestrus cycles, nor does the time of year appear to have much bearing, though it is thought that climate may be significant.

There are four recognized stages in the oestrus cycle of a bitch. The first is the pro-oestrus stage, when the vulva swells and a bloody discharge is seen from the vagina. This occurs before ovulation and is in no way equivalent to the menstruation of female humans and primates (Menstruation does not take place in female dogs). Dogs will be attracted to bitches during pro-oestrus, but their advances will not be reciprocated; although a pair may play together, any attempt at mounting by the male will be rebuffed by the female. Restlessness often accompanies this phase, which lasts an average of nine days, although it can range from two to 27 days.

The next stage is the oestrus stage, or sexual receptivity. The bloody discharge will become clear, and the bitch will allow mating to take place. Again, this period of the cycle extends over about nine days, but may be as short as three days or continue for three weeks. The release of ova from the ovaries – ovulation – usually occurs approximately two days after the start of oestrus.

In the following two or three months, the hormone progesterone controls the reproductive tract, whether the bitch is pregnant or not, and this period is known as dioestrus. During this phase a pseudo pregnancy may occur.

The longest stage of the cycle is anoestrus, when there is no sexual activity apparent, and this lasts until pro-oestrus next occurs. Bitches will normally continue to come on heat into old age and will remain fertile.

SOME MAJOR INHERITED AND CONGENITAL DISORDERS

Disorder	Observations	Breeds typically affected	
Clefts of lip and palate	May be hereditary in origin, but other factors, such as a nutritional deficiency in the bitch, may also be responsible.	American Cocker Spaniel American Staffordshire Terrier Beagle Bernese Mountain Dog Boston Terrier	Bulldog Dachshund German Shepherd Dog Shih Tzu
Deafness	Dog often appears unresponsive, even stupid, until this disorder is recognized.	American Foxhound Bull Terrier Collie Dachshund	English Foxhound Great Dane Scottish Terrier
Distichiasis	A double row of eyelashes; most common on upper lids. Causes severe irritation and excessive tear production. Surgery is the only effective treatment in the long-term.	American Cocker Spaniel Bedington Terrier Boston Terrier Boxer	Giffon Bruxellois Kerry Blue Terrier Lakeland Terrier Yorkshire Terrier
Ectropion	Eyelids directed outwards. Causes inflammation of the conjunctiva and cornea, with increased tear production. Needs to be corrected by surgery.	American Cocker Spaniel Bassett Hound Bloodhound	Bulldog Clumber Spaniel St Bernard
Entropion	Eyelids directed inwards, more commonly the lower lids. Eyelashes cause severe irritation of the cornea, with increased tear production. Again, requires surgical treatment.	Bloodhound Bulldog Chesapeake Bay Retriever Chow Chow	Irish Setter Labrador Retriever Rottweiler St Bernard
Hip dysplasia	Deformed hip (cox-femoral) joints. Signs extremely variable: lameness in severe cases, yet may pass unnoticed in a mild case. Detected by radiography. Inherited, hence the need to check potential breeding stock for this weakness.	American Cocker Spaniel Black and Tan Coonhound English Setter German Shepherd Dog	Giant Schnauzer Shetland Sheepdog
Intervertebral disc abnormalities	Symptoms influenced by locality of abnormality, as is the prognosis for treatment. Total, confined rest is essential for recovery, irrespective of other therapy. Surgery can be of assistance in some cases.	American Cocker Spaniel Beagle Boxer Dachshund	Dandie Dinmont Terrier Pekingese
Luxating patella	Results in lameness, typically about five months of age. Caused by movement of "knee bone" or patella. Degree of weakness variable. Surgical correction is the only treatment.	Boston Terrier Bichon Frise Chihuahua	Pomeranian Yorkshire Terrier
Progressive retinal atrophy	The first sign may be that the dog appears to be having difficulty seeing at night. As its name suggests, this disease is progressive, and ultimately blindness will result. The time span may extend from months to years. It appears to be an inherited condition, different forms of PRA are believed to be inherited in different ways, so it can be either a dominant or recessive trait.	Border Collie English Cocker Spaniel English Springer Spaniel Golden Retriever Gordon Setter Labrador Retriever Norwegian Elkhound	Pekingese Pointer Pomeranian Poodle Samyoed Shetland Sheepdog Welsh Corgi
Umbilical hernia	Distinct, noticeable swelling around the umbilicus or "belly-button", resulting from a partial protrusion of the abdominal contents. Can be corrected by surgery if necessary.	Basenji Bull Terrier Collie	Pekingese Pointer Weimaraner

MALE AND FEMALE REPRODUCTIVE ORGANS

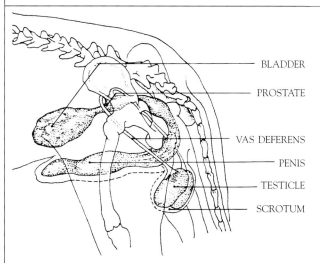

BLADDER

PROSTATE

VAS DEFERENS

PENIS

TESTICLE

SCROTUM

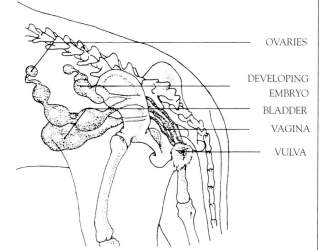

OVARIES

DEVELOPING
EMBRYO
BLADDER

VAGINA

VULVA

- The testicles are situated in the scrotum and they can vary greatly in size, according to breed. The spermatazoa and the male sex hormone testosterone are produced in the testicles, under the influence of the pituitary gland and various hormones. The distance of the testicles from the body can be muscularly regulated, which also serves as a thermoregulatory mechanism. Males remain sexually active into old age, although their fertlity declines.

- The ovaries in the bitch are located in the dorsal part of the abdominal cavity, near to the kidneys, at about the third or fourth lumber vertebra. The actual overyis about half an inch long and the shape of the lima bean – its size increases during the pro-oestrus phase, reaching its maximum at about the time of ovulation. The fallopian tube connects the overy with the uterine horns which are long and elliptical and unite caudally, forming the uterine body.

BREEDING

The choice of a mate for the bitch will be influenced by the purpose for which the puppies are required. Bloodlines are important for those who wish to exhibit, but the pet breeder is unlikely to worry about the finer points of a stud dog. Once the stud dog has been chosen, the owner of the dog should be approached well in advance of the anticipated date of mating, to make sure the stud will be available, and to ascertain the fee. As an alternative to payment, some owners will accept first choice of a puppy from the litter, especially if the bitch has a good pedigree.

It is a good idea to make an appointment to visit kennels and see the stud dog in advance. Ideally, it should excel in those points which are relatively poor in the bitch, so that it complements, rather than reinforces, her strengths and weaknesses. Before mating, the bitch should be given a booster vaccination to ensure that a high level of immunity will be passed to the puppies. Once pregnant, the bitch must not receive live vaccines, as these are extremely dangerous to the puppies. Both the bitch and stud dog should be checked for potential defects, such as hip dysplasia.

Establishing what is the best time for mating during the oestrus period can be difficult. The owner of the stud dog may be prepared to board the bitch for a short period, to ensure the maximum chance of a successful union. The right time is usually about ten days after the start of pro-oestrus, but again this can be variable. No increase in body temperature accompanies ovulation as it does in humans, and the only clinical test of value is examination of vaginal smears under a microscope to detect the characteristic changes in the cells.

Mating will probably take place twice, under controlled conditions, over the four-day period from the tenth day onwards. The reaction of the bitch to the dog should be monitored frequently. When ready to mate, she will stand with tail erect, over to one side.

Copulation is a protracted process. The male mounts the female, gripping with the forelimbs and, once penetration has taken place, the tip of the penis swells. The muscles of the vagina contract around the penis, holding it tightly in place, so that withdrawal is not possible. In male dogs there is a bone, known as the os penis, inside the penis, which helps to maintain its rigidity while it is lodged in the vagina. "Tying" or locking does not occur in every case, nor is it essential for fertilization.

The dogs remain joined together for about 20 minutes or so, rarely longer than three-

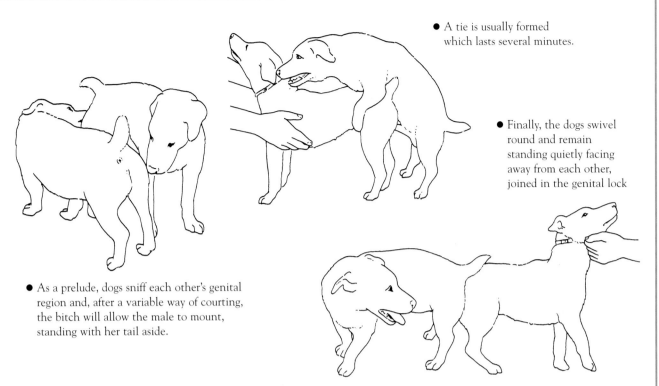

● A tie is usually formed which lasts several minutes.

● Finally, the dogs swivel round and remain standing quietly facing away from each other, joined in the genital lock

● As a prelude, dogs sniff each other's genital region and, after a variable way of courting, the bitch will allow the male to mount, standing with her tail aside.

quarters of an hour. The semen is ejaculated early during the tie, following the secretions produced by the urethral glands, and the dogs then alter their positions, so they face in opposite directions. Further ejaculation of prostate gland secretions helps to nourish the spermatozoa, and increase the chances of fertilization. A certain amount of struggling by the bitch is normal, but the tie will remain intact. Trying to break a tie can result in injuries to one or both partners. If the liaison is undesired, subsequent treatment to prevent implantation of any fertilized eggs is recommended as an alternative.

A bitchcan be artificially inseminated, using semen from a dog in another part of the country or even further afield, if permission is granted by the governing canine authority. As rabies can be transmitted by semen, its movement from country to country is often controlled strictly by licence. Fresh canine semen can be kept viable for nearly a week, or it can be frozen indefinitely. Tests will be required to ensure that the bitch is in the oestrus phase, and ready to mate. The semen is carefully introduced, using a pipette, and the bitch's hindquarters are kept raised, so that none flows back from the cervical region where it was deposited and out of the vagina. A gloved finger is then inserted for about five minutes into the vagina, to mimic the effect of the tie: this is supposed to improve fertility.

Above: Mating in dogs is usually supervised, certainly with a stud. Some ailments can be transmitted by sexual contact between dogs, notably the canine venereal tumour and brucellosis. Any signs of abnormal swelling should be reported to a veterinarian without delay.

THE BULBOUS URETHRA

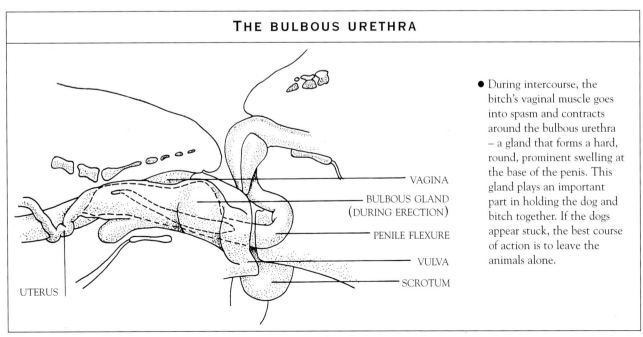

VAGINA

BULBOUS GLAND (DURING ERECTION)

PENILE FLEXURE

VULVA

SCROTUM

UTERUS

● During intercourse, the bitch's vaginal muscle goes into spasm and contracts around the bulbous urethra – a gland that forms a hard, round, prominent swelling at the base of the penis. This gland plays an important part in holding the dog and bitch together. If the dogs appear stuck, the best course of action is to leave the animals alone.

PREGNANCY

There are three major phases of pregnancy. First, the fertilized egg or eggs spend their early life in the uterus, and then implant into the wall. The placenta, which is responsible for nourishing the developing embryo and removing waste products, then develops, and the organs start to form. The major phase of growth takes place in the final part of pregnancy, from day 33 onwards. The gestation period lasts about 63 days in total, but breed variations of about a week are not uncommon. Any puppies born more than a week premature are unlikely to survive.

Pregnancy may not be apparent during the first month after mating, although a veterinarian can give an indication about four and a half weeks after mating. Such examinations have to be carried out carefully to prevent any damage to the developing puppies. Obesity, or well-developed abdominal musculature, complicates the task. Some bitches also tense their abdomens, making palpation impossible. The time of examination is quite vital; after five weeks, it is much harder

to detect pregnancy by this means, as the foetuses grow and feel like abdominal organs. By six weeks, abdominal distension is likely to be evident, in bitches which have not given birth before. The teats will become more conspicuous, and will turn pink if the skin is unpigmented, because of the increase in blood flow to the region. A day or so before birth, some clear fluid or milk may be apparent.

A recent innovation in the field of pregnancy detection is the use of ultra-sound machines, which can be divided into two categories, depending on their mode of action. Those of A-mode are quite reliable from about four-and-a-half weeks onwards, whereas Doppler machines can be used five weeks after mating. It is also possible to detect the foetuses on radiographs from the seventh week as their developing skeletons will contain sufficient calcium by this stage. Routine radiological examinations are not carried out, however, as unnecessary exposure to radiation must be avoided if at all possible, as it can cause malformations in the foetuses.

EMBRYOLOGY

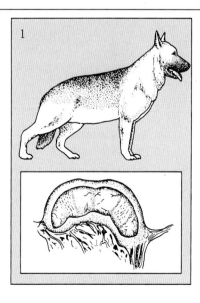

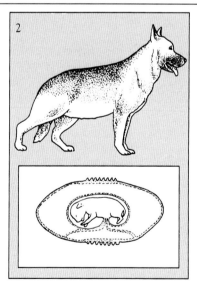

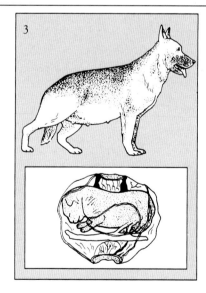

● Signs of pregnancy will not be apparent until about the fifth week. After fertilization, the egg becomes a zygote – a mass of dividing cells (1). The zygote implants into the uterine wall, and here the puppies develop, forming a placental connection with the mother.

● The bitch becomes progressively heavier and, by the fifth or sixth week her nipples and abdomen begin to swell. The embryo continues to develop, with the body organs being formed first. By the 35th day the head and limbs are formed and the external sex organs can be differentiated (2).

● As parturition approaches, the nipples become swollen and turgid, sometimes secreting milk, and the abnormal swelling is typically pear-shaped. By the 55th day (3), fetal movement becomes visible in the flank of the bitch. The embryo is fully developed, complete with body hair and color markings.

BIRTH

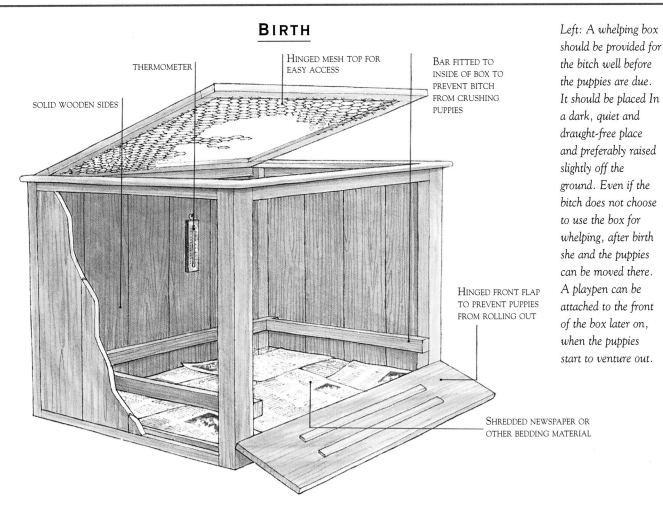

THERMOMETER

HINGED MESH TOP FOR EASY ACCESS

BAR FITTED TO INSIDE OF BOX TO PREVENT BITCH FROM CRUSHING PUPPIES

SOLID WOODEN SIDES

HINGED FRONT FLAP TO PREVENT PUPPIES FROM ROLLING OUT

SHREDDED NEWSPAPER OR OTHER BEDDING MATERIAL

Left: A whelping box should be provided for the bitch well before the puppies are due. It should be placed In a dark, quiet and draught-free place and preferably raised slightly off the ground. Even if the bitch does not choose to use the box for whelping, after birth she and the puppies can be moved there. A playpen can be attached to the front of the box later on, when the puppies start to venture out.

Preparation

A suitable box where the bitch can give birth will be necessary and should be placed in a quiet, warm part of the home, such as a spare room. The size of the box will depend on the bitch: it must be large enough to allow her to lie full length without difficulty. Whelping boxes are often made of either wood or cardboard. The bitch must have easy access, though the sides must not be so low that the puppies could roll or be pushed out. It is also useful to have a bar fitted inside the box around the sides so that the bitch does not accidentally lie on her puppies and kill them. The box should be lined with newspapers, rather than blanketing, as these can be replaced easily, can be torn up to make a nest, and are less likely to hide any puppies. The bitch should be encouraged to sleep in the bed for the last 10 to 14 days of pregnancy. She will not need much extra care for the majority of the gestation period. Exercise in moderation will help to keep a healthy muscle tone, but she should not be encouraged to jump at all, particularly in the latter stages. From the fourth week onwards, increased amounts of protein will be required. This extra food is best given in the form of an additional meal, as the expanding uterus will compress the stomach and reduce its capacity.

About four weeks before the birth is expected a veterinarian will provide the necessary tablets for worming the bitch, and advise on the need for dietary supplements. Beware that overdosing such tablets can have serious side-effects. On a balanced diet, little if any supplementation is strictly necessary. In the last few days of pregnancy, pressure from the uterus can result in constipation and if required, up to three teaspoonfuls of medicinal liquid paraffin can be added to the food.

Labor

The first stage of labor is characterized by restlessness. The bitch may cry out occasionally because of uterine contractions, and may tear up bedding. In order to facilitate birth, ligaments along the vertebral column slacken, and the pelvic bones become more obvious. Loss of appetite is fairly typical about a day before birth takes place, and a fall in body temperature, to about 99.5°F (37.5°C) lower, from the normal 101.5°F (38.5°C) is an indication that birth is imminent. A clear discharge will be apparent from the vulva, and the bitch will spend considerable time licking and cleaning this area. This stage lasts for a day, or possibly slightly longer in the case of a bitch giving birth for the first time. It is important that the bitch is kept quiet, with the

Above: As here, puppies are normally born head-first (1). It may take several minutes for a puppy to emerge fully (2). The bitch will pass the placenta within quarter of an hour or so after each puppy is born (3) and the puppies will begin suckling almost immediately (4).

minimum of disturbance, although food and water should be at hand if she wants them.

At the the second stage of labor, abdominal contractions, panting and straining will occur. The vulval discharge will become more noticeable, and the first sign of a puppy is likely to be the appearance of its enveloping water bag. This sac can rupture during labor, causing the fluid to pour out, or else it will be broken normally by the bitch once it emerges from the vulva. The umbilical cord connecting the puppy to its placenta will also be bitten through.

Finally, the bitch will pass the placenta or afterbirth within a quarter of an hour of the birth of the puppy. The bitch may eat the afterbirth but, if not, it should be removed and flushed down a toilet. One placenta should be voided for each puppy and it is important to keep a check on the number since they are sometimes retained, causing an infection in the uterus later. They are normally green in color, and this is not a sing of infection as a general rule.

Puppies are normally born at intervals of 15 to 30 minutes. In small litters, the gap between puppies may be longer, extending up to an hour or so. The whole litter should be born within about six hours from the onset of a second stage of labor, but in a few instances, a longer period of time may elapse.

General assistance

If the bitch fails to break the water bag of a puppy, carry this out for her, so the puppy can breathe. Make sure your hands are clean, then break through the membranes with the fingers and lift the puppy out. Hold its head slightly lower than the rest of the body to drain fluid forward, insert a finger in its mouth to stimulate breathing and check its nose is clean. The young dog can be dried gently with a towel which will also encourage it to breathe. Once the puppy is breathing satisfactorily, place it back with the bitch.

If the bitch has not bitten through the umbilical cord, do this by hand. Cutting rather than tearing the cord reduces the risk of injury, although blood loss is likely. Tie a piece of string tightly about 2in (5cm) from the puppy's body, then snip the cord with scissors on the side of the ligature closest to the placenta, leaving the tie in place. The remaining stump soon shrivels up and ultimately sloughs off naturally. It can be dabbed with iodine to minimize the risk of infection.

Problems during birth

Although no problems should arise during the birth process, there are certain serious conditions that require urgent veterinary attention. Notify the veterinarian of the expected date for the arrival of the puppies, particularly if difficulties have been encountered with the bitch before.

One problem is when the bitch goes into labor, yet produces no puppies. This is most likely to occur with individuals or small breeds expecting a large litter. If puppies do not begin to appear within two hours of the start of obvious uterine contractions, or if more than an hour elapses between births, call a veterinarian. If a puppy becomes stuck half way out of the birth canal, oxygen starvation may damage its brain irreversibly within five minutes or so. A veterinarian will be able to advise an owner on the best course of action in such an emergency.

Difficulties can also occur if the pelvic canal is relatively small or a puppy's head particularly large. Difficulties over the positioning of the puppy, or presentation, can be a source of concern. Puppies are normally born head first, but in some cases, reverse or breech presentations do occur. In such cases, a Caesarean section may have to be performed.

Sadly, some puppies may appear malformed at birth, or shortly afterwards. The first sign of a cleft palate, for example, is usually milk running back down the nose. Another highly unpleasant congenital defect is hydrocephalus. The skull of affected puppies is abnormally domed, and filled with fluid. Young dogs showing serious malformations usually do not live long, but should be put down by a veterinarian at the earliest opportunity. Some defects are relatively minor, and will not handicap the puppy in any way, although it will not be suitable for exhibiting. Double dew claws in the majority of breeds, and even extra toes are included in this category.

Post-natal care

After giving birth, the bitch will settle down with her puppies, licking them contentedly. They should respond by suckling, normally within 30 minutes of being born. It is vital that the puppies take milk as early as possible, as the first portion, known as colostrum, contains protective antibodies that will help to give immunity against illness until the puppy's own defence system is fully operational. The amount of colostrum ingested directly determines how long this maternal protection will last. The protection declines progressively and will disappear by the time the puppy is 12 weeks old. During their first week of life, puppies feed about every two hours, sucking the nipple with the forelegs raised, while pushing hard against their dam's body with their hindlimbs, taking whichever teat is available.

The right environment is very important during the early part of the puppies' lives. They are dependent at first on the temperature of their surroundings, since they are not yet able to regulate their body temperatures in the same way as adult dogs. The room in which they are housed should therefore be at least 70°F (21°C). If additional heat is needed, an infra-red lamp can be obtained. It is vital that this is positioned in such a way that there is no risk of actually burning the puppies or their dam. Lights of this type are produced exclusively for use with livestock; some emit heat with a minimum light output. They must not be covered, because the heat generated can present a fire risk. An alternative is to use a low wattage heating pad, positioned in the basket under a sheet of newspaper. The running costs of such pads are minimal, even when they are left on constantly. A heating element spreads heat evenly over the surface of the pad when the puppies are in contact with it.

At first puppies normally sleep together in a group, to maintain their body temperature. They will not make any noise, apart from the occasional grunt. Crying is a sign that the puppies are hungry or cold. Their senses are very limited at this stage. Born blind, it will take perhaps a fortnight for their eyes to open, and three weeks before they can hear.

Diet

The bitch will require increasing quantities of food as the puppies grow. Three or four meals may be necessary, with the actual amount of food depending on the breed concerned. As a guide, about one and a half times as much food as usual should be offered in the first week of lactation, twice as much as during the second week. Subsequently, until the fifth week, at least three times the normal food intake will be required. It is vital that a balanced diet is offered throughout this period, to prevent abnormalities such as rickets.

An adequate intake of fluid is also essential for a lactating bitch, and will help to ensure that sufficient milk will be produced for the puppies. Apart from water, one of the milk replacement foods used for rearing orphaned puppies can be given directly to the bitch. These are preferable to cow's milk, which contains relatively low levels of fats and proteins and a high level of sugar.

Weaning

Weaning is a gradual process, which usually starts when the puppies are about three weeks old. A little lean mince, or one of the special puppy foods, can be given, softened with water beforehand. The bitch will begin to leave her

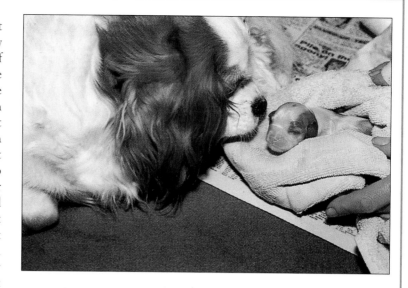

puppies for longer periods from three weeks onwards and the litter should be fed when she is not present. Puppies can be slow to feed themselves at first, and to tempt them, the food should be given on a flat saucer, which will make it easily accessible. It may be necessary to place a small amount on the puppies' tongues initially, until they acquire a taste for it. The puppies will take progressively more meat, and their dam will start to discourage them from suckling, as her milk production falls.

By the age of about six weeks, the puppies will be virtually independent, and will be acquiring their first, or deciduous, set of teeth. Once weaning is complete, they should be receiving four meals a day. The first and last meals of the day should be milk, perhaps with some soaked biscuit meal. Milk replacement foods mixed with water in the required quantity should be offered. The other two meals should consist of solid foods, given perhaps at midday and six o'clock in the evening. The use of a special canned puppy food, mixed with some fresh cooked items, is recommended. As the puppies get older, their meals can be gradually reduced in number, taking the milky foods out of the routine one at a time. By the age of six months, a young dog will be receiving two meals a day in increased amounts as it grows.

Above: Most bitches do not object to careful handling of their puppies, but disturbances should be kept to a minimum in the first few days.

Left: The puppies should be watched when they are suckling to ensure that all appear to be doing well.

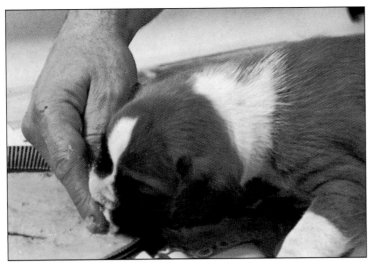

Above: Feeding puppies A puppy may need to be encouraged to feed on its own by offering it food on a finger. Most soon learn to eat from a dish, although it may be better to feed the puppies individually to ensure they all get an adequate share.

Rearing problems

Bitches very rarely harm their puppies, but it is safest to keep the sire of the litter away from them, even if he lives on the premises. The bitch will stay very close to the puppies for the first few days, and should not be disturbed unnecessarily. If, however, any teat appears sore and abnormally swollen, there may be a localized infection of the gland, known as mastitis. Veterinary advice must be sought without delay, and the teat should be covered to prevent puppies suckling from it. Antibiotic therapy will probably be required.

A particularly serious problem that occasionally occurs, is milk fever, also known as eclampsia. The most obvious signs are that the bitch becomes unsteady on her feet, neglects her puppies and loses her appetite. The condition results from a deficiency of calcium in the blood itself, and if not corrected, coma leading to death is inevitable. A veterinarian should be consulted as soon as symptoms become evident.

Eclampsia is one of the circumstances in which some or all puppies will have to be fostered or hand-reared, at least until the bitch recovers. If at all possible, try to transfer them to another bitch who has a smaller litter, or to a bitch that is already lactating, possibly after a pseudo pregnancy. A veterinarian may be able to suggest a suitable foster parent. When hand-rearing, use powdered milk replacements with special bottles and teats. It is worth obtaining a stock of such items before a bitch whelps, so that they are on hand for any emergency.

Hygiene is very important when rearing any young creature. Food should never be left standing, but mixed fresh before each feed. Any

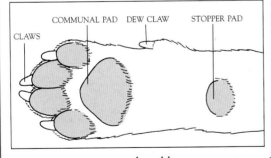

COMMUNAL PAD DEW CLAW STOPPER PAD
CLAWS

Above: Dew claws may be surgically removed when the dog is young to prevent problems later in life, as they are easily caught and torn.

stored in a refrigerator should be used within a day. Before feeding, check with a thermometer that the milk is warmed to about 100°F (38°C). It is vital not to rush a puppy that is being bottle-fed, as this increases the risk of choking. Any fluid that accidentally passes into the lungs may cause inhalation pneumonia. After feeding, the utensils used should be immersed in a proprietary product used for cleaning babies' bottles and then rinsed.

After each feed, the puppies' faces should be wiped with a cottonwool swab that has been moistened with warm water. Also rub he abdominal and anal regions with a clean swab, to mimic the dam's licking and stimulate the puppy to defecate and urinate after feeding.

Maintain the temperature of the puppies' environment carefully, reducing it gradually from about 85°F (30°C) in 5°F (2°C) stages from the end of the first week onwards.

Early surgery

There are a number of routine surgical procedures that are normally carried out early in a puppy's life.

The removal of a puppy's dew claws is a relatively minor operation if carried out in the first few days after birth. These claws, corresponding to the human thumbs and big toes, are vestigial in the dog, and serve no useful purpose. Only very few breeds must retain them in order to be exhibited. If the dew claws are not removed, particularly the hind claws, they often get caught up and torn quite seriously later in life.

A claw will bleed profusely if it is cut incorrectly, especially when inadequate tools are used for the task, and this will make the dog nervous of such treatment at a later date. Dew claws can also be removed on older dogs, but this is a more serious operation, which may have to be carried out if one is torn accidentally.

Tail docking was originally performed for practical reasons, to prevent hunting dogs being caught by their tails in thick undergrowth. Subsequently it has become fashionable just for show purposes. Approximately 45 breeds are required to be mutilated in this way. Breed standards specify the amount of tail which should remain. If such surgery is carried out, then a veterinarian will perform the task, using an anesthetic.

There are a number of other operations of a cosmetic nature which it is unethical for a veterinarian to perform on pedigree dogs, if these would disguise a fault which would be penalized under the show standards concerned. Obvious cases include alteration of ear and tail carriage.

REPRODUCTIVE DISORDERS

Diseases

Certain diseases are sexually transmitted in the dog. These include venereal tumors, which cause swellings close to, or on, the genitalia.

Infections acquired at the time of mating can lead to problems during pregnancy. A form of brucellosis, caused by *Brucell canis* was first identified in the US in 1966. The signs of infection are infertility in both sexes, or puppies being born dead or dying shortly after birth. In some cases of apparent infertility, the bitch may have actually conceived but the developing embryos died and were reabsorbed at an early stage. Abortion is also common, with a vaginal discharge being present for a long period afterwards. This discharge will be infectious, and the organism is likely to persist in the body for at least 18 months. Abortion is likely to occur again, if the bitch is mated again during this period.

The bacterium responsible for this disease can be present in aborted pups, as well as their dam. Like other forms of brucellosis, the canine type can be transmitted to humans, so protective clothing, including gloves, should be worn when dealing with dogs that might be infected. The signs of illness in humans are weakness, enlarged lymph nodes throughout the body and an accompanying fever, although generally this disease is less severe than brucellosis infections acquired from cattle.

Brucella canis is not the only cause of early death in puppies, and a variety of infectious causes can be implicated in the so-called "fading puppy syndrome". A dirty, cold environment is likely to lead to puppies dying early in life. Toxins produced by bacteria responsible for mastitis can be passed to puppies via contaminated milk and may prove lethal. Viruses can be implicated in some cases, with canine herpes virus being considered especially significant, partly because infection causes no apparent disease in older dogs, yet is invariably fatal to puppies under three weeks of age. Veterinary help must be sought urgently if a number of puppies are born dead, or die shortly afterwards. In breeding kennels, every effort should be made to keep the bitch and any surviving offspring isolated, especially from other pregnant dogs.

Contraceptives should not be confused with the various deodorant preparations which are marketed to disguise the bitch's output of pheromones – scents that attract male dogs. These deodorants have no actual contraceptive value. It must also be remembered that once a bitch has mated with a dog, this will not prevent her conceiving again if she mates with another dog shortly afterwards and both sets of puppies will be born in the same litter. This phenomenon is known as superfecundation.

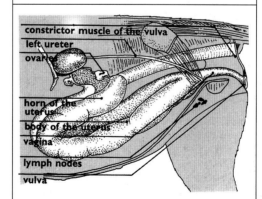

CASTRATION

- In castration, the testicles are removed by a single incision in the scrotum and the wound is then closed with a few external stitches. The operation is irreversible and is ideally carried out before the dog is sexually competent, yet sufficiently mature for surgery.

SPAYING

- This operation – an ovariohysterectomy – involves the removal of both the uterus and the ovaries. It is ideally performed in the period between heats (anestrus). The abdominal cavity has to be opened either at the flank or through the midline of the ventral surface. The wound heals quickly and stitches are normally removed about ten days afterwards.

When an unplanned mating is known to have taken place, it is possible to given an hormonal injection to ensure that conception does not occur. A veterinarian should be contacted at once to arrange this, as a delay can make such treatment worthless. A bitch that has mated with a dog of another breed or a mongrel will be able to conceive normally in the future. Research has been carried out into the possibility of reversible sterility by chemical means for a set period of time in male dogs, but no such treatments are yet available.

Neutering

The neutering operation (castration) is performed to decrease problems associated with male dogs, such as wandering and urinating in the home to leave their scent. The degree of success of this operation varies, but approximately 90 percent of male dogs show a decreased tendency to wander following castration. Mating behavior may persist if dogs have previously mated with bitches.

The risk of surgery is very slight but the operation is not reversible. The testes are removed via a single incision in the scrotum and the wound is then closed with a few external stitches. The best time for the operation is before the dog is sexually competent, yet sufficiently mature for surgery.

Both testes should have descended into the scrotum from the abdomen where they developed early in life, certainly by the time the puppy is six months old. In some breeds, there is an increased incidence of failure of one or both testes to descend normally. This condition is known as cryptorchidism and is potentially serious because a retained testis is very likely to become cancerous later in life, forming a sertoli cell tumor. Such dogs should always be castrated, with the testis being removed from the abdomen. They should not be used for breeding purposes, as this condition is likely to be inherited.

In the case of the female, neutering is referred to as spaying or, technically, as ovariohysterectomy, and involves the removal of both uterus and ovaries. Changes in behavior will be obvious and periods of heat will occur. Surgery is not normally carried out during a period of heat, or when a bitch is lactating. Ideally, the operation should be performed during anoestrus, although a case of pyometra will require immediate attention.

A bitch can be spayed either via the flank, through the midline of the ventral surface of the abdomen. The abdominal cavity has to be opened, but the wound will heal quickly and external stitches should be removed about 10 days after the operation. If the stitches break open before healing has begun, and if any of the abdominal contents, such as a loop of intestine, become evident through the incision, the veterinarian must be contacted without delay. The bitch should be kept quiet for several days after surgery, exercised on a lead and prevented from jumping if at all possible.

Once a dog of either sex has been neutered, it is very likely to start putting on weight, and its food intake must be reduced accordingly. Such dogs sometimes want less exercise as well, although they remain just as alert. The hair of neutered dogs can also become coarser, and it will take several months for hair to regrow fully over the site of the operation.

Pseudo pregnancy

This state is due to an ovarian disorder. Under normal circumstances, the corpora lutea, which form at the sites where eggs were released, produce the hormone progesterone for only a limited time. This hormone acts to ensure that the embryo implants successfully in the uterus, and also stimulates milk production. In cases of pseudo pregnancy, the corpora lutea persist, causing the typical signs of pregnancy six to eight weeks after oestrus. The effects can be variable in intensity. There can even be abdominal swelling as well as milk production. Behavioral changes are also likely. The bitch will attempt to make a nest, and adopt items such as slippers as part of the phantom litter. She is likely to be aggressive if such items are taken away.

Pseudo pregnancies often recur and will not necessarily be resolved by allowing the bitch to breed. Medication prescribed by a veterinarian will help to alleviate the symptoms if they become severe, but spaying is undoubtedly the best long-term solution.

Repeated pseudo pregnancies are also thought to make a bitch more prone to uterine infection, known as pyometra, later in life. Pyometra is first indicated by loss of appetite, and increased thirst and urination. Vomiting may also occur after drinking. If the condition is left untreated, the bitch will become increasingly weak and her abdomen will swell in size. A discharge from the vulva is likely to become evident. Pyometra is most common in bitches from the age of five years onwards, and follows a period of heat.

A veterinarian will be able to confirm a case of pyometra by radiography. Spaying will be necessary, although fluids may have to be given before surgery can be undertaken. As kidney failure can occur with pyometra, a period of convalescence under observation at the surgery is likely to be required.

Chemical control of the breeding cycle

To prevent a bitch in heat from breeding she must be kept isolated from other dogs and confined to the house, which can prove an intolerable burden. Contraception by chemical treatment is possible. This is particulartly useful when, for example, a bitch is being taken on holiday at a time when a heat is due. It also ensures that she will be able to breed satisfactorily at a later date if required.

The drugs used for contraception fall into two main categories: either those related to progesterone (progestagens), or male sex hormones (androgens). Neither group is free from side-effects. Progestagens are less likely than progesterone itself to stimulate the development of mammary tumours, but still can cause fluid retention, and lead to weight gain unless the diet is closely watched. Androgens may interfere with future reproductive cycles and cause physical problems such as a vaginal discharge and clitoral enlargement. A veterinarian will be able to advise and administer the safest preparation of this type. Drugs are administered by injection or tablets.

Below: A major responsibility for breeders is to find good homes for all the puppies. Pedigree puppies, especially those with champion parents, are likely to attract interest from other breeders.

CARING FOR ELDERLY DOGS

THE ELDERLY DOG

The problems of aging in dogs, as in humans, usually develop slowly and progressively. A range of diseases – cardiac, renal and tumorous – do become an increasing danger.

AS TIME PASSES, all dogs will begin to show signs of aging. However, an elderly dog will still provide years of pleasure.

How long can I expect my dog to live?

Generally, bigger breeds tend to have a shorter lifespan than their smaller cousins. Giant breeds such as the Irish Wolfhound are unlikely to live more than ten years, but some small terriers and toy dogs may live until well into their teens. There are of course exceptions to every rule, and dogs have lived into their thirties. While it is sometimes said that every year of our lives is equivalent to seven years in the life of a dog, this is essentially untrue.

What are the visible signs of aging?

Aging is a slow process, even in the dog, and changes tend to be gradual. They are not necessarily evident at a casual glance. The coat color is likely to become paler over successive sheddings. You are likely to notice a decrease in activity in your dog; it will not want to walk long distances and will walk rather slowly. Its teeth may show signs of wear, and it may appear reluctant to chew.

Obesity is a common adjunct to aging, because the dog's level of activity declines, but it often receives the same quantity of food it ate as a young adult dog. Failing senses may also be apparent, with a decline in eyesight being perhaps most noticeable. Deafness is also common but may not be detected by owners, who may just assume their dog is becoming more stubborn and disobedient in old age. But dogs are adaptable by nature, and an individual that is perhaps almost totally blind can live quite well without injuring itself in familiar surroundings.

Constipation may also afflict the older dog as the gut tone declines or as the uptake mechanisms in the gut begin to fail, the feces become more liquid, and diarrhea results. Urinary incontinence can also accompany the aging process, and treatment can prove difficult.

What can I do if my dog loses his teeth?

Certain breeds are more prone to dental decay than others. It is a good idea to provide hard items, such as dog biscuits, on a regular basis to reduce tartar accumulation. The teeth can also be cleaned with a special canine toothpaste. An older dog that has lost the majority of its teeth will still be able to eat adequately if offered soft foods. In any event, dogs do not use their teeth for chewing purposes but for catching prey and tearing strips of flesh that can be swallowed whole. Neither of these functions are of significance for the pet dog.

What skeletal problems may my dog encounter in old age?

These are likely to be degenerative conditions such as osteoarthrosis; a loss of the cartilage lining certain joints. This may cause lameness, especially in bigger dogs. If a dog is overweight, the problem is worse because the joints have to carry a greater burden than normal.

Slipped disks are more likely to occur in a slightly younger group of dogs, but the weakness remains throughout an affected individual's life. This can cause considerable pain, and result in paralysis of either the front or hind legs, depending on whether the disk concerned is in the neck or towards the tail.

Treatment tends to be supportive. The dog is kept as quiet as possible and confined to a small area so that it cannot injure itself further. Medical treatment decreases the inflammation and eases the pain. It makes sense to use a harness rather than a collar to remove stress from a sensitive part of the dog's anatomy.

Do many old dogs die of cancer?

The incidence of tumors in dogs averages about four in a thousand and about one-third of these are likely to prove malignant (cancerous). Older dogs are most likely to develop both benign and malignant tumors. A benign tumor is relatively slow-growing and does not spread and invade other tissues, so it can often be removed fairly easily. New tumors will not develop from it in other parts of the body, a process associated with malignant tumors and known as metastasis.

The skin is the most common site for tumors in the dog, and this facilitates early detection. Other likely sites include the mammary glands of bitches. Older dogs are increasingly susceptible to tumors in these two locations, but most of these tumors are not malignant. The incidence of major malignant tumors in dogs appears to peak between seven and ten years of age. These affect the skeleton and the lymphatic system. Large breeds are most likely to have bone cancer.

How can cancer be treated?

This depends largely on the type, size and locality of the tumor. It may be possible to operate and excise the tumor, but there is always a risk of recurrence, particularly with a malignancy.

Cryosurgery has a number of advantages over traditional surgery, particularly in the case of skin tumors. The patient does not always have to be fully anesthetized, which can be a distinct advantage with an old dog in declining health. There is no bleeding, which reduces the likelihood that malignant tumor cells will spread around the body to set up secondary tumors elsewhere. Using cryosurgery it is also possible to treat areas of the body, around the anus for example, that would bleed quite profusely if attempts were made to cut away the tumor. There is also less risk of an infection following surgery.

Cryosurgery does not provide a means of treating every tumor, especially those within the body. Here radiation therapy can lead to a remission, often in conjunction with chemotherapy. The side-effects of these drugs are not usually as unpleasant in dogs as in humans. If radiation therapy is not available in your area, you may have to travel to a veterinary school doing research into radiation therapy to obtain treatment.

My dog has been housebroken since puppyhood, but recently has started to wet indoors again. Could this be a sign of old age?

It may be linked to the kidneys. If the dog is drinking more, more urine will be produced, and the bladder will need to be emptied more frequently. For this reason, it is not unusual for older dogs to soil their quarters overnight while remaining clean for the rest of the day when someone is on hand to let them out to urinate more frequently. Keep a close check on the amount of fluid that your dog is consuming and inform your veterinarian. Note whether urine trickles out of the vulva in the case of a bitch, especially without its knowledge. This will stain the coat below the vulva. Be more responsive to your dog's requests to go out. Try to leave it alone in the home for only short periods, and let it out beforehand to empty its bladder.

Is heart failure a common cause of death in elderly dogs?

Dogs rarely succumb to coronary thrombosis (where blood clots occlude the pulmonary arteries nourishing the heart). Similarly, fatty deposits within the circulatory system are also uncommon. But the incidence of heart disease in elderly dogs is quite high and relates to the valvular structure of this vital organ.

The actual symptoms of valvular disease vary, depending on which valve in the heart is failing. Symptoms of bicuspid-valve failure include frequent coughing and exceptional tiredness when out for a walk. Symptoms of tricuspid-valve failure may include build-up of fluid in the tissues, because of increased pressure in the circulatory system from blood unable to enter the heart at the usual rate. Organs such as the spleen and liver may also become engorged with blood and swell in size. These changes can be detected when your veterinarian examines the dog. If both valves of the heart are failing, a combination of symptoms will be seen.

Above: The fading color on the head of this Golden Retriever is a typical sign of aging in a dog. Other more insidious and serious problems may be harder to detect in their initial stages – kidney failure and incontinence are common medical problems.

Once the condition has been diagnosed, it can be stabilized with drugs, and you should see an improvement in your dog's condition. The cardiac glycosides, of which digitalis is best known, control the heart rate. By slowing its pace and improving its contractibility, they increase cardiac output. Diuretic drugs remove excessive fluid and sodium salt from the blood via the kidneys and thus decrease the pressure on the heart itself. The initial dose of drugs will be higher than the maintenance dose, which will then be administered throughout the dog's life, especially if the dog is seriously ill. This may result in symptoms of toxicity such as vomiting. If you are concerned, contact your veterinarian.

The veterinarian treating my dog for bone cancer has recommended partial amputation of the affected leg. Is this fair, as he has always been such an active dog?
This choice ultimately has to be yours. Surprising as it may seem, dogs do adapt quite well to life on three legs and can live a relatively normal existence without appearing distressed. The idea may be abhorrent to you, however, and if so, you should opt to have your dog put to sleep before the malignancy spread further within the body. Before deciding, ask your veterinarian if you can see a former

Below: In old age, a dog's coat and nose color become pale. This Beagle is beginning to show white hairs, particularly around the muzzle.

patient that has undergone such surgery. This will give you a better idea of what to expect, and you can talk to the owner who, like you, would have been equally concerned at the outset. The surgery itself is unlikely to result in complications, but when you take your dog out for walks afterwards, be prepared for strange looks or comments from other people.

My dog is suffering from chronic kidney failure. Is this just part of the aging process?
All dogs are afflicted to a greater or lesser extent by kidney failure in old age. This is a progressive condition, and one of the first signs of it is the dog's foul-smelling breath (often linked with bad teeth). The body has a high reserve of functioning kidney tissue, but once the level falls to only 30 per cent of the total available, kidney or renal failure follows and the waste products of body metabolism that are normally filtered out of the body by this route remain in the blood. Various infectious causes of chronic renal failure exist and damage from such diseases at an early age will become more noticeable later in life.

Your dog will drink more fluid and urinate more often. The veterinarian may want to have a urine sample for testing, which can be collected in a broad plastic saucer. Once you have the sample, transfer it to a clean, dry, screw-top container. (Never use jars that have previously held jam as any remaining deposits of sugar are likely to interfere with the results.)

In cases of chronic renal failure, there is no effective curative treatment. But modifying the diet may help improve your dog's state of health. Special canned foods are available from your veterinarian for this purpose.

How will my dog be put to sleep?
The usual method involves the administration of a barbiturate by injection into a vein. It is quick and effective and mimics the procedure used when an intravenous barbiturate is given for anesthetic purposes but a stronger drug is used. Within seconds, the dog will be unconscious, and its heart stops almost immediately. With a dog that is known to be aggressive, a strong sedative in pill form may be given in meat beforehand to allow the process to be carried out efficiently.

After you reach the decision, arrange a time with your veterinarian to leave your dog at his office and say farewell. While you can stay to the end, it is usually preferable from everyone's viewpoint, including the dog's, if this unpleasant task is carried out with minimum fuss. Dogs are very sensitive to the mood of those around them and will detect the

emotion on this occasion. This could cause them to be more difficult. For this reason, it is better to have the task carried out at the veterinarian's office than at home.

What will happen to the body of my dog afterwards?

This will depend on your instructions. Many owners request that the veterinarian arrange the disposal of the body, or it may be possible to arrange a private cremation. In some areas, you can purchase a plot at a pet cemetery, and the organization concerned may arrange burial and a headstone if required. It is not always possible to bury your dog in your yard because of local laws. If you do opt for this method, make sure that the grave is at least three feet in depth to deter scavengers such as foxes that might otherwise be attracted to the carcass.

My mother's dog was put to sleep several weeks ago. She still seems very upset by this loss. How can I help her out of this depression?

The loss of a dog can be a devastating emotional blow, especially for people living alone with no other form of companionship. Indeed, it can be like losing a close relative, although the grieving process may remain largely unrecognized by society. Unexpressed grief may build up as the person feels unable to unburden his or her sense of loss. Try to persuade your mother to talk about her lost pet. This can be therapeutic.

It may be that another dog would help, but be prepared for the comment that it could never take the place of her previous dog. Be positive – tell her that a new dog would not be a direct substitute, but an individual in its own right. Given time, your mother is likely to accept a new dog with enthusiasm. If she feels that she cannot cope with another dog, suggest that she have a different pet. The positive benefits of pet ownership are increasingly appreciated, and in some countries such as France, dog ownership is a right for all citizens, embodied in the constitution.

How should I explain to my children that our dog has been put to sleep?

This depends to some extent on the age of your children; it may be easiest to explain it by saying that the family dog went to sleep and will not wake up again. Children are often very upset by the death of a pet. Lacking the acquired reserve of most adults, they may express their deep grief openly by crying and gradually come to terms with their sense of loss. The acquisition of another dog may also be helpful in overcoming this feeling.

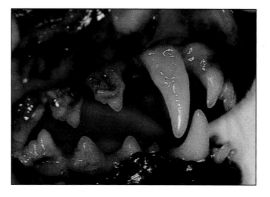

Left: Dental problems – such as this build-up of tartar which has led to gum disease – tend to affect older dogs. These teeth will have to be cleaned by a veterinarian, while the dog is under anesthetic.

How should I decide when the time has come for my dog to be put to sleep?

This is invariably a traumatic decision. Your veterinarian can guide you, but the ultimate responsibility must rest with you. Clearly, you do not want your dog to suffer unnecessarily when there is no hope of recovery. In the case of a paraplegic dog unable to stand on its own, you may be able to obtain a special dog cart to assist it, but the dog may not be happy with this, and you may not be in a position to provide the extra attention it needs. Or you may find the dog's state distressing.

Consider the normal daily habits of your dog: Can it walk? Is it able to eat and drink properly? Is it continent? Does it still appear to enjoy life? These are the type of questions that you must honestly ask yourself before arriving at your decision.

Euthanasia should always be carried out by a veterinarian. Do not be surprised or upset if you are asked to sign a consent form. This transfers the legal right of deciding your animal's future to your veterinarian.

Below: A bluish tinge on a dog's tongue may be an indication of a kidney failure, typical of an older dog.

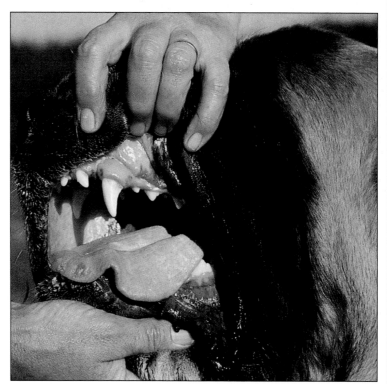

CREDITS

Quarto would like to acknowledge and thank the following for pictures reproduced in this book

D. Alderton; Ardea, London; T. A. Bazalik; Norvia Behling;
Jane Burton; Peter Clark; Anne Cumbers; K & D Dannen;
C. M. Di   H   l Eddi   Jean P. Ferrero; Paul Forrester;